The Best
AMERICAN
ESSAYS
2007

GUEST EDITORS OF
THE BEST AMERICAN ESSAYS

The Best AMERICAN ESSAYS® 2007

Edited and with an Introduction
By DAVID FOSTER WALLACE

Robert Atwan, Series Editor

HOUGHTON MIFFLIN COMPANY
BOSTON • NEW YORK   2007

www.houghtonmifflinbooks.com

ISSN 0888-3742
ISBN-13: 978-0-618-70926-7   ISBN-10: 0-618-70926-6
ISBN-13: 978-0-618-70927-4 (pbk.)   ISBN-10: 0-618-70927-4 (pbk.)

Printed in the United States of America

VB 10 9 8 7 6 5 4 3 2 1

Contents

Foreword

"THE ESSAY?" That's how Elizabeth Hardwick began her introduction to the first volume of *The Best American Essays* back in 1986. I can't imagine a more appropriate opening to the series: puzzlement. I confess that over two decades of considering the merits of hundreds of essays a year, I've encountered so many specimens of the form that I still find the genre as perplexing as Hardwick's very concise question suggests.

I do think there are certain things certain essays do, ways they behave (or misbehave) in prose that invite us to think that what we're reading is truly an essay. Sometimes the genre is unmistakable, like looking at an iambic pentameter poem that consists of three quatrains and concludes with a rhyming couplet. "Yes, of course," we say, "that's a Shakespearean sonnet." Similarly, there are essays that we recognize as essays with the same literary certainty, and there are many, many of them, courtesy of such authors as Montaigne, Joseph Addison and Richard Steele, Jonathan Swift, Samuel Johnson, Charles Lamb, Washington Irving, Robert Louis Stevenson, Agnes Repplier, Virginia Woolf, George Orwell, Loren Eisley, James Baldwin, E. B. White, Joan Didion, Joseph Epstein, and Annie Dillard. These essays — the older ones unfortunately nearly extinct — usually display several essential properties of the genre; they are autobiographical, self-reflective, stylistically engaging, intricately constructed, and provoked into being more often by internal literary pressures than by external occasions. Though nonfiction, these essays — go back and read Annie Dillard's *Teaching a Stone to Talk*, for example — clearly emerge from the same creative urgency as do short stories and poems.

Such essays have their founding father: Montaigne first used the term in 1580 when, without the inspiration of a literary movement or manifesto, he transformed by virtue of his dazzlingly digressive mind the conventional *leçon de morale* into the revolutionary *essai*. It was a leap of genius to turn customarily perceived flaws of composition into distinctive artistic features. But the lessons of the master were all implicit. He never defined his new literary production, and his intentionally casual and modest term (simply meaning "attempt" or "trial") has since been applied to all sorts of prose works, some as magisterial as John Locke's philosophical tome *Essay on Human Understanding* and others as minuscule as Francis Bacon's aphoristic and very un-Montaignean gems. Prose may not even be a requirement. At the same time that Addison and Steele were perfecting their brand of essay, Alexander Pope published in verse *An Essay on Criticism*.

So almost from the start the essay branched off in many directions and, more important for literary history, embedded itself in other genres ("Here is forcibly shown the great Montaigneism of Hamlet," Melville noted in the margin of his Shakespeare). But the hardy type of essay that evolved from Montaigne's innovative prose has long been identified as *the* essay, and it has received many labels over the centuries: the informal essay, the periodical essay, the moral essay, the anecdotal essay, the familiar essay, the personal essay, the true essay, and even — as William Dean Howells termed it — the "right" essay. True and right essays suggest that there might be such items on your bookshelves as false or wrong essays; the implied comparison, however, is between literary and non-literary, the essay intended as a literary work as opposed to prose put to a variety of expository, argumentative, and persuasive purposes.

From the start, this series rejected any sharp distinction, assuming one could be made, between essays that conducted themselves as literature and those that did not. One reason for this should be obvious: such a decision would automatically eliminate many of the finest and most interesting short prose works of our time, some of which defy classification. Another reason is that many writers and periodicals don't necessarily categorize works as essays to distinguish them from non-essayistic prose. What stands as an essay for one magazine might in several others be called an article, a report, a story, commentary, memoir, or a reflection. Although many literary quarterlies feature essays, these may often be found under

"Nonfiction," "Creative Nonfiction," "Prose," "Literary Non-fiction," or "Essays and Hybrid Forms." And some literary journals provide no labels at all, thus not infrequently — especially when it comes to prose narratives — leave the reader guessing.

In this volume alone, which is perhaps the most diverse in the entire series, the authors or periodicals have termed their various selections "Essay," "Comment," "Notes," "Letter," "Argument," and "Profile." There is narrative — in first, second, and third person — opinion, memoir, the essay-review, reportage, and a dispatch from Iraq. The philosopher Peter Singer makes a case for philanthropy, and the poet Molly Peacock constructs a mosaic tribute to a little-known but remarkable eighteenth-century woman artist. If one thinks a piece of writing must be fiction because the characters are imagined, then how does one assess the classic periodical essays of the pioneering journalists Addison and Steele, which depend on a cast of fictional characters and narrators, imagined events and gatherings, and even fabricated letters to the paper. With this bag of literary tricks, neither great essayist would qualify for a newspaper job today.

I once accepted a challenge to appear on a panel in which I would define the essay definitively. I had for years tried to avoid doing this, but then thought: Of all people, shouldn't I take on this thorny problem and settle the issue once and for all? Didn't I have a responsibility as the one annually in charge of a collection of America's best essays to clarify my standards and criteria? I struggled to develop a definition, starting broadly and then refining, and refining, and refining until I arrived at the essence of the genre in one sentence. When I finished delivering my long, discursive paper, I realized my attempt, my trial, was so hopelessly reductive that I would hereafter keep my feeble definition from circulation. To make matters worse, I went over my time limit and curtailed that of a friend and colleague. Now that I think about it, I should have simply stood up and with a Montaignean Gallic shrug uttered two words: *The essay?*

The Best American Essays features a selection of the year's outstanding essays, essays of literary achievement that show an awareness of craft and forcefulness of thought. Hundreds of essays are gathered annually from a wide assortment of national and regional publications. These essays are then screened, and approximately one hundred are turned over to a distinguished guest editor, who may add a few personal discoveries and who makes the final selections. The list of notable essays appearing in the back of the book is drawn from a final comprehensive list that includes not only all of the essays submitted to the guest editor but also many that were not submitted.

To qualify for the volume, the essay must be a work of respectable literary quality, intended as a fully developed, independent essay on a subject of general interest (not specialized scholarship), originally written in English (or translated by the author) for publication in an American periodical during the calendar year. Today's essay is a highly flexible and shifting form, however, so these criteria are not carved in stone.

Magazine editors who want to be sure their contributors will be considered each year should submit issues or subscriptions to: Robert Atwan, Series Editor, The Best American Essays, P.O. Box 220, Readville, MA 02137. Writers and editors are welcome to submit published essays from any American periodical for consideration; unpublished work does not qualify for the series and cannot be reviewed or evaluated. Please note: all submissions must be directly from the publication and not in manuscript or printout format.

As I was writing this Foreword, I was shocked and saddened to learn of the death of David Halberstam on April 23, 2007. His work will long be remembered by both the literary and journalistic communities. Once again, I extend my thanks to those at Houghton Mifflin who in many ways make this annual volume possible: Deanne Urmy, Nicole Angeloro, Larry Cooper, and Megan Wilson. It was an enormous pleasure and great intellectual fun to collaborate this year with one of America's finest writers and thinkers, David Foster Wallace. His multifarious interests are vividly reflected in this diverse and dynamic collection.

R. A.

Introduction:
Deciderization 2007 —
a Special Report

I THINK IT'S UNLIKELY that anyone is reading this as an introduction. Most of the people I know treat *Best American* anthologies
like Whitman Samplers. They skip around, pick and choose. There
isn't the same kind of linear commitment as in a regular book.
Which means that the reader has more freedom of choice, which
of course is part of what this country's all about. If you're like most
of us, you'll first check the table of contents for names of writers
you like, and their pieces are what you'll read first. Then you'll go
by title, or apparent subject, or sometimes even first line. There's a
kind of triage. The guest editor's intro is last, if at all.

This sense of being last or least likely confers its own freedoms.
I feel free to state an emergent truth that I maybe wouldn't if I
thought that the book's sales could really be hurt or its essays' audience scared away. This truth is that just about every important
word on *The Best American Essays 2007*'s front cover turns out to be
vague, debatable, slippery, disingenuous, or else 'true' only in certain contexts that are themselves slippery and hard to sort out or
make sense of — and that in general the whole project of an anthology like this requires a degree of credulity and submission on
the part of the reader that might appear, at first, to be almost un-
American.

. . . Whereupon, after that graceless burst of bad news, I'm betting that most of whichever readers thought that maybe this year they'd try starting out linearly with the editor's intro have now decided to stop or just flip ahead to Jo Ann Beard's 'Werner,' the collection's first essay. This is actually fine for them to do, because Beard's is an unambiguously great piece — exquisitely written and suffused with a sort of merciless compassion. It's a narrative essay, I think the subgenre's called, although the truth is that I don't believe I would have loved the piece any less or differently if it had been classed as a short story, which is to say not an essay at all but fiction.

Thus one constituent of the truth about the front cover is that your guest editor isn't sure what an essay even is. Not that this is unusual. Most literary readers take a position on the meaning of 'essay' rather like the famous one that U.S.S.C. Justice Potter Stewart took on 'obscene': we feel that we pretty much know an essay when we see one, and that that's enough, regardless of all the noodling and complication involved in actually trying to define the term 'essay.' I don't know whether gut certainty is really enough here or not, though. I think I personally prefer the term 'literary nonfiction.' Pieces like 'Werner' and Daniel Orozco's 'Shakers' seem so remote from the sort of thing that Montaigne and Chesterton were doing when the essay was being codified that to call these pieces essays seems to make the term too broad to really signify. And yet Beard's and Orozco's pieces are so arresting and alive and good that they end up being salient even if one is working as a guest essay editor and sitting there reading a dozen Xeroxed pieces in a row before them and then another dozen in a row after them — essays on everything from memory and surfing and Esperanto to childhood and mortality and Wikipedia, on depression and translation and emptiness and James Brown, Mozart, prison, poker, trees, anorgasmia, color, homelessness, stalking, fellatio, ferns, fathers, grandmothers, falconry, grief, film comedy — a rate of consumption which tends to level everything out into an undifferentiated mass of high-quality description and trenchant reflection that becomes both numbing and euphoric, a kind of Total Noise that's also the sound of our U.S. culture right now, a culture and volume of info and spin and rhetoric and context that I know I'm not alone in finding too much to even absorb, much less to try to make sense of or organize into any kind of triage of saliency or value. Such basic absorption, organization, and triage used to be what was required of an educated adult, a.k.a. an informed citizen — at least that's what I got taught. Suffice it here to say that the requirements now seem different.

A corollary to the above bad news is that I'm not really even all that confident or concerned about the differences between nonfiction and fiction, with 'differences' here meaning formal or definitive, and 'I' referring to me as a reader.* There are, as it happens, intergenre differences that I know and care about as a writer, though these differences are hard to talk about in a way that someone who doesn't try to write both fiction and nonfiction will understand. I'm worried that they'll sound cheesy and melodramatic. Although maybe they won't. Maybe, given the ambient volume of your own life's noise, the main difference will make sense to you. Writing-wise, fiction is scarier, but nonfiction is harder — because nonfiction's based in reality, and today's felt reality is overwhelmingly, circuit-blowingly huge and complex. Whereas fiction comes out of nothing. Actually, so wait: the truth is that both genres are scary; both feel like they're executed on tightropes, over abysses — it's the abysses that are different. Fiction's abyss is silence, *nada.* Whereas nonfiction's abyss is Total Noise, the seething static of every particular thing and experience, and one's total freedom of infinite choice about what to choose to attend to and represent and connect, and how, and why, etc.

There's a rather more concrete problem with the cover's word 'editor,' and it may be the real reason why these editorial introductions are the least appealing candy in the box. *The Best American Essays 2007*'s pieces are arranged alphabetically, by author, and they're essentially reprints from magazines and journals; whatever

---

*A subcorollary here is that it's a bit odd that Houghton Mifflin and the *Best American* series tend to pick professional writers to be their guest editors. There are, after all, highly expert professional readers among the industry's editors, critics, scholars, etc., and the guest editor's job here is really 95 percent readerly. Underlying the series' preference for writers appears to be one or both of the following: (a) the belief that someone's being a good writer makes her *eo ipso* a good reader — which is the same reasoning that undergirds most blurbs and MFA programs, and is both logically invalid and empirically false (trust me); or (b) the fact that the writers the series pick tend to have comparatively high name recognition, which the publisher figures will translate into wider attention and better sales. Premise (b) involves marketing and revenue and is thus probably backed up by hard data and thought in a way that (a) is not.

(light) copyediting they receive is done in-house by Houghton Mifflin. So what the cover calls your editor isn't really doing any editing. My real function is best described by an epithet that may, in future years, sum up 2006 with the same grim efficiency that terms like 'Peace with Honor,' 'Iran-Contra,' 'Florida Recount,' and 'Shock and Awe' now comprise and evoke other years. What your editor really is here is: the Decider.

Being the Decider for a *Best American* anthology is part honor and part service, with 'service' here not as in 'public service' but rather as in 'service industry.' That is, in return for some pay and intangible assets, I am acting as an evaluative filter, winnowing a very large field of possibilities down to a manageable, absorbable Best for your delectation. Thinking about this kind of Decidering* is interesting in all kinds of different ways;† but the general point is that professional filtering/winnowing is a type of service that we citizens and consumers now depend on more and more, and in ever-increasing ways, as the quantity of available information and products and art and opinions and choices and all the complications and ramifications thereof expands at roughly the rate of Moore's Law.

The immediate point, on the other hand, is obvious. Unless you are both a shut-in and independently wealthy, there is no way you can sit there and read all the contents of all the 2006 issues of all the hundreds of U.S. periodicals that publish literary nonfiction. So you subcontract this job — not to me directly, but to a publishing company whom you trust (for whatever reasons) to then subsubcontract the job to someone whom they trust (or more like believe you'll trust [for whatever reasons]) not to be insane or capricious or overtly 'biased' in his Decidering.

'Biased' is, of course, the really front-loaded term here, the one that I expect Houghton Mifflin winces at and would prefer not to see uttered in the editor's intro even in the most reassuring context, since the rhetoric of such reassurances can be self-nullifying

---

*(usage *sic*, in honor of the term's source)

†For example, from the perspective of Information Theory, the bulk of the Decider's labor actually consists of *excluding* nominees from the final prize collection, which puts the Decider in exactly the position of Maxwell's Demon or any other kind of entropy-reducing info processor, since the really expensive, energy-intensive part of such processing is always deleting/discarding/resetting.

(as in, say, running a classified ad for oneself as a babysitter and putting 'DON'T WORRY — NOT A PEDOPHILE!' at the bottom of the ad). I suspect that part of why 'bias' is so loaded and dicey a word just now — and why it's so much-invoked and potent in cultural disputes — is that we are starting to become more aware of just how much subcontracting and outsourcing and submitting to other Deciders we're all now forced to do, which is threatening (the inchoate awareness is) to our sense of ourselves as intelligent free agents. And yet there is no clear alternative to this outsourcing and submission. It may possibly be that acuity and taste in choosing which Deciders one submits to is now the real measure of informed adulthood. Since I was raised with more traditional, Enlightenment-era criteria, this possibility strikes me as consumerist and scary . . . to which the counterargument would be, again, that the alternatives are literally abysmal.

Speaking of submission, there was a bad bit of oversimplification two paragraphs above, since your guest editor is not really even the main sub-subcontractor on this job. The real Decider, in terms of processing info and reducing entropy, is Mr. Robert Atwan, the *BAE* series editor. Think of it this way. My job is to choose the twenty-odd so-called Best from roughly 100 finalists the series editor sends me.* Mr. Atwan, though, has distilled these finalists from a vast pool of '06 nonfiction — every issue of hundreds of periodicals, plus submissions from his network of contacts all over the U.S. — meaning that he's really the one doing the full-time reading

---

*It's true that I got to lobby for essays that weren't in his 100, but there ended up being only one such outside piece in the final collection. A couple of others that I'd suggested were nixed by Mr. Atwan — well, not nixed so much as counseled against, for what emerged as good reasons. In general, though, you can see who had the real power. However much I strutted around in my aviator suit and codpiece calling myself the Decider for *BAE* '07, I knew that it was Mr. Atwan who delimited the field of possibilities from which I was choosing . . . in rather the same way that many Americans are worried that what appears to be the reality we're experiencing and making choices about is maybe actually just a small, skewed section of reality that's been pre-chosen for us by shadowy entities and forces, whether these be left-leaning media, corporate cabals, government disinformers, our own unconscious prejudices, etc. At least Mr. Atwan was explicit about the whole pre-selection thing, though, and appeared to be fair and balanced, and of course he'd had years of hard experience on the front lines of Decidering; and in general I found myself trusting him and his judgments more and more throughout the whole long process, and there were finally only maybe about 10 percent of his forwarded choices where I just had no idea what he might have been thinking when he picked them.

and culling that you and I can't do; and he's been doing it since
1985. I have never met Mr. Atwan, but I — probably like most fans
of *BAE* — envision him as by now scarcely more than a vestigial
support system for an eye-brain assembly, maybe like 5'8" and 90
lbs., living full-time in some kind of high-tech medical chair that
automatically gimbals around at various angles to help prevent
skin ulcers, nourishment and wastes ferried by tubes, surrounded
by full-spectrum lamps and stacks of magazines and journals, a special emergency beeper Velcroed to his arm in case he falls out of
the chair, etc.

Given the amount of quiet, behind-the-scenes power he wields
over these prize collections, you're entitled to ask about Mr.
Atwan's standards for inclusion and forwarding;* but he's far too
experienced and cagey to encourage these sorts of questions. If his
foreword to this edition is like those of recent years, he'll describe
what he's looking for so generally — 'essays of literary achievement that show an awareness of craft and forcefulness of thought'
— that his criteria look reasonable while at the same time being
vague and bland enough that we aren't induced to stop and think
about what they might actually mean, or to ask just what principles
Mr. Atwan uses to determine 'achievement' and 'awareness' and
'forcefulness' (not to mention 'literary'). He is wise to avoid this,
since such specific questions would entail specific answers that
then would raise more questions, and so on; and if this process is
allowed to go on long enough, a point will be reached at which any
Decider is going to look either (a) arrogant and arbitrary ('It's literary because I say so') or else (b) weak and incoherent (as he
thrashes around in endless little definitions and exceptions and
qualifications and apparent flip-flops). It's true. Press R. Atwan or
D. Wallace hard enough on any of our criteria or reasons — what
they mean or where they come from — and you'll eventually get
either paralyzed silence or the abysmal, Legionish babble of every
last perceived fact and value. And Mr. Atwan cannot afford this;
he's permanent *BAE* staff.

I, on the other hand, have a strict term limit. After this, I go

*I believe this is what is known in the nonfiction industry as a transition. We are
now starting to poke tentatively at 'Best,' which is the most obviously fraught and
bias-prone word on the cover.

forever back to being an ordinary civilian and *BAE* reader (except for the introductions). I therefore feel free here to try for at least partial transparency about my Decidering criteria, some of which are obviously — let's be grownups and just admit it — subjective, and therefore in some ways biased.* Plus I have no real problem, emotionally or politically, with stopping at any given point in any theoretical Q & A & Q and simply shrugging and saying that I hear the caviling voices but am, this year, for whatever reasons (possibly including divine will — who knows?), the Decider, and that this year I get to define and decide what's Best, at least within the limited purview of Mr. Atwan's 104 finalists, and that if you don't like it then basically tough titty.

Because of the fact that my Decidering function is antientropic and therefore mostly exclusionary, I first owe some account of why certain types of essays were maybe easier for me to exclude than others. I'll try to combine candor with maximum tact. Memoirs, for example. With a few big exceptions, I don't much care for abreactive or confessional memoirs. I'm not sure how to explain this. There is probably a sound, serious argument to be made about the popularity of confessional memoirs as a symptom of something especially sick and narcissistic/voyeuristic about U.S. culture right now. About certain deep connections between narcissism and voyeurism in the mediated psyche. But this isn't it. I think the real reason is that I just don't trust them. Memoirs/confessions, I mean. Not so much their factual truth as their agenda. The sense I get from a lot of contemporary memoirs is that they have an unconscious and unacknowledged project, which is to make the memoirists seem as endlessly fascinating and important to the reader as they are to themselves. I find most of them sad in a way that I don't think their authors intend. There are, to be sure, some memoirish-type pieces in this year's *BAE* — although these tend either to be about hair-raisingly unusual circumstances or else to use the confessional stuff as part of a larger and (to me) much richer scheme or story.

---

*May I assume that some readers are as tired as I am of this word as a kneejerk derogative? Or, rather, tired of the legerdemain of collapsing the word's neutral meaning — 'preference, inclination' — into the pejorative one of 'unfairness stemming from prejudice'? It's the same thing that's happened with 'discrimination,' which started as a good and valuable word, but now no one can even hear it without seeming to lose their mind.

Another acknowledged prejudice: no celebrity profiles. Some sort of personal quota was exceeded at around age thirty-five. I now actually want to know *less* than I know about most celebrities.

The only other intrinsic bias I'm aware of is one that a clinician would probably find easy to diagnose in terms of projection or displacement. As someone who has a lot of felt trouble being clear, concise, and/or cogent, I tend to be allergic to academic writing, most of which seems to me willfully opaque and pretentious. There are, again, some notable exceptions, and by 'academic writing' I mean a particular cloistered dialect and mode; I do not just mean any piece written by somebody who teaches college.*

The other side to this bias is that I tend, as a reader, to prize and admire clarity, precision, plainness, lucidity, and the sort of magical compression that enriches instead of vitiates. Someone's ability

---

*Example: Roger Scruton is an academic, and his 'A Carnivore's Credo' is a model of limpid and all-business compression, which is actually one reason why his argument is so valuable and prizeworthy, even though parts of that argument strike me as either odd or just plain wrong (e.g., just how much humane and bucolic 'traditional livestock farming' does Scruton believe still goes on in this country?). Out on the other end of the ethicopolitical spectrum, there's a weirdly similar example in Prof. Peter Singer's 'What Should a Billionaire Give?,' which is not exactly belletristic but certainly isn't written in aureate academese, and is salient and unforgettable and unexcludable not despite but in some ways *because* of the questions and criticisms it invites. May I assume that you've already read it? If not, please return to the main text. If you have, though, do some of Singer's summaries and obligation-formulas seem unrealistically simple? What if a person in the top 10 percent of U.S. earners already gives 10 percent of his income to different, non-UN-type charities — does this reduce his moral obligation, for Singer? Should it? Exactly which charities and forms of giving have the most efficacy and/or moral value — and how does one find out which these are? Should a family of nine making $132,000 a year really have the same 10 percent moral obligation as the childless bachelor making 132K a year? What about a 132K family where one family member has cancer and their health insurance has a 20 percent deductible — is this family's failure to cough up 10 percent after spending $40,000 on medical bills really still the moral equivalent of valuing one's new shoes over the life of a drowning child? Is Singer's whole analogy of the drowning kid(s) too simple, or at least too simple in some cases? Umm, might my own case be one of the ones where the analogy and giving-formula are too simple or inflexible? Is it OK that I think it might be, or am I just trying to rationalize my way out of discomfort and obligation as so many of us (according to Singer) are wont to do? And so on . . . but of course you'll notice meanwhile how hard the reader's induced to think about all these questions. Can you see why a Decider might regard Singer's essay as brilliant and valuable precisely *because* its prose is so mainstream and its formulas so (arguably) crude or harsh? Or is this kind of 'value' a stupid, PC-ish criterion to use in Decidering about essays' literary worth? What exactly are the connections between literary aesthetics and moral value supposed to be? Whose moral values ought to get used in determining what those connections should be? Does anyone even read Tolstoy's *What Is Art* anymore?

to write this way, especially in nonfiction, fills me with envy and awe. That might help explain why a fair number of *BAE '07*'s pieces tend to be short, terse, and informal in usage/syntax. Readers who enjoy noodling about genre might welcome the news that several of this year's Best Essays are arguably more like *causeries* or *propos* than like essays per se, although one could counterargue that these pieces tend, in their essential pithiness, to be closer to what's historically been meant by 'essay.' Personally, I find taxonomic arguments like this dull and irrelevant. What does seem relevant is to assure you that none of the shorter essays in the collection were included merely because they were short. Limpidity, compactness, and an absence of verbal methane were simply part of what made these pieces valuable; and I think I tried, as the Decider, to use overall value as the prime triage- and filtering mechanism in selecting this year's top essays.

. . . Which, yes, all right, entitles you to ask what 'value' means here and whether it's any kind of improvement, in specificity and traction, over the cover's 'Best.' I'm not sure that it's finally better or less slippery than 'Best,' but I do know it's different. 'Value' sidesteps some of the metaphysics that makes pure aesthetics such a headache, for one thing. It's also more openly, candidly subjective: since things have value only to people, the idea of some limited, subjective human doing the valuing is sort of built right into the term. That all seems tidy and uncontroversial so far — although there's still the question of just what this limited human actually means by 'value' as a criterion.

One thing I'm sure it means is that this year's *BAE* does not necessarily comprise the twenty-two very best-written or most beautiful essays published in 2006. Some of the book's essays are quite beautiful indeed, and most are extremely well written and/or show a masterly awareness of craft (whatever exactly that is). But others aren't, don't, especially — but they have other virtues that make them valuable. And I know that many of these virtues have to do with the ways in which the pieces handle and respond to the tsunami of available fact, context, and perspective that constitutes Total Noise. This claim might itself look slippery, because of course any published essay is a burst of information and context that is by definition part of 2007's overall roar of info and context. But it is possible for something to be both a quantum of information and a

vector of meaning. Think, for instance, of the two distinct but related senses of 'informative.' Several of this year's most valuable essays are informative in both senses; they are at once informational
and instructive. That is, they serve as models and guides for how
large or complex sets of facts can be sifted, culled, and arranged in
meaningful ways — ways that yield and illuminate truth instead of
just adding more noise to the overall roar.

That all may sound too abstract. Let's do a concrete example,
which happens also to involve the term 'American' on the front
cover. In your 2007 guest editor's opinion, we are in a state of
three-alarm emergency — 'we' basically meaning America as a polity and culture. Only part of this emergency has to do with what is
currently called partisan politics, but it's a significant part. Don't
worry that I'm preparing to make any kind of specific argument
about the Bush administration or the disastrous harm I believe it's
done in almost every area of federal law, policy, and governance.
Such an argument would be just noise here — redundant for those
readers who feel and believe as I do, biased crap for those who believe differently. Who's right is not the point. The point is to try to
explain part of what I mean by 'valuable.' It is totally possible that,
prior to 2004 — when the reelection of George W. Bush rendered
me, as part of the U.S. electorate, historically complicit in his administration's policies and conduct — this *BAE* Decider would
have selected more memoirs or descriptive pieces on ferns and
geese, some of which this year were quite lovely and fine. In the
current emergency, though, such essays simply didn't seem as valuable to me as pieces like, say, Mark Danner's 'Iraq: The War of the
Imagination' or Elaine Scarry's 'Rules of Engagement.'

Here is an overt premise. There is just no way that 2004's reelection could have taken place — not to mention extraordinary ren-
ditions, legalized torture, FISA-flouting, or the passage of the Military Commissions Act — if we had been paying attention and
handling information in a competent grown-up way. 'We' meaning
as a polity and culture. The premise does not entail specific blame
— or rather the problems here are too entangled and systemic for
good old-fashioned finger-pointing. It is, for one example, simplistic and wrong to blame the for-profit media for somehow failing to
make clear to us the moral and practical hazards of trashing the
Geneva Conventions. The for-profit media is highly attuned to

what we want and the amount of detail we'll sit still for. And a ninety-second news piece on the question of whether and how the Geneva Conventions ought to apply in an era of asymmetrical warfare is not going to explain anything; the relevant questions are too numerous and complicated, too fraught with contexts in everything from civil law and military history to ethics and game theory. One could spend a hard month just learning the history of the Conventions' translation into actual codes of conduct for the U.S. military . . . and that's not counting the dramatic changes in those codes since 2002, or the question of just what new practices violate (or don't) just which Geneva provisions, and according to whom. Or let's not even mention the amount of research, background, cross-checking, corroboration, and rhetorical parsing required to understand the cataclysm of Iraq, the collapse of congressional oversight, the ideology of neoconservatism, the legal status of presidential signing statements, the political marriage of evangelical Protestantism and corporatist laissez-faire . . . There's no way. You'd simply drown. We all would. It's amazing to me that no one much talks about this — about the fact that whatever our founders and framers thought of as a literate, informed citizenry can no longer exist, at least not without a whole new modern degree of subcontracting and dependence packed into what we mean by 'informed.'*

In the context of our Total Noise, a piece like Mark Danner's 'Iraq: . . . Imagination' exemplifies a special subgenre I've come to think of as the service essay, with 'service' here referring to both professionalism and virtue. In what is loosely framed as a group book review, Danner has processed and arranged an immense quantity of fact, opinion, confirmation, testimony, and on-site experience in order to offer an explanation of the Iraq debacle that is clear without being simplistic, comprehensive without being

---

*Hence, by the way, the seduction of partisan dogma. You can drown in dogmatism now, too — radio, Internet, cable, commercial and scholarly print — but this kind of drowning is more like sweet release. Whether hard right or new left or whatever, the seduction and mentality are the same. You don't have to feel confused or inundated or ignorant. You don't even have to think, for you already Know, and whatever you choose to learn confirms what you Know. This dogmatic lockstep is not the kind of inevitable dependence I'm talking about — or rather it's only the most extreme and frightened form of that dependence.

overwhelming, and critical without being shrill. It is a brilliant, disciplined, pricelessly informative piece.

There are several other such service essays among this year's proffered Best. Some, like Danner's, are literary journalism; others are more classically argumentative, or editorial, or personal. Some are quite short. All are smart and well written, but what renders them most valuable to me is a special kind of integrity in their handling of fact. An absence of dogmatic cant. Not that service essayists don't have opinions or make arguments. But you never sense, from this year's Best, that facts are being specially cherry-picked or arranged in order to advance a pre-set agenda. They are utterly different from the party-line pundits and propagandists who now are in such vogue, for whom writing is not thinking or service but more like the silky courtier's manipulation of an enfeebled king.

. . . In which scenario we, like diminished kings or rigidly insecure presidents, are reduced to being overwhelmed by info and interpretation, or else paralyzed by cynicism and anomie, or else — worst — seduced by some particular set of dogmatic talking-points, whether these be PC or NRA, rationalist or evangelical, 'Cut and Run' or 'No Blood for Oil.' The whole thing is (once again) way too complicated to do justice to in a guest intro, but one last, unabashed bias/preference in *BAE '07* is for pieces that undercut reflexive dogma, that essay to do their own Decidering in good faith and full measure, that eschew the deletion of all parts of reality that do not fit the narrow aperture of, say for instance, those cretinous fundamentalists who insist that creationism should be taught alongside science in public schools, or those sneering materialists who insist that all serious Christians are as cretinous as the fundamentalists.

Part of our emergency is that it's so tempting to do this sort of thing now, to retreat to narrow arrogance, pre-formed positions, rigid filters, the 'moral clarity' of the immature. The alternative is dealing with massive, high-entropy amounts of info and ambiguity and conflict and flux; it's continually discovering new areas of personal ignorance and delusion. In sum, to really try to be informed and literate today is to feel stupid nearly all the time, and to need help. That's about as clearly as I can put it. I'm aware that some of the collection's writers could spell all this out better and in much less space. At any rate, the service part of what I mean by 'value' refers to all this stuff, and extends as well to essays that have nothing to do with politics or wedge issues. Many are valuable simply as exhibits of what a first-rate artistic mind can make of particular fact-sets — whether these involve the 17-kHz ring tones of some kids' cell phones, the language of movement as parsed by dogs, the near-infinity of ways to experience and describe an earthquake, the existential synecdoche of stagefright, or the revelation that most of what you've believed and revered turns out to be self-indulgent crap.

That last one's* of especial value, I think. As exquisite verbal art, yes, but also as a model for what free, informed adulthood might look like in the context of Total Noise: not just the intelligence to discern one's own error or stupidity, but the humility to address it, absorb it, and move on and out therefrom, bravely, toward the next revealed error. This is probably the sincerest, most biased account of 'Best' your Decider can give: these pieces are models — not templates, but models — of ways I wish I could think and live in what seems to me this world.

DAVID FOSTER WALLACE

---

*You probably know which essay I'm referring to, assuming you're reading this guest intro last as is SOP. If you're not, and so don't, then you have a brutal little treat in store.

The Best AMERICAN ESSAYS 2007

JO ANN BEARD

Werner

FROM TIN HOUSE

WERNER HOEFLICH spent the evening at his catering job, making white-wine spritzers and mixing vodka with Tab in a spacious apartment overlooking Central Park. There were orchids, thick rugs, a dog with long blond hair. He walked home late from the subway afterward, along the gated and padlocked streets of the Upper East Side. The trees on his block were scrawny and impervious, like invalid aunts.

Once he had seen a parakeet in one of those trees, staring down at him, shifting from foot to foot. The bird had sharpened both sides of its beak on the branch and then made a veering, panicky flight to a windowsill far above. Most of Werner's metaphorical moments were painterly — the juxtaposing of the wild bird and the tame tree, the shimmer of periwinkle, the splurt of titanium white that fell from it onto the pavement. He loved New York for its simple surprises, although in truth, Oregon and Iowa and Arizona and everywhere else had simple surprises as well. Cantaloupe-colored sunrises, banded cows, Dairy Queens, all kinds of things that didn't include black plastic mountains of trash and the smell of dog urine.

But on that night it wasn't like that; it was cold and fresh on the dark streets. He rounded the corner and his building came into view, a turn-of-the-century tenement, where right about then — just before midnight, December 19, 1991 — another kind of New York surprise was taking shape. Deep inside the walls, three floors below Werner's apartment, a sprig of cloth-wrapped wire sizzled and then opened, like a blossom.

*

From the street it looked like a single building but it was actually twin tenements, set next to each other and connected along the façade. Werner let himself into the entrance on the left, walked to the back, and climbed five flights to the top floor, where he was greeted by his cat, Two. She trotted ahead of him into the kitchen to wait for her bounty, served on an unfurled bed of tinfoil — a pale smear of liver pâté and several translucent strands of sashimi.

Feet up, Werner dialed Eugene, Oregon, and had a nice conversation with his mother. He liked to call home late, when they were just getting to the end of their West Coast day and he was still energized, sitting in his skivvies in the overhot apartment. The walls were bumpy and pocked, thick plaster reinforced with horsehair, but he had whitewashed them and hired someone to refinish the wood floors. They were hay-colored and gleamed in the lamplight. His paintings hung here and there, dark backgrounds with shapes emerging out of them — construction machinery, the camshaft of an ocean liner, simple tools, almost but not quite abstracted.

When Werner finally slept that night, it was like sinking slowly through water, fathom by fathom, to the ocean floor. He might have been dreaming when the wiring finally ignited, carrying fire upward through the building. He thought he could feel things swirling in the darkness, but when he tried to reach for them, the weight of the water pressed him to the bed.

Sometime between four and five A.M., the tenants in 2C woke to a heavy pounding noise in the ceiling, which then collapsed. Their upstairs neighbors in 3C heard the same sound and their ceiling collapsed as well; they made it to the fire escape and began screaming. The 2C tenants left through the stairwell with their children, although the wife became paralyzed with confusion and fear and the husband had to drag her. In the panic they left their door open.

The fire engulfed 2C and billowed out into the hallway.

Werner woke to the sounds of screaming. He was next to an open window, on a loft bed six feet off the floor. He sat up and pulled the string to the light, a bare bulb in the ceiling. Rectangular shapes jumped at him in the glare — wardrobe, doorway, rug. The screams were of a type Werner hadn't heard before.

His brain spun like a tire that wouldn't catch: the familiar terrain of his bedroom, the heavy scent of smoke drifting through the petals of the window fan, his own bent knees draped in a sheet.

He needed to get dressed and get to the street, help whoever was in trouble. He grabbed for his clothes but couldn't find the first thing he needed: underwear. He turned, and then turned back. He could see them in his memory — stacks of brightly colored boxers, and the other kind, folded neatly on a shelf — but there was something blocking him, an invisible membrane between Werner and the next step. He stood in front of the tall impenetrable wardrobe. He had been awake for approximately fifteen seconds. The screams were loud and prolonged, people coming unhinged.

Without his underpants he couldn't think.

It was a familiar scent, but distant — campfires in his past, in the Oregon woods. Boiled coffee, damp socks, Werner rooted to a stump, bow across his lap. Deer, someone had told him, needed two senses to pinpoint danger, some combination of sight, sound, smell; otherwise they just stood there, waiting.

Sound of screams, smell of smoke.

Werner bounded naked to the front door, flipped the locks, flung it open, and a wall of smoke hit him in the face. He slammed it shut, turned, and squinted into the apartment. More smoke was coming in through the living room. He saw the roof in his mind and the street below. Werner had been awake now maybe twenty-five seconds and had his first coherent thought. He thought he didn't want to be naked if he had to jump off the building.

He stepped back into the bedroom and a dry, papery gray cloud consumed him. He dropped to his hands and knees and put his cheek to the floor. With this nearsighted, close-up view, he could see smoke curling up through the floorboards, black specks inside the tendrils like a flock of birds banking and moving together. Dark geese rising into the Oregon sky. He wasn't going to find oxygen at the floor.

Time was starting to slow down.

His room was teeny and cramped; with the bare lightbulb it looked cheap and garish, like a torture site. He pulled the cord to the bulb on his way to the window, and then in darkness struggled to lift the sash. The window fan, set in the upper half of the casement, was blocking it. He thrust his fingers into the grating of the fan and tugged, but it wouldn't move. For an instant he became an animal, tearing at the immovable fan, panic surging upward, overtaking him like flames.

He let go of the fan. His arms dropped to his sides.

Once as a teenager he had gone hunting on the land of a man who was his father's patient. When his father introduced him to the man, Werner said, "Hi." Afterward his father lit into him, uncharacteristically, for not being more respectful — he explained that when he was called upon to meet someone, Werner should step forward and extend his hand. His father, a physician, was gentle and decent; that was about the only time he had ever been sharp with his son.

Now Werner made a shift. He spoke to himself, firmly but kindly, like a father. Werner, he said, you've got to calm down. You've dealt with this fan before.

He remembered: it was suspended from the top, by two neat hooks he had put there himself. After lifting it free, then shoving both panes of glass up and wedging them tightly into the frame, Werner stuck his whole torso out the window, sucking in air.

Everything suddenly became crystalline and calm; he could breathe. He looked around, listening, and heard sirens.

"Building's on fire! Call the fire department!" he yelled, leaning out the window.

Straight across was his building's twin, silent and dark. Off to the left, in back of the buildings, was a vacant lot surrounded by Cyclone fencing. Beyond that was Ninety-sixth Street. Sirens but no fire trucks. Directly below him, flames were shooting out of the third-floor windows and curling around the edge of the building.

He lost his fear. He was completely in the moment, experiencing instead of anticipating. Time stretched like rubber. Fascinated, he wandered around inside each moment as though it were a cavernous room.

Summer job at a retread factory, endless deafening days in which the hours were earned slowly through an accumulation of stiff, stinking cords of rubber to be stamped and stacked, and helpless imaginary encounters with every girl in his high school class. Ghost girls who joined him at his locker first thing and followed him out onto the floor. He had to brush past them in order to do his work; interference — one wrong move and your finger, hand, arm is gone. The clock would hop its minutes interminably and then suddenly everyone was poised, Werner and his colleagues, men in big gloves who had been out of high school for thirty years. When the buzzer went off, they were like a herd of steers aimed for a hole in the fence.

Get out while you can, they told him.

Sound clattered back into his head and he began to hear people screaming again, from the fire escapes on the other side of the building. Black smoke was billowing upward from the windows below. The fire was working its way up, floor by floor, the wind moving the smoke to the south, where the fire escapes were. His neighbors kept screaming, many voices, desperate and trapped. Werner was sure they were dying.

Beyond the end of the building and across the vacant lot, he saw between six and twelve people at the bus stop on Ninety-sixth, standing against the Cyclone fence and staring up at the building like people at a bonfire, their faces lit by flames.

He was still experiencing perfect clarity, assessing everything he could see in a clinical manner, sweeping back and forth between the people watching, the flames below him, and the strands of black smoke funneling out the windows.

He could see two options. There was taking a T-shirt, wetting it, draping it over his face, then leaving the apartment and making a run for the roof. Or there was crossing the living room to the fire escape and joining his neighbors in their cauldron of despair. The stairwell to the roof wasn't navigable; he'd already glimpsed it when he opened his door. The living room was dense with smoke; if he did make it across, there was no way he'd get the window gate unlocked. It was new, put in when Werner was out of town, crisscrossed bars with a key the super had placed somewhere along the ledge above.

He was trapped, nearsighted and naked in a burning building. He reached behind, groping, and found the robe that always hung from the loft bed. He put it on without pulling his head back into the room. He leaned farther out.

Werner had said just that night to his friend James that he was sick of being a caterer and wasn't going to do it anymore. He was thinking of taking a long-ago professor's advice to become a fireman, a good job for an artist. Not that his fellow caterers weren't artists too — painters, opera singers, designers — but this was 1991; AIDS and Reagan had happened, and Werner hadn't gotten out when everyone else did. No matter how depressing it got, his co-workers growing gaunt and dying, the economy surging and plummeting, he just hung in there.

He had seen a man nearly lose a hand once, not at the retread factory but later, in college during a gymnastics meet, a friend whose leather grip had somehow caught in the apparatus when he went up and over the bar. His hand tore loose as he finished the revolution, and he hung there by the glove until they could climb up and unbuckle him. The hand had looked so strange lying against the blue of the mat, the wrist bone jutting straight up, white and exposed, until someone put a Dixie cup over it.

The fire crew would have to come from behind the building, Werner realized, in order to climb up and save him, carrying their ladder through the vacant lot, over the Cyclone fences, and into the dark space between the two buildings. Growing up, Werner had worked his way around his family's property on a tall stepladder each summer, moving it a few feet at a time as he trimmed the eight-foot hedge that ran along the border. From a distance the hedge was squared off and stylized, like the neat shrubbery in a Grant Wood painting, but up close it was a dense chaotic bramble of bent twigs and thick, waxy leaves. Bay laurel. He knew its shades of green intimately. Once, far away from home, Werner dreamed of the bay laurel hedge, of stepping inside and finding it hollow, a cool rectangular box that he could lie down in.

Firemen weren't going to save him. They didn't even save cats anymore.

His cat! He turned to shout her name into the apartment.

He couldn't believe what was behind him — the smoke was everywhere, dark and billowing. He shouted into it and then listened. After a moment, coming from somewhere far away, he heard a meow. He kept calling, the meowing getting closer and closer until finally Two was at the open bedroom door. Werner took a breath and ducked back to snatch her up. She struggled, her fur matted and sticky with soot, so he held her in front of him, under the arms like you would a toddler. She yowled, raspy from swallowing smoke.

It was like trying to breathe through flannel. Werner realized he was going to die.

The dark back seat of a car in Iowa City, returning to campus from a gymnastics meet, junior year. Werner and Nate, the guy who would later nearly lose his hand, folded into the back seat, Clayton the all-around guy driving, somebody else shotgun, all of them high on exhaustion and victory. Werner had a simple but impeccable high-bar mount — vertical jump, grab the bar, swing forward straight-bodied, arch and then pike in to create the momentum that would shoot the legs straight up to a handstand. After that, the delirious, controlled fall into giant circles, the body as fully extended as it would go.

In the middle of campus, coming over a rise, they saw it just as they hit it: black ice on the downslope of a steep hill, the car in front of them hydroplaning sideways as their car hit the ice and shot forward like a bullet. Slowly revolving, the sideways car turned and headed back toward them broadside, gaining velocity, its blue flank growing larger and larger. It felt like five weeks, the time between the two cars starting to skid and the jarring impact.

That's what time felt like now, elongated and dreamlike, the outcome sliding toward him out of the cold night.

Inside the smoke, he turned with his cat, moving from the doorway back to the window, three long strides broken down into tiny, fractured increments of motion. Nude descending a staircase of absurdity — it wasn't even his fault, and this is how it ends? He almost laughed. Whatever had happened had happened on a floor below, some accident that had nothing to do with him, but he would be part of the outcome.

It wasn't so much that he never thought it would end this way as that he never thought it would end. His life was so absorbing — a series of long studio days pulling images out of the dark backgrounds. And he was moving away from that now, the backgrounds receding and the objects themselves seeming less iconic and barnacled and more . . . something else. He had wanted to see where he was going, was all, to follow the work.

He was thirty-six, midstride metaphorically and literally. His first studio in New York had been on the property of Cohen Carpentry. The scent of sawdust and the industrious buzz of power tools had become linked with the other accoutrements of creativity — the bristling arrangements of brushes in their jars, the silver tubes of paint, the tin echo inside the turp can as he lifted it to pour. On a grant he had gone to Europe and traveled for four months, drawn to the construction sites in each city he visited. Enormous crawling insects with men operating their pincers, thick sinewy cables like muscled arms, pulleys with long horselike faces, iron beams baled and lashed together like bundles of kindling, strands of rebar emerging from concrete, bent like giant, curling hairs. Werner, lonely and ecstatic, made drawings of it all.

The drawings, back home, became paintings. He painted his way through the objects to what was beyond; he painted the camshaft of the ocean liner until it was like a word repeated so many times that it became something new and foreign.

Even watching all his catering colleagues . . . growing stark, faltering with their trays, eyes getting larger as their flesh diminished . . . Werner had never realized that something unimaginable occurred when the end slithered up: it curled around your feet and entwined you; you became part of it instead of it becoming part of you.

Once, inside the laurel hedge, Werner had found an old Crush bottle hanging suspended, completely encased by tines. The hedge had sent feelers down inside it, twisting into the bottom and then twining back up through the neck. It was marvelous and beautiful and Werner tried to pull it free, but the hedge wouldn't let go of its prize.

He suddenly saw himself letting go, like stepping through the stiff green hedge into the cool rectangular space, taking a few deep breaths and then sleeping. He just wanted to rest. Sometimes a little brown bird would poke its way in and hop among the branches. If the leaves fluttered, Werner would rest the loppers for a moment, shift his weight on the ladder, then begin again.

He had an image now of himself as they would find him, arm around the cat, and was vaguely aware that people would be upset, although right then he couldn't have said who. The best he could conjure was a blurred impression, pointillist stabs of color that stood for sisters, parents, his girlfriend Jean Marie, friends he loved. Peter. Jeff. Chris, his old roommate, who used to set Two on his lap, get her very relaxed and purring, then put her head in his mouth. She had thick whiskers like barbed wire. Once while Werner was asleep she had set a live mouse on his naked belly, and he woke to feel it running up his torso and around his neck. They had been together for nine years now.

If he couldn't save himself, maybe he could help her. Holding the cat like a vessel in front of him, he put her through the open window and out into the air so she could breathe.

It was like being on drugs, the whole world surrounding him like a tidal pool, everything taking on equal significance and richness: the color of the skin on his hand, the eddies of refracted light, the amplified sound of sirens.

Please, he thought. If we can just hang on, the fire department will break in and save us.

Holding Two, both their heads out the window, he looked down and saw that the fire had reached the fourth floor. The smoke was thicker now, less porous. There would be no rescue.

The wind stopped. Holding Two, Werner suddenly couldn't see her. The wind had shifted, and like a fountain the smoke came rushing upward, his open window acting like a funnel, sucking the black cloud inside.

Two began to struggle desperately. Werner glanced backward and the bedpost, a foot and a half away, was gone. The smoke looked like oily Jell-O, granular, particles whirling all around him.

There was no oxygen between the particles now, no way to negotiate anything out of it. The opposite in fact; if air equals life, then non-air equals death, but this was a step beyond — it was non-air with poison.

In the stopped, strangled moment that followed, another thought burst loose and hung there, pale inside the black swirling column.

He would have to jump.

Five stories is too far to fall; he'd never survive it. He'd done it once long ago, a forty-five-foot drop, not onto concrete but into deep, still water. The bridge over Fall Creek, east of Eugene, a wood trestle built into bedrock, the surface of the water below tense and glittering, huge smooth boulders on either shore, his striped towel and white T-shirt draped over one where he would claim them after the jump when the next guy was standing there poised to sever his spine. He had looked down at his feet, which looked delicate at that height, wet sneakers sagging. Somebody hollered, "Hey, Werner," and then an obscenity, and others laughed. He thought he heard sympathy in the shouts, but that was useless, the sympathy of men. You still had to do it. He had made the mistake of pausing, and was momentarily stranded under a bored blue sky, just Werner on a trestle with his delicate-looking feet and the sunburned tops of his knobby knees. He realized he loved himself, gripping the trestle as the afternoon wind thumped at him. But love or no love, he still had to step off, and so he did.

Two didn't want to be held; she was going crazy. The black funnel had engulfed them completely now, and he tried not to breathe it. Hands clamped around Two's rib cage, Werner tried to take in glimpses of the window in the neighboring building straight across, perhaps eight feet away.

Four panes of glass, two over two. Stone sill on the outside. Orange-red drapes pulled shut, a lamp behind them giving off an incandescent glow.

The window would be like his, ancient and sturdy, the glass rippled, the wood thick with a century of paint. He wouldn't have the courage to climb out on his own ledge first — too much time to think — so he'd have to do it in one motion, hop up on the sill in the form of a racing dive. He had been a competitive swimmer from ages seven to twelve, a shivering, long-limbed boy in tight goggles and regulation trunks; he had a muscle memory of the stance, the bending, the tensing of the core. His toes would have to wrap around the sill to create the proper angle forward.

He thought it all the way through and then knew enough to stop thinking about it. He was completely adrenalized now. He cinched Two under his left arm, pressing her as securely as he could to his torso, then placed his right hand, knuckles down, against the wooden sill of the open window.

He spoke to his cat: "Looks like it's time to go."

In one motion, up and out.

He waited an instant for his toes to wrap around the sill — they were there but they hadn't all caught yet. When they did, he pushed off.

His skull broke the wood and shattered the glass into long daggers. He went in up to his knees, which landed on the stone sill, body all the way through onto somebody's bed, right into their apartment, clanging with brightness, lights on in every room.

Startling, everything now in fast motion, like a film whipping by: the orange-red curtains from this side were coarsely woven, the lamp knocked on the floor beaming out its white glare, the coverlet nubby, his shoulders webbed with stickiness.

He called out, his voice ringing with fright and embarrassment: "Is anybody home?"

No answer. He tried again, louder, and then walked swiftly past their belongings and furniture to the door. He felt a twinge of confusion over leaving it unlocked, moments racing past him in a blur as he hesitated in the corridor. This building wasn't on fire but it was being evacuated; in the stairwell there were people rushing around. He yelled down at someone he recognized, a man he'd seen but never talked to.

The man looked up, startled — but then kept going, hurrying down the stairs, carrying what looked like a box of figurines. Others were lugging televisions and computers. One woman in a nightgown and ski jacket was clutching a pot of Swedish ivy, hanger and all, thick strands of macramé slung over her shoulder.

Outside, the street was teeming. There were fire trucks, people running, all manner of blurry chaos, and all of it flashing.

Werner, barefoot, wearing only a bathrobe soaked in blood, walked up to a fireman. "I've hurt myself," he said.

The fireman had seen Werner come out of a building that wasn't on fire. He peered at Werner in the strobe of the red light, clearly confused. A second later, the fireman disappeared.

Werner began shaking uncontrollably. He didn't know what else to do, so he tried to follow the discombobulated fireman, staring into people's faces until he found him in the cab of a vehicle.

"Are you going to help me or what?" Werner asked. His arms were covered in blood, he realized. Everything was. He'd been ruined by the glass, torn up, the guy wouldn't even look at him.

Out of the night, another apparition appeared: a skinny little homeless man, possibly crazy, wearing a filthy red sweatshirt over a coat. Greasy hair, Fu Manchu. He took a close look at Werner, reached out, and tried to steer him away.

Werner wouldn't move.

"There's an ambulance down the block," Fu Manchu said. His features had receded into the grime on his face, but the voice was authoritative.

Werner resisted, backing up. In the chaos of these emergencies, he knew, people got themselves lured away from the lights and mugged. It happened. Anything could happen.

The homeless man sighed, reached under his filthy sweatshirt, and pulled out a badge.

NYPD Undercover.

The doors of the ambulance had a kind of quilted aluminum paneling on them, like a lunch truck, but inside it felt more like a camper, everything stowed in compartments, held secure with straps. Werner sat on one of the cots and the EMTs started questioning him.

"My building caught on fire and I had to jump across into another building," Werner explained, trying to stay calm. He was like a marionette someone was shaking.

The attendants looked at each other and then back at him.

It was predawn, the camper was warm. Somewhere, the deer were rising from their grass mats and moving into the woods, the bucks steering their antlers carefully, like women carrying kindling on their heads.

"We have to take your bathrobe off to examine you," one of the EMTs said.

Werner sat hunched as they lifted the soaking robe from his shoulders, peeling it from his back and sides. He'd seen it, every sportsman had, the frozen moment when the deer was still living, staring upward at the blackening world. Even Werner, so careful, had had to dispatch an animal at close range, the strangeness of shooting down instead of away, the surge of regret — why this? why did I do this? — before it was over and everything resumed, the bright neon of his vest, the green canopy overhead.

He looked down at his left shoulder, where there were three

cuts, large and startling, their pink interiors visible. His right shoulder — swooningly close — had a catastrophic wound, dark red and complicated, a fissure down into his body revealing something sinewy and glistening. He could see his own muscle, the broad deltoid that a man wears fitted over his shoulders like a cape. Werner began to cry.

He never could hold her if she didn't want to be held.

"I don't know what happened," he said. A wave of grief rose over him, pushing him forward into something new and unfamiliar. Failure, a bottomless black lake with something moving inside it.

He began crying so hard it sounded like a fit of choking.

The EMT guys were more or less unmoved by this. They kept sneaking assessing looks at his face as they put cotton over his wounds.

"All right," Werner said, pulling himself together, trying to sit up. The backs of his hands were like the hands of someone who has been murdered and left lying in his own blood. "You have to tell me what happened to my face," he said.

The men handed him a mirror so he could see what they were looking at — there were no cuts; his face was intact but so white it seemed like an emergency in itself, with black rings of soot circling his nostrils and mouth. He looked like one of those spectral creatures in a Japanese horror movie, the subliminal ones shown only in flashes.

Smoke inhalation, possibility of charred lungs.

The ambulance attendants had their walkie-talkies going, communicating with NYU's burn unit, getting clearance to leave the scene. Amid the clatter and static, the cop returned and asked if Werner wanted him to call anyone.

"Would you call my girlfriend?" he asked. "Tell her where they're taking me."

The cop took down the number as Werner was strapped onto the gurney, and asked if the girlfriend should bring anything.

Werner tried to think. "Maybe she could bring me a blanket," he said.

They conducted the ambulance through the New York streets, siren blaring. He had always wondered what this felt like. His mother didn't know where he was, none of the people he loved knew where he was right now, didn't have any idea that Werner had been forced to jump out of his life and into whatever this was.

He closed his eyes and sobbed for a moment inside his oxygen mask. The attendant reached over and adjusted it. Calmed, Werner shut his eyes. These gondolier guys were taking care of his physical self, placing their poles in the deep canal and pulling him along. He could relax, gliding forward over black water, the things that mattered falling like coins from his pockets.

He started crying again.

The ER at five A.M. was completely deserted. A ringing, fluorescent silence, then eight people crowded around to look at Werner. Poking, prodding, asking what happened.

The EMT told them that Werner had jumped out of a burning building into another building, one that wasn't on fire, thereby saving his own life. This caused a stir.

"We gotta call the newspaper," a doctor said.

"No," Werner said. He looked straight ahead, not at any of them. "I just want you to sew me up."

A young resident began babbling. He had worked in that ER for a long time, he had seen extreme things, people in bad circumstances, people shot in the head. Et cetera. You couldn't imagine the shit you hear, the stories people come in there with. "But yours is the most amazing," the resident exclaimed, his professionalism totally breaking down.

"Get him out of here," Werner said.

They wiped his face with something cool and antiseptic but left the rest of him covered with soot, dirt, and dried blood. They wheeled in a crash cart and took x-rays, Velcroed a foam brace around his neck without disturbing the gauze on his shoulders, and stuck EKG pads to his chest in a careful constellation.

"Can you relax that?" the nurse asked, nodding toward his right hand. She was popping open packages of sterile tubing, preparing to put two IVs in one arm, glucose and antibiotics.

Werner's left hand was open, but his right was clenched into a fist. He opened it for her.

Resting on his palm was the brass key to the old mahogany wardrobe in his bedroom, where his underwear was kept. He had snatched the key out instead of turning it. For a second, he had a grainy flashback of himself groping dumbly at the tall dark door, whirling in panic. He stared at the key, this thing he had brought with him from his old life.

"I dropped Two," he said.

The nurse stopped momentarily to glance down at her feet and then under the gurney. "I'm just about done," she reassured him. As she taped the needles in place and flicked her fingernail at the tubing, another nurse came in and without apology or ado reached under his sheet and inserted a catheter. It was swift and brutal, like plugging a burning wand into a socket, and Werner cried out, finally, in indignation.

Everyone left.

He was propped up on the gurney with things sticking out of him, unrecognizable to himself. He wiggled his toes. They were still his toes. He bent them and they bent.

The rolling table next to him was made to glide under and over a hospital bed; on its laminate wood-grain surface rested the brass key with its single tarnished tooth. Werner should have been dead, but instead he wasn't; that part, he still didn't get. Down at the bottom of the gurney were his toes. He moved them back and forth again like levers.

The officious pink curtain that moved on little ball bearings was quiet now, a thin membrane between Werner and the world.

He waited.

"Mr. Hoeflich," the doctor said.

Werner opened his eyes. It was the guy who seemed to be in charge, or anyway the one who was tallest. He was going bald in a handsome way, and seemed a little bit like an athlete, one of those TV doctors who played hoops out back on a slow night in the ER.

"When can I get sewn up and leave?" Werner asked him.

"We're sending you to intensive care," the doctor informed him. "Your blood gases show so much carbon monoxide we're guessing the lungs are scorched." He gave this time to sink in before he continued. "Very dangerous if that's what we've got. The sacs begin to fill up with water and you stop breathing."

Werner felt like swooning. Drowned by your own body. He had held Two, like a vessel, out the window. The whole thing seemed now like a succession of moments. In that moment, and the moment before, the smoke had been curling sideways around the building, a bolt of black cloth unwinding. Then it stopped and there was a moment of emptiness before the black current was swept upward, and he realized it wasn't like cloth at all; it was dark and viscid, like used motor oil, and they weren't breathing it, they were drinking it.

Those fucking people carrying their TVs out. He hadn't even saved his cat.

The dark lake that he thought was all around him was now seeping inside, swelling his lungs like wineskins.

"I just want to be sewn up," Werner said.

"Yeah, I don't know why you aren't," the doctor replied before disappearing.

He lay there some more, congealing.

The curtain rolled open a few inches and a janitor took a look at him, left, and then returned with Jean Marie, who was unprepared for what she found, the bloody mess on the gurney. She had been told only that she needed to come pick him up. Werner broke down at the sight of her. She was wearing blue jeans and a wool coat, blond hair still stuck inside her scarf, which she unwound without taking her eyes from Werner. Her face, her lovely off-kilter mouth. Like the brass key, Jean Marie had somehow made the leap with him to this new world. He put one hand over his eyes, crying.

"Two is dead. I dropped Two."

"Werner," Jean Marie said, touching him. "What do you want me to do?"

"You have to find her," he said. "Get somebody to go around back with you, under my window." Other things as well: his glasses, his wallet, five hundred dollars in a bureau drawer.

Jean Marie spoke quietly to him for a while and then stood up, rewinding her scarf, this time lifting her hair free of it before leaning over him again. She would come back. She would try to bring his friend Peter with her. He felt the soft knot of cashmere against his chest and then she was gone and someone else had materialized, another apparition. A Filipino woman in pink scrubs, blurry and beautiful, with coral nail polish as flawless as the finish on a new car.

"You haven't been sewn up," she informed him, lifting the gauze from his wounds. "Let's do that."

His muscle was exposed, the ragged opening leading down to it coagulated and angry. "And you are?" he asked her.

She was the ER surgeon. Using a tool that looked like a cross between a pair of scissors and a needle, she gave him fifty shots of lidocaine in his shoulders and torso. He looked up at the ceiling. In those paintings of Saint Sebastian, the eyes were always tipped toward the heavens. Orion in the night sky, drawing back his bow and shooting whatever was up there. All over Werner's upper body, small pains burned like stars. He didn't know if he could stand it, and then a numbness started to move across him, and he felt impassive in his suffering.

Before the Filipino doctor could stitch him up, a nurse poked her head in. "You're supposed to be down in *eleven*," she said to the doctor, who hustled out like a student caught by the hall monitor.

Werner waited.

A half hour later they flattened him out and trundled him along a series of tiled passageways. The hospital seemed both futuristic and worn out, like an old starship. Above him were fluorescent bulbs behind ribbed plastic panels. Wafers of light, one after the other, until he gave up and turned his head to the side. A man he couldn't see was steering the gurney expertly on its rubber treads, bumping it through doorways and, once, giving it a generous push and letting it glide alone down a quiet corridor, past a nurses' station where an African-American woman looked at Werner without curiosity.

It didn't seem utterly impossible that he had died and couldn't tell the difference, that no one here could, that they were all dead too, guiding gurneys, giving shots, whispering along in blood-spattered clogs. His lungs felt full and frightening in his chest, like cow udders.

They got him situated, off the gurney and onto a bed with a stainless steel trough around the edge. He tried to sit up and someone pushed him back down.

"I'm going to be your doctor," someone else said, a jovial Italian man surrounded by others. They all stared down at Werner as brown liquid was poured into his wounds. It was cold, and pooled up in the trough. The doctor had a big horse needle, curved. He slung his necktie over his shoulder and began sewing Werner's deepest cuts from the inside out.

He heard someone telling his story, the jump from one building to another, and a new embellishment, compliments of the lab: his blood gases had revealed that another ten seconds and he couldn't have done it, saved himself.

I didn't save myself, he thought, it was random.

You could spend your whole life swinging from rings and high bars, doing racing dives at seven A.M. into cold pools, but if the smoke happened to rise in a particular way, blocking the view of the window across the way, or if that window had a tall bureau in front of it instead of a bed, then your athletic ability was nothing more than an anecdote to be mentioned at your funeral.

This realization was new to Werner, like the sense of failure had been. It was a shameful, contaminating knowledge, jabbing him in the ribs like the finger of God. Werner felt a prodding, something being tugged upward and then released. It had been more than a half hour since the lidocaine.

"I'm starting to feel what you're doing," he told the doctor. "I can feel my shoulders." He was becoming agitated and hallucinatory; he could feel God plucking at the slippery muscle. Where were the people he knew, Jean Marie and the others? He was supposed to work that night for Glorious Foods, and it was all taking too long.

"Mr. Hoeflich, would you like a shot of morphine?" the Italian doctor asked. He stepped away from the table for a moment and then stepped back with a different needle.

Werner didn't even have to answer. They gave him a shot but he could still feel it; they gave him another, and a moment later he felt normal.

"My lungs," he said.

"Bronchoscopy," the Italian doctor said. "As soon as we're done here."

A few minutes passed.

"Will it hurt?" Werner asked.

"It won't be pleasant," the doctor said pleasantly.

One of the people standing around, a nurse wearing Christmas tree earrings, left to call him in sick at Glorious Foods. Werner couldn't remember the number, but she was happy to look it up.

"Ask for Jeff," Werner said. "Make sure you're talking to him." He closed his eyes for a moment; when he opened them the nurse was back.

"He was worried you were burned," she reported, and went to work unwinding from a portable machine a flexible steel shaft the size of a drinking straw. The shaft had a camera on the end of it and the doctor began feeding it into Werner's nose, inch by inch, driving it like a spike into his brain.

He arched up on the table, and people scattered for an instant, a flock of birds rising and then settling again, this time with three men on top of Werner, trying to hold him down. He came loose, flailing, and another man materialized and piled on. Werner fought silently, the spike probing into his head, his utterly private reaches.

"Give him a muscle relaxer!" somebody said, panting, and a moment later he couldn't move.

The thing pushed its way down until it was in his lungs. He felt like he was drowning. It was worse than the fire, being inanimate, like something already dead. He sank to the bottom of the lake, into the slippery weeds. The camera emitted a bead of light, peering at his cilia.

"It looks okay," he heard the Italian doctor say.

Up in the ICU he was still partially submerged as they tugged him from the gurney to a bed, a drowned man bumping against the pilings. The ICU was gleaming and technical, separated into pods, each with its own nurses' station.

"Whores," a man said to the ceiling. "Whoring *whores*."

The man was covered in gauze and a sheet; nothing but a blackened forearm and a pale horned foot were visible. It was like one of those all-night, labyrinthine dreams in which everywhere you turn there is some bizarre oversize thing occurring. Werner manually tugged one leg over and then the other, helping to arrange himself between the cool railings of the bed.

"Fuck," the man said intently through his teeth. "Fucking *fuck*."

"He's a homeless gentleman," the nurse confided, "set on fire by a group of kids."

"I'm sorry," Werner said.

"That's okay," the nurse said automatically.

She prepared a morphine shot for him, and as she gave it to him, two gowned and masked figures were ushered in to stand alongside his bed. They were wearing paper hats and booties. Werner recognized Jean Marie's eyes and then Peter's. He wept again, helplessly, as if he were seeing people from his distant past.

"Werner," they said through their masks, touching him on the legs.

They had found the wallet, the money, and the glasses, and taken two bottles of good champagne from his refrigerator. Nothing else was salvageable.

They were so sorry.

He closed his eyes and paddled away on his morphine raft. He watched himself throwing a series of baseballs through a window, making a bigger and bigger hole, then saw himself throwing his cat through it, a gentle, underhand toss. He saw Two plummeting off a bridge in a cartoon landscape, and he saw himself reaching down with a long, long arm to neatly catch her, a foot above the water, on a waiter's tray.

He roused himself to talk to Jean Marie and Peter. "I canceled my job for Glorious," he told them. "But I'm supposed to work for Sarah too. I think I can do it."

Their eyebrows rose.

The nurse left her station then to escort the visitors out, and Werner reclined into the cartoon landscape, a giant resting his back against a sand-colored butte. He reached out and grasped the cool railing. Giants had been the thing he liked best, back when he flew; they were preparation, momentum gathering for what would happen when he let go of the bar. He did his impeccable mount: swing forward straight-bodied, get a little tap, arch, pike, then straight up into a handstand. Now he was balanced over the railing of the bedrock bridge, high above Fall Creek.

"Fucking *doc,*" the charred man cried out.

The fall from the trestle all those years ago had been long enough to entertain regrets, although Werner had gone in just right — perpendicular, arms at his sides in tight fists, chin down. The impact was an explosion from below, like being hit with a plank on the soles of his feet and socked in the jaw at the same time. He plunged down and down, like a bullet shot into the water, the force of it lifting his arms. In the last moment of his descent, before he began to rise naturally and then to kick, Werner had looked up to see a pale green pillar of light leading to the surface.

*

When he woke, things were different. The female nurse had been exchanged for a male one, and the swearing man for an intubated patient with a sighing respirator. In the bed next to Werner's was a small white figure, a toddler covered in gauze. Her face was turned in his direction, but her eyes were closed.

He felt insubstantial and gossamer, as if he were spun out of glass. Still stoned but not enough. Everything hurt, even his gums. It would take a long time for the pain to go away, longer than ICU and step-down, longer than the ward filled with grizzled men watching blaring televisions. Both the pain and the residual pain, which seemed structural in nature: a kind of raw, bludgeoning happiness that would afflict him for months, until he managed to separate from his feelings altogether. Also long-term tinnitus, from the blow to the top of the skull, an interior clanging that would never allow him, even for a moment, to confuse himself with the old Werner.

Two weeks later, Frank, the super, took him around back, through the rubble of the fire, into the space between the buildings. Werner knelt to examine the cat Frank had found hidden in the shadow of an unused doorway. She had pulled her body through several feet of gravel and debris to a protected spot and died there. Werner recognized the tail, ringed gray and brown.

And that took care of that.

The Freedom to Offend

FROM THE NEW REPUBLIC

THE STRANGEST ASPECT OF Mel Gibson's drunken outburst in Malibu was not the anti-Semitic ranting. The notion that "the fucking Jews" are "responsible for all the wars in the world" (and pretty much everything else too) is neither new nor unusual. It has been an anti-Semitic cliché since the late nineteenth century. More disturbing, I think, was the peculiar mixture of sentimental religiosity and Hollywood arrogance that came after Gibson recovered from his hangover in jail. He wished to "meet with leaders in the Jewish community, with whom I can have a one-on-one discussion to discern the appropriate path for healing." As though no one else but "leaders" would do; as though these supposed leaders were priests, or psychiatrists, or yogis in the business of personal healing. As though anti-Semitism were a wound inflicted on Gibson by the outside world.

It should be no surprise that anti-Semitism still exists, just as bigotry against blacks, or Muslims, or Sikhs, or Tutsis, or indeed Catholics still goes on. That Jews were the victims of the most systematic genocide ever attempted lends a particularly sinister resonance to anti-Semitism, but as a prejudice it is hardly unique. Mass murder of Jews, at least in the Western world, is no longer on the agenda, and it is surely not what Gibson had in mind. But social prejudice is bad enough. It is at least one sign of progress that anti-Semitism, like racial prejudice against black people, is no longer socially acceptable. We cannot call people yids or niggers without being taken to task for it, and this is a good thing.

This progress probably would not have happened without the efforts of pressure groups and communal organizations, just as work-ers' rights would never have been expanded, or perhaps even granted, without trade unions. Such American organizations as the Anti-Defamation League or the National Association for the Ad-vancement of Colored People have made society more civilized. Activists and community leaders are there to make sure that it stays that way.

But like all forms of power, the power to advance the interests of vulnerable minorities is open to corruption. Just as trade-union fat cats sometimes abuse their position to accumulate power (and wealth) for its own sake, the community leaders and official watch-dogs of anti-racism can be tempted to advance their own interests and those of their organizations in a way that is not necessarily helpful to the people they are supposed to defend. When the whis-tle is blown too often, even when it is utterly uncalled for, or when offense is taken for self-serving reasons, even where none was in-tended, the guardianship of civil behavior can slip into a form of intimidation, which interferes with free speech.

One of the great powers appropriated by communal organi-zations, and by authoritarian national governments too, is the power over the use of language. They set the terms in which their communities can be discussed by others. These terms sometimes change quite suddenly to demonstrate the clout of the leaders. We are told to say Mumbai now instead of Bombay, because the leaders of the powerful Maharastran community in India decreed it. There is nothing offensive about the word Burma, except that the military junta decided that it had to be Myanmar.

What's in a name? Quite a lot, actually. NHK, the national Japa-nese broadcasting company, has a constantly updated list of appro-priate words for various minorities, including the socially discrimi-nated outcastes whose traditional occupations, such as butchering, slaughtering, or leather manufacturing, were considered to be pol-luted (Buddhism and Shinto have strong views on purity and death). These outcastes, or *burakumin,* still face many difficulties, and they are represented by various organizations, who define the precise terms in which the minority can be spoken about. But these terms change so fast, and for such complicated reasons, and are often enforced with such heavy-handedness, that NHK, and in-deed most Japanese media, prefer not to touch the subject at all.

This cannot be good for the *burakumin*. When a touchy subject can no longer be openly and rationally discussed, it is left up to the bigots to talk about it irrationally.

Intimidation is most effective when the fear is free-floating and threats can be left unspoken. One example is the current fear of saying anything that might be construed as being anti-Semitic, especially in the United States, where Jews are more secure than they have ever been anywhere at any time in history. Again, to guard against anti-Semitism is plainly a good thing. But this particular whistle has been blown so often and with such shrillness that exaggerated anxiety sometimes impairs serious discussion, and not only about Israel.

Recently I experienced an example of this myself. I was invited by a curator at the Metropolitan Museum of Art in New York to contribute an essay to the catalogue of an exhibition on the history of eighteenth- and nineteenth-century English dress and dandyism — not a particularly delicate subject. I wished to compare the relative openness of nineteenth-century English society with continental Europe, and so I cited the example of Benjamin Disraeli, a Jewish dandy who was elected prime minister. It was quickly made clear by the editor of the catalogue, as well as by the curator of the exhibition, that this reference to a Jewish dandy had to go. I was told that I didn't know "what things are like around here." And that "members of the board are very touchy on this topic." Perhaps they are, perhaps they aren't. No member of the board had seen the reference, let alone passed judgment on it. But fear of such judgment was enough to strike the "offending" words.

These spats over language and presentation actually cross communal lines. In the current climate a writer of Jewish or Muslim or Sikh extraction can just as easily be accused of offending the "community" as an outsider. Salman Rushdie is the most famous example. There are many others. In Birmingham, England, a play titled *Behzti* (*Dishonor*), by a British Sikh author named Gurpreet Kaur Bhatti, about sexual abuse and murder among British Sikhs, was discontinued after Sikhs staged a riot outside the theater. Few, if any, had read the play, but community leaders, invited to attend the dress rehearsal, had been offended by the "negative portrayal" of Sikhs. The police refused to guarantee the safety of the venue. So the show was canceled.

Monica Ali's best-selling novel *Brick Lane,* set among Bangladeshis in Britain, was going to be filmed in Brick Lane, the heart of the Bangladeshi area in East London. But then a local businessman named Abdus Salique organized the Campaign Against Monica Ali's Film Brick Lane, and threatened to burn her books, because he claimed that the novel did not present his community in the proper way. Salique and a small group of like-minded men call themselves community leaders, even though no one elected them, and most local Bangladeshis voiced no objection to the film or to Ali's novel. Still, the location for the film had to be changed.

No matter how much good may have been done in the past by communal pressure groups, the increasing prominence of "community leaders" and unelected figures who claim the right to define how others should talk about their ethnic or religious communities is having a damaging effect on our right to speak freely. Rushdie has made an important distinction between attacking people and criticizing what they stand for. We should treat individual Muslims, Christians, Jews, Sikhs, and the rest with courtesy and respect, but what they think or believe must not be exempt from criticism, or even from ridicule.

The problem is that many believers are unable to make such a distinction. The Dutch filmmaker Theo van Gogh was murdered in 2004 by a radical Islamist because he had "insulted the Prophet." Van Gogh often said offensive, even disgusting things, but he never mocked an individual Muslim. He mocked only the faith. For his killer, however, there was no difference. And our democratically elected leaders in government are more and more frightened into pandering to this sentiment.

The British government introduced a new law this year against stirring up hatred of people on the grounds of their religious beliefs. This sounds very progressive and noble-minded. In fact, it is not. Where exactly is the border between criticism or ridicule and "stirring up hatred"? Who defines the meaning of hatred? And who decides when it has been stirred up? In Salique's view, that is exactly what Ali, the daughter of a Bangladeshi, was doing with her gently satirical novel about a Bangladeshi family in London.

Allowing self-elected (or even popularly elected) leaders of minority communities to delegitimize criticism, to censor it by threatening violence (as happened in Birmingham), plays into the hands of bigots. Given his stated view that Jews run the world, it is no wonder that Mel Gibson wants to sit down with their leaders. The increasing number of people who throw their weight around on behalf of Jews and other minorities only confirm what sinister conspiracy theorists think anyway.

In one sense, leaders of minorities are a bit like bosses of criminal gangs. Crime syndicates, organized along ethnic lines, often claim to represent the interests of recent immigrants who have nowhere else to turn in an unfamiliar country. But which second- or third-generation Italian American or British Chinese would want to be represented by the Mafia or the Chinese triads? Most people, once they move into the middle class, want to be identified as national citizens anyway, rather than as members of ethnic or religious communities, although this does not exclude the possibility of belonging to both.

The problem of identification is not the same everywhere. The French republic goes out of its way to identify all its passport holders only as citizens, and pretends that ethnic and religious divisions are irrelevant. This is enlightened, but it makes it harder to discuss the particular problems faced by immigrants who still live in isolated communities. Officially, problems based on ethnic or religious background are not supposed to exist. The old idea of the melting pot in the United States was somewhat analogous to this: everyone, regardless of where hc or she came from, would become an American. But this has begun to unravel as the worship of ethnicity and the politics of "identity" emphasize and celebrate differences rather than a universal American civic identity.

There is a reactionary aspect to the ideal of multiculturalism as it is espoused in Britain and the Netherlands, and increasingly even in the United States. It presumes that minorities would rather be represented by ethnic or religious leaders than by national ones. This gives too much power to community leaders whose status is dependent on their ability to control the way we speak or think about the people supposedly in their charge, and it stops people from thinking of themselves as individuals and citizens. In fact, it thwarts rational discussion altogether. And rational discussion is a vital aspect of political education. It certainly was necessary to educate the mainstream of democratic societies to respect the rights of minorities, but now immigrants and their offspring must learn that to be offended is the price we all must pay for our freedom of speech and freedom of thought. Since many immigrants come from places where such freedom does not exist, they should be the first to appreciate its benefits.

MARK DANNER

Iraq: The War of the Imagination

FROM THE NEW YORK REVIEW OF BOOKS

Today, if we went into Iraq, like the president would like us to do, you
know where you begin. You never know where you are going to end.
— *George F. Kennan, September 26, 2002*[1]

I ask you, sir, what is the American army doing inside Iraq? . . . Saddam's
story has been finished for close to three years.
— *President Mahmoud Ahmadinejad of Iran to Mike Wallace,* 60 Minutes,
August 13, 2006

IN THE RUINED CITY of Fallujah, its pale tan buildings pulver-
ized by Marine artillery in the two great assaults of this long war
(the aborted attack of March 2004 and then the bloody, triumphant al-Fajr [The Dawn] campaign of the following November),
behind the lines of giant sandbags and concrete T-walls and
barbed wire that surrounded the tiny beleaguered American out-
post there, I sat in my body armor and Kevlar helmet and thought
of George F. Kennan. Not the grand old man of American diplo-
macy, the ninety-eight-year-old Father of Containment who, listening to the war drums beat from a Washington nursing home in the
fall of 2002, had uttered the prophetic words above. I was thinking
of an earlier Kennan, the brilliant and ambitious young diplomat
who during the late 1920s and 1930s had gazed out on the crum-
bling European order from Tallinn and Berlin and Prague and
read the signs of the coming world conflict.

For there in the bunkered Civil-Military Operations Center

(known as "the C-MOC") in downtown Fallujah, where a few score Marines and a handful of civilians subsisted in a broken-down bunkered building without running water or fresh food, I met young Kennan's reincarnation in the person of a junior State Department official: a bright, aggressive young man who spent his twenty-hour days rumbling down the ruined streets in body armor and helmet with his reluctant Marine escorts, meeting with local Iraqi officials, and writing tart cables back to Baghdad or Washington telling his bosses the truth of what was happening on the ground, however reluctant they might be to hear it. This young diplomat was resourceful and brilliant and indefatigable, and as I watched him joking and arguing with the local sheikhs and politicos and technocrats — who were meeting, as they were forced to do, in the American bunker — I thought of the indomitable young Kennan of the interwar years, and of how, if the American effort in Iraq could ever be made to "work," only undaunted and farseeing young men like this one, his spiritual successor, could make it happen.

This was October 2005, on the eve of the nationwide referendum on Iraq's proposed constitution, and I had come to Fallujah, the heart of rebellious Anbar province, to see whether the Sunnis could gather the political strength to vote it down. In a provision originally insisted on by the Kurds, a provision that typified an American-designed political process that had been intended to unify the country but that instead had helped pull it inexorably apart, the proposed constitution could be rejected if, in three of Iraq's eighteen provinces, more than two in three Iraqis coming to the polls voted no. During the first post-Saddam election the previous January, the televised extravaganza of "waving purple fingers" which had become perhaps the most celebrated of the many promised "turning points" of this long war, the Sunnis had boycotted the polls. This time, after Herculean efforts of persuasion and negotiation by the American ambassador, most Sunnis were expected to vote. What would draw them, though — or such, anyway, was the common wisdom — was the chance not to affirm the constitution but to doom it, and the political process along with it.

And so as I sat after midnight on the eve of the vote, scribbling in my notebook in the dimly lit C-MOC bunker as the young diplomat explained to me the intricacies of the politics of the battered city, I was pleased to see him suddenly lean forward and, with quick glances to either side, offer me a confidence. "You know, tomorrow you are going to be surprised," he told me, speaking softly. "Everybody is going to be surprised. People here are not only going to vote. People here — a great many people here — are going to vote yes."

I was stunned. That the Sunnis would actually come out to support the constitution would be an astonishing turnabout and, for the American effort in Iraq, an enormously positive one; for it would mean that despite the escalating violence on the ground, especially here in Anbar, Iraq was in fact moving toward a rough political consensus. It would mean that beneath the bloody landscape of suicide bombings and assassinations and roadside bombs a common idea about politics and compromise was taking shape. It would mean that what had come to seem a misbegotten political process that charted and even worsened the growing divisions among Iraqis had actually become the avenue for bringing them together. It would mean there might be hope.

I took the young diplomat's words as an invaluable bit of inside wisdom from the American who knew this ground better than any other, and I kept them in mind a few hours later as I traveled from polling place to polling place in that city of rubble, listening as the Fallujans told me of their anger at the Americans and the "Iranians" (as they called the leading Shiite politicians) and of their hatred for the constitution that they believed was meant to divide and thus destroy Iraq. I pondered the diplomat's words that evening when I realized that in a long day of interviews I'd not met a single Iraqi who would admit to voting for the constitution. And I thought of his words again several days later when it was confirmed that in Anbar province — where the most knowledgeable, experienced, indefatigable American had confided to me what he had plainly ardently believed, that on the critical vote on the constitution "a great many people here are going to vote yes" — that in Anbar ninety-seven out of every hundred Iraqis who voted had voted no. With all his contacts and commitment, with all his energy and brilliance, on the most basic and critical issue of politics on the ground he had been entirely, catastrophically wrong.

1

"You know where you begin. You never know where you are going to end." The ninety-eight-year-old George F. Kennan, sitting in the Washington nursing home as the war came on, knew from eight decades of experience to focus first of all on the problem of what we know and what we don't know. You know, though you spend your endless, frustrating days speaking to Iraqis, lobbying them, arguing with them, that in a country torn by a brutal and complicated war, those Iraqis perforce are drawn from a small and special subset of the population: Iraqis who are willing to risk their lives by meeting with and talking to Americans. Which is to say, very often, Iraqis who depend on the Americans not only for their livelihoods but for their survival. You know that the information these Iraqis draw on is similarly limited, and that what they convey is itself selected, to a greater or lesser extent, to please their interlocutor. But though you know that much of your information comes from a thin, inherently biased slice of Iraqi politics and Iraqi life, hundreds of conversations during those grueling twenty-hour days eventually lead you to think, must lead you to think, that you are coming to understand what's happening in this immensely complicated, violent place. You come to believe you know. And so often, even about the largest things, you do not know.

As this precious stream of flickering knowledge travels "up the chain" from those on the shell-pocked, dangerous ground collecting it to those in Washington offices ultimately making decisions based on it, the problem of what we really know intensifies, acquiring a fierce complexity. Policymakers, peering second-, third-, fourth-hand into a twilight world, must learn a patient, humble skepticism. Or else, confronted with an ambiguous reality they do not like, they turn away, ignoring the shadowy, shifting landscape and forcing their eyes stubbornly toward their own ideological light. Unable to find clarity, they impose it. Consider, for example, these words of Defense Secretary Donald H. Rumsfeld, speaking about the Iraq war on November 9, 2006, two days after the midterm elections and the day after President Bush fired him: "It is very clear that the major combat operations were an enormous success. It's clear that in Phase Two of this, it has not been going well enough or fast enough."[2]

Such analyses are not uncommon from Pentagon civilians; thus Dov Zakheim, a former Rumsfeld aide, to a television interviewer later that evening: "People will debate the second part, the second phase of what happened in Iraq. Very few are arguing that the military victory in the first phase was anything but an outright success."[3]

Three years and eight months after the Iraq war began, the secretary of defense and his allies see in Iraq not one war but two. One is the Real Iraq War — the "outright success" that only very few would deny, the war in which American forces were "greeted as liberators," according to the famous prediction of Vice President Dick Cheney, which he doggedly insists was in fact proved true: "true within the context of the battle against the Saddam Hussein regime and his forces. That went very quickly."[4] It is "within this context" that the former secretary of defense and the vice president see America's current war in Iraq as in fact comprising a brief, dramatic, and "enormously successful" war of a few weeks' duration leading to a decisive victory, and then . . . what? Well, whatever we are in now: a Phase Two, a "postwar phase" (as Bob Woodward sometimes calls it) that has lasted three and a half years and continues. In the first, successful, Real Iraq War, 140 Americans died. In the postwar phase, 2,700 Americans have died — and counting. What is happening now in Iraq is not in fact a war at all but a phase, a non-war, something unnamed, unconceptualized — unplanned.

Anyone seeking to understand what has become the central conundrum of the Iraq war — how it is that so many highly accomplished, experienced, and intelligent officials came together to make such monumental, consequential, and, above all, obvious mistakes, mistakes that much of the government knew very well at the time were mistakes — must see beyond what seems to be a simple rhetoric of self-justification and follow it where it leads: toward the War of Imagination that senior officials decided to fight in the spring and summer of 2002 and to whose image they clung long after reality had taken a sharply separate turn. In that War of Imagination victory was to be decisive, overwhelming, evincing a terrible power — enough to wipe out the disgrace of September 11 and remake the threatening world. In *State of Denial,* Woodward recounts how Michael Gerson, at the time Bush's chief

speechwriter, asked Henry Kissinger why he had supported the
Iraq war:

> "Because Afghanistan wasn't enough," Kissinger answered. In the con-
> flict with radical Islam, he said, they want to humiliate us. "And we need
> to humiliate them." The American response to 9/11 had essentially to
> be more than proportionate — on a larger scale than simply invading
> Afghanistan and overthrowing the Taliban. Something else was essen-
> tial. The Iraq war was essential to send a larger message, "in order to
> make a point that we're not going to live in this world that they want
> for us."

Though to anyone familiar with Kissinger's "realist" rhetoric of
power and credibility his analysis will come as no surprise, Gerson,
the deeply religious idealist who composed Bush's most soaring
music about "ending tyranny" and "ridding the world of evil,"
seems mildly disappointed: Kissinger "viewed Iraq purely in the
context of power politics. It was not idealism. He didn't seem to
connect with Bush's goal of promoting democracy."

Gerson, of course, was the author of what would come to be
called the Bush Doctrine, a neoconservative paean to democracy
that maintains that "the realistic interests of America would now be
served by fidelity to American ideals, especially democracy." Others in the administration, however, plainly did "connect" with
Kissinger's stark realism: Donald Rumsfeld, for example, whom
Ron Suskind depicts, in *The One Percent Doctrine,* struggling with
other officials in spring 2002 to cope with various terrifying warnings of impending attacks on the United States:

> All these reports helped fuel Rumsfeld's sense of futility as to America's
> ability to stop the spread of destructive weapons and keep them from
> terrorists. That futility was the fuel that drove the plans to invade Iraq
> . . . as soon as possible.
>
> Cheney's ideas about how "our reaction" would shape behavior —
> whatever the evidence showed — were expressed in an off-the-record
> meeting Rumsfeld had with NATO defense chiefs in Brussels on June 6.
> According to an outline for his speech, the secretary told those assem-
> bled that "absolute proof cannot be a precondition for action."
>
> The primary impetus for invading Iraq, according to those attending
> NSC briefings on the Gulf in this period, was to make an example of
> Hussein, to create a demonstration model to guide the behavior of any-
> one with the temerity to acquire destructive weapons or, in any way,
> flout the authority of the United States.

In the great, multicolored braid of reasons and justifications leading to the Iraq war, one might call this "the realist strand," and
though the shape of the reasoning might seem to Gerson to stand
as far from "democracy building" and "ending tyranny" as "power
politics" does from "idealism," the distance is wholly illusory, dependent on an ideological clarity that was never present. In fact,
the two chains of reasoning looped and intersected, leading inexorably to a common desire for a particular action — confronting
Saddam Hussein and Iraq — that had been the subject of the administration's first National Security Council meeting, in January
2001, and that had been pushed to the fore again by Defense Department officials in the first "war cabinet" meeting after the September 11 attacks.

Woodward describes a report commissioned by Paul Wolfowitz,
then deputy secretary of defense, intended to produce "the kinds
of ideas and strategy needed to deal with a crisis of the magnitude
of 9/11." After the attacks, Wolfowitz talked to his friend Christopher DeMuth, president of the American Enterprise Institute, who
gathered together a group of intellectuals and academics for a series of discussions that came to be known as Bletchley II (after the
World War II think tank of mathematicians and cryptographers set
up at Bletchley Park).[5] Out of these discussions, Woodward tells us,
DeMuth drafted an influential report, "Delta of Terrorism," which
concluded, in the author's paraphrase, that "the United States was
in for a two-generation battle with radical Islam":

> "The general analysis was that Egypt and Saudi Arabia, where most of
> the hijackers came from, were the key, but the problems there are in-
> tractable. Iran is more important, where they were confident and suc-
> cessful in setting up a radical government." But Iran was similarly dif-
> ficult to envision dealing with, he said.
>   But Saddam Hussein was different, weaker, more vulnerable. DeMuth
> said they had concluded that "Baathism is an Arab form of fascism trans-
> planted to Iraq." . . .
>   "We concluded that a confrontation with Saddam was inevitable. He
> was a gathering threat — the most menacing, active and unavoidable
> threat. We agreed that Saddam would have to leave the scene before the
> problem would be addressed." That was the only way to transform the
> region.

According to Woodward, this report had "a strong impact on President Bush, causing him to focus on the 'malignancy' of the Middle East" — and the need to act to excise it, beginning with an attack on Iraq that would not only serve, in its devastating rapidity and effectiveness, as a "demonstration model" to deter anyone thinking to threaten the United States but would begin a process of "democratic transformation" that would quickly spread throughout the region. The geopolitical thinking animating this "democratic domino theory" could be plainly discerned before the war, as I wrote five months before U.S. Army tanks crossed the border into Iraq:

> Behind the notion that an American intervention will make of Iraq "the first Arab democracy," as Deputy Defense Secretary Paul Wolfowitz put it, lies a project of great ambition. It envisions a post–Saddam Hussein Iraq — secular, middle-class, urbanized, rich with oil — that will replace the autocracy of Saudi Arabia as the key American ally in the Persian Gulf, allowing the withdrawal of United States troops from the kingdom. The presence of a victorious American Army in Iraq would then serve as a powerful boost to moderate elements in neighboring Iran, hastening that critical country's evolution away from the mullahs and toward a more moderate course. Such an evolution in Tehran would lead to a withdrawal of Iranian support for Hezbollah and other radical groups, thereby isolating Syria and reducing pressure on Israel. This undercutting of radicals on Israel's northern borders and within the West Bank and Gaza would spell the definitive end of Yasir Arafat and lead eventually to a favorable solution of the Arab-Israeli problem.
>
> This is a vision of great sweep and imagination: comprehensive, prophetic, evangelical. In its ambitions, it is wholly foreign to the modesty of containment, the ideology of a status-quo power that lay at the heart of American strategy for half a century. It means to remake the world, to offer to a political threat a political answer. It represents a great step on the road toward President Bush's ultimate vision of "freedom's triumph over all its age-old foes."[6]

It represented as well a breathtaking gamble, for if the victory in Iraq was to achieve what was expected — which is to say, "humiliate" the forces of radical Islam and reestablish American prestige and credibility; serve as a "demonstration model" to ward off attacks from any rogue state that might threaten the United States, either directly or by supplying weapons of mass destruction to terrorists; and transform the Middle East by sending a "democratic tsunami" cascading from Tehran to Gaza — if the Iraq war was to achieve this, victory must be rapid, decisive, overwhelming.

Only Donald Rumsfeld's transformed military — a light, quick, lean force dependent on overwhelming firepower directed precisely by high technology and with very few "boots on the ground" — could make this happen, or so he and his planners thought. Victory would be quick and awe-inspiring; in a few months the Americans, all but a handful of them, would be gone: only the effect of the "demonstration model," and the cascading consequences in the neighboring states, would remain. The use of devastating military power would begin the process, but once begun the transformation would roll forward, carried out by forces of the same thrilling "democratic revolution" that had erupted on the streets of Prague and Budapest and East Berlin more than a decade before, and indeed on the streets of Kabul the previous year. Here was an evangelical vision of geopolitical redemption.

2

Thus the War of Imagination draped all the complications and contradictions of the history and politics of a war-torn, brutalized society in an ideologically driven vision of a perfect future. Small wonder that its creators, faced with grim reality, have been so loath to part with it. Since the first thrilling night of shock and awe, reported with breathless enthusiasm by the American television networks, the Iraq war has had at least two histories, that of the war itself and that of the American perception of it. As the months passed and the number of attacks in Iraq grew, the gap between those two histories opened wider and wider.* And finally, for most

*Here are the number of daily attacks on U.S. forces at each of the Iraq war's purported "turning points":

July 2003: Bremer appoints Iraqi Governing Council; sixteen attacks per day.
December 2003: Saddam Hussein captured; nineteen attacks per day.
June 2004: Handover of sovereignty to Iraqis; forty-five attacks per day.
January 2005: Elections for Transitional Government; sixty-one attacks per day.
June 2006: Death of Abu Musab al-Zarqawi; ninety attacks per day.

See Anthony Cordesman, *Iraqi Force Development: Summer 2006 Update* (CSIS, 2006), p. 7.

Americans, the War of Imagination — built of nationalistic excitement and ideological hubris and administration pronouncements about "spreading democracy" and "greetings with sweets and flowers," and then about "dead-enders" and "turning points," and finally about "staying the course" and refusing to "cut and run" — began, under the pressure of nearly three thousand American dead and perhaps a hundred thousand or more dead Iraqis, to give way to grim reality.

The election of November 7, 2006, marks the moment when the War of Imagination decisively gave way to the war on the ground and when officials throughout the American government, not least the president himself, were forced to recognize and acknowledge a reality that much of the American public had discerned months or years before. The ideological canopy now has lifted. The study groups are at their work. Americans have come to know what they do not know. If confronted with that simple question the smiling President Ahmadinejad of Iran put to Mike Wallace last August — "I ask you, sir, what is the American army doing inside Iraq?" — how many Americans could offer a clear and convincing answer?

As the war drags on and alternatives fall away and American and Iraqi deaths mount, we seem to know less and less, certainly about "where we are going to end." Thus we arrive at our present therapeutic moment — the moment of "solutions," brought on by the recognition, three and a half years on, that we have no idea how to "end" Phase Two. This is now a matter for James A. Baker's Iraq Study Group and the military's "strategic review team" and the new Democratic committee chairmen, who will offer, to a chastened president who admits he thought "we would do all right" in the elections, the "new ideas" he now professes to welcome.[7] However quickly the discussion now moves to the geopolitical hydraulics, to weighing partition against partial withdrawal against regional conferences and contact groups and all the rest, the truth is that none of these proposals, alone or in combination, will end the war anytime soon.

It bears noticing that Kennan himself, having predicted that we will never know where we are going to end in Iraq, lived to see disproved, before his death at the age of 101 last March, what even he, no innocent, had taken as a given: that "you know where you begin." For as the war's presumed ending — constructed from carefully crafted images of triumph, of dictators' statues cast down

and presidents striding forcefully across aircraft carrier decks —
has flickered and vanished, receding into the just-out-of-grasp future ("a decision for the next president," the preelection President
Bush had said), the war's beginning has likewise melted away, the
original rationale obscured in a darkening welter of shifting intelligence, ideological controversy, and conflicting claims, all of it
hemmed in now on all sides by the mounting dead.

3

Out of this maelstrom, how does one fix now on "how we began" in
Iraq? One might do worse than the National Security Presidential
Directive entitled "Iraq: Goals, Objectives and Strategy," the top-se-
cret statement of American purpose intended to guide all the de-
partments and agencies of the government, signed by President
George W. Bush on August 29, 2002:

> U.S. goal: Free Iraq in order to eliminate Iraqi weapons of mass destruc-
> tion, their means of delivery and associated programs, to prevent Iraq
> from breaking out of containment and becoming a more dangerous
> threat to the region and beyond.
>
> End Iraqi threats to its neighbors, to stop the Iraqi government's tyr-
> annizing of its own population, to cut Iraqi links to and sponsorship of
> international terrorism, to maintain Iraq's unity and territorial integ-
> rity. And liberate the Iraqi people from tyranny, and assist them in creat-
> ing a society based on moderation, pluralism and democracy . . .
>
> Objectives: To conduct policy in a fashion that minimizes the chance
> of a WMD attack against the United States, U.S. field forces, our allies
> and friends. To minimize the danger of regional instabilities. To deter
> Iran and Syria from helping Iraq. And to minimize disruption in inter-
> national oil markets.

This secret document, disclosed by Bob Woodward, is presumably
the plainest, least ideological statement of what American officials
thought the country they led would be trying to achieve in the
coming war.[8] The words have now a sad and antique air, as if
scrawled on yellowed parchment and decipherable only by a historian skilled in the customs and peculiarities of a far-off time and
place. What can we say, as we look back at the Iraq of November
2006, about these official goals and objectives of the Iraq war?

The famous weapons of mass destruction are gone, most of
them probably fifteen years gone, and their absence has likely

damaged the United States and its power — the power, deployed daily, that depends on the authority of words and pronouncements and not directly or solely on force of arms — more severely than their presence ever could have. While no doubt convinced that Iraq had at least some chemical and biological weapons, Bush administration officials, like the cop framing a guilty man, vastly exaggerated the evidence, and in so doing — and even as they refused to allow UN inspectors to examine and weigh that evidence — severely undermined the credibility of the United States, the credibility of its intelligence agencies, and the support for the war and U.S. policy among Americans, among Muslims, and around the world.

The containment of Iraq, threatened only in the realm of policymakers' imaginations before the war, has been breached. The country's "threat to the region," with jihadis flowing from neighboring Sunni powers into Anbar and Baghdad and Iranian intelligence agents flowing into the Shia south, is growing daily, with the ultimate worst-case future, the confused and blackened landscape of a regional sectarian war, already standing clearly visible on the horizon as a possible consequence of an escalating conflict.

Though Saddam stands convicted of mass murder and condemned to death, and though an elected and ineffectual government deliberates within the Green Zone, it is hard to argue that the "tyrannizing" of the Iraqi population beyond its walls has not worsened. Every day on average a hundred or more Iraqis die from the violence of an increasingly complicated civil war. Sunnis attack Shia with bombs of every description — suicide bombers and car bombs and bicycle bombs and motorcycle bombs — and they maintain the pace of terror at an unprecedented, almost unimaginable rate. In the past six months alone Baghdad has endured 488 "terror-related bombings," an average of nearly three a day.*

---

*In the first year of the war Iraq saw 109 "terror-related bombings"; in the second year, 613; in the third year, 1,037; in the past six months, 1,002. See "The Geography of War," *Newsweek*, November 6, 2006. These numbers do not include attacks on American troops with improvised explosive devices, of which there were 2,625 in July alone (nearly double the 1,454 IED attacks in January). See Michael R. Gordon, Mark Mazzetti, and Thom Shanker, "Insurgent Bombs Directed at GI's in Iraq Increase," *New York Times*, August 17, 2006.

Shia leaders respond with death squads, whose members, drawn from party militias and often allied with the Ministry of the Interior and the Iraqi police, have by now tortured and assassinated thousands of Sunnis. As Iraqis do their shopping or say their prayers they are blown to pieces by suicide bombers. As they drive through the cities in broad daylight they are pulled from their cars by armed men at roadblocks who behead them or shoot them in the back of the neck. As they sit at home at night they are kidnapped by men in police or army uniforms who load them in the trunks of their cars and carry them off to secret places to be tortured and executed, their bound and headless bodies to be found during the following days in fields or dumps or by the roadside. These bodies, examined by United Nations officials in the Baghdad morgue, "often bear signs of severe torture including acid-induced injuries and burns caused by chemical substances, missing skin, broken bones (back, hands and legs), missing eyes, missing teeth and wounds caused by power drills or nails."[9]

As Iraqis know well, the power drills and nails were a favorite of Saddam's torturers — though now, according to a United Nations expert on torture, "the situation is so bad many people say it is worse than it has been in the times of Saddam Hussein."[10] The level of carnage is difficult to comprehend. According to official figures published by the United Nations, which certainly understate the case, 6,599 Iraqis were murdered in July and August alone. Estimates of the number of Iraqi civilians killed during the war range from a conservative 52,000, by the website Iraq Body Count, to 655,000, by the Johns Hopkins School of Public Health, with the Iraqi health minister recently announcing a cumulative total of 150,000.*

As for the country's links to international terrorism, we might look to the official consensus of the American intelligence agencies issued in April 2006 that "the Iraq jihad is shaping a new generation of terrorist leaders and operatives" and that "the Iraq conflict has become the 'cause celebre' for jihadists, breeding a deep resentment of U.S. involvement in the Muslim world and cultivating supporters for the global jihadist movement."[11] The Bush ad-

---

*The current rate of killing of one hundred Iraqis a day would be the equivalent, adjusting for population, of 1,100 Americans a day, or 33,000 dead a month. In the decade-long Vietnam War, about 58,000 Americans died.

ministration's fears about Iraq's possible collaboration with terror groups, largely conjectural, have since Saddam's fall attained a terrible reality.

Iraq's "unity and territorial integrity," meantime, has become the central issue as the war grows increasingly sectarian, cities and regions are "ethnically cleansed," and the Shia have pushed through a law, in the face of bitter Sunni opposition, making possible the autonomy of the south, the culmination of a political process that, beginning with the first vote boycotted by Sunnis, has served to worsen sectarian conflict.

The central question of how power and resources should be divided in Iraq and what the country should look like, a question that was going to be settled peacefully by the nascent political institutions of the "first Arab democracy," has become the critical political issue dividing Kurd from Sunni and Sunni from Shia, and also dividing the sectarian political coalitions themselves. Prime Minister Nuri al-Maliki, the leader of the "unity government," on whom President Bush repeatedly calls to "dismantle the militias," is in fact dependent for his own political survival on Moqtada al-Sadr, the creator and leader of the largest militia, the Mahdi Army. Indeed, the two most important militias are controlled by the two most powerful parties in parliament.

Increasingly the "unity government" itself, quarreling vituperatively within the Green Zone, serves as an impotent echo of the savage warfare raging beyond the walls. The partitioning of Iraq is now openly advocated by many — including such prominent American politicians as Senator Joseph Biden of Delaware, the incoming chairman of the Senate Foreign Relations Committee — desperate to find "a solution," however illusory, to the war, anything that will allow the Americans to withdraw, while avoiding any admission of defeat.

4

Kennan's problem of knowing "where you are going to end" begins, as he knew well, on the ground; but it does not end there. Information obtained by dedicated but deeply fallible humans travels from places like Fallujah by cable and e-mail and word of mouth into the vast four-mile-square bunker of the Green Zone, with its half-dozen concentric layers of concrete blast walls and sandbags and barbed wire, and from there to the great sprawling labyrinth of the Washington national security bureaucracy, up through the thousands of competing staffers in the layers of bureaus and agencies and eventually to the highly driven people at the tops of the organizational pyramids — the people who, it is said, "make the decisions." In the best managed of administrations there exists, between those on the ground who listen and learn and those in the offices who debate and decide, a great deal of bureaucratic "noise." And this, alas, as so many accounts of decision-making on the war make all too clear, was not the best managed of administrations. Indeed, its top officials, talented and experienced as many of them were, seem to have willingly collaborated, for reasons of ego or ambition or ideological hubris, in making themselves collectively blind.

Consider, for example, this striking but typical discussion in the White House in April 2003, just as the Iraq occupation, the vital first step in President Bush's plan "to transform the Middle East," was getting under way. American forces are in Baghdad but the capital is engulfed by a wave of looting and disorder, with General Tommy Franks's troops standing by. The man in charge of the occupation, Lieutenant General Jay Garner (retired), has just arrived "in country." Secretary of State Colin Powell has come to the Oval Office to discuss the occupation with the president, who is joined by Condoleezza Rice, then his national security adviser. Powell began, writes Woodward, by raising "the question of unity of command" in Iraq:

> There are two chains of command, Powell told the president. Garner reports to Rumsfeld and Franks reports to Rumsfeld.
> The president looked surprised.
> "That's not right," Rice said. "That's not right."
> Powell thought Rice could at times be pretty sure of herself, but he was pretty sure he was right. "Yes, it is," Powell insisted.
> "Wait a minute," Bush interrupted, taking Rice's side. "That doesn't sound right."
> Rice got up and went to her office to check. When she came back, Powell thought she looked a little sheepish. "That's right," she said.

What might Kennan, the consummate diplomatic professional, have thought of such a discussion among president, secretary of

state, and national security adviser had he lived to read of it? He
would have grasped its implications instantly, as the president and
his national security adviser apparently did not. Which leads to
Powell's patient — too patient — explanation to the president:

> . . . You have to understand that when you have two chains of command
> and you don't have a common superior in the theater, it means that
> every little half-assed fight they have out there, if they can't work it out,
> comes out to one place to be resolved. And that's in the Pentagon. Not
> in the NSC or the State Department, but in the Pentagon.

The kernel of an answer to what is the most painful and intractable
question about the Iraq war — how could U.S. officials repeatedly
and consistently make such ill-advised and improbably stupid decisions, beginning with their lack of planning for "the postwar" —
can be found in this little chamber play in the Oval Office, and in
the fact that at least two thirds of the cast seem wholly incapable of
comprehending the script. In Woodward's account, Rice, who was
then the official responsible for coordinating the national security
bureaucracies of the U.S. government, found what was being said
"a rather theoretical discussion," somehow managing to miss the
fact that she and the National Security Council she headed had
been cut out of decision-making on the Iraq war — and cut out,
further, in favor of an official, Secretary of Defense Rumsfeld, who,
if we are to believe Woodward, did not bother even to return her
telephone calls.

The Iraq occupation would have all the weaknesses of two chains
of command, weaknesses that would become all too apparent in a
matter of days, when Lieutenant General Ricardo Sanchez, the junior three-star in the entire army, replaced General Franks and L.
Paul Bremer replaced Garner, leaving the occupation in the hands
of two officials who despised one another and hardly spoke. And
both chains would end not in the White House but in the Pentagon, a vast bureaucracy not known for the delicate political touch
that would be needed to carry out an occupation of this degree of
complexity.

We hear again the patient explanation of Powell — whose fate in
the Bush administration seems to have been to play the role of Cas-
sandra, uttering grim prophecies destined to be ignored as reliably
as they were to be proved true — letting Woodward (but this time

not the president) know of his certainty that "the Pentagon wouldn't resolve the conflicts because Wolfowitz and Feith were running their own little games and had their own agenda to promote Chalabi."

The name of Ahmad Chalabi, the brilliant, charming, cunning impresario of the Iraqi exile community, evokes memories of disasters past and, from the Pentagon point of view, of dreams dashed: the king-to-be who was, alas, never crowned. He is an irresistible character and has served as the off-screen villain in the telling of many an Iraq war melodrama, with particular attention to his part in helping to supply intelligence to various willing recipients within the U.S. government, bolstering the case that Iraq had significant stockpiles of weapons of mass destruction. In fact, however, Chalabi had a much more consequential role, that of the Pentagon's ruler-to-be, the solution to that vexing question of what to do about "the postwar."

Inherent in the War of Imagination were certain rather obvious contradictions: Donald Rumsfeld's dream of a "demonstration model" war of quick, overwhelming victory did not foresee an extended occupation — on the contrary, the defense secretary abjured, publicly and vociferously, any notion that his troops would be used for "nation building." Rumsfeld's war envisioned rapid victory and rapid departure. Wolfowitz and the other Pentagon neoconservatives, on the other hand, imagined a "democratic transformation," a thoroughgoing social revolution that would take a Baath Party–run autocracy, complete with a Baath-led army and vast domestic spying and security services, and transform it into a functioning democratic polity — without the participation of former Baathist officials.

How to resolve this contradiction? The answer, for the Pentagon, seems to have amounted to one word: Chalabi. "When it came to Iraq," James Risen writes in *State of War,* "the Pentagon believed it had the silver bullet it needed to avoid messy nation building — a provisional government in exile, built around Chalabi, could be established and then brought in to Baghdad after the invasion."

This so-called "turnkey operation" seems to have appeared to be the perfect compromise plan: Chalabi was Shiite, as were most Iraqis, but he was also a secularist who had lived in the West for nearly fifty years and was close to many of the Pentagon civilians. Alas, there was one problem: the confirmed idealist in the White House "was adamant that the United States not be seen as putting its thumb on the scales" of the nascent Iraqi democracy. Chalabi, for all his immense popularity in the Pentagon and in the vice president's office, would not be installed as president of Iraq.

Though "Bush's commitment to democracy was laudable," as Risen observes, his awkward intervention "was not really the answer to the question of postwar planning." He goes on: "Once Bush quashed the Pentagon's plans, the administration failed to develop any acceptable alternative . . . Instead, once the Pentagon realized the president wasn't going to let them install Chalabi, the Pentagon leadership did virtually nothing. After Chalabi, there was no Plan B."

An unnamed White House official describes to Risen the Laurel-and-Hardy consequences within the government of the president's attachment to the idea of democratic elections in Iraq:

> Part of the reason the planning for post-Saddam Iraq was so nonexistent was that the State Department had been saying if you invade, you have to plan for the postwar. And DOD said, no you don't. You can set up a provisional government in exile around Chalabi. DOD had a stupid plan, but they had a plan. But if you don't do that plan, and you don't make the Pentagon work with State to develop something else, then you go to war with no plan.

5

Anyone wanting to answer the question of "how we began" in Iraq has to confront the monumental fact that the United States, the most powerful country in the world, invaded Iraq with no particular and specific idea of what it was going to do there, and then must try to explain how this could have happened. In his account Woodward resists the lure of Chalabi but not the temptation of melodrama, instead choosing, with typically impeccable political timing, to place Donald Rumsfeld in the role of mustache-twirling villain, a choice that most of the country, in the wake of the elections and the secretary's instant fall from power, seems happy to embrace. And the secretary — truculent, arrogant, vain — has shown himself perfectly willing to play his part in this familiar

Washington morality tale, setting himself up for the predictable fall by spending hours at the podium before fawning reporters and their television cameras during and after the invasion.

The Fall of Rumsfeld gives pace and drive to Woodward's narrative. No doubt this will please readers, who find themselves increasingly outraged at the almost unbelievable failures in planning and execution, rewarding them with a bracing wave of schadenfreude when the inevitable defenestration finally takes place — outside the frame of the book but wholly predictable from its story line. Indeed, the fact of *State of Denial*'s publication a month before the election, complete with the usual national television interviews and other attendant publicity, was not the least of the signs that the knives were out and glinting and the secretary's days were numbered.

Irresistible as Rumsfeld is, however, the story of the Iraq war disaster springs less from his brow than from that of an inexperienced and rigidly self-assured president who managed to fashion, with the help of a powerful vice president, a strikingly disfigured process of governing. Woodward, much more interested in character and personal rivalry than in government bureaus and hierarchies, refers to this process broadly as "the interagency," as in "Rice said the interagency was broken." He means the governing apparatus set up by the National Security Act of 1947, which gathered the government's major security officials — secretaries of state, defense, and treasury, attorney general, director of national intelligence, among others — into the National Security Council, and gave to the president a special assistant for national security affairs (commonly known as the national security adviser) and a staff to manage, coordinate, and control it. Through the National Security Council and the Deputies Committee and other subsidiary bodies linking the various government departments at lower levels, information and policy guidance are supposed to work their way up from bureaucracy to president, and his decisions to work their way down. Ron Suskind, who has been closely studying the inner workings of the Bush administration since his revealing piece about Karl Rove and John Dilulio in 2003 and his book on Paul O'Neill the following year,[12] observes that "the interagency" not only serves to convey information and decisions but also is intended to perform a more basic function: "Sober due diligence, with an eye for the way previous administrations have thought through a standard array of challenges facing the United States, creates, in fact, a kind of check on executive power and prerogative."

This is precisely what the president didn't want, particularly after September 11. Deeply distrustful of the bureaucracy, desirous of quick, decisive action, impatient with bureaucrats and policy intellectuals, Bush wanted to act. Suskind writes:

> For George W. Bush, there had been an evolution on such matters — from the early, pre-9/11 President, who had little grasp of foreign affairs and made few major decisions in that realm; to the post-9/11 President, who met America's foreign challenges with decisiveness born of a brand of preternatural, faith-based, self-generated certainty. The policy process, in fact, never changed much. Issues argued, often vociferously, at the level of deputies and principals rarely seemed to go upstream in their fullest form to the President's desk; and, if they did, it was often after Bush seemed to have already made up his mind based on what was so often cited as his "instinct" or "gut."

Woodward tends to blame "the broken policy process" on the relative strength of personalities gathered around the cabinet table: the power and ruthlessness of Rumsfeld, the legendary "bureaucratic infighter"; the weakness of Rice, the very function and purpose of whose job, to let the president both benefit from and control the bureaucracy, was in effect eviscerated. Suskind more convincingly argues that Bush and Cheney constructed precisely the government they wanted: centralized, highly secretive, its clean, direct lines of decision unencumbered by information or consultation. "There was never any policy process to break, by Condi or anyone else," Richard Armitage, the former deputy secretary of state, remarks to Suskind. "There was never one from the start. Bush didn't want one, for whatever reason." Suskind suggests why in an acute analysis of personality and leadership:

> Of the many reasons the President moved in this direction, the most telling may stem from George Bush's belief in his own certainty and, especially after 9/11, his need to protect the capacity to will such certainty in the face of daunting complexity. His view of right and wrong, and of righteous actions — such as attacking evil or spreading "God's gift" of democracy — were undercut by the kind of traditional, shades-of-gray analysis that has been a staple of most presidents' diets. This President's

traditional day began with Bible reading at dawn, a workout, breakfast, and the briefings of foreign and domestic threats . . . The hard, complex analysis, in this model, would often be a thin offering, passed through the filters of Cheney or Rice, or not presented at all.

. . . This granted certain unique advantages to Bush. With fewer people privy to actual decisions, tighter confidentiality could be preserved, reducing leaks. Swift decisions — either preempting detailed deliberation or ignoring it — could move immediately to implementation, speeding the pace of execution and emphasizing the *hows* rather than the more complex *whys*.

What Bush knew before, or during, a key decision remained largely a mystery. Only a tiny group — Cheney, Rice, Card, Rove, Tenet, Rumsfeld — could break this seal.

To the rest of the government, of course, this "mystery" must have been excruciating to endure; Suskind describes how many of those in the "foreign policy establishment" found themselves "befuddled" by the way the traditional policy process was viewed not only as unproductive but "perilous." Information, that is, could slow decision-making; indeed, when it had to do with a bold and risky venture like the Iraq war, information and discussion — an airing, say, of the precise obstacles facing a "democratic transition" conducted with a handful of troops — could paralyze it. If the sober consideration of history and facts stood in the way of bold action, then it would be the history and the facts that would be discarded. The risk of doing nothing, the risk, that is, of the status quo, justified acting. Given the grim facts on the ground — the likelihood of a future terrorist attack from the "malignant" Middle East, the impossibility of entirely protecting the country from it — better to embrace the unknown. Better, that is, to act in the cause of "constructive instability" — a wonderfully evocative phrase, which, as Suskind writes, was

> the term used by various senior officials in regard to Iraq — a term with roots in pre-9/11 ideas among neoconservatives about the need for a new, muscular, unbounded American posture; and outgrowths that swiftly took shape after the attacks made everything prior to 9/11 easily relegated to dusty history.
>
> The past — along with old-style deliberations based on cause and effect or on agreed-upon precedents — didn't much matter; nor did those with knowledge and prevailing policy studies, of agreements between nations, or of long-standing arrangements defining the global landscape.

What mattered, by default, was the President's "instinct" to guide America across the fresh, post-9/11 terrain — a style of leadership that could be rendered within tiny, confidential circles.

America, unbound, was duly led by a president, unbound.

It is that "duly led," of course, that is the question. Information, history, and all the other attributes of a deliberative policy may inhibit action but they do so by weighing and calculating risk. Dispensing with them has no consequences only if you accept the proposition that the Iraq war so clearly disproves: that bold action must always make us safer.

6

So there would be no President Chalabi. Unfortunately, the president, who thought of himself, Woodward says, "as the calcium in the backbone" of the U.S. government, having banned Chalabi's ascension, neither offered an alternative plan nor forced the government he led to agree on one. Nor did Secretary Rumsfeld, who knew only that he wanted a quick victory and a quick departure. To underline the point, soon after the U.S. invasion the secretary sent his special assistant, Larry DiRita, to the Kuwait City Hilton to brief the tiny, miserable, understaffed, and underfunded team led by the retired General Garner which was preparing to fly to a chaotic Baghdad to "take control of the transition." Here is DiRita's "Hilton Speech," as quoted to Woodward by an army colonel, Paul Hughes:

> "We went into the Balkans and Bosnia and Kosovo and we're still in them . . . We're probably going to wind up in Afghanistan for a long time because the Department of State can't do its job right. Because they keep screwing things up, the Department of Defense winds up being stuck at these places. We're not going to let this happen in Iraq."
>
> The reaction was generally, Whoa! Does this guy even realize that half the people in the room are from the State Department?
>
> DiRita went on, as Hughes recalled: "By the end of August we're going to have 25,000 to 30,000 troops left in Iraq."

DiRita spoke these words as, a few hundred miles away, Baghdad and the other major cities of Iraq were taken up in a thoroughgoing riot of looting and pillage — of government ministries, universities and hospitals, power stations and factories — that would virtually destroy the country's infrastructure, and with it much of the respect Iraqis might have had for American competence. The uncontrolled violence engulfed Iraq's capital and major cities for weeks as American troops — 140,000 or more — mainly sat on their tanks, looking on. If attaining true political authority depends on securing a monopoly on legitimate violence, then the Americans would never achieve it in Iraq. There were precious few troops to impose order, and hardly any military police. No one gave the order to arrest or shoot looters or otherwise take control of the streets. Official Pentagon intentions at this time seem to have been precisely what the secretary of defense's special assistant said they were: to have all but 25,000 or so of those troops out of Iraq in five months or less.

How then to secure the country, which was already in a state of escalating chaos? Most of the ministries had been looted and burned, and what government there was consisted of the handful of Iraqi officials whom Garner's small team had managed to coax into returning to work. In keeping with the general approach of quick victory, quick departure, Garner had briefed the president and his advisers before leaving Washington, emphasizing his plan to dismiss only the most senior and personally culpable Baathists from the government and also to make use of the Iraqi army to rebuild and, eventually, keep order.

Within weeks of that meeting in the Kuwait Hilton, L. Paul Bremer arrived in Baghdad, replacing Garner, who had been fired after less than a month in Iraq. On Bremer's first full day in country, in Woodward's telling, one of Garner's officials ran up to her now lame-duck boss and thrust a paper into his hand:

"Have you read this?" she asked.
"No," Garner replied. "I don't know what the hell you've got there."
"It's a de-Baathification policy," she said, handing him a two-page document.

The document was Bremer's "Coalition Provisional Authority Order Number 1 — De-Baathification of Iraqi Society," an order to remove immediately from their posts all "full members" of the Baath Party. These were to be banned from working in any government job. In every ministry the top three levels of managers would be investigated for crimes.

"We can't do this," Garner said. He still envisioned what he had told Rumsfeld would be a "gentle de-Baathification" — eliminating only the number one Baathist and personnel directors in each ministry. "It's too deep," he added.

Garner headed immediately to Bremer's office, where the new occupation leader was just settling in, and on the way ran into the CIA chief of station, referred to here as Charlie.

"Have you read this?" Garner asked.
"That's why I'm over here," Charlie said.
"Let's go see Bremer." The two men got in to see the new administrator of Iraq around 1 P.M. "Jerry, this is too deep," Garner said. "Give Charlie and I about an hour. We'll sit down with this. We'll do the pros and cons and then we'll get on the telephone with Rumsfeld and soften it a bit."
"Absolutely not," Bremer said. "Those are my instructions and I intend to execute them."

Garner, who will shortly be going home, sees he's making little headway and appeals to the CIA man, who "had been station chief in other Middle East countries," asking him what will happen if the order is issued.

"If you put this out, you're going to drive between 30,000 and 50,000 Baathists underground before nightfall," Charlie said . . . "You will put 50,000 people on the street, underground and mad at Americans." And these 50,000 were the most powerful, well-connected elites from all walks of life.
"I told you," Bremer said, looking at Charlie. "I have my instructions and I have to implement this."

The chain of command, as we know, goes through Rumsfeld, and Garner gets on the phone and appeals to the secretary of defense, who tells him — and this will be a leitmotif in Woodward's book — that the matter is out of his hands:

"This is not coming from this building," [Rumsfeld] replied. "That came from somewhere else."
Garner presumed that meant the White House, NSC or Cheney. According to other participants, however, the de-Baathification order was purely a Pentagon creation. Telling Garner it came from somewhere else, though, had the advantage for Rumsfeld of ending the argument.

*

Such tactics are presumably what mark Rumsfeld as a "skilled bureaucratic infighter," the description that has followed him through his career in government like a Homeric epithet. In fact, according to Bremer, he had received those orders at the Pentagon a few days before from Douglas Feith, Rumsfeld's undersecretary for policy. In Bremer's telling, Feith gave him the draft order, emphasizing "the political importance of the decree": "We've got to show all the Iraqis that we're serious about building a New Iraq. And that means that Saddam's instruments of repression have no role in that new nation."[13]

The following day, Bremer's second in Iraq, the hapless Garner was handed another draft order. This, Woodward tells us, was Order Number 2, disbanding the Iraqi ministries of Defense and the Interior, the entire Iraqi military, and all of Saddam's bodyguards and special paramilitary organizations:

> Garner was stunned. The de-Baathification order was dumb, but this was a disaster. Garner had told the president and the whole National Security Council explicitly that they planned to use the Iraqi military — at least 200,000 to 300,000 troops — as the backbone of the corps to rebuild the country and provide security. And he'd been giving regular secure video reports to Rumsfeld and Washington on the plan.

An American colonel and a number of CIA officers had been meeting regularly with Iraqi officers in order to reconstitute the army. They had lists of soldiers, had promised emergency payments. "The former Iraqi military," according to Garner, "was making more and more overtures, just waiting to come back in some form." Again, Garner rushed off to see Bremer:

> "We have always made plans to bring the army back," he insisted. This new plan was just coming out of the blue, subverting months of work.
> "Well, the plans have changed," Bremer replied. "The thought is that we don't want the residuals of the old army. We want a new and fresh army."
> "Jerry, you can get rid of an army in a day, but it takes years to build one."

Again Bremer tells Garner that he has his orders. The discussion attains a certain unintended comedy when the proconsuls go on to discuss the Iraqi Ministry of the Interior, which Bremer has also announced he will abolish:

"You can't get rid of the Ministry of the Interior," Garner said.

"Why not?"

"You just made a speech yesterday and told everybody how important the police force is."

"It is important."

"All the police are in the Ministry of the Interior," Garner said. "If you put this out, they'll all go home today."

On hearing this bit of information, we are told, Bremer looked "surprised" — an expression similar, no doubt, to Rice's when she and the president learned from the secretary of state that the civilian occupation authority would not be reporting to the White House but to the Pentagon. Unfortunately, in the Pentagon there coexisted at least two visions of what the occupation of Iraq was to be: the quick victory, quick departure view of Rumsfeld, and the broader, ideologically driven democratic transformation of Iraqi society championed by the neoconservatives. The two views had uneasily intersected, for a time, in the alluring person of Ahmad Chalabi, who seemed to make both visions possible. With a Chalabi coronation taken off the table by President Bush, however, determined officials with a direct line to Bremer were transforming the Iraq adventure into a long-term, highly ambitious occupation. Presumably as Garner woke up on May 17, reflecting that "the U.S. now had at least 350,000 more enemies than it had the day before — the 50,000 Baathists [and] the 300,000 officially unemployed soldiers," he could take satisfaction in having managed, by his last-minute efforts, to persuade Bremer to "excise the Ministry of Interior from the draft so the police could stay."

7

One can make arguments for a "deep de-Baathification" of Iraq. One can make arguments also for dismantling the Iraqi army. It is hard, though, to make an argument that such steps did not stand in dramatic and irresolvable contradiction to the Pentagon's plan to withdraw all but 30,000 American troops from Iraq within a few months. With no Iraqi army, with all Baath Party members thrown out of the ministries and the agencies of government, with all of Saddam's formidable security forces summarily sacked — and with all of these forces transformed into sworn enemies of the American occupation — who precisely was going to keep order in Iraq? And who was going to build that "new and fresh army" that Bremer was talking about?

These questions loom so large and are so obvious that one feels that they must have some answer, even if an unconvincing one. The simple fact is that these two enormously significant steps — launching a "deep de-Baathification" of the government and dissolving the Iraqi army — together with Bremer's decision, taken also during his first days, to downgrade to that of a figurehead the status of the group of Iraqi politicians known as the Iraqi Governing Council, transformed what had been the Pentagon's plan for a quick victory and quick departure into a long-running and open-ended occupation that would perforce involve the establishment of a new Iraqi army.

The political implications in Iraq were incalculable, for the de-Baathification and the dissolution of the army both appeared to the Sunnis to be declarations of open warfare against them, convincing many that they would be judged not by standards of individual conduct but by the fact of their membership in a group — judged not according to what they had done but according to who they were. This in itself undermined what hope there was to create the sine qua non of a stable democracy: a loyal opposition, which is to say an opposition that believes enough in the fairness of the system that it will renounce violence. "You Americans, you know," a young Sunni had told me in October 2003, when the insurgency was already in full flower, "you have created your enemies here."

It is unlikely that the Pentagon's vision of a rapid departure ever could have worked, Bremer or no Bremer. What is striking, however, is the way that the most momentous of decisions were taken in the most shockingly haphazard ways, with the power in the hands of a few Pentagon civilians who knew little of Iraq or the region, the expertise of the rest of the government almost wholly excluded, and the president and his highest officials looking on.

In the event, the Bush administration seems to have worked hard to turn Kennan's problem of knowing the facts on its head: the systemic failures in Iraq resulted in large part from an almost willful determination to cut off those in the government who knew anything from those who made the decisions. Woodward tells us, for example, that Stephen Hadley, then Rice's deputy and now her successor, first learned of the orders on de-Baathification and disbanding the military as Bremer announced them to Iraq and to the world. They hadn't been touched by the formal interagency process and as far as Hadley knew there was no imprimatur from the White House. Rice also had not been consulted. It hadn't come back to Washington or the NSC for a decision . . .

One NSC lawyer had been shown drafts of the policies to de-Baathify Iraq and disband the military — but that was only to give a legal opinion. The policymakers never saw the drafts, never had a chance to say whether they thought they were good ideas or even to point out that they were radical departures from what had earlier been planned and briefed to the president.

As for the uniformed military, the men who were responsible for securing Iraq and whose job would thus be dramatically affected both by de-Baathification and by the dissolution of the Iraqi army, they were given no chance to speak on either question. Woodward writes:

> General Myers, the principal military adviser to Bush, Rumsfeld and the NSC, wasn't even consulted on the disbanding of the Iraqi military. It was presented as a fait accompli.
>
> "We're not going to just sit here and second-guess everything he does," Rumsfeld told Myers at one point, referring to Bremer's decisions.
>
> "I didn't get a vote on it," Myers told a colleague, "but I can see where Ambassador Bremer might have thought this is reasonable."

Since it is the cashiered Iraqi troops who, broke, angry, and humiliated ("Why do you Americans punish us, when we did not fight?" as one ex-soldier demanded of me that October), would within days be killing Myers's soldiers with sniper fire and the first improvised explosive devices, one can't help regarding the general's expressed forbearance as uncommonly generous.

At the time, the civilians in the Pentagon had attained their greatest power and prestige. Rumsfeld's daily press conferences were broadcast live on the cable news channels, with an appreciative audience of journalists chortling at the secretary's jokes on national television. No one then seems to have questioned what Woodward calls his "distrust of the interagency." Instead, Woodward writes, "from April 2003 on, the constant drumbeat that Hadley heard coming out of the Pentagon had been 'This is Don

Rumsfeld's thing, and we're going to do the interagency in Bagh-dad. Let Jerry run it.'"

"Jerry," it might be said at this point, seems a well-meaning man, but he had never run anything larger than the United States embassy in the Netherlands, where he served as ambassador. He spoke no Arabic and knew little of the Middle East and nothing of Iraq. He had had nothing to do with the meager and inadequate planning the Pentagon had done for "the postwar" and indeed had had only a few days' preparation before being flown to Bagh-dad. He apparently never saw the extensive plans the State Department had drawn up for the postwar period. And as would become evident as the occupation wore on and he became more independent of the Pentagon civilians, he had no particular qualifications to make and implement decisions of such magnitude, decisions that would certainly prolong the American occupation and would ultimately do much to doom it. For Rumsfeld, however, Bremer's supposed independence in Baghdad has had its uses: "Rumsfeld later said he would be surprised if Wolfowitz or Feith gave Bremer the de-Baathification and army orders. He said he did not recall an NSC meeting on the subject. Of Bremer, Rumsfeld said, 'I talked to him only rarely . . .'"

It is impossible to believe, even in this administration, that Bre-mer decided on his own, on his second day in Baghdad, to dissolve the Iraqi army, and it is unlikely that Rumsfeld's own involvement in a matter of such magnitude would have slipped the defense secretary's mind. To the "skilled bureaucratic infighter," however, especially one with little or no oversight from president or Congress, what Woodward calls "the rubber-glove syndrome — the tendency not to leave his fingerprints on decisions" — can prove useful in avoiding responsibility for wreckage caused — for a time, anyway. It cannot, however, prevent the consequences on the ground, and in Iraq, it has not.

8

Nearly four years into the Iraq war, as we enter the Time of Proposed Solutions, the consequences of those early decisions define the bloody landscape. By dismissing and humiliating the soldiers and officers of the Iraqi army, our leaders, in effect, did much to recruit the insurgency. By bringing far too few troops to secure

Saddam's enormous arms depots, they armed it. By bringing too few to keep order, they presided over the looting and overwhelming violence and social disintegration that provided the insurgency such fertile soil. By blithely purging tens of thousands of the country's Baathist elite, whatever their deeds, and by establishing a musclebound and inept American occupation without an "Iraqi face," they created an increasing resentment among Iraqis that fostered the insurgency and encouraged people to shelter it. And by providing too few troops to secure Iraq's borders, they helped supply its forces with an unending number of Sunni Islamic extremists from neighboring states. It was the foreign Islamists' strategy above all to promote their jihadist cause by provoking a sectarian civil war in Iraq; by failing to prevent their attacks and to protect the Shia who became their targets, the U.S. leaders have allowed them to succeed.

To Americans now, the hour appears very late in Iraq. Deeply weary of a war that early on lost its reason for being, most Americans want nothing more than to be shown a way out. President Bush and his counselors, even in the weeks before the election, had begun redefining the idea of victory, dramatically downgrading the goals that were set out in the National Security Presidential Directive of August 2002. Thus Vice President Cheney, asked the week before the election about an "exit strategy" from Iraq, declared that "we're not looking for an exit strategy. We're looking for victory," but then went on to offer a rather modest definition: "Victory will be the day when the Iraqis solve their political problems and are up and running with respect to their own government, and when they're able to provide for their own security."[14]

This was before Americans had gone to the polls and overwhelmingly condemned the administration's Iraq policies — with the result that, as one comedian put it, "on Tuesday night, in an ironic turnaround, Iraq brought regime change to the U.S."[15] On the day after the election, the president, stripped of his majorities in Congress, came forward to offer a still more modest definition: victory would mean producing in Iraq "a government that can defend, govern and sustain itself."[16]

In fact, even these modest words have come to seem ambitious, and perhaps unrealistic. As I write, Operation Together Forward, the joint effort by American and Iraqi forces to secure the city of Baghdad, has failed. The American commander in the capital, faced with a 26 percent increase in attacks during the operation, declared the results "disappointing," an on-the-record use of direct language that a year ago would have been inconceivable coming from a senior U.S. officer.

Operation Together Forward was not only to have demonstrated that the Iraqis were now "able to defend themselves," as the president said, but to have made it possible for "the unity government to make the difficult decisions necessary to unite the country." The operation was intended to blunt the power of Sunni insurgents and thus clear the way for Prime Minister Nuri al-Maliki to lend his support to disarming and eliminating the Shia militias that are responsible for much of the death-squad killing in Baghdad. Unfortunately, the militias — in particular the Mahdi Army and the Badr Organization — remain a vital part of the unity government's political infrastructure. This inconvenient but fundamental political fact renders much of the Bush administration's rhetoric about its present strategy in Iraq almost nonsensical. The evident contradiction between policy and reality, and the angry reactions by al-Maliki to efforts by the U.S. military to rein in the militias by launching raids into Sadr City, have stirred rumors in Baghdad and Washington of a possible postelection coup d'état to replace al-Maliki with a "government of national salvation." It is hard to know what such a government, whether led by Ayad Allawi, a long-time Washington favorite who was briefly interim prime minister (and who derided the possibility of coming to power by a coup), or some other "strongman," might accomplish, or whether any gains in security could outweigh the political costs of conniving in the overthrow of a government that, however ineffectual it is, Iraqis elected. The establishment of that government stands ever more starkly as one of the few (if ambiguous) accomplishments remaining from the original program for Iraq.

To Americans the Iraq war seems to have entered its third and final act. Though the plans and ideas now will come apace, all of them directed toward answering a single, dominant question — How do we get out of Iraq? — none is likely to supply a means of departure that does not carry a very high cost. The present "sense of an ending" about Iraq has its roots more in American weariness and frustration than in any real prospect of finding a "solution" or "exit strategy" that won't, in its consequences, be seen for what it is: a de facto acknowledgment of a failed and even catastrophic policy.

Only a week before the midterm election, President Bush warned an interviewer about the consequences of an American defeat in Iraq:

> The terrorists . . . have clearly said they want a safe haven from which to launch attacks against America, a safe haven from which to topple moderate governments in the Middle East, a safe haven from which to spread their jihadist point of view, which is that there are no freedoms in the world; we will dictate to you how you think . . . I can conceivably see a world in which radicals and extremists control oil. And they would say to the West: You either abandon Israel, for example, or we're going to run the price of oil up. Or withdraw . . .[17]

A few days after the Republican defeat at the polls, the president's chief of staff, Josh Bolten, discussing the Iraqi government, put the matter in even starker terms:

> We need to treat them as a sovereign government. But we also need to give them the support they need to succeed because the alternative for the United States, I believe, is truly disastrous . . . We could leave behind an Iraq that is a failed state, a haven for terrorism, a real threat to the United States and to the region. That's just not an acceptable outcome.[18]

We are well down the road toward this dark vision, a wave of threatening instability that stands as the precise opposite of the Bush administration's "democratic tsunami," the wave of liberalizing revolution that American power, through the invasion of Iraq, was to set loose throughout the Middle East. The chances of accomplishing such change in Iraq itself, let alone across the complicated landscape of the entire region, were always very small. Saddam Hussein and the autocracy he ruled were the product of a dysfunctional politics, not the cause of it. Reform of such a politics was always going to be a task of incalculable complexity. Faced with such complexity, and determined to have their war and their democratic revolution, the president and his counselors looked away. Confronted with great difficulties, their answer was to blind themselves to them and put their faith in ideology and hope — in the dream of a welcoming landscape, magically transformed. The evangelical vision may have made the sense of threat after September 11 easier to bear, but it did not change the risks and the reality on the ground. The result is that the wave of change the president and his officials were so determined to set on course by unleashing American military power may well turn out to be precisely the wave of Islamic radicalism that they had hoped to prevent.

In the coming weeks we will hear much talk of "exit strategies" and "proposed solutions." All such "solutions," though, are certain to come with heavy political costs, costs the president may consider more difficult to bear than those of doggedly "staying the course" for the remainder of his term. George W. Bush, who ran for president vowing a "humble" foreign policy, could not have predicted this. Kennan said it in October 2002:

> Anyone who has ever studied the history of American diplomacy, especially military diplomacy, knows that you might start in a war with certain things on your mind as a purpose of what you are doing, but in the end, you found yourself fighting for entirely different things that you had never thought of before. In other words, war has a momentum of its own and it carries you away from all thoughtful intentions when you get into it.

If we are indeed in the third act, then it may well be that this final act will prove to be very long and very painful. You may or may not know where you begin. You never know where you are going to end.

Notes

1. See Albert Eisele, "George Kennan Speaks Out About Iraq," *The Hill*, September 26, 2002.
2. See "Rumsfeld Ruminates on Tenure at Pentagon," MSNBC, November 9, 2006.
3. See "Defense Secretary Donald Rumsfeld's Colleagues Debate His Legacy," *The NewsHour with Jim Lehrer*, November 9, 2006.
4. From Cheney's interview with Tim Russert on *Meet the Press*, September 10, 2006.
5. Among those taking part in Bletchley II discussions, according to Woodward, were Fouad Ajami, Reuel Marc Gerecht, Steve Herbits, Bernard Lewis, Mark Palmer, James Q. Wilson, and Fareed Zakaria.
6. See Mark Danner, "The Struggles of Democracy and Empire," *New York Times*, October 9, 2002.

7. See Michael R. Gordon, "Military Team Undertakes a Broad Review of the Iraq War and the Campaign Against Terror," *New York Times*, November 11, 2006.

8. See Bob Woodward, *Plan of Attack* (Simon and Schuster, 2004), pp. 154–155.

9. See "Civilian Deaths Soar to Record High in Iraq," *Guardian*, September 22, 2006.

10. See the statements of Manfred Nowak, "Torture in Iraq 'Worse Than Under Saddam,'" *Guardian*, September 21, 2006.

11. See "Declassified Key Judgments of the National Intelligence Estimate 'Trends in Global Terrorism: Implications for the United States' dated April 2006," found at www.dni.gov/press_releases/Declassified_NIE_Key_Judgments.pdf.

12. See Ron Suskind, "Why Are These Men Laughing?," *Esquire*, January 2003, and *The Price of Loyalty: George W. Bush, the White House, and the Education of Paul O'Neill* (Simon and Schuster, 2004).

13. See L. Paul Bremer, *My Year in Iraq: The Struggle to Build a Future of Hope* (Simon and Schuster, 2006), p. 39.

14. See "We're Not Looking for an Exit Strategy, We're Looking for Victory," *Time*, October 30, 2006, p. 35.

15. "Weekend Update," *Saturday Night Live*, November 11, 2006.

16. See John F. Burns, "Stability vs. Democracy: Could a New Strongman Help?," *New York Times*, November 12, 2006.

17. *This Week with George Stephanopoulos*, ABC News, October 22, 2006.

18. Ibid., November 12, 2006.

W. S. DI PIERO

Fathead's Hard Times

FROM THE THREEPENNY REVIEW

WHEN I'M STANDING at the opera — at ten dollars a ticket, it's the best cheap show in San Francisco — I look along the balustrade and think on the kinds and degrees of backache people will tolerate in exchange for a certain order of beauty. Regulars have to think things through in advance. The difference between the one-act *Salome,* a quick hundred minutes of sexed-up hysterics, and the nearly five-hour evening of the bitterly sweet *Così Fan Tutte* may entail significant medication. About opera I am the complete amateur, musically untrained, patchily familiar with the repertoire, but a concentrated listener and, like so many other hounds attracted by ripe scents, a helpless softie. Mostly I roll in it. Nothing else in my life induces the dark elation I feel at a performance of *Don Giovanni* or *Così.* Passages in *Rigoletto, Peter Grimes,* and *Jenufa* melt me down; and while I'm losing my mind during *Butterfly* I give no thought to Pound's crack in the *Cantos:* "Spewcini the all too human / beloved in the eyetalian peninsula / for quite explicable reasons."

I didn't grow up in the eyetalian peninsula, I grew up (in the 1950s and 1960s) in South Philadelphia, an operatic culture that gave no thought to opera. My neighborhood was working class, Italian Americans mostly, small congested squared-off red-brick row houses with shared stoops and walls, here and there a heroic sycamore, big voices aroused night and day, women's voices usually, shrieking at their misarranged ungrateful kids or at husbands coming home from miserable jobs. In the late 1950s through the 1960s, music of other sorts washed over every street and corner. They were the days of Berry Gordy's Motown Records and the sassy, big-finned-car vocals of Martha and the Vandellas, whose "Heat Wave" was an anthem to gluey city summers and sex. Phil Spector was crafting his "wall of sound" dynamics for the Ronettes, one of the early tough-girl groups, all beehive hairdos and goth eye shadow. ("Be My Baby" still kills.) One of Spector's groups, the Teddy Bears, performed their hit "To Know Him Is to Love Him" on the TV dance show *American Bandstand*, broadcast from Philadelphia, which soon had its own city sound in the Delfonics (featured in Quentin Tarantino's *Jackie Brown*), two of whose singers were born the same year I was, 1945.

I listened with sunny transport to doo-wop groups. The Delfonics and the Deftones. The Clovers and the Cadillacs. The names alone would entice any daydreaming misfit to become some sort of writer. Transistors fizzed their portable sounds around the clock, indoors and out. On August nights men slept in deck chairs on the sidewalk, radios tuned to Top Ten programs ("We're livin' in a heat wave / a pain in your heart"), which in those days still featured vocals by Tony Bennett, Della Reese, and Sinatra. On summer weekends certain guys (bad guys taking a break from badness) did pretty much what you see in movies, cluster and croon on corners, leaning into the central harmonies they made. I sang a little myself, a passable falsetto, though I didn't go off with them later to make trouble at the local dance. Our basso profundo occasionally brought along a shot-putter's shot, which he once laid against the head of a black kid, a dark-complexioned, kinky-haired boy who danced with a white girl but who, the shot-putter later learned, was actually Sicilian.

My experience of music took a hard-angled and inauspicious turn when as a young boy I entered Pat's parlor, with its deeply folded odors of tomato sauce, cabbage, and garlic, down the block from the house I grew up in. Pat played mandolin and violin, it was said, though nobody had actually ever heard him play. My parents, who didn't care much about music of any kind, didn't know what to do with me. A multidisk set of Sigmund Romberg's operetta *The Student Prince* had mysteriously turned up in our house. My father, who as staff handyman at a hospital had occasional access to useless pilfered goods like test tubes and fat rolls of butcher paper, might have acquired it after hearing me howl in the shower whatever stuck in my head from AM radio. (For weeks it was Jerry

Lewis's nasal "Rock-a-Bye Your Baby.") Or it may have been the remnant of opera sets some unknown immigrant uncle two generations back had owned. His collection, on acetate 78s, which in those days ran to twelve or more disks and weighed at least as much as a meat slicer, had all been given to the Salvation Army when he died, or moved away, or disappeared. (Nobody could tell me what became of him.) "For Chrissake," my mother would say years later. "If I knew you'd end up liking that stuff, I'd've kept them." For weeks I played *The Student Prince,* sang along with Mario Lanza (Alfredo Arnold Cocozza adopted his mother's name, Maria Lanza), a South Philly boy from Mercy Street, where he and my uncle Mike played stickball, lustily shredding my voice just as he was shredding his. Shredding, too, the already threadbare fabric of family peace. And so I was sent to Pat, as some parents send their children to Boy Scout camp or matinees.

I didn't expect so much silence. Pat spoke little English and taught me by the Italian method that had formed him. His parlor was like others in the neighborhood, an overcast weather with low clouds due to a high-pressure system — thickly upholstered, hard-spring furniture, statuettes of the Sacred Heart and Infant of Prague, and leaky table lamps. I was terrified. I didn't know what to expect but vaguely thought I'd soon hold an instrument. Instead, to learn tempo, I clapped, for weeks. Clapped, then waved my hand side to side, as if in benediction of a privileged moment that never arrived, because along with the clapping Pat tried to teach me to read music. He wrote down and told me to copy notes and phrases that to me meant nothing, because they weren't voiced or sounded. Each week he *showed* me music, then sent me home to study it, clapping. I lived in a constant state of anxious boredom, stupefied by abstraction, and as unwilling to master unvoiced notes on the stave as I was to memorize the Latin that would have cleared me to become an altar boy. I felt so alive when my puny voice swelled alongside Mario's light tenor. But music, while I was learning it, became not just dephysicalized — it's made of nothing, after all — but abstract, virtual, a metronomic code embodied only by that robotic clapping and waving.

Weeks passed and I still hadn't seen an instrument. The idea was to start with mandolin, then work up to violin. What did I know? One day Pat drifted off like a poltergeist and returned with a mandolin, which he played a bit and let me touch but not hold. Next week, out came the violin. Same routine. He held out the instrument so that I could stroke it with my hand as if it was his pet, but infinitely remote, an actuality (it seemed an extension of his body) sealed off in a medium of mere possibility. I was Tantalus in the Parlor. Tantalized all the more when he tickled the mandolin into sound, then coddled and stroked long sonorous lines from the fiddle. Why wasn't I ecstatic? What I had known as a physically enthralling medium that came straight onto my nerves in mysterious, scary ways was becoming Idea. Luckily, that part of my musical education didn't last long. When I was eighteen and finally experienced live performance, other than the snare drums and wheezing clarinets of wedding combos, it was at the Academy of Music during Eugene Ormandy's long stewardship of the Philadelphia Orchestra. Ormandy's predecessor, Leopold Stokowsky, had created the plush, deep sonorities that came to be known as the "Philadelphia sound," as specific and laudatory a designation in the classical world as the Delfonics' sound was in theirs. I couldn't get enough. In the mid-1960s the orchestra performed a lot of Bartók and Mahler — I remember feeling that I was listening to *Concerto for Orchestra* with my *stomach* — and I started paying attention to whatever was available on radio and the occasional LP I could afford. But my musical intake was what it still is, eclectic, a polite term for an indiscriminate mess that took in Sunday morning gospel broadcast live from local Baptist churches, early Beatles and Stones, and (critically, it turned out) jazz of any kind. In the end, probably because I always had rock-and-roll, *Bandstand,* and Mario singing "Golden Days" to fall back on, my interlude with Pat, instead of putting me off music or decisively cooling it into abstraction, jacked up music's nervous immediacy and made it even more systemic, brute, and ardent.

That physicality intensified when I was twenty years old and got sick, when music fused to physical pain. I've been in bondage, more or less, ever since, but it's a bondage — or bonding, a cellular hybridizing — I can't imagine living without. And it's formed by music of all sorts, especially, in my later life, by voice — Dawn Upshaw singing Marc Blitzstein, any good tenor's "Un aura amorosa" from *Così*, Sarah Vaughan accompanied by Clifford Brown, Dion's "The Wanderer," or Sting's a cappella "Roxanne" (which a dog I once knew, a Shih Tzu, sang along to, with sonorous conviction). Physical pain is like personality: it's involuntarily expressive and idiosyncratic, but expressive only to the person experiencing it, and so idiosyncratic that any verbal representation of it is sickly inadequate and, to listeners especially, tedious, though talking about pain is boring first and most of all to its owner. It's an idiolect, a language specific to one brain and comprehensible only to the nervous system that activates and networks messages from that brain. It's grotesquely companionable to the person experiencing it but unfriendly toward others. It islands and isolates. When Philoctetes, dragging around his evil-smelling wounded foot, describes his island to the visiting Neoptolemus, he's also describing the exile pain causes:

> There's no anchorage here, nowhere anyone
> can land or trade or have a good time.
> No sensible person sails this way,
> though now and then sailors come by,
> and when they do, they pity me,
> at least they say they do, and in their pity
> give me scraps of food and cast-off clothes.

Pain becomes you, becomes so capillary that even though it's local, it colonizes the entire body and is coextensive with it. It saturates perceptions and your sense of consequence. While it's active, just as we say certain pieces of music irrationally change our lives, it can permanently alter your sense of sense.

Ankylosing spondylitis is a severe inflammation that breaks down ligaments and cartilage and fuses them to bone. If in the vertebrae, you end up with "bamboo spine." If the lower back, the sacroiliac joints become an inelastic bony mass. In 1965 the syndrome was unknown, so the pain that put me in the hospital for three months, then plateaued for ten years (a steep plateau it was), and has faithfully stood by me in varying degrees — depending sometimes on the length of the opera — ever since, had no evident cause. The physical pain was fraught with the spiritual dread unknowingness creates. I was tested for slipped disk, neurological damage, and psychosomatic dysfunction (i.e., derangement). Because the pain wasn't identifiable, my body felt invaded and occupied by hostile unreason. A person my age whose AS went untreated now usually looks like a broken matchstick or twig, someone who, as a chiropractor friend of mine says, walks around looking at his shoes. (Imagine Groucho's scampish glide turned herky-jerky, Mr. Hyde-ish.) I've often seen old men in Chinatown shaped like grasshoppers, bent over a cane, looking up through inverted bifocals. Now I know why they look like that. My AS wasn't diagnosed until 2000, when a rheumatologist I consulted for a different ailment took an interest in my medical history and solved the mystery. He was rather surprised to see me standing upright. I *don't* walk around looking at my shoes, and for this I'm grateful to, among others, David "Fathead" Newman.

While in the hospital and for a long time thereafter, at night I kept by my ear a transistor radio like those the men who slept on sidewalks listened to. So whenever pain spiked me awake — *it* seemed deranged, because it migrated: now in my lower back, now knees, now upper legs — I had sounds running into my ear that instead of being a balm or distraction layered me more deeply into the pain, its rhythms and registers. The pain and its music, as one entity, took on the sort of casual familiarity Nietzsche describes in *The Gay Science:* "I have given a name to my pain and call it 'dog.' It is just as faithful, just as obtrusive and shameless, just as entertaining, just as clever as any other dog — and I can scold it and vent my bad mood on it."

My night music was jazz, spun by Joel Dorn at Philadelphia's FM station WHAT, which programmed around the clock. Early Nina Simone, Oliver Nelson's *The Blues and the Abstract Truth,* Miles Davis playing Gil Evans's arrangements, Oscar Peterson's sweet and melancholy *Canadian Suite,* and the celestial Charles Lloyd. Dorn, who went on to become an astute, adventurous record producer, hosted an evening show to which he brought some interesting backstory. In 1958, as a teenager already possessed by blues and jazz, he went to a small joint outside Philadelphia called the Ambler Sporting Club, where Ray Charles and his group were performing. Charles was mostly a rhythm-and-blues instrumentalist starting to break ground as a pop vocalist and jazz artist. The sax player in Charles's ensemble was a young and handsome fellow named David "Fathead" Newman. (When he flubbed an arpeggio in his high school band, the leader called him a fathead, and the moniker stuck.) Dorn cornered him during a break between sets and promised him that someday, when he became a DJ, he would use a number he heard that night, "Hard Times," as his theme song.

And so he did, every night at ten P.M. All day every day I felt the urge to take to my bed and settle into whatever occult infirmity waited there for me. I didn't know, of course, that if I did so, my body would shape itself to its illness, and once I put on my shoes I would spend a long time looking at them. We now know that certain rheumatic disorders require the body to stay in motion lest it stiffen for good. Some impulse, maybe fear of inertia — I became terrified, still am, by enforced immobility — or mule-headedness, made me want to stay in motion. With the help of stout canes given me by my Mario Lanza uncle Mike, who'd lost a leg in the war, I rode the bus into Center City, went up and down subway stairs and the stairs in our small dim house (occasionally harangued by my impossible mother about how much suffering I was causing her), and walked endless circles — ovals, actually — around the dining room table, to train my legs again, to walk the dog. Keep moving, I told myself, like jazz, which is most alive in its changes.

By late evening the pain was running high; I'd be exhausted and had to rest. "Hard Times," Charles on piano opening with a brief, tripping statement of theme, was always waiting for me. Fathead's sax line, a climbing plea resisting the drag of melancholy, became a resting place for (not from) pain, became pain's reliable nocturnal climate and substance. I loved the number all the more, with the kind of exasperated love that doesn't fade but gets more acute in memory, even after the pain dampened. I never owned the album, though, until a few months ago, when I ran down a remastered CD of the original 1958 LP, *Fathead: Ray Charles Presents David Newman*. "Hard Times" is the opening track, and when I played it, not having heard it for over thirty years, I wept like a child for the past, and then I whistled along.

In the hospital, I had nothing but time on my hands and pain in my brain. I spent time practicing apotropaic mind games I hoped would help with the pain. What they now call "pain management" is really a way of establishing terms of ownership. One tactic is to contrive likenesses. Pain is a language, a story, a journey, it's a busted gearbox's teeth, a bed of nails, a heat gun. Another, and one I practiced for years, is to imagine the means of eliminating it. Extirpating it. I imagined marking its boundaries, as one traces the frontiers of a small country on a map, then surgically knifing it out, carving it clear of its surrounding mass of nerve and flesh, as Filipino hoodoo men magically insert their hands into a sick person and extract the ailing part. I could, I thought, use a trowel or ice cream scoop or child's sand shovel and remove it cleanly. I wouldn't want to see it or dedicate it to science. I wanted an old high school pal, a racketeer trainee, to take it away and feed the gorgeously veined, placental mass to the rats and feral cats at the dump.

My reading kept pain company. I read Thomas Mann's *Doktor Faustus,* his "Nietzsche book" about the inseparability of sublimity and pain. Adrian Leverkühn, a prodigious young composer and inventor of tone-row music, in order to break through ("like a butterfly emerging from its chrysalis") to an original musical language for feeling, to something really new — it turns out to be plainsong — sells his soul to the devil by contracting the syphilis that kills him and bargaining away love. Immobilized, often in hip-harness traction ("counterindicated," they would now say), I moved laboriously through Mann's high-toned, immobile prose. What else was there to do? Except in movies and on TV, hospitals are generally uneventful places, the sick waiting to learn more about sickness, lose it, or succumb. So I was cheered by the occasional visits of an African-American orderly who would stop by on his rounds to chat with the poor young bastard in bed. Actually, I was cheered before he walked in. I knew he was approaching because he'd be whistling, pitch-perfect, some jazz standard, and so in addition to the emotional boost he brought, he reminded me of a character in *Doktor Faustus,* the violinist Rudolph Schwerdtfeger, who "whistled with such artistry that one laughed for sheer pleasure, whistled more like a violin than a flute, the phrasing masterly, the little notes, staccato or legato, coming out with delirious precision."

The eeriest jazz stylist then (featured, of course, on WHAT) was Morgana King. After cutting a few albums and drawing a small but devoted following, she shunted into an acting career, so that most people now know her only as Don Corleone's stolid wife in the

Godfather movies. Her repertoire was jazz classics and pop ballads like "A Taste of Honey," the title of her first LP. Some singers emulate the solidified sound of string instruments. King's voice went the opposite way. Her delivery was wound tight, breathy, flute-ish, air tremulously whisked into resonance, closer to moody, throaty whistling than to song. Her singing reminded me of the orderly's whistling. That was a time when you still heard people whistling everywhere, in hospital corridors and buses, in workplaces and on the street. I once read a lament by some poet about the passing of those sounds from public and private life. But they haven't entirely passed. The day I was reading the lament I could hear my adolescent daughter about the house whistling some Chopin she was working up on piano; that reedy vitality gave me a rush of affection and hope, for her and for all breath in life, but rattled me too, because it made me think of breath passing, my own, hers. And a childhood South Philly friend was visiting at the time, who in the many years I've known him whistles phrases the way people whoop at ball games and concerts, violent gusts and surging wingbeats of sound, but always only a phrase or two, which seems to exhaust him, because he never completes a melodic line. It's true enough that outdoors — I have no car so spend a lot of time waiting for and riding public transit — I hardly ever hear anybody whistling, and I don't have to catch myself if I start doing so because heads immediately turn my way, as if I'd burst into song. But who can say that's a bad thing? There's not much whistling going on because so many people are listening to music, ears muffed or buttoned up by headsets.

I tried another tactic while I was laid up, whistling through (or along with) the pain while the music was playing. Pain breathes forth its rhythms and tonalities through its instrument, the body. If I breathed too deeply, cleared my throat, or, God help me, coughed, the pain spiked. Once I sneezed and nearly passed out. ("Give that boy more Darvon and muscle relaxers.") When people around me whistle, I listen up, thinking I'll hear some essence revealed. I sat vigil with my mother until she stopped breathing. Before my father died his breath thinned to a hesitant narcotized hum. An old neighborhood friend of mine recently died in his sleep. Our lunch dates every couple of months were a ritual, the sort of little social celebration that refreshes and sustains affection:

we ate at the same time in the same neighborhood place, even ate the same dishes — I did, anyway; he flopped between two favorites. Inside the restaurant, when I sat or stood, the standard but by now dampened pain flicked its blowtorch, as it likes to do. (My darling remembers me.) But I was happy when we settled down to catch up, gossip, talk books and movies and mutual friends, then say goodbye with a peck on the cheek until next time. He loved to eat and drink and get lost. One night after dinner at my apartment, I was playing Dion and the Belmonts, and when he stood to leave he started juking and pumping his fists to "The Wanderer" — "I'm the wanderer, yeah the wanderer, I roam around around around around" — right there in my kitchen. Whenever I phoned to make a lunch date, while fumbling for his book he whistled in a way that bespoke his personality, a bit diffident, unobtrusive, more air than tone, and no tune really, just a happy-go-lucky breathy jaunt. Now I wait for a streetcar on our neighborhood corner where I sometimes ran into him, hearing no whistling at all, and feel as if he disappeared into his own breath, the small music he made, and took all that beautiful rough vitality with him.

GEORGE GESSERT

An Orgy of Power

FROM NORTHWEST REVIEW

I AM RELUCTANT to write about torture. It holds no special fascination for me — on the contrary, I find the subject repellent. But I
did not choose the times I live in, nor do I choose what I am compelled to write. As a writer I am committed to speaking from my
own experience, which may seem to counsel silence. I have not
been to Iraq, Afghanistan, or Guantánamo Bay. I am not a journalist or an authority on the history of torture. But the perimeters of
experience do not end with what is immediate. In today's world, almost everything connects with everything else. The coffee that fu-
els my editing was raised in Kenya, my shirt was made in China. Reports arrive daily from around the world. The problem is sorting
the relevant from the irrelevant, the true from the false, and as-
signing each bit of information something like its proper weight.
These things make learning gradual, writing slow, and these notes
very late.

In August 2002, following the battle of Konduz in Afghanistan, I
read puzzling reports on the Internet. More than two hundred
prisoners taken at Konduz had been found dead in a mass grave.
They had died of heat, dehydration, and suffocation after being
sealed in metal containers for transport to Shabarghan prison.
The U.S. role in the deaths was unclear, and to date has not been
properly investigated, although the number of victims is now put at
a thousand. However, the U.S. Army's Special Forces seems to have
been involved.[1]
    The media gave extensive attention to one captive, John Walker

Lindh. He was a twenty-one-year-old Californian who had converted to Islam, and trained in Afghanistan to fight the Northern Alliance. He had arrived at the front lines before September 11. We now know that he had no advance knowledge of the attacks on New York and Washington, D.C., and that reports he heard afterward were sketchy. Following his capture he was separated from other prisoners and allegedly tortured.

The accounts that I read at the time said that Lindh had been handcuffed, blindfolded, and photographed. Some of his captors were hostile to him and did not treat a wound in his leg. But how was this torture? I wondered if Lindh's family and lawyer were making exaggerated claims in an attempt to win public sympathy for the young man and save him from the death sentence he could face if charged with aiding the enemy. Only much later did I read that Lindh had had a bullet in his leg, and U.S. agents had left the bullet there while they interrogated him, which had gone on until the wound became "seeping and malodorous." Lindh received death threats, and his hands were cuffed so tightly that he was in intense pain. He was confined in a metal shipping container, and suffered extended exposure to cold.[2]

For almost a year after the battle of Konduz I read sketchy and ambiguous reports of prisoner mistreatment. I was not sure what to make of them. Then came the pictures from Abu Ghraib and overwhelming evidence that detainees had been tortured. They had been tortured not only in Iraq, but in Afghanistan and an archipelago of prisons around the world. Documents surfaced, such as the so-called torture memo of August 1, 2002, showing that very close associates of President Bush, apparently with his full approval, had encouraged torture.[3]

Lions and hyenas kill swiftly. Housecats play with their victims, but only to practice pouncing, not to cause pain. Tapeworms and the shingles virus keep their victims alive as sources of sustenance, not to cause pain. Only humans torture.

In many societies torture was open and acceptable. The Romans made elaborate forms of animal and human torture into public entertainments. During the Inquisition torture served the Church. But from the earliest days of the republic Americans have defined themselves as the people who are opposed to "cruel and unusual punishments." The Eighth Amendment to the Constitution provides a legal groundwork for putting this ideal into practice. By the twentieth century, the United States had become an international leader in outlawing torture. Along the way some Americans engaged in torture, but cruel and unusual punishments, variously defined, have been forbidden for so long as to seem somehow foreign and un-American. Consequently most Americans are unaccustomed to discussing torture, much less torture done with encouragement from the president.

A few days ago a letter appeared in our local newspaper repeating the familiar claim that nothing worse happened at Abu Ghraib than happens in fraternity hazings. This simile has cropped up in local and national media ever since Rush Limbaugh gave it his imprimatur on May 4, 2004, on his show "It's Not About Us; This Is War."

> CALLER: It was like a college fraternity prank that stacked up naked men . . .
> LIMBAUGH: Exactly. Exactly my point. This is no different than what happens at the Skull and Bones initiation . . . I'm talking about people having a good time, these people, you ever heard of emotional release? You ever heard of need to blow off some steam?

No doubt stress relief was a factor in what happened, and not only at Abu Ghraib. An army sergeant, describing events at Camp Mercury, near Fallujah, reported that "everyone in camp knew if you wanted to work out your frustrations you show up" at the PUC tent. PUC, pronounced "puck," stands for person under control, the term that has replaced POW, or prisoner of war, which evokes the Geneva Conventions. As an example of someone working out his frustrations, the sergeant told of a cook who on his day off went to the PUC tent and broke a prisoner's leg with a Louisville Slugger, a metal baseball bat.[4]

I am not shocked by war photographs. They are all too familiar. I have seen too many images of the dead and wounded, too many mutilated children, too many body parts in black-and-white and in color, and far too many grief-stricken survivors. Long ago, without ever making a conscious decision, I became detached. But my automatic defenses did not work with the photographs from Abu Ghraib. Their extraordinary power arose from the novelty of their subject matter, their striking resemblance to pornography, and their absolute authenticity. I doubt that any professional photographer or trained artist could have created such damning images.

The tormenters are my fellow countrymen and -women. They look like people on the street, and from all reports they are ordinary citizens. But the prisoners, in their fear, anguish, and humiliation, are more immediately recognizable as human beings — even with digitally blanked-out faces.

Of the many photographs from Abu Ghraib (the Pentagon may hold thousands), so far only about two dozen have entered the public realm.[5] After seeing a dozen or so photographs, I began to follow news about torture. This led me to pay attention to how public discussion was being framed. Beginning in March 2004, when the first photographs became public, the media adopted the administration's preferred word, "abuse," to describe what had happened at Abu Ghraib. "Abuse" covers a range of activities, but is not ordinarily used to describe attempted male rape, which is what some of the photographs show. We do not ordinarily call homicide "abuse," and yet one of the photographs is of a man who had evidently been beaten to death. The media could have corrected itself when those reports were confirmed, and when evidence emerged that detainees at Abu Ghraib, Guantánamo Bay, Bagram Air Base, and elsewhere had been forced to maintain stress positions until passing out, reports of cigarettes being put out in a detainee's ears, evidence of blows that liquefied muscles and produced strokes, and of many other clear instances of torture. But even today the media persists in using the unmodified word "abuse." Why? Perhaps reporters and media executives fear the administration. Fear is not unreasonable. The Bush administration has been unsparingly hostile and vindictive toward critics. Or perhaps mainstream reporters and those who manage the media fear the public, the greater part of which until very recently has supported the president. As I write, a *Newsweek* poll shows that about half of the American public approve of torture.[6] But whatever the reasons for the media's reluctance to use the word "torture," at what point do denial, fear, and caution shade into complicity?

To the media's credit, it has brought news of torture to the attention of U.S. citizens and to the world. Who is ultimately responsible, the major media or individuals, for determining the moral weight of tossing the body of a murdered man into his sister's cell, as reported by the *Los Angeles Times*? Is it torture when a man is nearly drowned by having his head forced into a toilet, as we learn happened at Guantánamo Bay from an article in the *Washington Post*? Is a broken jaw less painful if it is noted on page 10 rather than on page 1?

The United States may not have as monumental a literature of war as Russia, or as desolating a one as Germany, but in any good public library one can find vivid descriptions of Americans at war, read about the ordeals and boredom and camaraderie of soldiers, gain some sense of the appeals and horrors of combat, and learn about its aftermath. We also have literature about the home front, about the women and children, the parents waiting for the knock on the door — typically with neighbors determinedly oblivious of what is happening.

But torture plays only the most minor role in our literature. *The Pit and the Pendulum,* if it can be said to describe torture at all, reads like an overheated fantasy. In Faulkner's *Sanctuary* an impotent gangster named Popeye rapes a girl with a corncob. A mob mutilates and murders Joe Christmas in *Light in August.* In Robert Stone's *Dog Soldiers* two drug dealers use a heated clothes iron to terrorize a man into surrendering heroin that he has smuggled into California. In *A Flag for Sunrise* an American nun is tortured in a fictitious Central American country. But such passages only underscore a near absence in our literature. Our literature does not fathom torture. Torture by Americans has spread in a vacuum of language.

Painting and filmmaking have prepared us slightly better. Leon Golub devoted much of his career to painting torturers and their victims. During the Vietnam War Peter Saul painted terrifying, cartoonlike fantasies that map a peculiarly American approach to torture. And *Reservoir Dogs* brought unaestheticized images and sounds of torture to a mass audience. In small ways, perhaps, our visual culture has helped educate us to see the photographs from Abu Ghraib.

Susan Sontag observed that the grins on the faces of U.S. soldiers in photographs from Abu Ghraib resemble those on white faces in photographs of lynchings.[7] Schoolyard bullies have the same smile. The truth that the bully and the torturer share is the truth of unrestrained power, but the bully only glimpses it, while the lyncher and the torturer realize it.

Jean Améry, who was tortured by the Gestapo in Fort Breendonk in Belgium in 1943, remembered the faces of his torturers as "not 'Gestapo faces' with twisted noses, hypertrophied chins, pockmarks and knife scars, as they might appear in a book, but rather faces like anyone else's. Plain, ordinary faces." During torture, these plain, ordinary faces became "concentrated in murderous self-realization. With heart and soul they went about their business, and the name of it was power, domination over spirit and flesh, an orgy of unchecked self-expansion."[8]

Hannah Arendt's insight into the banality of evil applies to bureaucrats and ordinary citizens far removed from the suffering that they cause, but according to Améry does not apply to the men and women who do the actual work of destruction. Améry claims an authority in this regard that exceeds Arendt's, since Arendt was never tortured. The act of torture, he writes, destroys ordinary social bonds and relationships, and propels the torturer far beyond the realm of daily life. The torturer engages in what Elaine Scarry calls "the unmaking of civilization . . . [and the] uncreating of the created world."[9]

"An orgy of unchecked self-expansion": Améry's phrase, with its Sadean grandiosity, is consistent with the smiles on American faces at Abu Ghraib. The reward of torture, according to Améry, is "murderous self-realization." Self-realization in this context suggests a return, however brief, to infantile omnipotence. The smile of the torturer is latent within everyone.

The torturer and his or her superiors mimic God. They and they alone determine who is guilty, what is right, and what is wrong. It comes as no surprise, then, that according to the International Committee of the Red Cross, between 70 and 90 percent of the thousands detained at Abu Ghraib had been arrested "by mistake."[10] Reportedly these were among the victims of torture. At least one hundred prisoners were children. We have less information about the prisoners at Guantánamo Bay, but we know that among them are children and demented old men. Destruction of the innocent is the most incontrovertible proof of power.

Unchecked self-expansion is also consistent with what we know about the Bush administration's efforts to legitimize torture. Many military and intelligence experts claim that torture does not yield reliable information, endangers U.S. prisoners of war, and can serve enemies as a recruitment tool. Other intelligence experts disagree, claiming that torture can yield useful information, and may terrorize opponents, but comes at too high a price: loss of American prestige internationally and corruption of the military. Pragmatic objections to torture are convincing only if national honor and the well-being of our troops and citizens are primary concerns. The administration has had a very different, overriding concern: that the president not be restrained by the Geneva Conventions or the Constitution as traditionally interpreted. We do not need to psychoanalyze George W. Bush or understand the inner life of Dick Cheney to recognize broad patterns in their behavior. Their primary concern is and has been power, irrespective of traditional morality or law.

As every dreamer learns sooner or later, and as the framers of the Constitution, who were hardly sentimental about humankind, knew very well, something in us would sculpt the universe. In itself this is neither good nor bad; it is simply a psychological phenomenon. It informs everything from law to art to child rearing to exploration of the solar system. But it also produces tyranny.

Améry considered torture an essential feature of totalitarian rule. Under German fascism, torture became "the total inversion of the social world . . . in the world of torture man exists only by ruining the other person who stands before him."[11] Améry's insights are relevant to us because although the United States is profoundly unlike Nazi Germany, our society accommodates not only democratic practices but undemocratic ones, including outright totalitarian rule as at Abu Ghraib and Guantánamo Bay. For several decades torture has been a feature of U.S. proxy wars, clandestine campaigns, CIA actions, and partnerships with military regimes and death squads. From the 1970s to the 1990s American involvement in torture, especially in Latin America, surfaced from time to time in the media. Numerous reports focused on the School of the Americas (renamed the Western Hemisphere Institute for Security Cooperation in 2001). In 1996 the Pentagon was forced to release school training manuals that taught torture. However, the mainstream media usually characterized the role of the School of the Americas in torture as indirect, and downplayed instances of direct involvement as aberrations.[12]

Until photographs from Abu Ghraib were aired on national television, most Americans probably did not know that their government sometimes encouraged torture. Or, if they did know, they could tell themselves that it was quite rare — this was what I believed. I believed that torture by Americans existed, but involved very few people and played a very small role in American foreign policy. Relative to other extremely serious problems, such as mass extinctions, global warming, the spread of nuclear weapons, and the population explosion, torture was distinctly less important. I still think that in a very general way this is true, but my failure to comprehend what was happening arose from not wanting to think about torture, from a sense of having no personal connection with torture or the tortured, and from the reports themselves. Arriving intermittently from distant places, the words seemed ghostly and insubstantial in their horror. They needed a catalyst to gain psychological substance. Photographs from Abu Ghraib provided the catalyst.

Writing these notes, I held on to the belief that I had no personal connection to the tortured. I had almost completed my notes (or so I thought) when I began to think about the long-term effects of torture. I began to think about friends who had lost family in the Holocaust — was torture involved? How does torture affect the second and third generations? How does not knowing whether a close relative had been tortured affect a family? I thought about a boy I played with when I was in junior high school. His family was from Armenia. I recalled his mother telling me that the family had arrived in the United States in 1920, but I never learned more. Then there was the doctor from El Salvador who for a short time cleaned house for my mother. What was his story? What was his family's story? I realized that I did not know my degrees of separation from the tortured, or from torturers.

But this too was a trick that I played on myself. Years ago, at a conference in São Paulo, I became acquainted with an amateur scholar of Paracas culture. He was Brazilian, perhaps fifteen years my senior, tall and distinguished-looking, and one evening at dinner he told me in excellent, German-inflected English about his many visits to Nasca to see the ancient earthworks there. The Nasca Lines, which were scraped into the earth some eighteen hundred years ago and stretch for miles across the desert floor, are some of the largest artworks in the world. What they meant to their creators no one knows, but because weaving played a central role in Paracas culture, some authorities believe that the lines diagram the loom of the stars.

I asked him if he had ever seen the lines at night.

"Once," he said. "It was as I imagine the beginning of the universe, and the end." For me that was the beginning of our friendship.

Over the next twelve years we corresponded, mostly about Paracas art but also about ourselves. His father, I learned, had been involved in the 1944 attempt to assassinate Hitler. But we did not discuss this. He made it clear that he did not want me to ask questions. "I never think about it," he wrote. I could only begin to imagine his situation. I had read that the plotters were tortured to death after they were captured. His father had sent him to boarding school in Switzerland, which probably saved his life. From there his mother took him to Brazil.

Several years ago, in declining health, he shot himself. He bungled the attempt and took two months to die.

Writing these notes, I turned to novels for relief, a safe haven from the subject of torture, or so I assumed, typically American. The title character in J. M. Coetzee's *Elizabeth Costello* is a distinguished novelist, navigating the mildly hazardous waters of literary fame. She uses her renown to speak out for animals suffering under industrialism, comparing them with the victims of the Holocaust. Strongly criticized for making this comparison, she reads Paul West's *The Very Rich Hours of Count von Stauffenberg*, a history of the

1944 plot to assassinate Hitler. West recounts in detail how the plotters were tortured to death, and their agonies were filmed so that the Führer could replay them at his leisure. Elizabeth Costello is so wounded by horror that she publically attacks the author and tells him that he should never have written his book. There is such a thing as too much knowledge.

I found myself arguing with her. The written word, except for a few works of poetry, never provides more than incomplete knowledge. Reading cannot provide too much knowledge, but timing is everything. The art of reading involves intuiting when to read and when not. As readers, we do not enlarge ourselves by taking no risks, but even a masterpiece read at the wrong time is a waste of time, or worse.

If I knew then what I know today, I could have been a better friend. Right now I do not have the heart to read more about what happened to my dead friend's father. But when the time is right I will do the reading.

The outbreak of torture today is different from previous torture by Americans in three significant ways. First, the Bush administration carefully laid the groundwork for torture. In previous wars torture did not result directly from White House planning, even if commanding officers and their civilian superiors were willing to avert their eyes when it occurred. Second, the administration and the Pentagon, for all of their formidable skills in managing imagery, did not take digital cameras and the Internet into account. Third, more information about torture by Americans is available today than ever before.

The election of 2004 was an indirect referendum on torture. Neither George Bush nor John Kerry made torture an election issue, but reports about what had happened at Abu Ghraib and what was happening at Guantánamo Bay and elsewhere appeared intermittently in the major media throughout the campaign. The election confirmed what both candidates apparently knew from the beginning, that torture would bear no political price.

As I write, all that is necessary to practice torture outside the country on noncitizens, and on citizens such as John Lindh, is to maintain a measure of secrecy abroad, and appearances domestically. President Bush has attempted to accomplish the latter by condemning torture as not reflecting American values. "Freedom from torture," he said in a typically hypocritical speech, "is an inalienable right."[13]

On November 4, 2004, the greater part of the electorate became implicated in torture. Nothing like this had happened in any previous American war. The closest parallel to the present situation is, of course, not a previous war but the heyday of lynching. During the half century from the 1880s to the 1930s, most of the American public, along with much of the press and Congress, ignored or downplayed atrocities, and by doing so tacitly endorsed them.

Consider the contrast with the French in the early 1960s, when evidence of torture in Algeria became public. Half the nation rose up in protest. That largely put a stop to torture.

Will new categories of victims emerge, such as foreign nationals living within the boundaries of the United States or citizens suspected of supporting terrorism, ever more broadly defined? Only time will tell, but this much is certain: torture, and the imperial project that favors it, has a price. One part of the price is loss of American innocence.

Improbable as it may seem today, at one time the United States had a genuine claim to innocence. Although the republic was conceived amid genocide and slavery, the sheer daring of the experiment in representative government allowed informed men and women of good faith to believe that even the worst crimes were vestiges of an older order in the process of being outgrown.

Balzac considered the virgin to be the most terrifying of all figures. This is because we are fallen but she is pure. Her inexperience and spiritual invincibility do not predispose her to be merciful to us for our failings. Throughout the nineteenth century America's virginity made the nation invincible, to itself first of all, as it projected itself onto the world. But such innocence cannot indefinitely survive empire. The rhetoric of the Bush administration mimics the old moral invincibility, but today American innocence, except for those elements that have changed to disillusionment or that we share with all other peoples, has completed its transformation into kitsch.

Kitsch has its own powers, and great ones too — the powers of ignorance and public relations. Kitsch innocence is cartoonlike and amplified, all smiles and snarls and formulaic sincerity, rapt with faith one minute, boundlessly cynical the next, but always tuned to public desires. None of this is new, of course. Europe knows all about it. European history cautions against any leader who talks like a cartoon. And Europe is littered with the remains of empires. Many of our leaders, to widespread domestic applause, scorned Old Europe, but amid the cheers America had become like the Europe we read about in books, the Europe of the unromantic past, the genuine Old Europe. The spectacles and orgies of self-expansion, the murderous hypocrisy, the denial and religious fanaticism and systemic corruption of language, and above all the tragic waste began to look familiar. They began to look like what centuries of immigrants crossing oceans to begin again dreamed that they had left behind forever.

According to Jean Améry, the source of torture is our innate drive for unchecked self-expansion. If this is true, the possibility of torture will always be with us. How are we to deal with this today?

Machiavelli summarized the relationship of ordinary people to power as a shadow play of deceptions brought by the people on themselves. A prince "should seem to be all mercy, all loyalty, all sincerity, all humanity, all religion. And nothing is more necessary to seem to have than [religion] . . . Everybody sees what you appear to be, few feel what you are, and those few will not dare to oppose themselves to the opinion of the many, who have the majesty of the state to defend them . . . Let a prince therefore conquer and maintain his state: his means will always be judged honourable and praised by everyone, for ordinary people will always be taken by appearances and by the outcome of action."[14] To put this into contemporary language, presidents are encouraged in evil by the people, who are eager to be deceived.

Machiavelli wrote about the nature of power after his political career had ended in disaster. He had been accused of plotting against the Medici, and tortured. The experience of torture may have convinced him that human beings are fundamentally evil. His insights into power are brilliant, but his assessment of human nature is as reductive as the belief that human beings are fundamentally good. Such formulations are alluring. They voice our hopes and fears, but they bring only factitious clarity to experience by ignoring evidence that does not fit. The overwhelming lesson of history and of daily life is that human beings are capable of beautiful behavior and terrible behavior, individually and collectively. What this implies is that although taboos, information, empathy, moral intelligence, uncorrupted law, and democratic practices are crucial lines of defense against torture, the single most important defense is the separation of powers. The more concentrated power becomes, the fewer the obstacles to extremity, including torture. The deeper our society descends into militarism, one-party rule, and rule by a single branch of government, the more embedded the practice of torture will become in American life.

Notes

1. Jennifer K. Harbury, *Truth, Torture, and the American Way* (Boston: Beacon Press, 2005), pp. 2–4.

2. Ibid., pp. 4–5.

3. The memo of August 1, 2002, defines torture as applying only to acts that produce "physical pain . . . equivalent in intensity to the pain accompanying . . . organ failure . . . or even death." The memorandum goes on to say that "even if the defendant knows that severe pain will result from his actions, if causing such pain is not his objective, he lacks the requisite specific intent." What this means is that if extracting information is a torturer's objective, he or she is not legally responsible for causing pain, no matter how intense and no matter how lasting the damage.

For about two years the memo guided the administration and provided legal protection for torturers and their superiors. After the publication of photographs from Abu Ghraib, the administration revised the guidelines, but in a footnote protected the August 1 memo's extremely limited definition of torture.

4. Human Rights Watch, *Leadership Failure: Firsthand Accounts of Torture of Iraqi Detainees by the U.S. Army's 82nd Airborne Division: Summary*.

5. In February 2006, while this manuscript was being prepared for press, hundreds of additional images were released by the Australian news show *Dateline*.

6. "44 percent of the public thinks that torture is often or sometimes justified to obtain important information . . . a clear majority — 58 percent — would support torture to thwart a terrorist attack." Evan Thomas and Michael Hirsch, "The Debate over Torture," *Newsweek*, November 21, 2005, p. 29.

7. Susan Sontag, "Regarding the Torture of Others," *New York Times Magazine*, May 23, 2004.

8. Jean Améry, *At the Mind's Limit*, trans. Sidney Rosenfeld and Stella P. Rosenfeld (Bloomington and Indianapolis: Indiana University Press, 1980), p. 25.

9. Elaine Scarry, *The Body in Pain* (New York: Oxford University Press, 1985), p. 45.

10. *Report of the International Committee of the Red Cross (ICRC) on the Treatment by the Coalition Forces of Prisoners of War and Other Protected Persons by the Geneva Conventions in*

Iraq During Arrest, Internment, and Interrogation, Section 1.7, February 2004. Brigadier General Janice Karpinski, who oversaw Abu Ghraib at the time that the photographs were taken, provides a slightly different, but substantially similar assessment: "The vast majority of them [prisoners] were [arrested for] minor crimes. They were missing curfew. They were subjected to a random inspection and a weapon was found in their trunks . . . they were minor crimes, nonviolent crimes." Interview with Marjorie Cohn, *Truthout,* August 24, 2005.

11. Jean Améry in ICRC report, p. 35.

12. The School of the Americas' involvement in torture may not always have been indirect. At the school's interrogation classes in Panama, street people may have been used to demonstrate torture techniques. In Uruguay, four homeless people were reportedly used as guinea pigs in an "anatomy class" and tortured to death. Jennifer Harbury in ibid., pp. 95–96.

13. George W. Bush, Reuters, June 26, 2005.

14. Niccolò Machiavelli, *The Prince,* trans. Wayne Rebhorn (New York: Barnes and Noble, 2003), pp. 76–77.

MALCOLM GLADWELL

What the Dog Saw

FROM THE NEW YORKER

IN THE CASE of Sugar v. Forman, Cesar Millan knew none of the facts before arriving at the scene of the crime. That is the way Cesar prefers it. His job was to reconcile Forman with Sugar, and, since Sugar was a good deal less adept in making her case than Forman, whatever he learned beforehand might bias him in favor of the aggrieved party.

The Forman residence was in a trailer park in Mission Hills, just north of Los Angeles. Dark wood paneling, leather couches, deep-pile carpeting. The air conditioning was on, even though it was one of those ridiculously pristine Southern California days. Lynda Forman was in her sixties, possibly older, a handsome woman with a winning sense of humor. Her husband, Ray, was in a wheelchair, and looked vaguely ex-military. Cesar sat across from them, in black jeans and a blue shirt, his posture characteristically perfect.

"So how can I help?" he said.

"You can help our monster turn into a sweet, lovable dog," Lynda replied. It was clear that she had been thinking about how to describe Sugar to Cesar for a long time. "She's ninety percent bad, ten percent the love . . . She sleeps with us at night. She cuddles." Sugar meant a lot to Lynda. "But she grabs anything in sight that she can get, and tries to destroy it. My husband is disabled, and she destroys his room. She tears clothes. She's torn our carpet. She bothers my grandchildren. If I open the door, she will run." Lynda pushed back her sleeves and exposed her forearms. They were covered in so many bites and scratches and scars and scabs that it was as if she had been tortured. "But I love her. What can I say?"

Cesar looked at her arms and blinked: "Wow."

Cesar is not a tall man. He is built like a soccer player. He is in his mid-thirties and has large, wide eyes, olive skin, and white teeth. He crawled across the border from Mexico fourteen years ago, but his English is exceptional, except when he gets excited and starts dropping his articles — which almost never happens, because he rarely gets excited. He saw the arms and he said "Wow," but it was a "wow" in the same calm tone of voice as "So how can I help?"

Cesar began to ask questions. Did Sugar urinate in the house? She did. She had a particularly destructive relationship with newspapers, television remotes, and plastic cups. Cesar asked about walks. Did Sugar travel, or did she track — and when he said "track" he did an astonishing impersonation of a dog sniffing. Sugar tracked. What about discipline?

"Sometimes I put her in a crate," Lynda said. "And it's only for a fifteen-minute period. Then she lays down and she's fine. I don't know how to give discipline. Ask my kids."

"Did your parents discipline you?"

"I didn't need discipline. I was perfect."

"So you had no rules . . . What about using physical touch with Sugar?"

"I have used it. It bothers me."

"What about the bites?"

"I can see it in the head. She gives me that look."

"She's reminding you who rules the roost."

"Then she will lick me for half an hour where she has bit me."

"She's not apologizing. Dogs lick each other's wounds to heal the pack, you know."

Lynda looked a little lost. "I thought she was saying sorry."

"If she was sorry," Cesar said softly, "she wouldn't do it in the first place."

It was time for the defendant. Lynda's granddaughter, Carly, came in, holding a beagle as if it were a baby. Sugar was cute, but she had a mean, feral look in her eyes. Carly put Sugar on the carpet, and Sugar swaggered over to Cesar, sniffing his shoes. In front of her, Cesar placed a newspaper, a plastic cup, and a television remote.

Sugar grabbed the newspaper. Cesar snatched it back. Sugar picked up the newspaper again. She jumped on the couch. Cesar took his hand and "bit" Sugar on the shoulder, firmly and calmly. "My hand is the mouth," he explained. "My fingers are the teeth." Sugar jumped down. Cesar stood and firmly and fluidly held Sugar down for an instant. Sugar struggled briefly, then relaxed. Cesar backed off. Sugar lunged at the remote. Cesar looked at her and said, simply and briefly, "Sh-h-h." Sugar hesitated. She went for the plastic cup. Cesar said, "Sh-h-h." She dropped it. Cesar motioned for Lynda to bring a jar of treats into the room. He placed it in the middle of the floor and hovered over it. Sugar looked at the treats and then at Cesar. She began sniffing, inching closer, but an invisible boundary now stood between her and the prize. She circled and circled but never came closer than three feet. She looked as if she were about to jump on the couch. Cesar shifted his weight and blocked her. He took a step toward her. She backed up, head lowered, into the farthest corner of the room. She sank down on her haunches, then placed her head flat on the ground. Cesar took the treats, the remote, the plastic cup, and the newspaper and placed them inches from her lowered nose. Sugar, the onetime terror of Mission Hills, closed her eyes in surrender.

"She has no rules in the outside world, no boundaries," Cesar said finally. "You practice exercise and affection. But you're not practicing exercise, discipline, and affection. When we love someone, we fulfill everything about them. That's loving. And you're not loving your dog." He stood up. He looked around. "Let's go for a walk."

Lynda staggered into the kitchen. In five minutes, her monster had turned into an angel.

"Unbelievable," she said.

Cesar Millan runs the Dog Psychology Center out of a converted auto mechanic's shop in the industrial zone of South-Central Los Angeles. The center is situated at the end of a long narrow alley, off a busy street lined with bleak warehouses and garages. Behind a high green chain-link fence is a large concrete yard, and everywhere around the yard there are dogs. Dogs basking in the sun. Dogs splashing in a pool. Dogs lying on picnic tables. Cesar takes in people's problem dogs; he keeps them for a minimum of two weeks, integrating them into the pack. He has no formal training. He learned what he knows growing up in Mexico on his grandfather's farm in Sinaloa. As a child, he was called *el Perrero,* "the dog boy," watching and studying until he felt that he could put himself inside the mind of a dog. In the mornings, Cesar takes the pack on a four-hour walk in the Santa Monica Mountains: Cesar in front, the dogs behind him; the pit bulls and the rottweilers and the German shepherds with backpacks, so that when the little dogs get tired Cesar can load them up on the big dogs' backs. Then they come back and eat. Exercise, then food. Work, then reward.

"I have forty-seven dogs right now," Cesar said. He opened the door, and they came running over, a jumble of dogs, big and small. Cesar pointed to a bloodhound. "He was aggressive with humans, really aggressive," he said. In a corner of the compound, a Wheaton terrier had just been given a bath. "She's stayed here six months because she could not trust men," Cesar explained. "She was beat up severely." He idly scratched a big German shepherd. "My girlfriend here, Beauty. If you were to see the relationship between her and her owner." He shook his head. "A very sick relationship. A *Fatal Attraction* kind of thing. Beauty sees her and she starts scratching her and biting her, and the owner is, like, 'I love you too.' That one killed a dog. That one killed a dog too. Those two guys came from New Orleans. They attacked humans. That pit bull over there with a tennis ball killed a Labrador in Beverly Hills. And look at this one — one eye. Lost the eye in a dogfight. But look at him now." Now he was nuzzling a French bulldog. He was happy — and so was the Labrador killer from Beverly Hills, who was stretched out in the sun, and so was the aggressive-toward-humans bloodhound, who was lingering by a picnic table with his tongue hanging out. Cesar stood in the midst of all the dogs, his back straight and his shoulders square. It was a prison yard. But it was the most peaceful prison yard in all of California. "The whole point is that everybody has to stay calm, submissive, no matter what," he said. "What you are witnessing right now is a group of dogs who all have the same state of mind."

Cesar Millan is the host of *Dog Whisperer,* on the National Geographic television channel. In every episode, he arrives amid canine chaos and leaves behind peace. He is the teacher we all had in grade school who could walk into a classroom filled with rambunctious kids and get everyone to calm down and *behave.* But what did that teacher have? If you'd asked us back then, we might have said that we behaved for Mr. Exley because Mr. Exley had lots of rules and was really strict. But the truth is that we behaved for Mr. DeBock as well, and he wasn't strict at all. What we really mean is that both of them had that indefinable thing called presence — and if you are going to teach a classroom full of headstrong ten-year-olds, or run a company, or command an army, or walk into a trailer home in Mission Hills where a beagle named Sugar is terrorizing its owners, you have to have presence or you're lost.

Behind the Dog Psychology Center, between the back fence and the walls of the adjoining buildings, Cesar has built a dog run — a stretch of grass and dirt as long as a city block. "This is our Chuck E. Cheese," Cesar said. The dogs saw Cesar approaching the back gate, and they ran, expectantly, toward him, piling through the narrow door in a hodgepodge of whiskers and wagging tails. Cesar had a bag over his shoulder, filled with tennis balls, and a long orange plastic ball scoop in his right hand. He reached into the bag with the scoop, grabbed a tennis ball, and flung it in a smooth practiced motion off the wall of an adjoining warehouse. A dozen dogs set off in ragged pursuit. Cesar wheeled and threw another ball, in the opposite direction, and then a third, and then a fourth, until there were so many balls in the air and on the ground that the pack had turned into a yelping, howling, leaping, charging frenzy. Woof. Woof, woof, woof. *Woof.* "The game should be played five or ten minutes, maybe fifteen minutes," Cesar said. "You begin. You end. And you don't ask, 'Please stop.' You demand that it stop." With that, Cesar gathered himself, stood stock still, and let out a short whistle: not a casual whistle but a whistle of authority. Suddenly there was absolute quiet. All forty-seven dogs stopped charging and jumping and stood as still as Cesar, their heads erect, eyes trained on their ringleader. Cesar nodded, almost imperceptibly, toward the enclosure, and all forty-seven dogs turned and filed happily back through the gate.

Last fall, Cesar filmed an episode of *Dog Whisperer* at the Los Angeles home of a couple named Patrice and Scott. They had a Korean jindo named JonBee, a stray that they had found and adopted. Outside, and on walks, JonBee was well behaved and affectionate. Inside the house, he was a terror, turning viciously on Scott whenever he tried to get the dog to submit.

"Help us tame the wild beast," Scott says to Cesar. "We've had two trainers come out, one of whom was doing this domination thing, where he would put JonBee on his back and would hold him until he submits. It went on for a good twenty minutes. This dog never let up. But, as soon as he let go, JonBee bit him four times . . . The guy was bleeding, both hands and his arms. I had another trainer come out too, and they said, 'You've got to get rid of this dog.'"

Cesar goes outside to meet JonBee. He walks down a few steps to the back yard. Cesar crouches down next to the dog. "The owner was a little concerned about me coming here by myself," he says. "To tell you the truth, I feel more comfortable with aggressive dogs than insecure dogs, or fearful dogs, or panicky dogs. These are actually the guys who put me on the map." JonBee comes up and sniffs him. Cesar puts a leash on him. JonBee eyes Cesar nervously and starts to poke around.

Cesar then walks JonBee into the living room. Scott puts a muzzle on him. Cesar tries to get the dog to lie on its side — and all hell breaks loose. JonBee turns and snaps and squirms and spins and jumps and lunges and struggles. His muzzle falls off. He bites Cesar. He twists his body up into the air in a cold, vicious fury. The struggle between the two goes on and on. Patrice covers her face. Cesar asks her to leave the room. He is standing up, leash extended. He looks like a wrangler taming a particularly ornery rattlesnake. Sweat is streaming down his face. Finally Cesar gets the dog to sit, then to lie down, and then, somehow, to lie on its side. JonBee slumps, defeated. Cesar massages JonBee's stomach. "That's all we wanted," he says.

What happened between Cesar and JonBee? One explanation is that they had a fight, alpha male versus alpha male. But fights don't come out of nowhere. JonBee was clearly reacting to something in Cesar. Before he fought, he sniffed and explored and watched Cesar — the last of which is most important, because everything we know about dogs suggests that, in a way that is true of almost no other animals, dogs are students of human movement.

The anthropologist Brian Hare has done experiments with dogs, for example, in which he puts a piece of food under one of two cups placed several feet apart. The dog knows that there is food to be had but has no idea which of the cups holds the prize. Then

Hare points at the right cup, taps on it, looks directly at it. What happens? The dog goes to the right cup virtually every time. Yet when Hare did the same experiment with chimpanzees — an animal that shares 98.6 percent of our genes — the chimps couldn't get it right. A dog will look at you for help, and a chimp won't.

"Primates are very good at using the cues of the same species," Hare explained. "So if we were able to do a similar game, and it was a chimp or another primate giving a social cue, they might do better. But they are not good at using human cues when you are trying to cooperate with them. They don't get it: 'Why would you ever tell me where the food is?' The key specialization of dogs, though, is that dogs pay attention to humans when humans are doing something very human, which is sharing information about something that someone else might actually want." Dogs aren't smarter than chimps; they just have a different attitude toward people. "Dogs are really interested in humans," Hare went on. "Interested to the point of obsession. To a dog, you are a giant walking tennis ball."

A dog cares, deeply, which way your body is leaning. Forward or backward? Forward can be seen as aggressive; backward — even a quarter of an inch — means nonthreatening. It means you've relinquished what ethologists call an "intention movement" to proceed forward. Cock your head, even slightly, to the side, and a dog is disarmed. Look at him straight on and he'll read it like a red flag. Standing straight, with your shoulders squared rather than slumped, can mean the difference between whether your dog obeys a command or ignores it. Breathing evenly and deeply, rather than holding your breath, can mean the difference between defusing a tense situation and igniting it. "I think they are looking at our eyes and where our eyes are looking, and what our eyes look like," the ethologist Patricia McConnell, who teaches at the University of Wisconsin, Madison, says. "A rounded eye with a dilated pupil is a sign of high arousal and aggression in a dog. I believe they pay a tremendous amount of attention to how relaxed our face is and how relaxed our facial muscles are, because that's a big cue for them with each other. Is the jaw relaxed? Is the mouth slightly open? And then the arms. They pay a tremendous amount of attention to where our arms go."

In the book *The Other End of the Leash*, McConnell decodes one of the most common of all human-dog interactions, the meeting between two leashed animals on a walk. To us, it's about one dog sizing up another. To her, it's about two dogs sizing up each other after first sizing up their respective owners. The owners "are often anxious about how well the dogs will get along," she writes, "and if you watch them instead of the dogs, you'll often notice that the humans will hold their breath and round their eyes and mouths in an 'on alert' expression. Since these behaviors are expressions of offensive aggression in canine culture, I suspect that the humans are unwittingly signaling tension. If you exaggerate this by tightening the leash, as many owners do, you can actually cause the dogs to attack each other. Think of it: the dogs are in a tense social encounter, surrounded by support from their own pack, with the humans forming a tense, staring, breathless circle around them. I don't know how many times I've seen dogs shift their eyes toward their owner's frozen faces and then launch growling at the other dog."

When Cesar walked down the stairs of Patrice and Scott's home then, and crouched down in the back yard, JonBee *looked* at him intently. And what he saw was someone who moved in a very particular way. Cesar is fluid. "He's beautifully organized intraphysically," Karen Bradley, who heads the graduate dance program at the University of Maryland, said when she first saw tapes of Cesar in action. "That lower-unit organization — I wonder whether he was a soccer player." Movement experts like Bradley use something called Laban Movement Analysis to make sense of movement, describing, for instance, how people shift their weight, or how fluid and symmetrical they are when they move, or what kind of "effort" it involves. Is it direct or indirect — that is, what kind of attention does the movement convey? Is it quick or slow? Is it strong or light — that is, what is its intention? Is it bound or free — that is, how much precision is involved? If you want to emphasize a point, you might bring your hand down across your body in a single, smooth motion. But how you make that motion greatly affects how your point will be interpreted by your audience. Ideally, your hand would come down in an explosive, bound movement — that is, with accelerating force, ending abruptly and precisely — and your head and shoulders would descend simultaneously, so posture and gesture would be in harmony. Suppose, though, that your head and shoulders moved upward as your hand came down, or your

hand came down in a free, implosive manner — that is, with a kind
of a vague, decelerating force. Now your movement suggests that
you are making a point on which we all agree, which is the opposite of your intention. Combinations of posture and gesture
are called phrasing, and the great communicators are those who
match their phrasing with their communicative intentions — who
understand, for instance, that emphasis requires them to be bound
and explosive. To Bradley, Cesar had beautiful phrasing.

There he is talking to Patrice and Scott. He has his hands in
front of him, in what Laban analysts call the sagittal plane — that
is, the area directly in front of and behind the torso. He then leans
forward for emphasis. But as he does, he lowers his hands to waist
level and draws them toward his body, to counterbalance the intru-
sion of his posture. And when he leans backward again, the hands
rise to fill the empty space. It's not the kind of thing you'd ever notice. But when it's pointed out, its emotional meaning is unmistakable. It is respectful and reassuring. It communicates without being intrusive. Bradley was watching Cesar with the sound off, and
there was one sequence she returned to again and again, in which
Cesar was talking to a family and his right hand swung down in a
graceful arc across his chest. "He's dancing," Bradley said. "Look at
that. It's gorgeous. It's such a gorgeous little dance.

"The thing is, his phrases are of mixed length," she went on.
"Some of them are long. Some of them are very short. Some of
them are explosive phrases, loaded up in the beginning and then
trailing off. Some of them are impactive — building up and then
coming to a sense of impact at the end. What they are is appropriate to the task. That's what I mean by 'versatile.'"

Movement analysts tend to like watching, say, Bill Clinton or
Ronald Reagan; they had great phrasing. George W. Bush does
not. During this year's State of the Union address, Bush spent the
entire speech swaying metronomically, straight down through his
lower torso, a movement underscored, unfortunately, by the presence of a large vertical banner behind him. "Each shift ended with
this focus that channels toward a particular place in the audience,"
Bradley said. She mimed perfectly the Bush gaze — the squinty,
fixated look he reserves for moments of great solemnity — and
gently swayed back and forth. "It's a little primitive, a little re-
gressed." The combination of the look, the sway, and the gaze was,

to her mind, distinctly adolescent. When people say of Bush that he seems eternally boyish, this is in part what they're referring to. He *moves* like a boy, which is fine, except that, unlike such movement masters as Reagan and Clinton, he can't stop moving like a boy when the occasion demands a more grown-up response.

"Mostly what we see in the normal population is undifferentiated phrasing," Bradley said. "And then you have people who are clearly preferential in their phrases, like my husband. He's Mr. Horizontal. When he's talking in a meeting, he's back. He's open. He just goes into this, this same long thing" — she leaned back and spread her arms out wide and slowed her speech — "and it doesn't change very much. He works with people who understand him, fortunately." She laughed. "When we meet someone like this" — she nodded at Cesar, on the television screen — "what do we do? We give them their own TV series. Seriously. We reward them. We are drawn to them, because we can trust that we can get the message. It's not going to be hidden. It contributes to a feeling of authenticity."

Back to JonBee, from the beginning — only this time with the sound off. Cesar walks down the stairs. It's not the same Cesar who whistled and brought forty-seven dogs to attention. This occasion calls for subtlety. "Did you see the way he walks? He drops his hands. They're close to his side." The analyst this time was Suzi Tortora, the author of *The Dancing Dialogue*. Tortora is a New York dance-movement psychotherapist, a tall, lithe woman with long dark hair and beautiful phrasing. She was in her office on lower Broadway, a large, empty, paneled room. "He's very vertical," Tortora said. "His legs are right under his torso. He's not taking up any space. And he slows down his gait. He's telling the dog, 'I'm here by myself. I'm not going to rush. I haven't introduced myself yet. Here I am. You can feel me.'" Cesar crouches down next to JonBee. His body is perfectly symmetrical, the center of gravity low. He looks stable, as though you couldn't knock him over, which conveys a sense of calm.

JonBee was investigating Cesar, squirming nervously. When JonBee got too jumpy, Cesar would correct him with a tug on the leash. Because Cesar was talking and the correction was so subtle, it was easy to miss. Stop. Rewind. Play. "Do you see how rhythmic it is?" Tortora said. "He pulls. He waits. He pulls. He waits. He pulls. He waits. The phrasing is so lovely. It's predictable. To a dog that is all over the place, he's bringing a rhythm. But it isn't a panicked rhythm. It has a moderate tempo to it. There was room to wander. And it's not attack, attack. It wasn't long and sustained. It was quick and light. I would bet that with dogs like this, where people are so afraid of them being aggressive and so defensive around them, that there is a lot of aggressive strength directed at them. There is no aggression here. He's using strength without it being aggressive."

Cesar moves into the living room. The fight begins. "Look how he involves the dog," Tortora said. "He's letting the dog lead. He's giving the dog room." This was not a Secret Service agent wrestling an assailant to the ground. Cesar had his body vertical, and his hand high above JonBee holding the leash, and, as JonBee turned and snapped and squirmed and spun and jumped and lunged and struggled, Cesar seemed to be moving along with him, providing a loose structure for his aggression. It may have looked like a fight, but Cesar wasn't fighting. And what was JonBee doing? Child psychologists talk about the idea of regulation. If you expose healthy babies repeatedly to a very loud noise, eventually they will be able to fall asleep. They'll become habituated to the noise: the first time the noise is disruptive, but by the second or third time they've learned to handle the disruption and block it out. They've regulated themselves. Children throwing tantrums are said to be in a state of dysregulation. They've been knocked off-kilter in some way and cannot bring themselves back to baseline. JonBee was dysregulated. He wasn't fighting; he was throwing a tantrum. And Cesar was the understanding parent. When JonBee paused to catch his breath, Cesar paused with him. When JonBee bit Cesar, Cesar brought his finger to his mouth, instinctively, but in a smooth and fluid and calm motion that betrayed no anxiety. "Timing is a big part of Cesar's repertoire," Tortora went on. "His movements right now aren't complex. There aren't a lot of efforts together at one time. His range of movement qualities is limited. Look at how he's narrowing. Now he's enclosing." As JonBee calmed down, Cesar began caressing him. His touch was firm but not aggressive; not so strong as to be abusive and not so light as to be insubstantial and irritating. Using the language of movement — the plainest and most transparent of all languages — Cesar was telling JonBee that he was safe. Now JonBee was lying on his side, mouth relaxed, tongue out. "Look at that, look at the dog's face," Tortora said. This was not defeat; this was relief.

Later, when Cesar tried to show Scott how to placate JonBee, Scott couldn't do it, and Cesar made him stop. "You're still nervous," Cesar told him. "You are still unsure. That's how you become a target." It isn't as easy as it sounds to calm a dog. "There, there" in a soothing voice, accompanied by a nice belly scratch, wasn't enough for JonBee, because he was reading gesture and posture and symmetry and the precise meaning of touch. He was looking for clarity and consistency. Scott didn't have it. "Look at the tension and aggression in his face," Tortora said when the camera turned to Scott. It was true. Scott had a long and craggy face, with high, wide cheekbones and pronounced lips, and his movements were taut and twitchy. "There's a bombardment of actions, quickness combined with tension, a quality in how he is using his eyes and focus — a darting," Tortora said. "He gesticulates in a way that is complex. There is a lot going on. So many different qualities of movement happening at the same time. It leads those who watch him to get distracted." Scott is a character actor with a list of credits going back thirty years. The tension and aggression in his manner made him interesting and complicated — which works for Hollywood but doesn't work for a troubled dog. Scott said he loved JonBee, but the quality of his movement did not match his emotions.

For a number of years, Tortora has worked with Eric (not his real name), an autistic boy with severe language and communication problems. Tortora videotaped some of their sessions, and in one, four months after they started to work together, Eric is standing in the middle of Tortora's studio in Cold Spring, New York, a beautiful dark-haired three-and-a-half-year-old wearing only a diaper. His mother is sitting to the side, against the wall. In the background, you can hear the soundtrack to *Riverdance,* which happens to be Eric's favorite album. Eric is having a tantrum.

He gets up and runs toward the stereo. Then he runs back and throws himself down on his stomach, arms and legs flailing. Tortora throws herself down on the ground just as he did. He sits up. She sits up. He twists. She twists. He squirms. She squirms. "When Eric is running around, I didn't say, 'Let's put on quiet music.' I can't turn him off, because he can't turn off," Tortora said. "He can't go from zero to sixty and then back down to zero. With a typical child, you might say, 'Take a deep breath. Reason with me' — and that might work. But not with children like this. They are in their world by themselves. I have to go in there and meet them and bring them back out."

Tortora sits up on her knees and faces Eric. His legs are moving in every direction, and she takes his feet into her hands. Slowly and subtly she begins to move his legs in time with the music. Eric gets up and runs to the corner of the room and back again. Tortora gets up and mirrors his action, but this time she moves more fluidly and gracefully than he did. She takes his feet again. This time she moves Eric's entire torso, opening the pelvis in a contralateral twist. "I'm standing above him, looking directly at him. I am very symmetrical. So I'm saying to him, I'm stable. I'm here. I'm calm. I'm holding him at the knees and giving him sensory input. It's firm and clear. Touch is an incredible tool. It's another way to speak."

She starts to rock his knees from side to side. Eric begins to calm down. He begins to make slight adjustments to the music. His legs move more freely, more lyrically. His movement is starting to get organized. He goes back into his mother's arms. He's still upset, but his cry has softened. Tortora sits and faces him — stable, symmetrical, direct eye contact.

His mother says, "You need a tissue?"

Eric nods.

Tortora brings him a tissue. Eric's mother says that she needs a tissue. Eric gives his tissue to his mother.

"Can we dance?" Tortora asks him.

"Okay," he says in a small voice.

It was impossible to see Tortora with Eric and not think of Cesar with JonBee: here was the same extraordinary energy and intelligence and personal force marshaled on behalf of the helpless, the same calm in the face of chaos, and, perhaps most surprising, the same gentleness. When we talk about people with presence, we often assume that they have a strong personality — that they sweep us all up in their own personal whirlwind. Our model is the Pied Piper, who played his irresistible tune and every child in Hamelin blindly followed. But Cesar Millan and Suzi Tortora play different tunes in different situations. And they don't turn their back and expect others to follow. Cesar let JonBee lead; Tortora's approaches to Eric were dictated by Eric. Presence is not just versatile; it's also reactive. Certain people, we say, "command our attention," but the verb is all wrong. There is no commanding, only soliciting. The dogs in the dog run wanted someone to tell them when to start and stop; they were refugees from anarchy and disorder. Eric wanted to enjoy *Riverdance*. It was his favorite music. Tortora did not say, "Let us dance." She asked, "Can we dance?"

Then Tortora gets a drum and starts to play. Eric's mother stands up and starts to circle the room in an Irish step dance. Eric is lying on the ground, and slowly his feet start to tap in time with the music. He gets up. He walks to the corner of the room, disappears behind a partition, and then reenters, triumphant. He begins to dance, playing an imaginary flute as he circles the room.

When Cesar was twenty-one, he traveled from his hometown to Tijuana, and a "coyote" took him across the border for a hundred dollars. They waited in a hole, up to their chests in water, and then ran over the mudflats, through a junkyard, and across a freeway. A taxi took him to San Diego. After a month on the streets, grimy and dirty, he walked into a dog-grooming salon and got a job, working with the difficult cases and sleeping in the offices at night. He moved to Los Angeles and took a day job detailing limousines while he ran his dog-psychology business out of a white Chevy Astrovan. When he was twenty-three, he fell in love with an American girl named Illusion. She was seventeen, small, dark, and very beautiful. A year later, they got married.

"Cesar was a machoistic, egocentric person who thought the world revolved around him," Illusion recalled of their first few years together. "His view was that marriage was where a man tells a woman what to do. Never give affection. Never give compassion or understanding. Marriage is about keeping the man happy, and that's where it ends." Early in their marriage, Illusion got sick, and was in the hospital for three weeks. "Cesar visited once, for less than two hours," she said. "I thought to myself, This relationship is not working out. He just wanted to be with his dogs." They had a new baby, and no money. They separated. Illusion told Cesar that she would divorce him if he didn't get into therapy. He agreed, reluctantly. "The therapist's name was Wilma," Illusion went on. "She was a strong African-American woman. She said, 'You want your wife to take care of you, to clean the house. Well, she wants something too. She wants your affection and love.'" Illusion remembers Cesar scribbling furiously on a pad. "He wrote that down. He said, 'That's it! It's like the dogs. They need exercise, discipline, *and* affection.'" Illusion laughed. "I looked at him, upset, because why the hell are you talking about your dogs when you should be talking about us?"

"I was fighting it," Cesar said. "Two women against me, blah, blah, blah. I had to get rid of the fight in my mind. That was very difficult. But that's when the lightbulb came on. Women have their own psychology."

Cesar could calm a stray off the street, yet, at least in the beginning, he did not grasp the simplest of truths about his own wife. "Cesar related to dogs because he didn't feel connected to people," Illusion said. "His dogs were his way of feeling like he belonged in the world, because he wasn't people friendly. And it was hard for him to get out of that." In Mexico, on his grandfather's farm, dogs were dogs and humans were humans: each knew its place. But in America dogs were treated like children, and owners had shaken up the hierarchy of human and animal. Sugar's problem was Lynda. JonBee's problem was Scott. Cesar calls that epiphany in the therapist's office the most important moment in his life, because it was the moment when he understood that to succeed in the world he could not just be a dog whisperer. He needed to be a people whisperer.

For his show, Cesar once took a case involving a Chihuahua named Bandit. Bandit had a large, rapper-style diamond-encrusted necklace around his neck spelling "Stud." His owner was Lori, a voluptuous woman with an oval face and large, pleading eyes. Bandit was out of control, terrorizing guests and menacing other dogs. Three trainers had failed to get him under control.

Lori was on the couch in her living room as she spoke to Cesar. Bandit was sitting in her lap. Her teenage son, Tyler, was sitting next to her.

"About two weeks after his first visit with the vet, he started to lose a lot of hair," Lori said. "They said that he had Demodex mange." Bandit had been sold to her as a show-quality dog, she recounted, but she had the bloodline checked, and learned that he had come from a puppy mill. "He didn't have any human contact," she went on. "So for three months he was getting dipped every week to try to get rid of the symptoms." As she spoke, her hands gently encased Bandit. "He would hide inside my shirt and lay his head right by my heart, and stay there." Her eyes were moist. "He was right here on my chest."

"So your husband cooperated?" Cesar asked. He was focused on Lori, not on Bandit. This is what the new Cesar understood that the old Cesar did not.

"He was our baby. He was in need of being nurtured and helped and he was so scared all the time."

"Do you still feel the need of feeling sorry about him?"

"Yeah. He's so cute."

Cesar seemed puzzled. He didn't know why Lori would still feel sorry for her dog.

Lori tried to explain. "He's so small and he's helpless."

"But do you believe that he feels helpless?"

Lori still had her hands over the dog, stroking him. Tyler was looking at Cesar, and then at his mother, and then down at Bandit. Bandit tensed. Tyler reached over to touch the dog, and Bandit leaped out of Lori's arms and attacked him, barking and snapping and growling. Tyler, startled, jumped back. Lori, alarmed, reached out and — this was the critical thing — put her hands around Bandit in a worried, caressing motion and lifted him back into her lap. It happened in an instant.

Cesar stood up. "Give me the space," he said, gesturing for Tyler to move aside. "Enough dogs attacking humans, and humans not really blocking him, so he is only becoming more narcissistic. It is all about him. He owns you." Cesar was about as angry as he ever gets. "It seems like you are favoring the dog, and hopefully that is not the truth . . . If Tyler kicked the dog, you would correct him. The dog is biting your son, and you are not correcting hard enough." Cesar was in emphatic mode now, his phrasing sure and unambiguous. "I don't understand why you are not putting two and two together."

Bandit was nervous. He started to back up on the couch. He started to bark. Cesar gave him a look out of the corner of his eye. Bandit shrank. Cesar kept talking. Bandit came at Cesar. Cesar stood up. "I have to touch," he said, and he gave Bandit a sharp nudge with his elbow. Lori looked horrified.

Cesar laughed incredulously. "You are saying that it is fair for him to touch us but not fair for us to touch him?" he asked.

Lori leaned forward to object.

"You don't like that, do you?" Cesar said, in his frustration speaking to the whole room now. "It's not going to work. This is a case that is not going to work, because the owner doesn't want to allow what you normally do with your kids . . . The hardest part for me is that the father or mother chooses the dog instead of the son. That's hard for me. I love dogs. I'm the dog whisperer. You follow what I'm saying? But I would never choose a dog over my son."

He stopped. He had had enough of talking. There was too much talking anyhow. People saying "I love you" with a touch that didn't mean "I love you." People saying "There, there" with gestures that did not soothe. People saying "I'm your mother" while reaching out to a Chihuahua instead of their own flesh and blood. Tyler looked stricken. Lori shifted nervously in her seat. Bandit growled. Cesar turned to the dog and said "Sh-h-h." And everyone was still.

MARK GREIF

Afternoon of the Sex Children

FROM N+1

NOT LONG AGO, I took part in one of the conversations you're not supposed to have. It turned on whether Vladimir Nabokov, author of *Lolita*, really desired underage girls. The usual arguments came out: Nabokov was a master of personae, and Humbert Humbert a game to him. Kinbote, analogous narrator of *Pale Fire*, didn't make you think Nabokov loved boys. The late novels were Nabokov's allegories of the seductions of aestheticism, which transfigures the forbidden into the beautiful; or moral paintings of our acceptance of crime, when crime is presented alluringly. So love of the wrong object becomes a metaphor for art, ethics, personality, and so forth.

I was reluctant to say that I felt these explanations were inadequate and even in bad faith. The trouble with *Lolita* is plainly its ability to describe what a sexual twelve-year-old looks like. What her dress is like when it brushes her knees, what her toes are like with painted nails, how the color sits on the plump bow of her lips — the phrase for this is that it is "too real"; that's the scandal. It continues to be the scandal fifty years after publication, and it will be a scandal whenever any adult acknowledges the capacity to up-end his vision and see a child, protected larval stage of the organism, as a sexual object. The girl is still a child, only now she is a sex child. Yet this makes me feel Nabokov was not a pedophile but something he is not credited with being — a social critic.

You, too, see it, or should. The trend of these fifty years has been to make us see sexual youth where it doesn't exist, and ignore it as it does. Adults project the sex of children in lust, or examine children sexually with magnifying glasses to make sure they don't appeal to us. But these lenses became burning glasses. The hips of Betty Grable melted and disappeared. The breasts of Marilyn Monroe ran off and were replaced with silicone. The geography of fashion created new erogenous zones — pelvic midriff, rear cleavage — for dieters starving off their secondary sex characteristics, and for young teens, in the convergence of the exerciser and the pubescent child. The waif and the pixie became ideal. Mama and daughter look the same again before the bedroom mirror — not dressed up in Mama's pearls and heels this time, but in children's wear. The dream belongs to sixteen, or to those who can starve themselves to sixteen.

The critic Philip Fisher used to note that *Lolita,* tightly plotted as it is, repeats one scene twice. Humbert spies a lit window far opposite. Because he longs to see a nymphet, he sees one. The wave of arousal returns, its tide dampening him up to his knees. As he nears the climax, the form is refocused as an adult woman or man. Disgusting! But this is a simple inversion of a characteristic experience of our time. A man will see a distant form, in low-cut top and low-slung jeans, and think he is on the trail of eroticism; draw near, and identify a child. Revolting! The defenses against it continue the problem. The more a whole nation inspects the sex characteristics of children to make sure it is not becoming aroused by childishness, and slyly hunts around to make sure its most untrustworthy members are not being so aroused, the more it risks creating a sexual fascination with the child. However you gaze, to accept the fantasy or to assure yourself you see nothing, you join in an abomination.

We live in the afternoon of the sex children; Nabokov just saw the dawn.

Now children from junior high to high school to college live in the most perfect sex environment devised by contemporary society — or so adults believe. Now they are inmates in great sex colonies where they wheel in circles holding hands with their pants down. Henry Darger, emblematic artist of our time with his girl armies, made for our sensibilities what Gauguin's Tahitian beauties were to the French nineteenth-century bourgeoisie — repositories of true, voluptuous, savage inner nature.

Yet in public we want to believe that children are not prepared for sex as we are, do not understand it, and have a special, fragile, glassy truth inside them that will be endangered by premature use — as if the pearls of highest value for us, our chase after sex, our truth of "sexuality," should not also be the treasure for them.

It took the whole history of postwar American culture to make the sex child. It required a merging of old prurient fantasies, dating from the Victorians and Progressives, with the actual sexual liberation of children after midcentury. You needed the expansion of the commercial market for children — selling to kids with sex as everything is sold with sex. You needed the bad faith of Madison Avenue advertisers and Seventh Avenue fashion writers. You needed the sinister prudery of Orange County evangelicalism and the paraliterature of child sex that arises in anti-pedophilia crusades (*Treacherous Love; It Happened to Nancy*) — erotica purveyed to middle school libraries. You needed the Internet.

Victorian child-loving is only loosely the background for our current preoccupation with the pedophile and the sexual child. With Lewis Carroll and Alice, John Ruskin and Rose La Touche, the fantastic young bride and her gauzy innocence, we know we are in the realm of adult prurience. It is *child sexual liberation* that transforms the current moment. We can no longer say it is *only* fantasy that exists about the sex lives of children. Or, rather — maybe this is the better way to say it — children have been insistently invited into our fantasy too, and when they grow up they'll furnish the adult continuity of this same madness.

Is it necessary to say that the majority of the sex children we see and desire are not legally children? The representatives of the sex child in our entertainment culture are often eighteen to twenty-one — legal adults. The root of their significance is that their sexual value points backward, to the status of the child, and not forward to the adult. So there is Britney, famous at the age of eighteen for a grind video to "Oops! . . . I Did It Again" ("I'm not that innocent"); Paris, nineteen years old in her amateur porn DVD (*1 Night in Paris);* alumnae of the Mickey Mouse Club like Christina, licking her lips at twenty on the *Rolling Stone* cover, miniskirt pulled open above the headline "Guess What Christina Wants"; and Lindsay, veteran of Disney children's films, whose breast size, extreme dieting, and accidental self-exposures on the red carpet are the stuff of

Entertainment Tonight. It's important that these are not adult "stars" in the way of Nicole Kidman or Julia Roberts, not called beautiful, and rarely featured in adult films. Instead they furnish the core of entertainment news to two distinct audiences: children nine to fourteen, who enjoy their music and films on these works' own terms, and adults who regard them — well, as what?*

Oddly, those of us who face these questions now have been sex children ourselves; we come after the great divide. You would think we'd remember. Our sex was handed to us, liberated, when we appeared in the world. We managed to feel like rebels with all the other twelve-year-olds, deluded, but not to be blamed for that. A great tween gang of sexual ruffians, trolling the basement TV for scrambled porn, tangling on couches, coming up for air in clouds of musk, shirts on backward; what did we learn? Having lived in the phantasm evidently does not diminish the phantasm. One still looks at those kids enviously; that is one of the mysteries to be solved. It is as if crossing the divide to adulthood entailed a great self-blinding in the act of seeing what is not, precisely, there; and forgetting what one oneself experienced. If we turn to the sex children as avidly as anyone, it must be because they are *doing something for us, too,* as participants in this society and as individuals. And the supplement will not be found in their childhood at all, but in the overall system of adult life.

The lure of a permanent childhood in America partly comes from the overwhelming feeling that one hasn't yet achieved one's true

---

*The entertainment does not seem to be only for adult men. It's a difficult question whether there is strict symmetry by gender, so that boys should also become sex objects for adult women, and adult male fashion regress to youth. In the private realm, schoolteachers keep being revealed as molesters when they get pregnant by their seventh-graders; so that is one kind of appeal. And in the popular culture, "Abercrombie & Fitch" names a certain iconography of high school musclebound male toplessness, teen depilation, and wrestling as signs of eros — an eroticism drawn from gay men's pleasure in the college boy and teen, repurposed for heterosexuality. But it does seem the popular culture is still just testing the waters to find the extent of adult women's desire. This is the meaning of the aphasic silences, for example, around Demi's Ashton and Gabi's lawn-boy lover on *Desperate Housewives.* The logic of our society should ultimately even out private fantasies between the genders. But perhaps because there is always so great a capacity for fantasy and pleasure in self-display — not just in pursuit of one's opposite number — for now adult women's investment in the sex children, at least in public, remains largely oriented toward youthful girls.

youth, because true youth would be defined by freedom so total that no one can attain it. Presumably even the spring-break kids, rutting, tanning, boozing with abandon, know there is a more perfect spring break beyond the horizon. Without a powerful aspiration to become adult, without some separate value that downplays childhood for sharper freedoms in age and maturity, the feeling of dissatisfaction can proceed indefinitely, in the midst of marriage, child rearing, retirement, unto death.

The college years — of all times — stand out as the apex of sex childhood. Even if college is routinized and undemanding, it is still inevitably residential, and therefore the place to perfect one's life as a sex child. You move away from home into a setting where you are with other children — strangers all. You must be patient for four years just to get a degree. So there can be little to do but fornicate. Certainly from the wider culture, of MTV and rumor, you know four years is all you will get. The semester provides an interruption between institutionalized sex jubilees: spring break, or just the weekends. The frat-house party assumes a gothic significance, not only for prurient adults but for the collegians themselves, who report, on Monday, their decadence.

As a college student today, you always know what things *could* be like. The *Girls Gone Wild* cameras show a world where at this very moment someone is spontaneously lifting her shirt for a logoed hat. You might think the whole thing was a put-on except that everyone seems so earnest. The most earnest write sex columns — "Sex and the (Elm) City" — in which the elite and joyless of Yale aspire to be like the déclassé and uninhibited of Florida State. The new full-scale campus sex magazines — for example, Boston University's *Boink* (2005) and Harvard's *H Bomb* (2004) — seek truth in naked self-photography and accounts of sex with strangers, as if each incident were God's revelation on Sinai. The lesson each time is that sleeping with strangers or being photographed naked lets the authors know themselves better. Many of these institutions are driven by women. Perhaps they, even more than young men, feel an urgency to know themselves while they can, since America curses them with a premonition of disappointment: when flesh sags, freedom will wane.

From college to high school, high school to junior high, the age of sex childhood recedes and descends. "The Sexual Revolution

Hits Junior High," says my newspaper, reporting as news what is
not new. Twice a year *Newsweek* and *Time* vaunt the New Virginity.
No one believes in the New Virginity. According to polls of those
who stick with it, their abstinence is fortified with large measures of
fellatio. Eighty percent of people have intercourse in their teens,
says the Centers for Disease Control and Prevention. (Why this
government agency keeps records of sexual normalcy, unsmilingly
pathologized as an "epidemic," is its own question.) My newspaper
tells me that menstruation starts for girls today at eleven, or as
early as nine. No one knows why.

Yet the early reality of sex childhood is its restrictive practical di-
mension. It exists only in the context of the large institutions that
dominate children's lives, the schools. In these prisonlike closed
worlds of finite numbers of children, with no visible status but the
wealth they bring in from outside (worn as clothes) and the domi-
nance they can achieve in the activities of schooldays (friend-mak-
ing, gossiping, academic and athletic success), sex has a different
meaning than in adult licentiousness or collegiate glory. Sex appeal is demanded long before sex, and when sex arrives, it appears
within ordinary romantic relationships. New sexual acts are only
substitutes for any earlier generation's acts, as you'd expect. Where
petting was, there shall fellatio be.

It will simply never be the case that children can treat sex with
the free-floating fantasy and brutality that adults can, because we
adults are atomized in our dealings with others as children in
school are not. If I do something rotten on a blind date, I never
need to see the only witness again. A child does something rotten,
and his date is sitting next to him in homeroom. The adult world
sends down its sexual norms, which cannot blossom in a closed institution (though alarmists say they *originate* there) but which the
children tuck away to fulfill just as soon as they can. Children are
the beneficiaries of a culture that declares in all its television,
jokes, talk, and advertising that if sex isn't the most significant
thing in existence, it is the one element never missing from any ac-
tivity that is fun. They are watchers, silent, with open eyes, and they
grow in the blue light.

So much for the decadent reality of childhood.

But adults then look back from exile and see wrongly, thinking the
children are free because we've hemmed them in with images of a

transitory future freedom. Never mind that we ourselves led carnal lives that would make old men weep. Those lives hardly counted: inevitably we were caught in actual human relationships with particular people, in a matrix of leaden rules and personal ties. Envy of one's sexual successors is now a recurrent feature of our portion of modernity. Philip Larkin, in his 1960s poem "High Windows," sees a "couple of kids" and enviously imagines they're "fucking" and "she's / Taking pills or wearing a diaphragm," free of all his generation's worries. Then he stops to think that his parents' era might once have envied *him*. Larkin's solace in the poem was high windows and the icy blue of eternity; in real life, an enormous collection of pornography.

The dirty magazines and their supposedly legitimate counterparts in fact play a significant role in the system of sex childhood. In Larkin's life, the poetry of longing went hand in hand with the fulfillments of porn, and all of us share in this interchange at a more banal level. The colloquialisms "men's magazines" and "women's magazines" generally seem to name two very different sets of publications. "Women's magazines" are instructional — how to display oneself, how to serve men, and nowadays (maybe always) how to steal sexual and emotional pleasure from men, outwitting them, while getting erotic and affective satisfactions too, in the preparations for your self-display. "Men's magazines," for their part, are pornographic — how to look at women, how to fantasize about women, how to enjoy and dominate, and what one becomes while fantasizing this domination. The two genres are distinct, but continuous.

The women's advice and fashion magazines — *Cosmopolitan, Glamour, Elle, Vogue* — hold a permanent mandate for an erotic youthfulness, though not literal sexual youth. They provide shortcuts to staying young for old and young alike: how to keep your skin young, how to keep your muscles young, how to keep your ideas young, how to feel perpetually young, how to siphon vitality from elsewhere to be "young" even if you're not literally young, and how to use your youth if you are. You learn early what you'll lose late, and get accustomed to denying the aging that you might never have minded as much without this help.

Men's magazines fix readers' desires in the range of women's shapes and bodies and modes of seduction and subordination — fragmenting the market by body part and sex act and level of ex-

plicitness, but also by age. Pornography has a special investment in
youth. The college girl is a central feature of *Playboy* in its "Girls of
the Big Ten" pictorials; *Hustler* has a relentless *Barely Legal* fran-
chise in magazines and videos, aped by *Just 18* and *Finally Legal* and
all the bargain titles behind the convenience-store counter. In the
demimonde of the Internet, an even more central category of all
online pornography is "teen." Of course it is profoundly illegal in
the United States to photograph sexually anyone under eighteen;
in what is called 2257 compliance, producers of pornography
must keep public legal records proving that every model is eighteen or older. Technically, therefore, there are only two ages, eighteen and nineteen, at which "teen" models can be actual teens. Nor
do the models ever seem to be sexually immature; child pornography doesn't seem to be what the sites are for. Rather, putative teen
models are made *situationally* immature — portrayed with symbols
of the student life, the classroom, the cheerleading squad, the college dorm, the family home, the babysitting, the first job; not the
husband, not the child, not the real estate brokerage or board-
room or bank office, never adult life.*

Thus a society that finds it illegal to exploit anyone below the
age of legal majority is at the same time interested in the simula-
tion of youth — often by people who are sexually mature but still
only on the cusp of adulthood. And in its legitimate publications,
as in its vice, it encourages a more general, socially compulsory female urgency to provision youth across the life span, and a male
rush to take it.

Though the young person has never been old, the old person
once was young. When you look up the age ladder, you look at
strangers; when you look down the age ladder, you are always looking at versions of yourself. As an adult, it depends entirely on your
conception of yourself whether those fantastic younger incarna-
tions will seem long left behind or all too continuous with who you

*Feminist critiques of pornography rooted in an idea of male violence and revenge
against the threat of women's liberation might have predicted a different outcome
in our age of equality: wider representations of the literal humiliation or subordination of adult women in power. What they did not anticipate was a turn to sexualized
youth. Though the two lines of critique are not at all incompatible (that is,
youth still may be a way of denying adult equality), one sees now that feminist critiques of youth and aging are proving to be more significant historically than the
MacKinnon-Dworkin line of pornography criticism.

are now. And this conception of yourself depends, in turn, on the culture's attitudes toward adulthood and childhood, age and youth. This is where the trouble arises. For in a culture to which sex furnishes the first true experiences, it makes a kind of sense to return to the ages at which sex was first used to pursue experience and one was supposedly in a privileged position to find it. Now we begin to talk, not about our sex per se, but about a fundamental change in our notion of freedom and what our lives are a competition for.*

We must begin to talk directly about the change that was well begun in Nabokov's day and is well advanced in ours, the transformation that created the world in which we are both freed and enslaved. That was sexual liberation.

Liberation implies freedom to do what you have already been doing or have meant to do. It unbars what is native to you, free in cost and freely your possession, and removes the iron weight of social interdiction. Even in the great phase of full human liberation that extended from the 1960s to the present day, however, what has passed as liberation has often been *liberalization*. (Marcuse used

---

*I want to acknowledge two popular lines of thought that insist on the attraction to sexually mature children as natural, not social, contravening my account. One is the commonsense historical argument that until recently sexually mature children of the middle teen years *were* adults, because human beings used to marry in their teens. Natasha, the dream of Russian womanhood in *War and Peace*, one of the greatest novels of the nineteenth century, set in that century's early years, is fourteen when she becomes the object of her first suitors' attention — and admirable suitors too: hussars in the czar's army and a count. Her girlishness is treated matter-of-factly by those who are drawn to it as an appealing aspect of her personality, and it is considered realistically by her parents, who are concerned she may be too immature yet to leave home and run a household. In the United States, as the historian Philip Jenkins has summarized, the standard age of sexual consent was ten years old until the 1890s, when it was raised to sixteen or eighteen, depending on the state.

The other argument is one occasionally offered explicitly, but much more often implicitly, in the field of evolutionary psychology. Evolutionary psychology explains behavioral dispositions in modern human beings by the optimal strategies for passing on genes, through patterns hard-wired into our brains by our evolutionary past and the continuing reproductive demands of the present. "Youth is a critical cue," writes evolutionary psychologist David M. Buss in the standard book on the subject of sex, "since women's reproductive value declines steadily with increasing age after twenty. By the age of forty, a woman's reproductive capacity is low, and by fifty it is close to zero" (*The Evolution of Desire*). The desire for children from the moment of visible pubescence (say, twelve today) to the maximum age before reproductive de-this distinction.) Liberalization makes for a free traffic in goods formerly regulated and interdicted, creating markets in what you already possess for free. It has a way of making your possessions no longer native to you at the very moment that they're freed for your enjoyment. Ultimately you no longer know *how* to possess them, correctly, unless you are following new rules that emerge to dominate the traffic in these goods.

In sexual liberation, major achievements included the end of shame and illegality in sex outside marriage (throughout the twentieth century); the disentangling of sex from reproduction (completed with the introduction of the oral contraceptive pill in 1960); the feminist reorganization of intercourse around the female orgasm and female pleasure (closer to 1970); and the beginning of a destigmatization of same-sex sexuality (1970 to the present). The underlying notion in all these reforms was to remove social penalties from what people were doing anyway.

But a test of liberation, as distinct from liberalization, must be whether you have also been freed to be free *from* sex, too — to ignore it, or to be asexual, without consequent social opprobrium or imputation of deficiency. If truly liberated, you should engage in sex, or not, as you please, and have it be a matter of indifference to

---

cline (age twenty) may therefore be the best means for passing on genes. This inclination would be set beneath the level of consciousness, as men's desire is targeted to females who are fertile, healthy, and poised for the longest period of childbearing possible before the decline sets in. On evolutionary-biological presuppositions, it ought to be the case that human males today and yesterday, and in every society, should be maximally attracted to newly postpubescent girls unless it be determined statistically that there is some ramping up of reproductive success in the years after menarche — in which case, certainly, no later than fourteen or fifteen.

Neither the historical nor the biological argument seems to meet the problem of the sex child as we now know it, because I think neither captures our current experience of desire, in which the sex children come in only secondarily, through some kind of mediation of fancy; in our real lives adults feel the sexual appeal of other adults. Unless sexual desire is wholly unconscious, not plastic and social, and the social level entirely a screen or delusion — a very complex delusion to cover biological determinism — then with the sex children it's my sense that we are dealing primarily with the sexual appeal of *youth* rather than the actual determinative sexual attractiveness of *youths*. It would be something like a desire for the sex child's incipience, the child's taste of first majority before the rules clamp down: youth as eternal becoming, in eternal novelty of experience. Apart from such fancies, the appeal of sexually mature children seems to me particularly weak, not strong. But I understand that introspection is not science, and I am aware this may not satisfy partisans of the "natural" views.

you; you should recognize your own sex, or not, whenever and however you please. We ought to see social categories of asexuals who are free to have no sex, just as others are free to have endless spectacular sex, and not feel for them either suspicion or pity. One of the cruel betrayals of sexual liberation, in liberalization, was the illusion that a person can be free only if he holds sex as all-important and exposes it endlessly to others — providing it, proving it, enjoying it.

This was a new kind of unfreedom. In hindsight, the betrayal of sexual liberation was a mistake the liberators seemed fated to make. Because moralists had said for so many centuries, "Sex must be *controlled* because it is so powerful and important," sexual liberators were seduced into saying, in opposition, "Sex must be *liberated* because it is so powerful and important." But in fact a better liberation would have occurred if reformers had freed sex not by its centrality to life, but by its triviality. They could have said: "Sex is a biological function, and for that reason no grounds to persecute anyone. It is *truthless* — you must not bring force to bear on people for the basic, biological, and private; you may not persecute them on grounds so accidental. You must leave them alone, neither forcing them to deny their sex nor to bring it into the light."

This misformulation of liberation became as damaging as it did only because another force turned out to have great use for the idea that sex is the bearer of the richest experiences: commerce. The field of sex was initially very difficult to liberate against a set of rival norms that had structured it for centuries: priority of the family, religious prohibitions, restraint of biology. Once liberation reached a point of adequate success, however, sex was unconscionably easy to "liberate" further, as commerce discovered it had a new means of entry into private life and threw its weight behind the new values. What in fact was occurring was liberalization by forces of commercial transaction, as they entered to expand and coordinate the new field of exchange. Left-wing ideas of free love, the nonsinfulness of the body, women's equality of dignity, intelligence, and capability, had been hard-pressed to find adequate standing before — and they are still in trouble, constantly worn away. Whereas incitement to sex, ubiquitous sexual display, sinfulness redefined as the unconditioned, unexercised, and unaroused body, and a new shamefulness for anyone who manifests a *non-sexuality* or, worst of all, willful sexlessness — that was easy.

Opposition to this is supposed to be not only old-fashioned but also joyless and puritanical — in fact, ugly. Sex talk is so much a part of daily glamour and the assurance of being a progressive person that one hates to renounce it; but one has to see that in general it is commercial sex talk that's reactionary, and opposition that's progressive. Liberalization has succeeded in hanging an aesthetic ugliness upon all discussions of liberation, except the purely ornamental celebrations of "the Woodstock generation" one sees on TV. Original liberators are ogres in the aesthetic symbolism of liberalization. They don't shave their legs! They're content to be fat! They have no fun. To say that a bodily impulse is something all of us have, and no regimentation or expertise or purchases can make one have it any more, *is* to become filthy and disgusting. It is to be nonproductive waste in an economy of markets, something nonsalable. It is not the repression of sex that opposes liberation (just as Foucault alerted us), but "inciting" sex as we know it — whatever puts sex into motion, draws it into *publicity,* apart from the legitimate relations between the private (the place of bodily safety) and the public (the sphere of equality).

The question remains why liberalization turned back to gorge itself on youth.

How should a system convince people that they do not possess their sex properly? Teach them that in their possession it is shapeless and unconditioned. Only once it has been modified, layered with experts, honeycombed with norms, overlaid with pictorial representations, and sold back to them can it fulfill itself as what its possessors "always wanted." Breasts starved away by dieting will be reacquired in breast implant surgery — to attain the original free good, once destroyed, now re-created unnaturally.

How to convince them that what appears plentiful and free — even those goods that in fact are universally distributed — is scarce? Extend the reach of these new norms that cannot be met without outside intervention. Youth becomes a primary norm in the competition for sex. The surprise in this is not that youth would be desirable — it has always had its charm — but that you would think youth ought to be competitively *ineffective,* since it is

universally distributed at the start of life. Yet youth is naturally eva-
nescent, in fact vanishing every single day that one lives. It can be
made the fundamental experience of a vanishing commodity, the
ur-experience of obsolescence. Plus, it was everyone's universal
possession at one time; and so artful means to keep it seem justified by a "natural" outcome, what you already were; and youth can
be requalified physically as an aspect of memory, for every single
consumer, in minutiae of appearance that you alone know (looking at yourself every day in a mirror, you alone know the history of
your face and body), even while other people don't. We still pretend we are most interested in beauty, and it covers our interest in
youth. Beauty is too much someone else's good luck; we accept
that it is unequally distributed. Youth is more effective precisely because it is something all of us are always losing.

From the desire to repossess what has been lost (or was never
truly taken advantage of) comes, in the end, the ceaseless extension of competition. It is easily encouraged. It doesn't require anything nefarious or self-conscious, certainly not top-down control,
though it's sometimes convenient to speak of the process metaphorically as a field of control. All it requires is a culture in which
instruments of commentary and talk (news, talk shows, advice
magazines) are accompanied and paid for by advertisers of aesthetic and aestheticizable products — everything from skin cream
to Viagra to cars. This is supremely prosaic, but this is it. Once people can be convinced that they need to remain young for others to
desire them, and that there are so many instrumentalities with
which they can remain young; once they can be encouraged to suspect that youth is a particularly real and justifiable criterion for desire, then the competition will accelerate by the interchange of all
these talkers: the professional commentators and product vendors
and the needy audiences and ordinary people. Norms will not be
set in advance but are created constantly between the doubting individual and the knowing culture, or between the suddenly inven-
tive individual and the "adaptive" and trend-spotting culture, a dia-
lectic ultimately reproduced *inside* individuals who doubt ("I'm
growing old") but seek know-how ("I'll be young") — in the chan-
neling of desire in the bedroom, in conversation, in the marketplace.

For our object lessons and examples, it becomes advantageous for those searching for sexually desirable youthfulness to follow the trail to those who actually have youth. Thus young people in all forms of representation — advertising, celebrity-following, advice literature, day-to-day talk, and myth — augment the competitive system of youth whether or not they are the "target market" of any particular campaign.

And yet the young are off-limits sexually, by law and morality and, more visibly, because of institutions that instruct and protect them. An adult simply will not get his or her hands on a college student — in large part because that student is in a closed institution. Professors have increasingly learned to stay away from students by threat of firing and public shaming. An adult should never wind up in sexual contact with a high school student unless conscience is gone and jail holds no fear, but neither will he run into many of them. The real-world disastrous exceptions of abuse, as we well know, come from those inside the institutions that instruct and protect the child: teachers, priests, babysitters, and, far and away most frequently, parents and family members. This criminal subset has an ambiguous relation to the wider fascination. For society as a whole, gazing at those youths who are sexually mature but restricted from the market institutionally or legally, sex children become that most perfect of grounds for competition, a fantastic commodity unattainable in its pure form.

Hence the final double bind of social preoccupation with the sex children in a commercial society regimented by a vain pursuit of absolute freedom. On one side, the young become fascinating because they have in its most complete form the youth that we demand for ourselves, for our own competitive advantage. They are the biologically superrich whose assets we wish to burgle because we feel they don't know the treasures they keep; they stand accidentally at the peak of the competitive pyramid. *Desire for sex childhood is thus a completion of the competitive system.* On the other side, the sex child as an individual is the only figure in this order who is thought to be *free* from competition, who holds sex as still a natural good, undiminished, a capability, purely potential — not something ever scarcer and jeopardized by our unattractiveness and our aging. For sex children, sex remains a new experience of freedom and truth that retains its promise to shape a better self. The kids are not innocent of carnality, but they are innocent of competition. *Desire for sex childhood thus becomes a wish for freedom from the system.* The sex child can be a utopia personified, even as she props up the brutal dystopia to which her youth furnishes the competitive principle.

As I attempted the first draft of this essay, the news was filled with reports about a twenty-two-year-old North Dakota college student, Dru Sjodin, who was abducted and murdered as she left her retail job at Victoria's Secret. Police arrested a fifty-year-old "level-three sex offender" who had been identified in the mall parking lot, though he lived thirty miles away in Minnesota. The man had Sjodin's blood in his car; police couldn't find the girl. But the news kept showing a college glamour picture, comparing her to other abducted youths, and dwelling on her workplace with its lingerie.

At the time, I thought: We can expect this to keep happening as long as sex with the sex children is our society's most treasured, fantasized consumer good. There was something inevitable about a murderer going to the mall to abduct a sex child — though under the circumstances it seemed terrible to say so. The whole tragedy was too depressing. So I stopped writing.

During the second attempt, I reached the clinical literature on child molestation. Some of it is tolerable. This includes the accounts of abused children who enter therapy and meet child psychologists who then record their cures in a whole hopeful literature on the side of healing. What is mostly intolerable, on the other hand, is the literature about child molesters. There are valuable contributions to criminology and psychology on the library shelves which outline the problems of pedophilia and sexual abuse and molestation, often with in-depth interviews. I couldn't read very much of them. Sorry as I felt for these men, it seemed clear to me they should be destroyed. But this was really insane and went against my other beliefs. So I began to consider: What is the meaning of abomination today, in a nonreligious age? It must be that there are points of cultural juncture at which phenomena are produced that, though explicable, are *indefensible* in the terms of any of the structures that produce or analyze them. You don't want to appeal to trauma, rehabilitation, socialization, or biological inclination. You can't just run away from the phenomena, and yet they can't be brought into the other terms of social analysis without an unacceptable derangement of values. This explains the impasse in which the annihilative impulse takes hold. So I stopped a second time.

In an increasingly dark mood, I came to the darkest way to frame the enigma of the sex children. A fraction of young people are extraordinarily highly valued, emulated, desired, examined, broadcast, lusted after, attended to in our society. These legal ex-children are attended to specifically as repositories of fresh sexuality — not, say, of intellect or even beauty. As their age goes up to seventeen, eighteen, and nineteen, the culture very quickly awards them its summit of sexual value. Yet as their age goes down from some indefinite point, to sixteen, fifteen, fourteen, and so on, the sexual appeal of childhood quickly reaches our culture's zone of absolute evil. Worse than the murderer, worse than the adult rapist of adults, and even worse than the person who physically and emotionally abuses children is the person who sexually tampers with a child in any degree — who can then never be reintegrated into society except as a sex offender — or is simply the author of monstrous thoughts, a cyberstalker netted in police stings in chatrooms or found downloading underage images to his hard drive. This is the "pedophile" whether or not he acts. Since the two zones — maximum *value* of sex and maximum *evil* for sex — are right next to each other, shouldn't we wonder whether there's some structural relation in society between our supergood and absolute evil?

The most direct explanation is that we may be witnessing two disparate systems as they come into conflict at just one point. System A would be the sexual valuation of youth, spurred by the liberalization of sex and its attachment to youth in a competitive economy. System B would be adult morality, the moral impulse to shield beings who need protection from sexual tampering and attention — because of the cruel nonreciprocity inflicted on a young child who doesn't yet have sexual desire (in true pedophilia, molestation of those beneath pubescence); the equally cruel coercion of those old enough to desire but not to have an adult's power to consent or to see how their actions will look to a future self (molestation of adolescents); and the deep betrayal, in all acts of sexual abuse, of the order of society and of its future, in something like a society-level version of the taboo on incest. Now, System A (sexual value, commerce) possesses a major flaw in its tendency to drive sexual attention down the age scale relentlessly — even to those legal children who hold sex in its newest and most inaccessible form. System B would fight this tendency, trying to provide necessary restraints; but perhaps it becomes most destructively punitive just where it refuses to disavow System A entirely. By otherwise accepting the sexual value of youthfulness, in other words — with such threatening possible side effects — morality would have to narrow itself vengefully upon the single point of visible contradiction and overpunish whoever pursues too much youth, or does so too literally.

What's really striking to anyone who watches the news is of course the *intensity* of punitive violence where the two systems clash. From the point of view of morality, the overpunishment of the pedophile and the sex offender (barred from living anonymously, unrehabilitatable, hounded from town to town, unable to return to society) makes perfect sense because of the extreme moral reprehensibility of abusing a child — combined with a dubious contemporary doctrine that *desires* can never be rehabilitated. It would also make sense, however, if we feared that the ruthlessness of this interdiction of pedophilia helped rationalize or reinforce the interests that confer extreme sexual value on youth just a bit up the ladder. *One fears our cultural preoccupation with pedophilia is not really about valuing childhood but about overvaluing child sex.* It would be as if the culture understood it must be so ruthless to stop tampering with real children just because it is working so hard to keep afloat the extreme commercial valuation of youth and its concrete manifestations in the slightly older sex child. Does the culture react so vehemently at just this point because were the screen of morality to collapse, the real situation would have to be confessed — the child's extreme uninterest in adults; the child's sexual "liberation" as a subeffect of our own false liberation; the brutalization of life at all levels by sexual incitement?

One further step into the darkness has to complete the critique. The most pitiful and recondite form of pedophilia is sexual attachment to children below the age of sexual maturity — true pedophilia, which seems so utterly unmotivated, a matter of strict pathology. But a certain amount of the permanent persistence of child molesting as a phenomenon must come not from a fixed psychic category but from the misdirecting of the sexual impulse to

young people who temporarily fill a place of temptation or fascination — especially in the desire for teens who are sexually mature
but to whom an adult may still do a profound wrong by addressing
sexually. It seems likely that an incessant overvaluing of the sex
of the young will *train* some people toward wrong objects. This
should swell the numbers of the class of incipient or intermittent
wrongdoers who might no longer see a bright line between right
and wrong — because social discourse has made that beam wob-
ble, then scintillate, attract, and confuse.

If this is so, such immoral attention is not just a matter of a
"loosening" of morality, but the combination of liberalization (*not*
liberation) with a blinkered form of cultural interdiction. The
pedophilic sensibility of the culture is strengthened. Thus we may
produce the obsession we claim to resent; the new pedophile
would become a product of our system of values.

One rehabilitative solution would be to try to extinguish the worship of youth. Childhood is precisely the period when you can't do
what you like. You are unformed and dumb. It is the time of first
experiences; but first experiences can be read either as engravings
from which all further iterations are struck and decline in clarity
or as defective and insufficient premonitions of a reality that will
only develop in adulthood. We know the beauty of the young,
which it is traditional to admire — their unlined features, their un-
worn flesh — but we also can know that the beauty of children is
the beauty of another, merely incipient form of life, and nothing to
emulate. One view of the young body is as an ideal. The other is as
an unpressed blank.

A second solution would be the trivialization of sex altogether.
This is much harder, because every aspect of the culture is so much
against it, counterliberators and prudes included. Aldous Huxley
warned of a world in which we'd arrange sexual intercourse as we
make dates for coffee, with the same politeness and obligation.
That now seems like an impossibly beautiful idyll. At least coffee
dates share out assets pacifically. You meet for coffee with people
you don't really want to see, and people who don't want to see you
agree to meet you, and yet everyone manages to get something out
of it. If only sex could be like coffee! But sex has not proved adapt-
able to this and probably never will, despite the recent overcoming

of a heretofore limiting condition — the inability to control physical arousal at will. The new pharmacopoeia of tumescence drugs will soon give way, according to reports of current clinical trials, to libido drugs that act directly on the brain rather than the vascular system — and for both men and women. I'm still not optimistic they will produce a revolution in etiquette.

The reason it seems a sex of pure politeness and equal access does not work is that the constant preparation to imagine any and every other person as a sexual object (something our culture already encourages) proves to be ruthlessly egocentric and antisocial, making every other living body a tool for self-pleasure or gain. At times I wonder if we are witnessing a sexualization of the life process itself, in which all pleasure is canalized into the sexual, and the function of warm, living flesh in any form is to allow us access to autoerotism through the circuit of an other. This is echoed at the intellectual level in the discourse of "self-discovery." The real underlying question of sexual encounter today may not be "What is he like in bed?" (heard often enough, and said without shame) but "What am I like in bed?" (never spoken). That is to say, at the deepest level, one says: "Whom do I discover myself to be in sex?" — so that sex becomes the special province of self-discovery.

Meanwhile the more traditional way of trivializing sex, by subordinating it to overwhelming romantic love, has diminished as an option as the focus on self-discovery has increasingly devitalized full romantic love. Self-discovery puts a reflecting wall between the self and attention to the other, so that all energy supposedly exerted in fascination, attraction, and love just bounces back, even when it appears to go out as love for the other. When self-discovery is combined with the notion of a continually new or renewed self, and this newness is associated with literal or metaphorical youth — well, then you simply have a segment of the affluent First World at the present moment.

This means the trivialization of sex and the denigration of youth will have to start with an act of willful revaluation. It will require preferring the values of adulthood: intellect over enthusiasm, autonomy over adventure, elegance over vitality, sophistication over innocence — and, perhaps, a pursuit of the confirmation or repetition of experience rather than experiences of novelty.

The trivialization of sex and the denigration of childhood can still be put on the agenda of a humane civilization. However, I think it's basically too late for us. Perhaps I simply mean that I know it is too late for me. If you kick at these things, you are kicking at the heart of certain systems; if you deny yourself the lure of sex, for example, or the superiority of youth, you feel you will perish from starvation. But if I can't save myself or my children, I still might help my grandchildren. The only hope would be, wherever possible, to deny ourselves in our fatuousness and build a barricade, penning us inside, quarantining this epoch that we must learn to name and disparage.

Let the future, at least, know that we were fools. Make our era distinct and closed so that the future can see something to move beyond. Record our testament, that this was a juvenile phase in liberation that must give way to a spiritual adulthood! Turn back to adults; see in the wrinkles at the side of the eye which catch the cobalt, the lines of laughter in the face, the prolific flesh, those subtle clothes of adulthood, the desire-inspiring repositories of *wisdom* and *experience*. Know that what we wish to be nourished upon is age and accomplishment, not emptiness and newness. Then, in sophisticated and depraved sexuality, rather than youth's innocence and the fake blush of truth, let our remaining impulses run in the sex of the old for the old — until they run out. Make a model for a better era. Once more, my moderns — in a superior decadence, in adult darkness rather than juvenile light — rise to the occasion! One effort more if you wish to be called liberators.

MARIONE INGRAM

Operation Gomorrah

FROM GRANTA

I REMEMBER that the summer in Hamburg in 1943 was unusually dry and hot. Three of us now lived in the fifth-floor apartment on Hasselbrook Strasse: my mother, my baby sister, Renate, and me. I was eight years old and a respectful, obedient child. But one day in late July my mother asked me to do something and I disobeyed her, and I shall be forever glad that I did. She asked me to take my baby sister to my cousin Inge's apartment in another part of the city and wait for her there. We set off. I was thrilled to be outdoors, unsupervised, in charge. A cooling salt breeze from the North Sea blew through the streets and seemed to calm Renate as I pushed her along inside a gray wicker carriage with spoked wheels and a handle as high as my chin. But after a while I turned back and then began to hurry. Something wasn't right with my mother. She had cried for most of the night and hadn't told me why.

When I think of myself then, hurrying home with the pram, I also think of all the things that were unknown to me. German officials who had placed our names on deportation lists; Royal Air Force officers studying aerial photographs of our city; bombers revving on runways in the flat fields of eastern England. All of them were about to impinge on my life.

I opened the door to our apartment that afternoon and found Mother slumped on the floor in front of the kitchen stove, and for a moment I just stood there, listening to the gas jets hiss like angry geese. Because she had a six-pointed yellow star on her dress, there was no one I could call upon for help. It hadn't always been that way, but this was the summer of 1943 and those who might have helped in the past had long since been silenced.

Trying not to inhale too much gas, I pulled Mother away from the stove, tugging first one limp arm and then the other. I managed to get her head and a shoulder into the dining room, but there her clothes bunched and clung to the carpet, making further progress slow and difficult. So I took down the blackout drape that covered the dining room window, swung back the glass pane, and welcomed the air into the room and into my lungs. Mother was lying partly on one side but mainly on her back, with her eyes shut and her lips slightly parted. She was very pale and completely limp, but she seemed to be breathing.

I was sitting on the floor with her head in my lap, trying to think what to do, when coming from the bottom of the stairwell where I'd left the pram I could hear the faint sounds of my baby sister's whimpering. I slipped out from under my mother's head and ran down to fetch Renate, and then laid her beside our mother on the floor in the hope that her hunger cries would wake her. They didn't. I put a pillow under my mother's head and began to look around for something that Renate and I could eat. I found a few potatoes and filled a pot with water. Then I scratched a match and tried to light the stove, which caused a frightening flash and a loud pop and the smell of singed hair. I tried again and again, until at the third or fourth attempt the gas ring produced a steady flame. And then I cooked and mashed the potatoes and fed and changed Renate and put her on the bed where all three of us slept together when Father was away.

A year earlier there had been four of us, but Father had managed to place my middle sister, Helga, with a family that lived on a farm on the outskirts of Hamburg. With her light blond hair, green eyes, and pale skin, she was easily accepted as one more city kid farmed out among relatives to escape the bombing raids. Father wasn't Jewish. He was serving with the Luftwaffe in Belgium, not as a combat pilot but as a member of Reichsminister Göring's procurement command, which kept Germans relatively well fed at the expense of the occupied peoples. He'd been recruited by a group of storm troopers who had beaten him almost to death — permanently injuring his kidneys — and given him the choice of joining up or dying together with his Jewish wife and children. Father's work enabled him to supply us with enough food to survive after our ration cards were canceled. He was also, though I didn't fully understand this then, an effective member of the Resistance — like his brother, my uncle Eugene Oestreicher, who was serving in occupied France when he chose to kill himself rather than be interrogated and tortured by an SS unit known as the Ascension Commandos. On his last visit home, my father told us that his room in his Brussels pension had been searched by the Gestapo. My mother believed that Eugene's death drew suspicion on us all and that the Gestapo (to whom she had to report every week) took more than the usual interest in us as Jews.

That night I transferred Renate from the bed to the floor, put her on two pillows beside Mother, covered them with a cotton sheet, and lay down next to them. There were no air raids to disturb us, though I woke up often to see if she was still unconscious. At last, in the morning, she opened her eyes and hugged and kissed Renate with tears pouring down her face.

Soon after, my cousin Inge arrived. She was the daughter of Father's half brother, and her parents ran a grocery store. They also had a Jewish woman living in their apartment, which took courage and conviction.

Inge was breathing hard after her climb up the five floors to our apartment. "I was so worried about you," she said, "but I couldn't come earlier. Our lodger got a deportation order yesterday. She tried to take her own life while we were out at the store."

I looked at Mother and I understood. She dried her eyes and explained that she too had received a deportation order: in five days we were supposed to report to Moorweide Park, the place from which all our Jewish aunts, uncles, grandparents, and cousins had been taken, along with almost all of the other Jews in Hamburg. Mother told Inge that, in a desperate bid to save her children, she had asked me to take Renate to Inge's home and then tried to take her own life, hoping the authorities would not go further after finding her dead. Inge didn't say anything but simply leaned forward and took Mother's hands. Still joined, the two women sat down and searched each other's eyes and then began to talk while I made tea. The authorities had disconnected our telephone. Inge promised that she would let Father know about the deportation order as soon as possible. When she left, she took Renate with her.

*

That night it was unnaturally hot even for the last week of July, and breathlessly still despite the distant flashes of dry lightning. Mother and I went to bed soon after sunset. Although I was tired and glad to be in the same bed as her, I couldn't sleep because of the heat and because Mother soon began writhing and gasping and occasionally crying out in her sleep. I didn't know whether this was because of all the gas she had inhaled or because she was so upset by our deportation order. Both thoughts distressed me, and I was still wide awake less than an hour later when the air-raid sirens began to wail again.

An explosion shook the building seconds later. Walls, ceilings, and windows shattered and showered us with plaster and glass. Lamps and picture frames were hurled around the room. A second blast sent gale-force winds gusting through the apartment, crashing the front door to the floor, stripping moldings, sills, and sashes, overturning bookcases and tables. Then a sheet of flame flashed outside our window as a third explosion seemed to detonate inside my skull. The shock wave sent our bed skittering across the room until it tipped and spilled us onto the floor.

I was stunned. I couldn't catch my breath and I desperately had to pee, but I was too worried about Mother to stay on the floor for long. The air was thick with plaster dust and the floor slippery with broken glass. As I urinated on a crumpled heap of rug, managing somehow to remain upright and keep my panties dry, I thought I could see Mother doing the same in another corner. I tried to call out to her but we were entirely surrounded by screaming bombs and explosions. Through a large hole that had been a window I watched as the balconies of the building next door were sprayed with shards of white phosphorus, some landing on tabletops, where they glowed and smoldered like strange food from outer space. Every geranium on every balcony was clearly visible in the glare of the flames. As I searched for my shoes, an incendiary bomb thudded through the roof of our building. I found one shoe and Mother the other. Unable to speak, we embraced and felt each other all over. Finding that nothing seemed to be broken or missing, we cautiously picked our way down the darkened, debris-cluttered stairway toward the courtyard at the bottom.

Draping blankets over our heads like huge shawls, we ran to the large metal door that led to the basement shelter. Mother took the nozzle of a fire extinguisher and banged on the door until it opened. A man's head in a large steel helmet poked out: it was our neighbor Block Warden Wiederman. "What are you doing here?" he demanded.

An ear-splitting explosion answered and he slammed the door. Mother banged some more and Herr Wiederman's head reappeared. We wedged our way inside.

"You have to let us stay!" Mother shouted. "We've been bombed out! It's certain death outside!"

Several of the people lying or sitting on bunks in the shelter got up and came over to the door. One, a rumpled, whiskered walrus of a man, held a lantern near Mother's face.

"It's the Jews!" a woman shouted. "The Jews! The damned Jews!"

The voice was neither young nor old, and there was no quality of mercy in it. In fact, it seemed that the woman had progressed from surprise to indignation to outrage as she repeated herself. Explosions smothered whatever else she said and I desperately hoped others would be more compassionate; the explosions, although horrific, were much less frightening inside the bunker. But the next voice to rise above the din was Frau Wiederman's. She yelled at her husband that he had to put us out because he was in charge and it was his duty to enforce the rules against sheltering Jews.

"You'll be held responsible!" she yelled. "Think of your family."

"Think of us, Daddy!" It was their daughter Monika, my former playmate. She was holding her favorite doll, holding it tight and turning slightly away as if she feared I might try to snatch it from her. "Think of us!"

The man with the lantern spoke up, his voice and breath thick with schnapps: "Listen to your family! Put the Jews out!"

"They're going to be deported in two days," Herr Wiederman said. "I've seen the order myself."

"All the more reason to boot them out," the walrus man said.

Herr Wiederman turned to tell us to leave, but Mother interrupted, pleading with him and with the others to allow me, at least, to stay, an idea that was very upsetting to me but seemed to find some support from others in the shelter. To my relief, louder voices shouted down the softhearted.

"The Bolshevik Jews are behind this!" a hoarse voice growled. "They sold us out. They told the English where to bomb."

I found the idea exciting, but Mother said it was ridiculous.

"My husband is in the Luftwaffe," she shouted. "He's on his way here now. You will answer to him if you put us out!"

The response was angry insistence on our immediate expulsion. Frau Wiederman gave her husband a shove and he pushed open the door. Instead of going out, Mother stepped deeper inside the shelter.

"You will answer . . ." she shouted, and the room became silent. She didn't say anything more, but stood for several seconds looking into their faces, her eyes glistening in the lantern light. She looked hurt and angry, but cleansed of fear, almost triumphant. Instead, many of the faces in the gloom began to look fearfully at us, apparently sensing that they had damned themselves by refusing to share their private donjon. When another explosion shook the building, Mother bent with a calm, protective look and adjusted my blanket so that it covered my head. Herr Wiederman grabbed her arm to force her toward the door, but she wrenched free. Then she picked me up and walked into the street as the door slammed behind us.

A false dawn lit the southeastern sky, rouging Mother's cheeks and painting the walls of buildings on our side of the street a lurid red. Through the openings of blasted windows we could see orange and yellow flames dancing beside pianos, making bonfires of bookcases, curling around bedposts. A torrent of hot wind coursed down Hasselbrook Strasse, bending trees almost double, stripping off branches and leaves and tugging at our blankets. Although antiaircraft guns banged away and searchlights still probed the sky, the bombing seemed to have diminished. Along the street a gusher of water rose more than three feet above the pavement. Everything was unreal. We went back through the arched entrance to our courtyard and saw pink tulips of flame sprouting along the roofline not far from our apartment.

There were firemen in the street, which was encouraging because normally they didn't come out of their shelters while a raid was in progress. The firemen had unraveled a hose, but it was flat. Although some water pressure had been restored after the raids on Sunday and Monday, the mains had been hit during the first waves of tonight's raid, creating gushers like the one we had just seen.

Some firemen across the street were working with crowbars to open the metal door of a cellar shelter while a fireman at the top of a long ladder chopped a hole in the roof of the building next door. Although we were afraid to approach for fear of being reported, I went close enough to hear one fireman yell to another that smoke from the building next door had entered the shelter through an exit tunnel. I thought how horrible it must be for those suffocating inside the shelter and was glad for a moment to be in the street. But even as the firemen succeeded in opening the shelter door and began bringing people outside, the terrifying shrieks of falling bombs, followed by thundering explosions, announced a new wave of Lancasters or Halifaxes. Both my eardrums seemed to burst at once as a large bomb landed much too close and collapsed the wall of the building next to the shelter. We watched and moaned, "No! No! No!" as the fireman who had chopped a hole in the roof fell with his ladder into the flames.

More bombs struck in quick succession. Most of the firemen abandoned the smoke victims and began to run for their own bunker. Two who didn't run were ripped by shrapnel and flying debris from another explosion. One fell on his face on top of a smoke victim and the other sat down on the sidewalk, holding his groin and screaming. Two firemen returned to retrieve their screaming comrade and carry him in the direction of their bunker. Many of the smoke victims were lying where they had been placed on the grassy strip beside the street, but some were staggering about, coughing and blinded, clutching at trees or lampposts for support. We lay in the gutter and watched as two or three from the shelter ran after the firemen. Following another nearby explosion we got up and chased after them, hoping that the firemen might allow us into their bunker. We ran down a narrow side street between high walls of flame until we came to a large commercial avenue. The firemen's bunker was on the other side, about fifty yards away, but the wind blowing down the avenue was filled with flying brands and was so strong that I could hardly stand in it. I lost my footing and would have gone tumbling into the flames, but Mother held on to my hand and hauled me to her side. We ducked back around the corner just as another bomb exploded between the firemen's bunker and us, spraying shrapnel into the wall we crouched behind.

After we'd caught our breath, we started running again, wanting desperately to get away from the flames and explosions erupting all around us. We would run down a street that seemed to have been missed by the bombers and cower for a time in an archway or entrance, but soon more flames would shoot up in front of us. Fleeing the intense heat, we tried to move away from what seemed to be the main flight path of the bombers, but often we found the way blocked by a huge crater or a hillock of smoldering bricks and flaming wood that had toppled into the street. Sometimes we tried to pick our way over the debris, but often we gave up and turned back. Everywhere the bellowing wind drove the flames into a frenzy, but the larger streets leading from Alster Lake were the worst. Hot air and gases flew down these streets with incredible force, carrying everything that wasn't anchored toward the blazing incinerator that an hour or so earlier had been the districts of Hamm and Hammerbrook.

We found some partial shelter in a basement entrance, but soon that, too, was ablaze. It was obvious that we couldn't stay where we were; pieces of the building had begun to fall onto the sidewalk. Despite the sustained roar of the wind and the sporadic explosions, I could sometimes hear the great cracking sounds made by the fire. I didn't see how we could avoid being crushed by the collapsing building if we stayed, or consumed by flames if we tried the street. I looked at Mother's face and read that she was undecided about whether it would be worse to stay or to leave. When there was a pause in the bombing, however, she wordlessly wrapped me like a mummy in my blanket. I could hardly breathe, and coughed miserably as she picked me up and edged back into the wind. By sticking close to walls and taking advantage of every possible windbreak, she eventually managed to get us to a more sheltered side street.

We were both exhausted — limping, blistered, and bleeding from the ears and nose — when we stumbled into a shallow crater with some water at the bottom. The crater appeared to be in the small front garden of what had once been a handsome brick house with bays and turrets but was now a smoldering shambles. Mother thoroughly dampened her blanket and draped it over us. The terrible explosions seemed to have abated, although hundreds of incendiary bombs had fallen close by, some landing in rubble no more than a dozen yards away. A canister of liquid phosphorus had hit an office building just down the avenue. As the phosphorus burned and dripped its way through floor after floor, it looked as if the lights were being turned on one after the other by someone descending methodically through the building. Before the phosphorus reached the ground, flames were leaping from the windows of the upper floors.

Then a woman carrying an infant came running down the street along the same route we had taken. She was followed by a young man dressed in the khaki shorts and shirt of a Hitler Youth. I thought they must be fleeing from a bomb shelter that had been damaged, possibly the one Mother had been heading for when we first left our apartment building. The woman looked to be about Mother's age. Her dress and her plaited pigtails appeared to have been burned, and she was almost completely naked below the waist. Despite his agile build and hiking shoes, the boy seemed to be having trouble keeping to his feet. I thought his difficulty might be the hot wind roaring down the avenue in front of us and almost expected to see him lifted up as he ran. Instead, after passing us at a gallop, he slowed to a grotesque caricature of walking, more like slow-motion skating, one leaden foot moving seconds after the other, with his arms spread out at his sides for balance. It took a while before I realized that both he and the woman were wading in molten asphalt. The woman slipped a couple of times and touched the pavement with one hand but managed to recover. Then she slowly fell head-first toward the street, twisting at the last moment so that she landed on her back with the baby on her chest. The boy tried to reach her but slipped and fell, got up and fell again, and then again. Despite the incredible noise, I thought I could hear their screams and ducked down into the crater with my eyes closed and my hands over my ears.

Mother climbed to the edge of our crater, and for a moment I worried that she was going to dash out to try to save the baby. But the hot wind burned her face and forced her back down. We lay in the crater beneath the blanket, getting hotter and hotter as the strong winds drove the flames into the sky. The image of the woman and the Hitler Youth writhing in hot asphalt remained vivid in the sweltering darkness until I realized that I was gasping for breath like a fish on land. No matter how deeply I inhaled, I couldn't get enough air into my lungs. When it seemed that I was about to suffocate, I pulled the blanket away and stuck up my head. Flaming logs and lumber, some of the planks several feet long, were sailing about in the air, along with millions and millions of sparks swirling at such speed they seemed to be tiny streaks of light. Without thinking, I opened my mouth wide and tried to suck in as much air as I could, until sharp needles of pain in my chest told me this was a bad mistake. I slumped back, more terrified than ever. When I closed my eyes it felt as if we were lying between railroad tracks while an endless train rumbled over us so swiftly that sparks from the wheels prickled my face.

I passed out for a time, awakening to find that breathing was still painful but that the explosions had stopped and the wind, though still almost as hot as steam, was not as strong. The heat was intense and so was our thirst, and we couldn't remain in the crater any longer without trying to drink the stinking water in the bottom. When we emerged we seemed to be in a winter snowstorm, with white flakes of ash flying in the wind. They looked so cool that I wanted to stick out my tongue to taste them, but there was still enough fire left in them to burn painfully. I'd lost my blanket, but Mother wrapped us both in hers and we tried to walk so that the hot ashes were not blowing directly at us.

We hadn't progressed very far when we began to see bodies. Before leaving the area of the crater, Mother had cautiously confirmed that the woman and her child and the Hitler Youth were dead, but she had shielded me from the sight. Although earlier we hadn't seen many other people in the streets, after the raid they seemed to be everywhere. Some, the obvious victims of exploding bombs, had been terribly torn and dismembered. Fire or heat had killed many more. Most were lying face-down. The flames had shorn their hair and clothes, seared and swollen their buttocks, split their skin and raised their hips a few inches off the ground. Though unmistakably human, they looked like huge bratwursts. The smell of burnt flesh wrenched our stomachs and made us want to cry, but we hadn't enough water in us for tears or throwing up. Instead, I clasped Mother and buried my face in her dress.

Desperate for something to drink, we headed toward the Eilbek Canal. Although we couldn't have been more than six or seven blocks away, it took us another hour to get there. Hundreds of people were still in the water, most of them near the opposite shore, where the canal was shallow, much shallower than usual because of the lack of rain during the past few months. Even more were on the banks, quite a few of them obviously dead. Some had faces as swollen and red as Chinese lanterns: their heads had been cooked while their bodies had been under water. Piteous moans, whimpering, and cries of anguish rose from the canal. The screams of children seemed to hang in the air like paper kites. Now and then someone on the shore would start shrieking and jumping about and then they would leap into the water.

Normally, Hamburgers were extremely stoical. Sometimes they muttered curses or shouted insults, but typically they clamped their jaws and endured adversity in silence. That morning, they voiced their pain.

Listening to the voices in the water, I realized that they had been burned by phosphorus. Just as it burned through the floors of a building, it quickly penetrated living flesh and bone. Judging from the grotesque shapes and expressions of the dead, many had died in agony. Those still in the canal had discovered that the phosphorus became inactive when it was immersed, but if they left the water it would start burning again as fiercely as before.

When another series of air-raid alarms announced that more bombers were within thirty minutes of Hamburg, a spontaneous wailing and cursing arose from the sufferers, and then quickly subsided, as if the effort had been too taxing or embarrassing. A few people started moving toward the church, whether to pray or to take shelter in the basement I couldn't say. Most, like us, remained by the canal. At the second alarm, signaling bombers within fifteen minutes, Mother recovered our blanket and wet it again in the canal, and we were sitting with our feet in the water when the final siren announced that the bombers were overhead. The unexpected quickness of their arrival gave us hope. If the bombers were moving so much faster than expected, they were probably the smaller British Mosquitoes rather than Lancasters or American Flying Fortresses returning to pulverize whatever was still standing. We lay on the bank for roughly two hours, listening to an occasional Mosquito buzz across the sky to drop a few more bombs into the billowing smoke. Long before the all clear sounded, Mother and I began to have stomach cramps and to vomit the canal water we had drunk earlier.

Where could we go? Brandsende, where Inge and Renate were staying, was impossible to reach because soldiers had cordoned off the streets near the city hall. A rescue worker told us to go to the Stadtpark. There we would at least be safe from the fires and could try to get transportation out of the city. On our way we saw that the Karstadt department store had collapsed on its two air-raid shelters. People disinterred from the shelter reserved for store employees and city officials were dazed but unhurt, but rescue workers had taken hundreds of dead women and children from the other shelter and were bringing out more as we passed. Mother squeezed my hand to signal her relief that we had not been in the shelter of the dead.

There were thousands of refugees in the park by the time we got there: police and other city officials were loading people into every type of vehicle and sending them off without much inquiry into who was going where. Baby buggies and other paraphernalia stood where they'd been left; abandoned cats and dogs chased one another through the park.

I didn't think that Mother had decided to leave the city, but when a policeman herded us toward the back of a truck with a canvas cover she didn't pull away or resist. The truck driver demanded some money and answered her question about our destination with a single word: "South!" And so we left the city. British fighters were reported to have strafed columns of fleeing refugees, and we stayed off the road the next day, parked in an orchard under trees laden with unripe apples to which we helped ourselves. I found swallowing painful, but the tart flavor was heavenly. Mother and I took as many apples as we could carry, and we still had some when we were dumped in the Bavarian village of Hof at around two in the morning. I was more asleep than awake as arrangements were made to stay in a room over a tavern beside a trout stream.

I can't remember much of the next few days other than the pain that came with breathing and eating, and that my mother was now my savior, my beautiful hero. She had outwitted the Gestapo and faced down the Nazis in the shelter and everywhere else. She had held my hand and led me through exploding streets; she had never let go.

Then came news of my father. Mother told me she had talked to him on the telephone, that he'd arrived in Hamburg the day after we left and was staying with Inge in Brandsende. Though the British had made another massive raid on the city, Renate and Inge and her family had survived the bombs. Father arranged for us to hide on the farm of Marie Pimber, the woman who had been taking care of my middle sister, Helga, on the understanding that she was a Christian evacuee. Frau Pimber was part of a network of people, mainly communists or former communists, that Father called upon for Resistance help of one sort or another. Frau Pimber didn't much like the idea of hiding Jews, an offense for which she could be killed, but she had been childless until my sister arrived and had become so attached to her that she thought of Helga as her own. Faced with the prospect of losing Helga or letting us live on the farm, and offered as much material support as Father could muster, Frau Pimber agreed.

Two years passed. The war ended. A fortnight after the Allies formally accepted Germany's surrender, on May 8, 1945, Father arrived at Frau Pimber's farm and we returned to Hamburg. My parents spent the next few months examining official and unofficial lists of survivors and waiting at railway stations for refugees to arrive. Father volunteered to help the British relief work among the refugees and displaced persons, pointing out that he was fluent in several languages and familiar with the cultures and countries from which many of the refugees had come. A British officer told him that he couldn't possibly be of any assistance because he was married to a Jew.

The joy of having escaped death made the unearthly ruins of Hamburg seem more like a smoldering paradise than the purgatory other people thought our once lovely city had become. After years of fear and hiding, I skipped down rubbled streets, flashing a smile and a thumbs-up at every British soldier I saw. I desperately wanted the British to know that I wasn't like the rest, that Winston Churchill was my hero, that I was glad they had come, and that I wanted them to stay to protect the handful of Jews who had somehow survived.

The bombings had left me with such a fear of fire that my heart would begin to pound whenever I heard a siren, and something within me would shiver long after the sound died away. I was extremely uncomfortable in enclosed spaces and I dreaded elevators, tunnels, cellars, and windowless rooms. I was also aware that thousands of Hamburg's children had been killed or maimed by the bombings, possibly even more than had been condemned to death for being Jews. And I hated all such killing with a passion that I couldn't always control.

At the same time I was glad that the intensive bombing of Hamburg by the British and the Americans during the summer of 1943 had enabled my mother and me to escape the fate of a death camp. Since we lived near the center of the firestorm, the authorities who had ticketed us for Auschwitz assumed that we must have been among the thousands of the unrecognizable dead. Because our neighbors would not let us share their shelter, I escaped being roasted alive. If the smile I flashed at British soldiers two years later sometimes appeared a trifle tight-lipped, that was because, while I wanted other Hamburgers to see how I felt, I was also afraid of what they might do when the tommies packed their gear and went home. Only a hundred or so Jews were left in Hamburg; another 17,000 had been killed or had fled.

Many Hamburgers must have felt some remorse for the suffering Germany had inflicted — when they saw, for example, pictures of the mountain of children's shoes at one of the death camps. That photograph made my father weep and place his large hand on my shoulder, while Mother had cried out and almost crushed Renate in her arms. But most people seemed too embittered by their own war experiences to give much thought to the suffering of others, especially of people whom they had been taught to hate. Every Hamburg family had experienced losses, most of them in the ten days of Operation Gomorrah, when somewhere between 45,000 and 70,000 civilians had died. Long after those raids, thousands of Hamburgers had to burrow beneath the rubble to sleep in cold cellars and basements. Whatever sparks of penitence smoldered beneath the ashes of the ruined city, the only expressions of regret I saw or heard in the streets, shops, and schools of Hamburg were laments for the hardships of defeat.

GARRET KEIZER

Loaded

FROM HARPER'S MAGAZINE

> That rifle hanging on the wall of the working-class flat or labourer's
> cottage is the symbol of democracy. It is our job to see that it stays there.
> — *George Orwell*

ENGLAND WAS NOT ENGAGED in a war against Islamo-fascists
when Orwell penned the words above, only a war against Nazi fascists — or, as one now feels obliged to say, *fascist* fascists — and the
rifle he referred to was in use by the British Home Guard. Still, his
reasons for wanting the rifle to stay on the wall obviously had to do
with a different sort of homeland security than the War Office had
in mind. Otherwise, why specify the gun owner's *class?*

In fact, Orwell was anticipating a time when the rifle might have
a revolutionary purpose. His hopes were not altogether in vain,
though supporting examples tend to be about as well known as the
quotation itself, and for much the same reason.

Here is one from 1947, three years before Orwell's death.
In Monroe, North Carolina, a motorcade of Ku Klux Klansmen
pulled up to a funeral home to "claim" the body of Bennie Mont-
gomery, a black sharecropper recently tried and executed for killing his white boss. With the help of a skilled mediator and a regi-
men of trust-building exercises, the night riders might have been
persuaded to settle for a limb or a chunk of Bennie's torso, but instead they were met by forty African Americans armed with rifles
and shotguns. Among them was a former army private named Robert Williams (1925–1996), whose career as a rogue civil rights ac-

tivist and NAACP officer, a story he tells in his 1962 book, *Negroes with Guns*, seems to have begun with that (ultimately bloodless) incident.

Although the rifle club he formed in his community had a National Rifle Association charter, there is, as far as I'm aware, no "Rob Williams Armed Citizen Award" offered by that organization, no essay contest bearing his name sponsored in the public schools. Nor does Williams appear in the official narrative of the civil rights movement, where Negroes with guns are seldom permitted to upstage folksingers with guitars.

To talk about guns in America is inevitably to talk about race. Both sides of the so-called gun debate have strange fruit in their family trees. The Second Amendment speaks of the importance of "a well regulated militia," and although framers like James Madison saw the local militia and the right "to keep and bear arms" as a check on the tyranny of standing armies, some historians have noted that one probable function of a well-regulated militia was to keep slaves in their place.

Likewise, one of the regulatory questions of Colonial times was what, if any, access slaves ought to have to guns; what, if any, role free blacks ought to have in the militias. Neither slavery nor the militias lasted as long as that dilemma. When Robert Williams aimed his gun at a racist mob during a campaign to integrate a public swimming pool, an old white man burst into tears and cried, "What is this God damn country coming to that the niggers have got guns?" From the beginning, gun control in America has had much to do with that question.

With antecedents like these, one might suppose that adversaries in the ongoing gun debate would have a harder time maintaining their stridency. I happen not to suppose anything of the kind, but then, my suppositions in regard to the limits of human reasonableness are one reason I own a gun.

As with its sister issue abortion, the debate over guns amounts to a clash of absolutes. the right of bodily self-determination versus the right to be born, the right of self-defense versus the right to walk down the street without being shot. In both cases the debate is frequently conducted by pretending that the opponent's concerns hardly deserve mention and by an inevitable transference of opprobrium from the adversary's position to his or her cultural "type." I wonder, for instance, as I read the various pro- and anti-gun polemics, who the actual enemy is supposed to be: the marauding outlaws who might be deterred by an "armed citizen," or the execrable Clintons, who, according to an editorial in the *American Rifleman,* attacked the Second Amendment *every day.* Are we supposed to be more incensed by the shady dealer who sells guns to Murder Incorporated or by the straight-arrow collector who thinks Charlton Heston could act? Issue-driven politics in red-and-blue America is like a man whose appetite for a steak is greatly enhanced by his contempt for vegetarians.

The gun issue is further complicated by a good deal of silliness, and in this it differs noticeably from the politics of the womb. Guns are either objects of superstition (they will just about *make* you commit suicide, according to some accounts) or pieces of pornographic paraphernalia, the things that get whipped out at the climax of a thousand socially smutty plots, on TV, in our heads, and then, insanely, in an actual event in which real people die. We all know what the Terminator said and the Taxi Driver said, but who recalls, much less ponders, what Thoreau said in his *Plea for Captain John Brown* (1853): "I speak for the slave when I say that I prefer the philanthropy of Captain John Brown to that philanthropy which neither shoots me nor liberates me . . . I do not wish to kill nor to be killed, but I can foresee circumstances in which both these things would be by me unavoidable."

Unfortunately, a progressive, as someone with my politics has come to be called, does not like to ponder such mortal circumstances. Notice the telling grammatical shift by which the adjective "progressive" becomes a titular noun — comparable to a godly person who begins to speak of himself as a god. As the living embodiment of progress itself, a progressive is beyond rage, beyond "the politics of yesterday," and certainly beyond anything as retro as a gun. More than I fear fundamentalists who wish to teach religious myths in place of evolution, I fear progressives who wish to teach evolution in place of political science. Or, rather, who forget a central principle of evolutionary thought: that no species completely outgrows its origins.

Like democracy, for example. What is that creature if not the offspring of literacy and ballistics? Once a peasant can shoot down a knight, the writing is on the wall, including the writing that says, "We hold these truths to be self-evident." Self-evident because Sir Galahad doesn't appear to be moving. *Guns, Germs, and Steel* is a good title for a book about European imperialism; *Guns, Fonts, and Ballots* would serve for a book about the rise of the European democratic state.

There are those who will insist, and many do, that what might have been true in the days of James Madison and Henry David Thoreau — and even in the days of Robert Williams — is no longer true in the days of neo-Nazis and Guantánamo Bay. But that questionable premise gives rise to an even more interesting question: If the Second Amendment is a dispensable anachronism in the era of school shootings, might not the First, Fourth, and Fifth amendments be dispensable anachronisms during a "war on terror"? Small wonder if some of those who readily make the first concession were equally ready to queue up behind the Republican right in ratifying the second.

Historians of weaponry tell us that one effect of the gun was to change the ideal of courage on the battlefield from a willingness to engage in hand-to-hand combat to an ability to stand firm under fire. At this point in our history, I'll take any form of courage I can get, but had Congress the smallest measure of the gunner's kind, the Patriot Act might still be a doodle on Dick Cheney's cocktail napkin.

I grew up with guns, and I live in a region where many people have them. They have guns because they hunt for meat, and they have guns for the same reason that many of them also have ponds dug close to their barns and houses. In a community with no fire hydrants, you want water for the fire engine. And in an area where a handful of state police and part-time sheriffs patrol a vast web of back roads spread across three counties, you might want the means to defend yourself. I own a fire extinguisher, a first-aid kit, and a shotgun. Not to own any of these would strike me as an affectation.

I hope that I shall never have to confront anyone with my gun, but owning a gun has forced me to confront myself. Anyone who owns firearms for reasons other than hunting and sport shooting (neither of which I do) has admitted that he or she is willing to kill another human being — as opposed to the more civilized course of allowing human beings to be killed by paid functionaries on his or her behalf. Owning a gun does not enhance my sense of power; it enhances my sense of compromise and contingency — a feeling curiously like that of holding down a job. In other words, it is one more glaring proof that I am not Mahatma Gandhi or even Che Guevara, just another soft-bellied schlimazel trying to keep the lawn mowed and the psychopaths off the lawn.

If the authorities attempted to confiscate my gun in a house-to-house search, I believe I would offer resistance. What I would not offer is a justifying argument; the argument is implicit in the ramifications of a house-to-house search. But all of this is so much fantasy, another example of the disingenuousness that tends to color our discussion of guns. The Day When All the Guns Are Gathered Up — what the paranoids regard as the end of the world and the Pollyannas as the Rapture — it's never going to happen. There are nearly 1.4 million active troops in the U.S. armed forces; there are an estimated 200 million guns in private hands. The war over the proper interpretation of the Second Amendment is effectively over. The most reasonable and decent thing that gun groups could do at this point is to declare victory and negotiate terms with the generosity that is so becoming in a victor. *Five-day waiting periods? Agreed, but our sense of honor compels us to insist on ten.* (Oh, to have been born in a time of so many guns and so little gallantry! Perhaps we ought not to have shot Sir Galahad after all.) *No assault rifles owned by civilians — also agreed, so long as no assault rifles are used on civilians.*

Of course, none of this is going to happen either. It would require a confidence that scarcely exists. One need only peruse the ads and articles in gun magazines to see the evidence of its rarity — to see that poignant, ironic, and insatiable obsession with overwhelming force. That cry of impotence. The *American Rifleman* I recall from my boyhood was closer to *Field & Stream* than to *Soldier of Fortune,* more like *Popular Mechanics* than *National Review.* My father and my uncles were do-it-yourself guys; their guns were just something else to lube. When I was a kid, I thought a liberal was a person who couldn't fix a car. But the cars aren't so easy to take apart anymore; the "check engine" light comes on and only the dealership has all the codes. As in Detroit, so in Washington: the engineering works the same. I am not the first to point out the sleight of hand that bedevils us: the illusion of power and choice perpetuated to disguise a diminishing sphere of action. A person dry-fires his Ruger in the same reverie of preparedness as another aims her cursor at her favorite blog. What precision, what access, what an array of options! Something's going to happen one of these days, and when it does, man, I'm going to be ready. In the meantime, just listen to that awesome sterile click.

Recreational purposes aside, the problem with guns is that their only conscionable private use is defensive. Even Robert Williams was insistent on this point. Hannah Arendt says as much when, in her book *On Violence,* she writes, "Rage and violence turn irrational only when they are directed against substitutes." Whom are you likely to shoot in a modern uprising if not a substitute?

The other trouble with guns is their reductive effect on the question of violent versus nonviolent resistance. They predispose us to think of violence exclusively as gun violence. Arendt herself seems close to this assumption when she defines violence as the forceful use of "implements." Her definition makes sense to me only if the human body also counts as an implement.

In that regard it may be instructive to look at the political history of violent confrontations in America. None has been pretty; perhaps a few led to reform. But of the latter, not all or even many have involved guns. Shootouts always follow a predictable script. They are like bullfights: the matador may get gored but the bull always dies. Red flags wave and perhaps a white flag after that, but with a few exceptions, like Harpers Ferry and Matewan, one finds very little to salute.

The prospect changes when we consider certain mostly unarmed, often spontaneous engagements. They include the worst instances of mass behavior and, if not also the best, at least some of the most defining for their times. One thinks of the Boston Massacre, Haymarket Square, Kent State, Stonewall, Watts. Some of the participants carried signs and some did not, but in retrospect they all seem to be massing under the same banner: "If you are so afraid of 'the mob' that you would deny us our place at the table, then we will remind you what a real mob looks like." Aeschylus put the Furies under the hill of the Areopagus; that is, under the taming influence of rational persuasion. Under the pretext of taming them further, overweening governments only manage to let them loose.

This is the lesson our leaders seem to have forgotten and that the more comfortable among us would just as soon forget: when the rules of participatory government are broken, the governed have a tendency, a right, and an obligation to become unruly.

Saul Alinsky liked to say that a liberal is someone who leaves the room when an argument is about to turn into a fight. We are currently in need of a liberalism that goes back into the room and starts the fight. We are possibly in need of some civil unrest. This is not a conclusion I come to lightly. I have always believed in the superiority of nonviolent noncooperation. The Hindu sage Sri Ramakrishna is supposed to have said that if a person could weep for a single day because he had not seen God, he would behold his heart's desire; I continue to believe that if the mass of Americans refused to earn or spend a dollar for a single day following a fishy election — no matter whose guy won — by the dawn's early light we would behold our country. But the likelihood of achieving that kind of solidarity brings us back to the subject of weeping.

The harvest is great but the laborers are few. Still, if asked to choose between an urban guerrilla armed with an AK-47 and a protester armed with a song sheet and a map showing how to get to the designated "free speech zone," I would decline on the grounds of insufficient faith and negligible inspiration. Rather, give me some people with very fanatical ideas about the sanctity of habeas corpus and the length of time an African American or any other American ought to have to wait on line to vote. Give me some people who are not so evolved that they have forgotten what it is to stand firm under fire or even to squat near the fire in a cave. Give me an accountant who can still throw a rock.

Petrified

FROM THE NEW YORKER

IN FEBRUARY 1995, the thirty-seven-year-old British actor and comedian Stephen Fry was starring with another popular British comic, Rik Mayall, in the West End production of Simon Gray's *Cell Mates*. Fry had the role of George Blake, a spy and traitor who is sprung from Wormwood Scrubs, where he is serving a forty-two-year sentence, by a prison friend, Sean Bourke, and who then, through a series of stratagems, keeps Bourke living with him in Moscow for two years. Fry, a multifaceted performer (he was Oscar Wilde in the 1997 film *Wilde* and a featured player on Rowan Atkinson's TV comedy *Blackadder*), had "the manners of a convivial prelate," as Gray subsequently wrote in *Fat Chance*, his account of the production. On the Sunday after the show's opening, when the weekend reviews hit the stands, however, Fry woke up feeling a "sort of clammy horror." He told me, "I had something to do, something annoying — I had agreed I would do narration for *Peter and the Wolf* in a church somewhere. I woke up. I looked at the ceiling. I thought, I can't let this person down on *Peter and the Wolf*. But I can't go back to the theater. I cannot." He added, "It was just a feeling of impossibility. It's inexplicable. I'd never, ever had stagefright and I'd done things like appear in front of close to eighty thousand people at Wembley for Nelson Mandela's birthday."

Fry fulfilled his *Peter and the Wolf* obligation at midday, returned to his apartment, wrote a series of letters to his cohorts, and then went into the garage to kill himself. "My finger was on the ignition key," he said. "But then pictures of your mother appear in front of your eyes. You cannot do that to your parents. At least I couldn't. I had tried when I was seventeen." Instead, Fry fled. "I drove to Bruges and struck east through to Germany. I had it in my head that the tip of Jutland would somehow suit me. I would buy a small wooden, quite well-heated hut. I just somehow imagined that British people didn't go there. I would learn Danish. I kind of liked the idea of going around in a big white pullover and a pipe and teaching English in some school in Denmark, meanwhile writing peculiar novels." He added, "I thought I had burned every bridge." Fry's disappearance was a subject of scandal and concern in England, where it dominated the headlines. A substitute was found for *Cell Mates,* but the production never recovered, and it closed prematurely three weeks later, with a loss of some three hundred thousand pounds. "I really believed I would never come back to England," Fry said in his documentary *The Secret Life of the Manic Depressive.* "I couldn't meet the gaze of anyone I knew."

In a sense, the term "stagefright" is a misnomer — fright being a shock for which one is unprepared. For professional performers, the unmooring terror hits as they prepare to do the very thing they're trained to do. According to one British medical study, actors' stress levels on opening night are equivalent "to that of a car-accident victim." When Sir Laurence Olivier was in his sixties, he considered retiring from the stage because of stagefright. It "is always waiting outside the door," he wrote in *Confessions of an Actor.* "You either battle or walk away." The Canadian piano virtuoso Glenn Gould, who suffered from disabling stagefright, did walk away, abandoning the public platform for the privacy of the recording studio. "To me the ideal artist-to-audience relationship is one to zero," he said.

Stagefright is a traumatic, insidious attack on the performer's expressive instrument: the body. According to the psychoanalyst Donald Kaplan, who studied this morbid form of anxiety, the trajectory of stagefright begins with manic agitation and moodiness, proceeds to delusional thinking and obsessional fantasies, and then to "blocking" — the "complete loss of perception and rehearsed function." The actor stiffens, trembles, and grows numb and uncoordinated. His mental and aural processes seize up. His throat tightens, his mouth goes dry, and he has difficulty speaking. The experience, with the metabolic changes it sets off — sweating, confusion, the loss of language — is a simulacrum of dying. "I died out there" or "I corpsed," actors say. In defense against the immobilizing terror, sufferers often split off. They disassociate. They report out-of-body experiences, a sense of watching themselves go by. ("It's a negative ecstasy," Fry says. "Remember that 'ecstasy' means 'to stand outside.' You stand outside yourself.") The actor's feeling of physical as well as mental coherence disintegrates. Instead of being protected, as usual, by the character he is playing, he suddenly stands helpless before the audience as himself; he loses the illusion of invisibility. His authority collapses and he feels naked, as if he were exposing to the judgmental spectators "an image of the man behind the mask," as the anthropologist Erving Goffman puts it. Actors sometimes refer to this momentary collapse as "drying": nothing flows from them to the audience or from the audience to them. "There is this catastrophic loss of confidence," the American psychoanalyst Christopher Bollas, who has treated many stage and screen actors, says. "You lose your radar — like a surfer. You can ride a ten-foot wave with real confidence, not thinking about it, just doing it. Then, all of a sudden, you become too self-aware. You think too much. You get wiped out." The paradox of acting is that, like surfing, it requires both relaxation and concentration. If there is concentration without relaxation, or relaxation without concentration, the performance doesn't work.

"Composure is repose," the playwright Clifford Odets observed in his diary. What the public wants, and what the performer sells, is the illusion of control, of never being at a loss. The actor is a model of perfect personality, "one who is not wounded, or worried, or maimed, or in danger," as Wilde described it. The performer's poise works as a defense against shame and social threats, both signaling security and creating it, projecting confidence and neutralizing aggression. Poise, according to the analyst Leo Rangell, is a way of recapturing the blissful state of the infant, who develops strategies to ensure his mother's collaboration and to prevent the agitation that would lead to his being "put down" or "dropped." Poise is an expression of the desire to be wanted and loved — a form of social security, which is never at play in solitude, when, Rangell writes, "there is no danger from without, no fear of ridicule: one is not at the moment being observed and judged." Actors, of course, watch themselves like hawks. Some, like Noël Coward, turn poise into a philosophy of life: their careers are a perpetual performance of charm. "I have taken a lot of trouble with my public face," Coward said. "Lose yourself and you lose your audience." The psychoanalyst Harvey Corman, speaking of his friend Barbra Streisand, who suffers from chronic stagefright, says, "Her greatest talent isn't acting or singing; it's her ability to hide her fear." ("Break a leg" and "*Merde*" — the backstage mantras for good luck — are acknowledgments of the actor's terror of losing control of his body and of making a mess.)

"Performers don't talk much about stagefright," Ian McKellen wrote in a defense of Fry that was published in the London *Times* in 1996. "The spectre of a tongue turned to stone and vomit where the lines should be is all too frightening to be evoked." One of the few to describe the trauma in detail is the British actor Ian Holm, who abandoned theater for nearly fifteen years because of it. In 1976, before the final preview of the Royal Shakespeare Company production of *The Iceman Cometh,* in which he played the central role of Hickey, Holm, as many sufferers do, had a presentiment of disaster. "I knew — I *knew* — that something was going to happen," he writes in *Acting My Life:*

> Somehow I got through the first part of the play, though I do remember sweating in the wings while I was waiting to go on, suddenly feeling cold and clammy, and people asking me if I was all right. Although I did not realize it, I had started to seize up . . . Then the moment arrived when I knew I would not be able to continue. I was giving a monologue from a chair at the front of the stage. The rest of the cast was behind me and, despite their previous efforts, now unable directly to intervene or assist me. I kept drying, even at one point addressing the audience with something like, "Here I am, supposed to be talking to you . . . there are you, expecting me to talk . . ." Getting off the stage was quite complicated and involved a choreographed manoeuvre through and past the other actors, who were frozen in a kind of tableau . . . I had only been off stage for a few moments before I knew some kind of buffer had been reached, that the game was up. I walked briskly past the stage manager, who waved a flimsy arm at me and uttered something polite like, "But you're due back on almost immediately, Mr. Holm."
> "I'm off," I replied. "And I'm not coming back." . . .
> By the time I got back to the dressing-room area, I had even lost the

ability to walk. The black curtain which slowly cowled my brain had become a complete hood . . . I experienced complete meltdown. I was unable to speak or to focus on anything. My eyes were wild and staring.

Holm ended up being comforted by a fellow actor backstage. "We
were both on the floor, my head in his lap," he writes. "He was caressing me like a child."

The poster for Alfred Hitchcock's 1950 film *Stage Fright* reads,
"Hands that applaud can also kill." In fact, it's not the hands of the
audience but their observing eyes that are lethal. The pianist and
critic Charles Rosen writes, in his mischievous essay "The Aesthetic
of Stage Fright," "The silence of the audience is not that of a public that listens but one that *watches,* like the dead hush that accompanies the unsteady movement of the tightrope walker poised over
his perilous space." Without an audience, or the fantasy of one,
there is no stagefright. The actor's success depends on his ability
to conquer the audience, which is why the encounter is so often fraught with excitement and danger. "The relationship is
undoubtedly sexual," the British character actress Anna Massey
says. "You get to know an audience very, very quickly. Within the
first five minutes. They become your friends or they become difficult to woo. Sometimes they're never won." Fry, before his first
professional engagement — in Alan Bennett's *Forty Years On* — was
found by Paul Eddington, one of the show's seasoned stars, peep-
ing through a hole in the curtain at the sea of strangers. "Never
look at the enemy," Eddington told him. Performance is, for the
actor, a form of battle — as the idioms of theatrical success make
clear: "I killed 'em," "I slaughtered 'em," "I knocked 'em dead."

In the 1989 show *Back with a Vengeance!*, Barry Humphries, as the
"housewife/superstar" Dame Edna Everage, perfectly parsed the
role of the audience and the effect that its cruel gaze can have on
frightened actors; he also made the audience itself feel the fear. At
one point in the show, Dame Edna patrolled the edge of the stage
in her high heels and diamanté harlequin glasses, looking for
someone from the first six rows "to do nude cartwheels onstage."
"And now the mood has completely changed, hasn't it?" she said.

> "I don't know what you'd call it. Blind terror, I think, don't you . . .
> But don't be nervous. Please . . . Supposing I chose, for argument's sake
> . . . you! In the third row. Yes. Yes. What is your name?"

"Emma."

"Hello, Emma. Have you done much cartwheel work? We've found audiences prefer an amateur nude cartwheelist, they do. They have a way of falling over which is vulnerable . . . and, well . . . strangely appealing. Don't scratch your eczema, Emma. Because you will not know you're doing these cartwheels, Emma. Do you know why? You'll be in deep shock, Emma. You will. Because whenever we women are very, very frightened, our bodies do a funny thing . . . Did you know, Emma, that we women have a little wee gland about half the size of a little fingernail tucked in an intimate nook? . . . This gland of ours, Emma, has a duct jointed on to it . . . And whenever we women have to do something a little, oh, unacceptable or even a little bit yucky, Emma, you know what this funny little gland of ours does? Do you? It squirts. It squirts. And it oozes. And drips. And we black out, Emma . . . And that'll be you. You will literally not know that you've been tonight's nude-cartwheel girl until you're leaving the theatre and you notice people pointing and laughing at you. And saying things like 'She wasn't a natural blonde, was she?'"

All the central traumas of childhood — being alone, abandoned, unsupported, emotionally abused — are revived for an actor when he appears before the paying customers, who have the power to either starve him of affection or reward him with approval. What the child gets from his mother — rapt focus, adoration, a sense of self — is what the actor needs from the audience. When things are going well, the stage and the house merge and a sort of imaginative union is achieved. The intimacy is palpable on both sides of the footlights; the audience seems to breathe with the actors. "There is brilliant intellectual clarity, a sense of boundless, inexhaustible energy as the chambers of the brain open up," Holm says of a successful performance. "Your whole existence is lit up by a dazzling sense of potential." Fry, explaining why he put himself through the stress of acting, says, "You're trying to recapture the 'first fine, careless rapture.' The first time you felt king of time and space, the first spinning joy of it all."

When the actor cannot make contact and the audience withholds its affection, however, the experience brings back a primal anxiety. "Every time I went onstage, there was that heavy feeling," Fry says. "I felt the audience was not on my side almost from the get-go . . . It was a sweaty sense of not being in control . . . constantly behind rather than ahead." He adds, "Everybody else had some transformative magic power that was completely denied me. I had no business being there." Fry blames his attack of stagefright partly on a scene that he had to perform in his underwear. "I was putting on a lot of weight," he says. "I was clearly a middle-aged man with a big gut." The audience, he adds, "sees the shriveled penis in your head." For Olivier, whose much-loved mother died when he was twelve, the audience was, to some degree, his parsimonious father. "My father couldn't see the slightest purpose in my existence," Olivier wrote. "Everything about me irritated him. I was an entirely unnecessary extra burden on the exchequer." In what seemed to be a gesture of preemptive defiance, before a show Olivier used to stand behind the curtain muttering at the audience over and over, "You bastards." Shirley MacLaine, contemplating the unfathomable energy and fierce focus of Frank Sinatra, with whom she worked for a time, came to the conclusion that "it has more to do with remaining a perpetual performing child who wants to please the mother audience." She continued, "He desperately needed her to love him, appreciate him, acknowledge him, and never betray his trust. So he would cajole, manipulate, caress, admonish, scold, and love her unconditionally until there was no difference between him and her."

The parent in the audience who needs to be won over is also, in some cases, a theater critic. In *Fat Chance*, Simon Gray makes it clear that a bad review played a large role in Fry's stagefright. Gray remembers reading Fry's "ambiguous suicide letter" to one of the producer's associates, Peter Wilkins. "Wherever he was going, whether to his untimely end, or into a hospital, or a monastery, or just into hiding," Gray writes, "the letter made it unequivocally clear that (a) he wasn't going to appear in 'Cell Mates' again, indeed was never going to act again, and (b) the reason for this was he believed that he was letting Rik, me and the whole production down." Gray added, "He followed this with a kind of spiteful lampoon on himself — 'the lumpen, superior "act" which I inflict on a bored audience every time I open my mouth.'" Gray recalls hearing Wilkins let out "something that sounded like a gasp":

WILKINS: But that's the *Financial Times* review.
ME: What?
WILKINS: Almost word for word. The *Financial Times* review.

Fry, who claimed not to read reviews, had gone out and bought the Sunday papers; if the actor couldn't actually see the judgmental eye of the audience from the stage, the words of the critic were in cold type and impossible to miss. "Fry is the all-time façade: so damnably English on the one hand, and so perplexingly inexpressive on the other," Alastair Macaulay had written in the *Financial Times*. The impact of the review was, Fry says, "phenomenal." He describes the sense of acute self-consciousness and loss of confidence that followed as "stage dread," a sort of "paradigm shift." He says, "It's not 'Look at me — I'm flying.' It's 'Look at me — I might fall.' It would be like playing a game of chess where you're constantly regretting the moves you've already played rather than looking at the ones you're going to play." Fry could not mobilize his defenses; unable to shore himself up, he took himself away. E-mails from his father and from Hugh Laurie, his friend and comedy partner, eventually found Fry in Hamburg and coaxed him to return briefly. By then, he'd seen his name in headlines and pictures of the police clamoring around his family's home in Norfolk. After a stint in America, staying first at John Cleese's Santa Barbara beach house and then at an apartment he'd bought in New York, Fry went back to his London flat in the fall of 1995. Around that time, he was asked to star in the Oscar Wilde biopic. "The idea that so much faith was put in me was a big thing," he says. "The film was one of the happiest experiences of my life." Since "the Debacle," as he calls it, Fry has written six books, appeared in several films, including the Academy Award–winning *Gosford Park*, and made a handful of documentaries. He has not, however, returned to the stage.

Stagefright, with its ties to both terror and shame, inspires a powerful desire to hide. "I was always looking for exits, literally looking for ways to escape," the singer and songwriter Carly Simon, who suffers from chronic stagefright, told me. "It felt claustrophobic being in the spotlight and being expected to finish a song. So I left myself the leeway of being able to leave the stage at the end of every song. What I tell myself now is 'If I just get through the song, I'll be able to leave.'" Olivier wrote of his famous performance in *Othello*, "I had to beg my Iago, Frank Finlay, not to leave the stage when I had to be left alone for a soliloquy, but to stay in the wings downstage where I could see him, since I feared I might not be able to stay there in front of the audience by myself."

The entertainer's journey through fear is the burden and the blessing of performance; it's what invests the enterprise with bravery, even a kind of nobility. "There was no other treatment than the well-worn practice of wearing *it* — the terror — out," Olivier wrote. The battle takes many strange and creative forms. Some performers drink to give themselves courage; some pop beta-blockers; some meditate or practice various other tension-reducing exercises; some play inspirational videos in their dressing rooms; some, like Charles Rosen, simply see stagefright as an inevitable and appropriate result of a virtuoso's perfectionism. "Stagefright is not merely symbolically but functionally necessary, like the dread of a candidate before an examination or a job interview, both designed essentially as a test of courage," Rosen writes. "Stagefright, like epilepsy, is a divine ailment, a sacred madness . . . It is a grace that is sufficient in the old Jesuit sense — that is, insufficient by itself but a necessary condition for success."

One of Olivier's ways of coping with stagefright was to ask his fellow actors not to look him in the eye. "They generously agreed, and managed to look attentively to either side of my face," he wrote of his performance as Shylock in the National Theatre production of *The Merchant of Venice* in 1970. "For some reason this made me feel that there was not quite so much loaded against me." Fry had the opposite experience. "If you're going well, the one thing you hate is being onstage with an actor who won't look you in the eye," he says. "If they're not going to meet your eye, there's something wrong with them, or they think there's something wrong with you."

Sviatoslav Richter, whom Prokofiev thought "the best pianist . . . in the whole world," coped with his stagefright by turning the lights on the audience and — except for a reading light on his sheet music — off himself. The illusion of invisibility freed Richter and allowed the listener, he said, "to concentrate on the music rather than on the performer." Some performers, like Carly Simon, on the other hand, choose to have the lights on the audience "because of the empathic reaction." She says, "When I feel I don't have the audience, when they're not warm, I'll pick out one person, usually in the first four rows, and sing a song directly to that person. He or she will get embarrassed and turn to people on his right or left. Therefore the embarrassment, or the focus I'm putting on him, takes it away from me."

On tour in 1995, Simon discovered that another way to handle her stagefright was to lie down onstage. "Rock-and-roll is so good because it accepts so much," she said. "I had a couch onstage so that I could be languorous . . . I could ease my way up to the mike. I do it in stages. I'm lying down on the couch, then I put my knees around and I sit up, and then I stand up at the end of the first song." These days, Simon says, 80 percent of the time she has beaten her stagefright before she's vertical. As part of her arsenal of attack, she keeps a hairbrush under the couch cushions so that she can brush her hair during the set, a gesture that helps to calm her palpitations. Simon has found that physical pain often trumps psychological terror. "If you have something that's hurting you physically, the pain is the hierarchy," she said. To that end, she has been known to take the stage in tight boots, to jab her hand with clutched safety pins, and even, just before going on, to ask band members to spank her. At a celebration for President Bill Clinton's fiftieth birthday, at Radio City Music Hall in 1996, Simon, terrified of following Smokey Robinson, invited the entire horn section to let her have it. "They all took turns spanking me," she says. "During the last spank the curtain went up. The audience saw the aftermath, the sting on my face. I bet Olivier didn't do that."

The acting coach Susan Batson, whose clients include Juliette Binoche, Jennifer Lopez, and Nicole Kidman, advises her students to try to displace the fear onto the role they're playing, to make it part of the performance, part of what she calls the "previous circumstances" of the character. When one of her actors has stagefright, she says, her response is "Can we use this?" Batson considers stagefright a "civilian issue," not an artistic one. "If you are a people pleaser" — worried about whether the audience is going to like you — "you're bound to have stagefright," she told me. "If you have an issue of not feeling like you're good enough, you're bound to have stagefright. The people who survive it are the ones who can take control of the situation and override it."

Kidman falls into Batson's "people pleaser" category. "My job with her is to scare her, really terrify her, tell her that she'll do awful work if she continues that kind of shit," Batson says. "Then she

gets the courage, and she's okay." In the early nineties, Kidman
wanted to audition for the part of the icy Las Vegas hustler Ginger
McKenna, opposite Robert De Niro, in Martin Scorsese's *Casino*, a
role for which all the Hollywood swamis said she was wrong. "She
worked like a dog to prove that she could do it," Batson recalled.
On the day Kidman went for her audition, according to Batson,
"she felt awkward" and "lost it." Scorsese took her in to meet
De Niro, Batson recalled. "She could feel everything just falling
apart." Her legs got wobbly and she felt hives coming on, but she
pushed ahead and went straight into a scene that required her to
strike her costar. "All she could think of was 'Stay in the character's
circumstances.' She reared back, and she slapped the shit out of
De Niro." Batson added, "They didn't give her the part" — it
went to Sharon Stone — "but they were impressed. That's literally the artist overcoming the terror. She had no choice. She said,
'I was gone. The only thing to do was to do the slapping. To
get through.'" Courage generates more courage. "Once you go
through it and lift it, you feel very, very courageous. It's a high that
you pray everybody has," Batson said. "I'm always terrified of the
person who doesn't have it, because it means that the commitment
is not fully there."

LOUIS MENAND

Name That Tone

FROM THE NEW YORKER

THERE IS A NEW cell-phone ring tone that can't be heard by most people over the age of twenty, according to an NPR report. The tone is derived from something called the Mosquito, a device invented by a Welsh security firm for the noble purpose of driving hooligans, yobs, scamps, ne'er-do-wells, scapegraces, ruffians, tosspots, and bravos away from places where grownups are attempting to ply an honest trade. The device emits a 17 kilohertz buzz, a pitch that is too high for older ears to register but, as we learn from additional reporting by the *New York Times,* is "ear-splitting" for younger people. A person or persons unknown have produced a copy of the Mosquito buzz for use as a cell-phone ring tone, evidently with the idea that it will enable students to receive notification of new text messages while sitting in class, without the knowledge of the teacher.

The *Times,* in a welcome but highly uncharacteristic embrace of anarchy, celebrated this development as an ingenious guerrilla tactic in youth's eternal war against adult authority — "a bit of techno-jujitsu," as the paper put it. But it's not entirely clear which side is the winner here. When you hear the tone, it apparently sets your teeth on edge, which means that, if the entire class suddenly grimaces, it's a good bet that one of the students just got a text message. (Which probably says "sup." Youth, as George Bernard Shaw correctly observed, is wasted on the young.) Anyway, what was wrong with "vibrate only"?

The real interest of the story, of course, lies elsewhere. The news is not that students are fooling their teachers, which was never news, even in ancient Greece, or that technology is rapidly unraveling the fabric of trust and respect on which civil society depends, which everyone already knows. It is that one more way for middle-aged people to feel that they're losing it has been discovered. The public concern over natural hearing loss — the *Times* explains that the medical term is "presbycusis" — is part of a trend that started when Bob Dole told the nation that he had trouble getting an erection. Now television commercials inform us that thirty million American men may have trouble getting an erection. Wow. And these are big, friendly, touch-football-playing guys, with George Clooney smiles and luscious, adoring, patient wives. Decay is everywhere discussed, though it is always, weirdly, disguised. Young women with luminous skin explain the importance of fighting premature wrinkling. Thirty is the new forty. We know that this is just anxiety manufactured to sell products, but it does have an impact. People worry about being old before they get old. Americans are living longer but, somehow, aging sooner.

People tend to regard the gradual yet irreversible atrophying of their faculties as a bad thing. Is it, though? Sure, it's tied up with stuff that you don't want to think too much about. One day, you learn that you can't hear a sound that is perfectly audible to teenagers and dogs. (Any significance in that symmetry, by the way? Do we feel diminished as a species because dogs can hear a noise that we can't?) Soon after that, you realize that you have forgotten how to calculate the area of a triangle, and how many pints there are in a quart. From there, it's not long until you find that you are unable to stop talking about real estate, which is the first step down an increasingly rocky and overgrown path that leads, almost always — all right, always — to death. What is there to like about any of this?

Well, first of all, who *wants* to hear someone else's cell phone? The Mosquito tone is like the squirrel's heartbeat that George Eliot refers to in *Middlemarch:* "If we had a keen vision and feeling of all ordinary human life, it would be like hearing the grass grow and the squirrel's heart beat, and we should die of that roar which lies on the other side of silence. As it is, the quickest of us walk about well wadded with stupidity." The Mosquito tone is one of those things you're better off not knowing. The world is probably full of such things (though how would you know?). Maybe the area of a triangle isn't that important either. Maybe, in the end, it *is* all about real estate.

The point is that mental and physical development never stops, no matter how old you are, and development is one of the things that make it interesting to be a being. We imagine that we change our opinions or our personalities or our taste in music as we ripen, often feeling that we are betraying our younger selves. Really, though, our bodies just change, and that is what changes our views, our temperament, and our tolerance for Billy Joel. We can't help it. The chemistry has altered.

This means that some things that were once present to us become invisible, go off the screen; the compensation is that new things swim into view. Ramps are an example. Try getting a teenager to appreciate a grilled ramp. Try getting a teenager to appreciate another person, for that matter. We may lose hormones, but we gain empathy. The deficits, in other words, are not all at one end of the continuum. Readers who are over twenty may not hear the new ring tone; if they had it on their phones, it might as well be silent. But most readers who are under the age of twenty will not be able to "hear" this Comment. Yes, they will see the words, and they will imagine that they are reading something, and that it makes sense; but they can never truly "get it." The Comment is simply beyond the range of their faculties. For all intents and purposes, if you're under twenty, this page might as well be blank.

DANIEL OROZCO

Shakers

FROM STORYQUARTERLY

> Whoever you are! motion and reflection are especially for you,
> The divine ship sails the divine sea for you.
>
> — *Walt Whitman, "A Song of the Rolling Earth"*

THEY ARE CALLED P-WAVES. They are the primary waves, the
first and the fastest, moving at up to six miles per second, near
top speed through the fold and furl of basalt layer, and slowing
when they hit the granite massifs, the slabs of continent borne
upon magmatic flows inside the earth's crust. P-waves are sound
waves that move through solid rock and that compress and dilate
the solid rock they move through, coming at you peristaltic and
slinkylike, radiating upward and outward from the seismic event. S-
waves follow four to twelve seconds later, depending on where you
are from the epicenter. L-waves follow soon after. These last are the
slowpokes, the long-period surface waves that arrive like laggards
in the seismic sequence, languid and weary, but powerful enough
to do all the damage you will read and hear about when it is all
over. But P-waves come first.

When they hit, rats and snakes hightail it out of their burrows.
Ants break single-file ranks and scatter blind, and flies roil off garbage bins in shimmering clouds. On the Point Reyes Peninsula,
milk cows bust out of feed sheds and bolt for open pasture. Inside
aquariums in dentists' offices and Chinese restaurants and third-
grade classrooms, fish huddle in the corners of their tanks, still as
photos of huddled fish. Inside houses built on the alluvial soils

of the Sacramento Delta, cockroaches swarm from behind walls, pouring like cornflakes out of kitchen cabinetry and rising in tides from beneath sinks and tubs and shower stalls. Crows go mute. Squirrels play possum. Cats awaken from naps. Dogs guilty of nothing peer guiltily at their masters. Pigeons and starlings clatter fretfully on the eaves and cornices of buildings, then rise en masse and wheel away in spectacular rollercoaster swoops. Pet shop parakeets attempt the same maneuver in their cages. In the San Francisco Zoo, every single Adélie penguin dives and swims around and around their Plexiglas grotto, seeking the safety of what they believe to be open ocean. Big cats stop pacing, tortoises drop and tuck, elephants get antsy as pee-prone toddlers. The chimps on Monkey Island go ape-shit. Horses everywhere go mulish and nippy. Implacable cattle get skittish as deer. And a lone jogger on a fire trail on Mount Diablo gets lucky, for the starving cougar stalking her gets spooked by the subsonic pulse that rolls under its paw pads, and breaks off the hunt and heads for the hills, bounding silent and unseen up a hidden defile and leaving behind only a shudder of knotweed grass burnished amber by the waning light of an Indian-summer dusk.

Subsonic pulses register in measuring devices throughout the state, in boreholes surrounding sag ponds in Big Pines and Lost Lake; in austere concrete vaults strung along an abandoned railway through Donner Pass and on the peripheries of rest stops along Highway 99 through the San Joaquin Valley; inside an array of seemingly derelict, rust-pocked, and listing corrugated-steel shacks smack in the middle of nowhere. Subsonic pulses register in instruments in firehouses, transformer substations, and the watershed property surrounding every dam in the state. In university labs and USGS offices, ink styli twitch against seismograph drums, unnoticed for now. In field stations, in Latrobe and Bear Valley and Mercy Hot Springs, the pulses are registering inside wide-band seismometers, flat steel cylinders painted green and bolted onto bedrock outcrops, squat and solid as toads. In Colusa, in Cloverdale and Coalinga and Arbuckle, pulses are registering inside sleek steel-cased tubes stashed down sixty-meter boreholes. Pulses are registering in tubular, yam-sized instruments embedded in grabens and scarps and streambeds in fault zones everywhere. The devices are called geophones, and their urethane casings are pumpkin orange, and there are hundreds of them pimpling vistas everywhere, from Cape Mendocino and across the geologic fretworks of the Carrizo Plain and down to the crusted shorelines of the Salton Sea, near marshes where migrating gulls think they are starfish and try to eat them.

To look at them, these field instruments — these containers embedded and tucked and stashed about — seem benign and dumb and exquisitely unperturbed. But inside them, everything is going crazy. Within precisely calibrated tolerances, tiny leaf springs recoil and pea-sized bobs pendulate between capacitor plates. Feedback circuits open wide, resistors hum, and a wee electrical impulse begins a journey. Precambrian time and the making of mountains and the heat and energy that has extruded ocean floors and shoved continents apart — all is rarefied and reduced and squeezed into the gauge and extent of a titanium filament, whose vibration releases a speck of data that will join the million others in a telemetric stream that, when it is all over, will tell the story of this earthquake.

Southeast of Palmdale, at a conduit box atop a phone pole along a stretch of Pearblossom Highway, a telephone lineman testing relays sways in his cherry picker. He looks down, around the perimeter of his truck thirty feet below, then at the traffic whipping past. He squints out into the desert, the horizon a laminate of browns and ochres wiggly in the heat. It is near dusk. The air is still. He listens. And there it is again, like a wave rolling under him, and his heart skips, and he lets out a hoot. His life thus far, untroubled and unremarkable — in other words, a good life has passed without a California earthquake. He hollers: Shakers, baby! Whoo-hoo! He whirls his hips, does the tiniest of hulas in his basket high off the ground. This is never smart, but especially now — the S-waves that are following the P-waves he is dancing to will resonate with the same frequency as the vibration his hula is inducing in the hydraulic lift. When frequencies match, vibrations will increase, and the hydraulic lift will shudder and lurch, and both it and the truck will keel over. The cherry picker will snap in two, and our telephone lineman will ride his basket all the way down in his first earthquake, slamming into the macadam below and the traffic streaming on it. He will be the first to die.

In the landing area of a timber tract in the Headwaters Forest, two loggers are intent on the problem of unhooking a trouble-some choke line, and feel nothing. But soon the forest will keen and low, and the grinding of tree roots in the unsettled earth will grow to a deafening roar, and the loggers will drop their grapples and watch with trepidation the rumbling decks of logs stacked ten feet high all around them.

A slack-jawed teen playing Grand Theft Auto in the basement of a house in San Francisco's Sunset district is too stoned to know or care whether he's winning, too stoned to remember that he's had a frozen pizza going in the microwave oven upstairs for over an hour. Yet he feels it, up through the dune sands his neighborhood was built on and through the foundation and flooring of his mother's house and through his sneakers and up deep and weird into the lengths of his shin bones.

In houseboats and fishing sleds on Shasta Lake and in sailboats bobbing in their slips along the Sausalito marina, they feel it as a series of nonrandom thumps, as if water had somehow acquired the wherewithal to come together and knock polite but resolute on the hulls of their vessels, and sounding nothing like the slap and slosh they are used to, and being disconcerting enough to give pause — beers and forks stilled halfway to expectant mouths, quesadillas and turkey patties suspended midflip.

Thousands give pause, hesitate, stop short. Thousands take a moment — to weigh up and sort out, to digest and to process and to see what's what. Hygienists stop flossing, butchers stop cleaving, priests stop absolving. Coupled lovers in their throes stop for just a second. Inside vehicles up and down the Nimitz and the Bayshore and strung along the Ventura and the Van Nuys, thousands of commuters cease their prattle and yammer, and — abruptly compelled to ponder the Now — give pause, then speak the exact same phrase into their cell phones: Did you feel that?

A checkout clerk at end of shift in a grocery store in Watsonville feels it just as she nicks a carton of Lucky Strikes and tucks it into her backpack, and stands up and looks at everyone looking at each other. And when the shaking starts she will hang on and watch awe-struck as every single item on every single shelf leaps off in a slow-motion mass suicide and piles up three feet deep in the aisles. She will hear the great shattering of every window blowing out. And when the shaking stops she will pick herself up and take that carton of cigarettes and step over debris and return it to its now empty shelf, and see that her hands and arms are covered with blood and embedded with broken window glass, and drop like a hammer in a dead faint.

Inmates in Folsom Prison's dining hall stop eating and glare at one another as century-old mortar shakes off the ceiling and sifts down, dusting the tops of their heads like cannolis.

In Oxnard, the local earthquake prognosticator shuffles down an alley behind Taqueria Row. A forgotten and once ascendant surf god of the 1960s — a Hurricane Nationals champ, a Duke Kahanamoku protégé — he now lives under a footbridge on the beachfront along Point Mugu, and on this day, diving Dumpsters for supper, he feels — and prognosticates — nothing.

And at a vast and bustling gas station and travel center in Tracy, just off the I-205, a girl with spiky green hair climbs into a very tidy cream-colored Ford Econoline. She is nineteen but looks younger, and she is traveling light — the clothes on her back and a midsized duffel — and heading east. She tells her ride that her name is Neve, and her ride — a compact, neatly dressed man in his forties who looks older — tells her he's meeting his wife and kids in Yosemite Village. He backs the van out of its space, and as he shifts into first, his palm slips on the gear knob and he pops the clutch and kills the engine, so flustered and thrilled is he to have gotten this girl, this Neve. And before he can start the engine again, before they can be on their way, the van will begin to pitch and yaw and the cars parked around them will rise and fall as if heaved by cresting seas. Neve's ride is terrified, unable to breathe, and Neve's hand will come from nowhere and snatch his and squeeze it hard, and his hand will squeeze hers back. And for the next thirty-seven seconds they will in this fashion watch light poles and freeway signs bow deeply to each other, and watch the parking lot pavement in front of them snap and ripple then settle like a bed sheet. They will watch an espresso cart stagger drunk across their field of view and stagger back. They will see the treetops on hills in the distance shimmy and shake on this still and windless day. A chorus of car alarms will rise up around them. And when it is over, they will let go of each other and survey the damage — very little, as it happens — and they will both laugh crazily. The man will rub his hand and go: Wow, you're strong! They'll laugh some more. And then he will start up the van and ease out of the lot and onto the I-205 and take this girl where she wants to go. The radio will be on low and they'll listen to the damage that has occurred elsewhere. They won't talk much; they won't need to because they've been through something together, and that is enough. They will cross a reservoir and veer north, away from the water and into the foothills. She'll stare hard at the landscape while giving him directions, as if matching what she sees with the memory of it in her head. And just before dark she'll point to where she wants to be let off, at a busted cattle gate with the barest trace of a road behind it and nothing but arroyo and scrub all around. He'll ask her if she's sure, and she'll say: Yep, this is the place. She'll get out with her duffel and thank him. We had some ride, didn't we? she'll say. And he'll say: We sure did! And he'll give her a twenty from his wallet and wish her luck and mean it. And all this he will do instead of what he was going to do to her, because of the touch of her hand which made her human, and the fear she saw in his face that made him human like her and that made them both the same. She will grow small and dim in his rearview mirror, and when she waves, he'll wave back. And as he returns to the travel center in Tracy to get another girl, he'll wonder what will become of this girl — this Neve — out here in the middle of nowhere.

The middle of nowhere. In Death Valley, a string of ultra-marathoners at mile sixty-five of a hundred-mile course weaves along a sticky blacktop road in 115-degree heat, sucking hard at unyielding air and being trailed by ESPN news crews in satellite vans. Miles from nowhere in Sierra Nevada high country, on a mudflat of lakebed sun-baked hard and gray as pavement, hundreds camp out for a motocross rally. Somewhere along a desolate stretch of sea cliff due west of the Coast Highway, through cypress and thickets of scrub oak, then over the edge and seventy-five feet straight down and under cold black water, divers feel along cleft and crag with numbed fingers, poaching abalone. Deep inside the old-growth woods of Plumas or Lassen or Kings Canyon — regions so remote that rangers have yet to map or break trail therein — pot farmers dangle fishhooks at eye level around their crops, and a meth cooker crazy from isolation and from paint thinner and acetone fumes sets punji stakes inside pits dug around his makeshift lab. On a map, the roads end in the Granite Mountains north of the Mojave. Dotted lines, then white space — nothing. But in the Granite Mountains, air force personnel in air-conditioned Nissen huts play foosball, microwave corn dogs, and watch Oprah on TV. In terrains unreachable by road or trail, mountain bikers whoop and tear up and down the broken, rain-rutted slopes of hidden gullies, and hang gliders pitch off bluffs, wheeling high above tiny golden fans of virgin beach and an ocean inflamed by the sun dropping into it. In the middle of nowhere, phone company technicians rappel down slopes and hack through Doug fir and sugar pine to erect cell towers disguised as Doug fir and sugar pine. And in Joshua Tree National Park, a day hiker off trail in the Pinto Mountains lies at the bottom of a ravine with a broken left ankle and a mangled right knee. He lies prone and still to avoid the grinding pain when he moves either leg. His water bottle is empty. His cell phone is gone, lost on the craggy slopes above him — his cigarettes are somewhere up there too, and his sunglasses — and he has no warm clothing for the cold desert night coming on. He is hoarse and thirsty, and feeling humbled and stupid, and wondering whether he really could die out here, just three miles from his car, parked in the lot of a gift shop that sells trail maps and nature guides, and bottled water and sunglasses, and tote bags and key chains and postcards — *Hotter'n Hell in Joshua Tree! Wish You Were Here!*

It is like this here: Get off the interstate, get anywhere off it, and drive away, onto State Route 16 to Gold Country, or Route 36 into Trinity Wilderness, or 178 toward the Piutes. Find a smaller road and take it, then a smaller road and take that — the one that squiggles like a heartbeat's trace along a skinny ridge; the one that winds through an endless wold of identical hummocks; the road cut that is barely road or cut, cinched tight across the midsection of sheer mountain wall; or the straightaway that shoots into the empty flats below you and fades into the distant haze, becoming more an erasure of a road than a road itself. Keep going. Go past signs with the names of towns on them that make you chuckle: Peanut and Fiddletown and Raisin City, Three Rocks and Copperopolis, Look Out and Rescue and Honeydew. Listen to the static on your radio, which picks up nothing here in the middle of nowhere. Marvel at how fucking big this state is. Allow yourself to be seduced by notions of vastness and desolation. Do this, and a pickup truck crammed with paint cans and ladders or bundles of steel pipe or a dining room set will rise up and loom in your mirrors and rattle past you like the clamorous armies of Death himself, late for the Apocalypse. Do this, and in the middle of boundless farmland, devoid of human landmarks to all horizons, you will come across a sprinkler going. On the shoulders of derelict roads you will see mailboxes huddled like abandoned old men, weathered and stooped, and among them today's paper inside a bright blue tube. Around a curve that brings into view an unbroken panorama of brown mesas and buttes, you will see graffiti, bold and crass, painted high on a rock face: baroque gang tags or cryptic acronyms, or GO TITANS! or I LOVE YOU VANESSA! Chained to a lone dead tree you will see a lidless, rust-cankered garbage can — forsaken, forlorn, God's Last Garbage Can — filled with fresh, logoed trash from Taco Bell and Hardee's. At sunset, the spectacular scenery that you've begun to ignore will recede into shadows, into night, until you are hurtling through a tube of darkness. In the wedge of your headlights the road sweeps under you, and there is only the ember glow of the dashboard, and the thump and thrum of the tires, and the static on the radio turned low and hissing steady like a whisper of distant rain. And just when you succumb once again to the romance of solitude, you see lights up ahead. You tap your brakes, and this is what glides past you: a neat little cottage with a fence and a lawn, the porch light a fever of beetles and moths; in the windows, the water of light from a TV; from the chimney, a steady white finger of smoke; and in the gravel driveway, a freshly washed car, beaded and gleaming. And then it is gone, sailing into the night, and for a moment you're not sure you saw what you saw. But there it is, glimmering small and bright in your rearview mirror for a long time until it finally drops into a dip of road behind you. And you realize you couldn't get lost here if you tried. And you've tried. The middle of nowhere is always somewhere for somebody.

Down a densely wooded gorge in the Siskiyou Mountains, the bones of a hiker lay scattered in the underbrush, long picked clean by coyotes and crows and grown brown and mossy in the cool dirt. Inside the mud at the bottom of San Francisco Bay, hundreds of commuters rustle and sway on trains rattling through the Transbay Tube. In a ninth-floor dorm room on the UCLA campus, two students who've just tearfully broken up have breakup sex on a futon in the corner. One room over, a young woman gingerly presses her entire body against the wall to listen, rapt as an acolyte apprehending the mystery of the divine. And four floors down, an unfinished letter to Mom sits atop the rubble of a desk. Its last line is: I hate it here. And its author is cross-legged on the floor, tearing the pages from hundred-dollar engineering textbooks and gazing as if sunblind into a floodlit vision of disappointment and ruin.

In an efficiency studio high up a tower block in Bakersfield, or in an upscale-ish condo on the fringes of a dicey neighborhood in Inglewood, or in an in-law unit wedged beneath a house that clings to the Oakland Hills, or in a loft or duplex or railroad flat in Rio Linda or Citrus Heights or Gilroy, you are watching TV.

You are sitting in a leather club chair in the middle of an otherwise spare room. You are home early from the office, having feigned a headache worse than the one you really do have. You are drinking a beer, watching the local news anchor read. Her name is Wendy Something, and you have a crush on her. You moved here only months ago — from Cedar Falls, from Monroe or Meridian, from Canton, Grand Forks, Eau Claire — and you have yet to make friends. The weekly drink with coworkers has drifted into a less occasional gathering, then none at all, as you've gradually discovered you have little in common, and you get along well at work anyway, so why even bother? People are hard to get to know out here, inside their bubbles, with their benign, almost tender indifference toward you and their studious gestures of intimacy — the banter that is devoid of subtext and the How-are-you! that is never a question and the See-you-later! that simply signals the end of conversation. It has been lonely. You come home in the evenings and eat a takeout burrito over the kitchen sink and stroll through your half-furnished rooms, with books in alphabetized stacks on the floor and unpacked boxes as end tables and nothing on the walls. You have pondered this metaphor for an unfinished life — or, better, the beginning of a new one — and you remind yourself why you moved here, why everyone moves here. And you may be lonely like this forever, but out here at least it feels transitory — a step on a journey, a blip on a timeline, and all that.

Joists groan overhead. A window frame stutters in its casement and is shot open. A kitchen chair is scraped across a floor. Movement above you. The sound of other people.

The sun will set within the hour. It is a time of day you love, between the room growing dark and you turning the lights on.

They crow about their light out here. In the early twentieth century, artists came in droves to paint in California light, adjusting color schemes and developing a choppy brush stroke and applying the paint quickly so as to capture on canvas the fleeting quality of the light — the "temporal fragment," the "instantaneous view." Out here they go on about how the light chisels, how it polishes and defines the edges of whatever it falls upon and imparts a dazzling clarity. They go on about how the light comes down around you in curtains or how it pours and spills like honey. It gleams and glints, it sparks and flares. The light has weight, it has density, it is palpable. Sometimes you can even hear it, zinging metallic and bright! What crap. When they aren't steeped in the clichéd golden hues of a shampoo commercial, the skies most days are an insipid palette of white and bluish white and yellowish white. Every vista is dull and bleary, a sun-bleached smudge in the distance. And nothing is chiseled. Everything you look at is foreshortened, flat and common as a souvenir poster. Although there can be days — those mornings of unseasonable fog when the sunlight is filtered through a fragile veil of cloud that renders the air itself luminous as milk; or the clear, cloudless afternoon when you're walking under a canopy of trees or through the lobby of a building downtown, and just before moving out of the shade, you take off your sunglasses and stand there a moment and anticipate entering the world of sunlight.

You take a swig of beer. You catch the whiff of a cigarette — the woman above you, smoking out of her window. You've said hello to her. She's said hello back.

On the TV, something is up with Wendy Something. She stops midsentence and looks off-camera. You feel a bump beneath you, then another. The ceiling joists begin to groan loud and steady, and all of your windows are rattling like maracas. Wendy is hanging on to her bucking desk, that on-air equanimity of hers that you love pretty much gone. She is looking right at you, and then the screen goes to snow and the TV tips over. There is a pounding like the fists of giants against the building you live in. There is a muffled cry from the woman above you, and you finally apprehend what is happening. You take a breath, chug your beer, toss the empty bottle over your shoulder. You hang on tight to your fat, heavy, chocolate-leather chair — your gift to yourself for finally making the move out here. You hang on and you think: The shaking will either stop or keep going. Life is lived from moment to moment.

On a grassy knoll overlooking an ocean view in Pacific Grove, two lovers on a blanket sip wine from plastic cups, reveling in a silence between them that goes on and on. A rice farmer, shin-high in flooded fields, stops brooding over weed infestation and a late harvest to watch the sunlight shatter and reshatter on the surface of the waters. A tiny old woman seated on a crowded bus barreling along an express lane peels a tangerine with the gravity and precision of bomb disposal. A grill cook on break from a hellish workday lolls on a bed of flattened boxes in an alley, and with absolutely nothing on his mind — hellish day gone! — watches a queue of mare-tailed clouds file across a slot of sky high above him.

A Riverside County sheriff loops through the parking lot of the Oasis Visitor Center in Joshua Tree National Park. The center is closed and the lot is empty except for a silver Honda hatchback. His last stop before going off shift, the sheriff idles in the middle of the lot inside his beautiful new-issue Chevy Tahoe. The sun moves behind a row of fan palms, their long shadows reaching for him. It is windless and still. He lingers in this anticipatory moment, then punches the gas and cranks the wheel and hangs on, going around and around, reduced to breathlessness and gooseflesh from the thunder of 240 horses in his bones and the delicious centrifugal tug on his innards, and the darkling hills and mustard skies of a desert dusk streaking and smearing all tilt-a-whirl around his head.

Three miles to the southeast, the owner of a forgotten Honda hatchback lies at the bottom of a ravine. He is very thirsty. His skin is sunburn pink. A line of shadow slices his body in two, and in the shaded half it's cold already. His ankle swells inside a boot he can't reach to untie and take off, and his right knee is big as a cantaloupe and awful to look at. Plus, there's something wrong with his elbow; he can't move his arm. All in all, a shitty day. And then the earth begins to move. The rock debris in the talus he is lying in shimmies and shudders and shoves him around. Scree chatters down the slopes of the ravine. He is pelted with stones and submerged in a cloud of desert dust. The quake subsides, the cloud settles. His eyes are cut and raw from grit, and his mouth is filled with sand. He hacks and coughs, igniting his legs with pain, and his heaving soon gives way to sobs. He is desolate and alone. He is so dehydrated that tears do not come.

And hours from now, after the sun has gone down, when he is shivering from the cold, when the cold is all he can think about, something remarkable will happen. A diamondback rattlesnake will home in on his heat-trace and unwind itself from the mesh of a creosote bush and drop to the ground and seek the warmth of his body against the chill evening, slicing through the sand and sweeping imperiously between his legs and turning into itself until coiled tight against his groin and draped along his belly with the offhand intimacy of a lover's arm. He will watch its dumpling-sized head in repose on his sternum go up and down with his breathing, its eyes open and indifferent and exquisitely wrought — tiny bronzed beads stippled black and verdigris. And his breaths will soon come slow and steady, and his despair will give way to something wholly unexpected. He is eyeball to eyeball with a rattlesnake in the powdery moonglow of Mojave Desert. He can hear birds calling back and forth — birdsong! — in the middle of nowhere. He can look up at a night sky that is like gaping into a chasm boiling with stars as if the celestial spigots were opened wide and jammed, and he can remember nothing of the life he's lived up to now. And he will shake, not from cold or fear or from any movements of the earth, but from some vague and elemental conviction about wholeness or harmony or immortality. He will shake, resolute in a belief in the exaltation of this moment, yet careful not to disturb the lethal snake on his chest. How cool is this! he will think. Wish you were here! he will think.

CYNTHIA OZICK

Out from Xanadu

FROM THE NEW YORK TIMES BOOK REVIEW

IN MY LATE TEENS and early twenties I was a mystic. It was Blake and Shelley who induced those grand intoxications, and also Keats and Wordsworth and Coleridge. At New York University, where Thomas Wolfe had once taught freshman composition, his shade — *O lost, and by the wind grieved, ghost, come back again!* — sometimes still flickered. Dylan Thomas, not yet in his cups and not yet renowned, came to a handful of students in an ordinary classroom and chanted, as if to a hall of hundreds, *The force that through the green fuse drives the flower,* syllables instinct with divine afflatus. Meanwhile I was writing an undergraduate thesis on the Romantic poets, and though I knew neither the word nor the concept, I was at that time seriously antinomian. Nothing was distinct, or of its own indivisible nature, nothing was fixed, nothing was demanded: all was wavering spirit and intuition. Rapture and ecstasy, ecstasy and rapture! — these were imagination's transports, abetted by the piercing sweetness of melancholy. The sage was withered from the lake, and no birds sang; or else they chorused thrillingly, like celestial choirs.

Besides being a mystic and an antinomian, I was also a believing monist: all things were one thing, watercolor worlds leaching and blending and fading into porous malleable realms. Yearning and beauty were the heart's engines, shocking the waiting soul (mine, anyhow) into a pulsing blur of wonderment. In Xanadu, where Alph the sacred river ran, you might actually see the Blessèd Damozel leaning over the bar of heaven! As for where the Spirit of God dwelled . . . well, where else but in you and me? (Primarily, of course, in me.) The Ten Commandments? In Xanadu nobody had ever heard of them.

At twenty-four I blundered, I no longer recall where or how, into "Romantic Religion," a book-length essay — or manifesto, or scholarly credo — by Leo Baeck. His name, his stature, his personal history, his transcendent learning were all unfamiliar. That he was of that remarkable German-Jewish generation that included, among many other humanist eminences, the historian Gershom Scholem and the philosophers Martin Buber and Walter Benjamin, I had yet to discover. Nor did I know that Baeck was a rabbi consumed, beyond the vastnesses of his own multifaceted tradition, by Greek and Christian thought; or that he was of that minute fraction of Jewish humanity to have come out of Theresienstadt alive. When I stumbled into the majesties of "Romantic Religion," I was as one (so it seemed to me afterward) who had conversed with Socrates while ignorant of Socrates' origins and identity.

Not that Baeck was Socratic in his tone or approach. The essay was a formidable looking glass. In a dissenting voice more analytic than scornful (though scorn seethed behind it), he told me off. For the romantic, he wrote, "everything dissolves into feeling; everything becomes mere mood; everything becomes subjective . . . Fervently, the romantic enjoys the highest delight and the deepest pain day after day; he enjoys the most enchanting and the most sublime; he enjoys his wounds and the streaming blood of his heart . . . Experiences with their many echoes and billows stand higher in his estimation than life with its tasks; for tasks always establish a bond with harsh reality. And from this he is in flight. He does not want to wrestle for his blessing, but to experience it, abandoning himself, devoid of will, to what spells salvation and bliss." And again: "Everything, thinking and poetry, knowledge and illusion, all here and all above, flows together in a foaming poem, into a sacred music, into a great transfiguration, an apotheosis. In the end, the floods close over the soul, while all and nothing become one."

In the hundred energetic pages of Walter Kaufmann's translation from the German (Kaufmann was himself a Princeton philosopher), under headings such as "Ethics," "Humanity," and "The Sentimental," Rabbi Baeck had me dead to rights. I had been surrendering my youth to *Weltschmerz*, to *Schwärmerei*, to *Welttrun-kenheit*, all those unleashed Wagnerian emotions which, Baeck pointed out, Hegel had once dismissed as the displacement of "content and substance" by "a formless weaving of the spirit within itself." The opposite of all that besottedness was "the classical, ethical idea of history" as manifested in "the Kantian personality who confronts us as the bearer of the moral law" — the law of act and deed that is itself "an essential part of that honesty which man owes to himself: the test of criticism." Who could criticize a dream? And what was that dream but immersion in fantasy and illusion? "Ethics evaporates into exaltation," Baeck declaimed. "Justice is to be reduced to a mere feeling and experience; the good deed is effected not by human will but by divine grace; man himself is a mere object and not a personality. The will becomes supernatural, and only concupiscence remains to man . . . Something more diametrically opposed to ethics than Romanticism would be hard to find."

And reading on and on in a fever of introspection, I was beginning to undergo a curious transformation: not the spirit's visionary turning, but one willed and chosen. I had become the Ancient Mariner — only in reverse. Gazing down at the water snakes writhing below, Coleridge's mystical sailor is all at once seized by a burst of joyous sanctification: to his transfigured senses the repulsive creatures of the sea are now revealed as blessèd things of beauty. But I, pursuing passage after passage of Baeck's reprise of the incantatory romantic — its transports and exultations, its voluptuously nurtured sorrows, its illusory beauty anchored in nothing but vapor — I came to see it all as loathsome, no different from those mindlessly coiling water snakes. What did it lead to? The self. What did it mean? Self-pride. What did it achieve? Self-delusion and delirium. That way lay Dionysus. I chose Rabbi Baeck.

More decades than I wish to admit to have fled away since I first looked into "Romantic Religion." And just recently, when I revisited my old copy — battered from many coerced lendings (it was I who did the coercing), and almost always returned unread — I was still impressed by its bold intellectual and moral cogency. But its power seemed somehow diminished, or, if not exactly that, then a tiny bit stale. I had, after all, assimilated those ideas from multiple sources over the years (not counting the Bible), and by now they were locked, as we have learned to say, into my DNA. "Romantic Religion," with its emphasis on humane conduct over the perils of the loosened imagination, remains an essay to live by. It is not an essay to write stories by; stories crave the wilderness of untethered feeling. But once — even though I wanted then more than anything on earth to write stories — it left me dazzled and undone.

Passion Flowers in Winter

FROM PMS

1

IMAGINE STARTING your life's work at the age of seventy-three, as Mrs. D. did. (That is what they call her in the Print Study Room at the British Museum.) Mrs. Mary Delany, a student of Handel, a sometime dinner partner of Jonathan Swift, and a devoted subject of mad King George invented the precursor of what we call collage. One afternoon in 1773, she noticed that a piece of colored paper matched the dropped petal of a geranium. She made this vital imaginative connection shortly after the death of her beloved second husband, Dr. Patrick Delany, while she was staying at a friend's house. (Some house! It was Bulstrode, the British estate, ancestral home of the Duchess of Portland, Mrs. Delany's lifelong friend.) She picked up her scissors (I'd guess they were embroidery scissors) and cut out the exact petal shape from the paper and began to paste up a replica of the flower. The Duchess couldn't tell the paper flower from the real one. Mrs. D. dubbed her paper-and-petal paste-up a *flower mosaik,* and in the next ten years she completed nearly a thousand cut-paper botanicals so shockingly accurate that botanists still refer to them and so energetically dramatic that each one leaps out from the dark as onto a lit stage.

Her flowers are staged, actually, because unlike the usual pale botanical drawings, they are done on deep black backgrounds. Mrs. D. drenched the front of white laid paper with India ink, waited for it to dry, and then began to paste hundreds — and I really mean hundreds into the thousands — of the tiniest slices of brightly colored paper onto the backgrounds. How she had the eyesight to do it, let alone the physical energy (didn't her arm muscles seize up?), let alone the dexterity (one passion flower alone has 230 slivers of paper whorled into the central mob of its pistils), is absolutely beyond me. I have seen and held this *flower mosaic,* called *Passiflora Laurifolia, Bay Leaved,* and looking at it did not make it any less fantastic than merely hearing about it. It seems to be beyond everyone who looks at them, since everyone I've ever talked with about Mrs. D. gasps to think of the enterprise.

Seventy-three years old. It gives a person hope.

I am fifty-eight, and now I have a role model. I hold out hope that I might start a memorable life's work at seventy-three. Of course I have had many role models throughout my life, beginning with my mother, but they are few and far between at my present age. I've led a life of a certain amount of accomplishment, and I don't need a role model for making a mark. What interests me is that a life's work is always largely unfinished, and it requires creativity till the day a person dies. But where are the models? Where are the readily apparent models for all of us who still consider that we are inventing a life?

Because the process of inventing your life seems to go on all your life, I have found that my search for role models has beat quietly on, in a sub-rosa way, long past my adolescence. It's not a focused search; it's almost the opposite, involving wandering, and full of happenstance. The wandering began with teachers and slightly older girlfriends, then progressed to professors, then older colleagues and therapists, and always led through the forests of characters' lives in stories and novels. At times the role models proliferated; then the need for them paled. Yet a blurry sort of casual sorting, as if I were looking for something at the back of the drawers of experience, always goes on.

And now the role models I turn up no longer tend to come from the ranks of the living. Mrs. Delany (1700–1788), for instance, or even Mrs. Peacock, my mother (1919–1992), whose life I so deeply internalized that now its postlife suggestions are succinct and piquant. They are like the imagined scent that might arise from Mrs. Delany's blooms. A dead role model is ideal; everything about the life is complete, cut and pasted. The stilled life is something like a still life: rich with the captured curves of the passiflora's purple petals, bristling with the leaf. The life of such a role model, now completed by its end, feels something like a work of art: still breathing, listening, and feeling, as works of art, even when finished, seem quite alive.

2

Seventy-three. That is something of a magical number for these two women, Mrs. Delany beginning her life's work at this age, and Mrs. Peacock dying at the very same age. My mother's death gave me the realization that, just as in a sonnet, the end gives the lived life a shape. You can see it in time. You can take the silhouette of another's life and place it against your own.

Mary Delany was born Miss Mary Granville, in 1700, matching her life with the beginning of a new century — the eighteenth century of the American musket, the French guillotine, Handel's *Messiah,* George Washington striding into the Continental Congress, King George III's passion for botany and the opening of Kew Gardens, Jonathan Swift's cudgel of an essay on the Irish potato famine, the import into the West of wallpapers from China, women's embroidered stomachers, Jacobites thrown into the Tower of London, and forced marriages. Mary was the first daughter of Colonel Bernard Granville, who was the second son of his family. (His older brother, George, held the title of Lord Lansdowne.) Little Mary had every expectation of being a maid in waiting to the Queen, like her aunt Stanley, except that when Queen Anne died in 1714, the Granvilles came out on the wrong side of the Jacobite controversy, and her uncle Lord Lansdowne was thrown into the Tower. In the middle of that night her father ushered her hysterical mother, little sister, older brother, and Mary herself into a carriage and took them away to a small house in the country to live in a kind of Jane Austenesque exile away from intrigue.

But intrigue happens in the country too. By the time Mary was sixteen, her uncle had gotten himself out of the Tower and back to the family seat, busily consolidating his political power. He needed some new friends. And he was conscious of his responsibility toward his brother, who had little money except what he, the eldest, the Lord, gave him. But perhaps Mary was a kind of money.

What I am describing here isn't so much a role model as a story, but it's a real story. The early life of Mary Delany, née Granville, is external to me. It's history. But history shapes the events of lives, even the ones — especially the ones — you insert in your soul. When you internalize a role model, you internalize the role model's past as well as what you see directly.

As in an Austen novel, Mary was invited to stay at her uncle's estate as a way of her coming out into society. And as a way for Lord Lansdowne to consolidate his power in the county. At his table one evening there appeared a drunken squire about sixty years old. His behavior fascinated her. It disgusted her. (I identify with this in a strange way because when I was about sixteen, contemplating my first sexual adventure — with the boy who, it turned out, after decades of separation, became my husband, thirty years after this first escapade — my father's alcoholism was at its most energetic. He fascinated and disgusted me.)

We know all about how Mary felt because she wrote a memoir late in life, and she also wrote letters at the time to her younger sister Anne. Anne kept the letters, and so did Anne's descendants. And today we know about Mary because of Ruth Hayden, a current descendant and the author of *Mrs. Delany, Her Life and Her Flowers.* In the book's dedication Hayden thanks her children and late husband for tolerating her obsession with her ancestor, and I have to thank Ruth Hayden for beginning mine. I became so entranced by Mrs. D.'s collages that I spent a week's worth of mornings in the Print Study Room of the British Museum, where, if you are pleasant and are willing to don a pair of white cotton gloves, you can look at these miracles of drama and precision, and see all 230 pistils of that collage passion flower for yourself.

But back to Lord Lansdowne's dinner table.

Squire Alexander Pendarves held political cards that were necessary to complete the Lord's hand, and so he was invited to stay awhile. Mary was always at table, observing and recoiling in the intense repulsion a sixteen-year-old girl might feel at the sight of a slobbering man. Then one day her uncle invited her to a special tête à tête in which he informed her that he had found an ideal suitor for her, one who could provide a large house and an income, although the majority of this suitor's estate was already pledged to a relative and would not come to her at his death. However, what was that compared to a comfortable life, especially as it would relieve her father of the responsibility of keeping her when her father, as the Lord no doubt did not have to remind her, depended on him, his brother, for income. She had not once seen Alexander Pendarves — forty-four years her senior — sober, or even with his shirt properly tucked in.

For obvious reasons, and very much unlike a fictional Austen heroine, Mary had to say yes to Pendarves. Upon her arrival at his estate, she found a dilapidated house, so dark, dank, and gloomy that, when she saw light at the end of a corridor, she raced toward it, anticipating at last a room she could live in, but discovered when she got there that it had appeared so bright because there was a gaping hole in the roof. She threw herself down on a damp divan and wept.

She was a young woman who had heard a heavy door clang shut on her life. It stayed locked for ten years, until Pendarves died, when she was twenty-six.

I did not hear such a door clang so distinctly shut in my own life, but I continually thought it might. In a house dominated by a violent alcoholic father, I lived in fear of something happening that would prevent me from getting out of Buffalo, going on to college and my own life. Sometimes I even feared I would die. There is a strange way in which the atmosphere of Mary's life at sixteen can enter my own life retrospectively, laying a ghostly silhouette of her emotional circumstances onto the atmosphere of my own experiences. I was not a sexual victim of my father (and she may not have been of Pendarves either — there were no children), but as my father stomped through the house in his underpants, throwing furniture, he exuded an aura of sexual threat that seemed as much a part of the atmosphere of the house as the alcohol-and-smoke-fumed air. As I read the story of the servants helping the drunken Pendarves up the stairs night after night, and undressing him, and shoving him into the bed with Mary, I entered into memories of my father. The image of the girl and drunken older man is so potent that every single woman I've told it to has audibly gulped.

3

At the age of sixteen my mother, graduating early from high school, cut off her hair, got a factory job, and bought a car, a

Model A. It was 1935. With her first paycheck she made a down payment on new furniture for her parents and bought clothes in a store, vowing never to sew another stitch. My grandmother — her mother — embroidered, crocheted, quilted, cut dress patterns, and sewed clothes for everyone. (Watching her, as her grandchild, I knew firsthand the creative power of a pair of scissors.)

By the time she was twenty-two, with six years of semi-independent living under her slender belt (she still lived with her parents), my mother packed her car to head for a new life in California. I think of her California as the equivalent of Mrs. D.'s Ireland. It was Sunday night, December 7, 1941. She planned to set out with her two best girlfriends from the factory the next morning. But by breakfast on the eighth, the news that Pearl Harbor had been bombed reached their hamlet in upstate New York. My grandmother, the embroiderer, pleaded with my mother not to go to California — where she would surely die when the Japanese invaded. But my mother and her friends had the car packed! Their compromise was to drive one and a half hours to Buffalo instead and get assembly-line jobs at Bell Aircraft. My mother's boss was Mary Peacock, my father's aunt. Soon my mother would become Mrs. P., and a door would be shutting for her, too.

4

In the years before he died, Alexander Pendarves suffered from gout. The inflammation of his foot was so severe that he could not bear to be near heat of any kind. He sat in a room without the fireplace on, where dutiful Mary came to read to him. Her teeth must have chattered as she sat for hours next to the cold dead fireplace and read — what, I can only imagine — perhaps Jonathan Swift, whom she would meet later in life.

The absent fire and the warmth of the reading voice remind me of my mother's reading. A creeping depression overtook her after she stopped working at her aircraft job to care for her two young daughters at home, and her former exhilaration dissolved into hours of fantasy reading. Mrs. P. was never without a book, usually a fantasy novel or a Western. She read while she cooked; she read in the bathroom, of course; she read in bed eating chocolate-covered cherries; she read behind the cash register of Peacock's Superette, our grocery store, always with a cigarette ash growing a curved, stemlike shape before it dropped to the page, sometimes burning a little spark-hole in the paper before it went out. She read inside the closed, locked door of her own life. It was the mid-twentieth century, and one would have thought she could have gotten out of the marriage to a degenerating alcoholic, but locked doors can be psychological as well as sociological, and it took her twenty years to extricate herself.

My mother might have felt that Mary got off easy when the Squire kicked the bucket in 1726. After all, she might have reasoned, Mary was only twenty-six, and she was about to embark on a solo life. Mary Granville Pendarves, a charming, amiable widow lacking an inheritance, embarked on almost twenty years as a houseguest, installing herself for weeks at a time in her relatives' houses or on her friends' estates. In those twenty years, she conducted a dead-end flirtation with Lord Baltimore, and wrote in her letters that she didn't think that having children was all it was cracked up to be. Eventually she traveled to Dublin with one of her friends, where she dined at Jonathan Swift's, looking down toward the end of the table to spy a particularly kind face. It was Dr. Patrick Delany, a vicar whom she would later marry, when she was forty-five, against the wishes of her wellborn family. Modest Dr. Delany would, through Mary's connections, become the Dean of Downe, and their twenty-five-year marriage would flourish, allowing her time and space to paint, collect wildflowers, entertain, and collaborate with her husband on their garden.

My mother was forty-five and the mother of two rambunctious young women when she contemplated divorcing my father and embarking on a single life. She sold Peacock's Superette and got a job as a secretary in a hospital.

At the age of forty-five, more like Mrs. Delany than my mother, I embarked on my second marriage, to the man who had been the boy I'd dated in high school, and I am astonished that both my husband and I could experience such a calm and secure midlife happiness.

Is it ridiculous of me to compare my role models — my own mother, who died at seventy-three, and Mrs. Delany, who literally came into a second flowering? I wonder if I am overmanufacturing these links between my role models and myself. Are these details really silhouettes within silhouettes, upside down and inverted, tissue thin?

5

After Patrick Delany's death, Mary would, perhaps as an act of mourning, perhaps as an act of survival, begin the work of her life, collages for which her education, scant in our terms, might have been preparing her since she was a child. Before she was whisked off from London in the middle of the night during the Jacobite crisis, she attended Mademoiselle Puelle's school with almost twenty other little girls. There she learned the art of cutting silhouettes. Perhaps you have seen these silhouettes: complicated affairs with outlines of men in top hats, women in gowns, and children accompanied by dogs or cats chasing balls of yarn. Sometimes the figures play at a game of cards, sometimes they dance. The eye-hand coordination required to make these silhouettes defeats me before I even start to imagine the steps. The miniature scissors! The carefulness of the observation! I cannot even paint my own fingernails successfully. I don't have the focus, and I feel, strangely, that I don't have the time, even though on occasion I have the time to sit in a nail salon and watch with fascination as someone else does it.

One of my mother's prize possessions was a silhouette of me that my teacher did in the early 1950s, when I was in elementary school. At the time I hated it, because my ponytail had gone slack and the teacher had cut out each loose tendril of hair in the silhouette paper. (She had asked each child to step into the light of a projector and to stay still — a feat we accomplished only after being told again and again not to move — while she drew each of our silhouettes onto a piece of construction paper. Later she cut the figure of each child's head and shoulders out of the paper.) I was fascinated by the teacher's dexterity. And my mother was over the moon! She marveled at the tendrils that embarrassed me, and at the fact that the teacher even cut out the tiny lines of my eyelashes.

Now I, too, see the tendrils as moving. The fact that the teacher cared so much for details moves me, and the profile of myself from so many decades ago, so foreign to the profile I have now — I could be a grandmother to myself — moves me as well. Who was that girl? Well, I know, and I don't know. In her collage of the passion flower, Mrs. Delany pays particular attention to the tendrils of the vines, cutting the thin-thinner-thinnest line, almost like pencil lines, out of yellow-green paper. Her devotion to the detail is moving because to notice with such concentration is to be full of emo-

tion. I cannot help but see her project of the *flower mosaiks* as portraits of her midlife passion, portraits of perhaps the woman she
was in the twenty years she was married to Patrick Delany. It is as if
she delved into the details of her happiness. She cut into them.
She snipped them out and touched them again and again as she
positioned them and pasted them on black paper in an act every
bit as tactile as making a pastry or giving a massage or having sex.

They became her next life.

In the British Museum's Print Study Room, as the curator carefully, carefully heaves up one of the volumes Mrs. D. herself pasted
together, and places it on the foam-rubber supports in front of
you, sometimes pieces shred from the jostling. Some curators feel
gloves are essential; others feel gloves only make you clumsier and
don't recommend them. In either case, the fact that a visitor with a
good justification is allowed to touch the edges of these beautiful
oddities — any square inch of which might be replicated and
blown up to become an abstraction very much like an Henri
Matisse cutout — is almost an overwhelming honor. I dreaded
touching them as much as I was hopelessly anxious to be in contact
with them. What if I did something ruinous? Yes, according to one
of the curators, a very helpful young woman named Marta, sometimes a little shower of paper particles accompanies the turning of
a page.

6

At the end of the twenty-year lockup of her marriage, Mrs. Peacock
had the Great Throw Out. She called both of her daughters and
asked them if they wanted anything. Otherwise, it was getting
pitched. My seventh-grade teacher, Mrs. Baeumler, to whom I owe
my writing life, told me later that she hated my mother for pitching
my assignments, including my Revolutionary War diorama picturing events in upstate New York at the time of Mrs. Delany's *flower
mosaiks*. According to Mrs. Baeumler, the diorama was exquisitely
cut out and pasted. (I don't remember it.) I only remember shouting at my mother from the telephone in my college dorm, "I don't
care, Polly! Do what you want!" In my fury I called her by her first
name. (But I had saved some of my artwork in a portfolio that my
mother kept, and she kept the silhouette. I have it still.)

Then Mrs. P. started her new life. I was resentful and wished she
had started it earlier, but I was happy because she had come into
her own energy. She seemed to fill out her own outline, to embody
her silhouette.

Mrs. P. never remarried. Once was absolutely enough. She cared
for her sister, who died in her forties. She cared for her father,
then her mother, until each of them died. Every Friday night, she
drove from her secretarial job at Buffalo General Hospital to the
little house-and-general-store that my grandfather had built in the
early 1920s near Perry, New York, to take care of them, and then,
after they were all gone, to indulge herself in another Great Throw
Out, this time pitching drawerfuls of paper goods: sheet music and
dress patterns of the thirties and forties as well as all of my grandmother's correspondence. On one of my visits I rescued the diaries.

I think of Anne, Mrs. Delany's sister, saving her letters, and generations saving her embroidery. I saved some of my grandmother's
embroidery. To save, one must value. And to throw out, one must
value *moving on*. Interestingly, though she threw out a great deal, I
don't think my mother did move on. Wholesale throwing out only
closes a door against the past, like the door that closed on her life
when she married. You have to sort through the details of the past
in order to process what happened, and then to move. You have to
keep opening and closing the door, ordering and reordering. In
throwing it all away, I think my mother actually stopped herself
from that slow growing, that layering upon layering that is growth
in maturity. She had her great triumph of energy when she got rid
of so much, including my father, but that energy diminished. Eventually, she even sold the little house-and-store, by then a dilapidated shell, enervated, like my mother, and far from its singular
energy when my grandparents were alive.

Patrick and Mary Delany's house and garden, near what has become Dublin's Botanic Gardens, survived until the mid-twentieth
century, when the house, too, was torn down.

7

How is it that Mary Delany, two hundred years before my mother,
who was born at the edge of the Roaring Twenties, seems to have

led a life of greater liberty? Personality and heredity aside, there is the little matter of class. When I first walked along the south side of St. Stephen's Green searching for the bishop's mansion where Mrs. Delany stayed on her first visit to Ireland, and actually found that, though the house she lived in later was demolished, this mansion still existed, now as a government building, what shocked me was the substantial difference in our wealth. Mrs. Delany was related to royalty, to kings and queens, and the mansion she visited, so solid, with its pillars of stone so anchored that the Irish government felt it was solid enough to govern from, was so different from the ephemeral house my grandfather had built near a busy road all by himself, and quickly, with no foundation, just a dirt crawl space underneath. It never had bathrooms or running water, and its electricity was makeshift: one bulb hung down from a socket in each ceiling . . .

Yet the house of my grandfather, who was descended from Northern Irish people, like those farmers to whom the Dean of Downe and his wife Mrs. Delany ministered, charmed the landscape. It was set in an orchard. It was neat and trim as a cottage. Attached to the side of the house and out to the road was a general store and gas station and a garage adorned by gas pumps with round glass heads, like the figures of ghosts children are taught to draw at Halloween. Geraniums at the frosty windowsills bloomed in January. And the view of the rolling landscape of the fruit and wine country west of the Finger Lakes in upstate New York was worthy of the photo shoot *Gourmet* magazine would feature on the happiness of the upstate weekend. I was shocked when I saw the layout. The photographer must have positioned the camera in places I stood to take my own snapshots.

But my branch of the family — farmers and small-business people on my mother's side, truck drivers and factory workers on my father's — had little wealth. And curiously, this seems tied to the fact that they had little wealth of memory.

8

Mrs. P. thought about things she might do and things she might have done, but she never actualized them. She never seemed to decide anything. Drifting from stage to stage in her life, she had ill-formulated goals and never seemed to go after things in a straight-forward way. She settled for less in every situation except friendship, whether it was the choice on a menu or the choice of a divorce lawyer. Was this the limitation of class or the limitation of the post–World War II return to traditional society? Or was it due to the very close mental quarters that were the result of her depressive personality? Or to the fact that she did no art or craft?

Craft is engaging. It results in a product. The mind works in a state of meditation in craft, almost the way we half meditate in heavy physical exercise. There is a marvelously obsessive nature to craft — only an obsessive could have completed nearly a thousand cut-paper botanicals — that allows a person to dive down through the ocean of everyday life to an ocean floor of meditative, repetitive making. It is an antidote to what ails you. It was the method by which Mrs. D. survived her mourning. She had no children. She had likely entered perimenopause before she married the Dean. I haven't any children either, another crucial parallel in our lives. I worry about what I would do if my adored husband predeceases me. If I could dive into an act of mourning like this, repeating the cutting that cut my love from my life, then my role model would teach me how to survive my widowhood.

At about the age of thirty-six, my mother executed six paint-by-number paintings, three winter landscapes and three exotic jungle-scapes prominently featuring peacocks. She spread the work out on the kitchen table and, over several happy years, went at it. One can lose oneself, even in paint-by-number, and the loss of the self within safe confines nurtures the imagination. Craft leads to a contented heart. To ornament one's existence, even with six paint-by-number paintings, is a key to understanding one's personal wealth — and acknowledging that wealth in others, too.

But she stopped. For the next thirty-seven years, she did no making.

Mrs. Delany took her exercise. She walked for miles.

Mrs. Peacock walked to her car and drove to the Family Restaurant for lunch. I loved lunch with my mother. We gossiped, conjectured about the gossip, then drove home the long way around, tucked ourselves in for a nap, then woke to read our novels. After that we would get up from the couches and make supper. Last we would watch TV. When my husband (he is my second husband, *my* Dr. Delany) expressed horror at the fact that I could spend two whole weeks with my mother, I told him that, if I stayed away from certain subjects, it was like a rest cure.

Mrs. P. spent the last half of her life resting up from the first half.

Mrs. D. made all kinds of visually alluring things (I'm not even venturing into the painting, embroidery, and decorative shellwork projects), and she wrote, too: long letters, and even a memoir. In my life I never received a full-length letter from my mother. I have a few scraps of notes in her hand. She refused to write to her own mother or to anyone else. A postscript on a Christmas card was the most you'd get. She generally refused to make social phone calls, though she would answer the phone. You had to come to her. The fury this ignited in me was lifelong. Yet I called. I wrote. Refusing to make, she made me into a maker — into a writer, in fact. Mrs. P. inched her way forward in life, making me seize every opportunity. I had to leap, I had to bound. In not making, she denied herself play, which is the source of the creativity of everyday life. She did nothing fanciful and nothing ornamental except putting her makeup on. She was an attractive woman who drew a line of red lipstick with assurance. She drove a car exceptionally well, and even knew how to fix one.

Why go on comparing these essentially uncomparable women? Have I secretly never outgrown the fantasy everyone has that they have been swapped at birth? That really I'm the daughter of a childless 247-year-old mother? That I could throw away my mother's motto and adopt Mrs. Delany's? Did Mrs. D. even have a motto? If she did, it might have been *You never know what will happen!* Mrs. P.'s motto was *People never change.* But they do. They grow. And they grow old. And despite her motto, Mrs. P. changed.

She gave up smoking. An intense two-pack-a-day lifelong smoker (since the age of fourteen), she up and went cold turkey at the age of sixty-five, eliminating a terrible habit. I had done this some years before, but it had taken me eleven tries, and finally I stopped through a Cancer Society group that held my hand at every stage. My mother walked away from smoking like a gunslinger from a shootout, turning on her heel and striding out of town. Well. There's hope. An imagination activated a vision of a future life.

9

When I was twenty-nine years old, just out of graduate school and at a tiny conference held by the funders of the fellowship that had supported me and some other writers and scholars through graduate school, I felt absolutely exhausted by the prospect of creating my life. In the cushy, quiet living room of a large house commandeered by the conference for the purpose of debriefing their newly degreed students, I heard an exasperated voice belting out of me. "I'm sick of being a pioneer!" I declared, but I found I couldn't really answer any questions about what I was pioneering, and so the conversation among the new elite eddied around me until I calmed down and joined in again. What I meant was, I was sick of the loneliness of leaving my working-class family. Not that I loved them in a fairytale way — you can't love depression or alcoholism in that way — but my family was a family; bleak and bizarre as it all was, Mrs. P. encouraged me to make my own life. She firmly felt it was possible for me, but she didn't know how to show me. One thing her life did give me was a hatred of being adrift. I like to be doing things, creating things, going places.

One day in February 2003, in the heart of the happiness of midlife, having just left Oxford University, where my husband had given a lecture and I had given a poetry reading, we ended up in London, having just enough time to peek into the new atrium of the British Museum and be enthralled by the winter light. Unusually, it had just snowed. My husband went to make a phone call, which seemed to be taking ages. I wanted to sit down, so I found a bench outside the gift shop, where I became restless. That phone call was really going on and on . . . I ventured into the gift shop and found a catalogue called *Mrs. Delany, Her Life and Her Flowers*.

There it was! When I was in my thirties, I had been thrilled by the *flower mosaics* of Mary Delany when they had traveled to New York, to the Morgan Library, to be displayed in a special exhibition. I went back several times. I was so poor at the time (teaching seventh grade in a private school and trying to write poetry) that I would sublet my apartment at the end of the month and move in with my boyfriend for the weekend in order to get the money to pay my rent. I would have loved to purchase the catalogue, but it was too expensive. I passed it up. Now here it was again, popping up just when I needed it, just as answers pop up if you are always carrying on a sub-rosa search for them. I read the book. I found a role model, one born at the start of a century I had previously ignored. The phone call was over and it was time to go to the airport. I had no time to find the prints at the museum during that trip. But I could buy and read the book and find out some things, just the way my mother taught me to. And so I did.

As I was reading, I had that familiar but blurry role-model-searching-wandering feeling, that looking-through-the-back-of-the-drawers-of-experience sensation. As I looked at the passion flower in the book, *Passiflora Laurifolia, Bay Leaved,* a mosaic of images bobbed up and down in my mental stream, carried by a current of years from my grandmother's seed catalogues to my mother's high school prize for Latin vocabulary to the shockingly vulvular purplish pinks of the 230 petals cut out by the gray-haired, bonnet-wearing, black-clad lady thought to be Mary Delany, in a painting by Benjamin West. I leaned closer, bedazzled by the slenderest ivory veins in the leaf of the passion flower, also cut from paper, and the tendrils finer than a girl's hair, and the shading of greens: there are olives, browns, dark greens, medium greens, beige-ivories . . . Counting the colors of the pieces of paper is as bewildering as counting the papers themselves. I saw a complex world.

Complexity! That was it. I saw the vision of a person who was not remotely interested in simplification, in the lessening of experience in order to smooth out the complicated contrariness of its elements. Mrs. D. took those scissors and she got it all, every single wisp in the field of her vision. On the day several years later when I was looking at the original of this cut-paper *mosaik* in the British Museum, a botanist writing about geraniums had come to check something against the reliably factual vision of Mrs. Delany, still utterly dependable after 230 years. She did work that could be searched. She was someone for whom I had searched, feeling always how complicated life is, what a multitude of vectors brings us to the moment where we are, and where we love, or cough, or say the wrong thing, or fail, or feel our fate in what we fear, or to a moment when clarity descends and we understand the world simply from having observed it. To search a drawer or a pocketbook, feeling for one's conscience or one's heart, even to search the world, or only to search a website, means to look for something that will complete — with a key, a tissue, a truth, a love, a victory, a sliver of knowledge — an instant of one's being, or perhaps one's whole life.

That is why we need our role models long past adolescence. It is because figuring out how to go on from one place in life to another repeats the confusion of youth. Living a full life requires invention, as Mrs. Delany shows us nearly a thousand times with each of her botanicals. All invention requires a previous pattern, if only to react against, as I've often reacted against my mother's, or, more positively, to refigure in the making of something new. The work of these other lives provides a balm of answering likeness.

PHILLIP ROBERTSON

In the Mosque of Imam Ali

FROM TRIQUARTERLY

Sungsu Cho

CHO IS DOING SOMETHING to a cigarette with his fingers. He's rolling it back and forth until the tobacco falls out onto a sweat-damp handkerchief full of black hash. He mixes the tobacco with the stuff we scored in Baghdad and then puts it back in the cigarette like a surgeon. Cho is the acknowledged master of this art and executes his moves with precision, with the same fingers that sold vegetables in a market in Seoul. Cho would go anywhere in the war, and if he wanted you to stick around, he would say, "Yeah, you stay here with me, okay?" Distracted and tired, he would make you dinner with the kimchi he had flown in from Seoul. I wrote the captions for his photographs because it wasn't easy for him. Cho's father was a retired South Korean military officer, and I always wanted to know what had happened that drew Cho to war zones. It was something his father never got over. I want to weep, seeing him there in the car next to his pile of forgotten Nikons.

Up front, Cho's driver, Ibrahim, is getting upset. From the back seat I can see him twisting around, trying to figure out what will stop Cho from going through with it, but Ibrahim is forced to watch the road for speeding traffic, for insurgents hunting the roads for American convoys. We are passing Hilla and Babylon, heading north at eighty miles an hour into a highway of bombs and ten-mile traffic jams. Ibrahim is spooked because his passengers are going to get high and fill his car with hash fumes. He keeps twisting around in the driver's seat to give us a look, but there's nothing he can do. I can tell he thinks that the trip is another bad-luck proposition from the nervous animal sounds coming from his throat.

We speed down the road while Ibrahim swerves away from other cars and twitches the wheel back and forth. "It's total fucking bullshit," Cho says, and lights up just as we cross into the Sunni Triangle. He is referring to everything. Thirty miles south of Baghdad, the highway that runs through the towns of Latayfiya and Yusufiya is one of the most violent stretches of road in the country. It is a major artery for religious pilgrims on their way to Najaf and a critical supply route for goods from Kuwait. In a zone from Al Haswa to the outskirts of Baghdad, the sons of Sunni farmers attack U.S. forces and anyone connected to the provisional government. Everyone is a potential target. After the bombs detonate, throwing columns of oil-black smoke into the air, the fighters disappear into a network of irrigation canals and palm groves. American patrols have never come close to owning this road. Instead, they roll down it at high speed with their guns up, waiting for the high signaling crack of a Kalashnikov and the blood-starved spirits of the air.

I watch the low dust-colored buildings retreat along the sides of the highway, hiding men with rocket launchers and rifles who watch the stream of cars between Baghdad and Shiite central Iraq. We have white rimes of salt under our arms from the sun. It is Friday afternoon, the terminal stages of July, and we are going steadily through light that is gold and then red as it falls on the stands of palms along the Euphrates River. The sun is burning in the west under the empty screen of the sky.

Cho has this handsome Frankenstein face. He takes a drag and lets it out and the car fills with the smell of dope. We smoke in the back and hide our faces from boys selling soft drinks by the side of the road. Children work as spotters for kidnapping teams. When Ibrahim cracks a window, the vapors stream out behind the car in a comet's tail and the purified dread washes out of us. Riding through this dark stretch that spawns hundreds of fear myths, we are outside the war. The hash makes us feel invisible.

A few weeks earlier, during the first clashes between the U.S. military and the Mahdi Army, I found a driver in front of the Hamra

Hotel who panicked on the way south to Najaf. His name was Hekmat, and he finally lost it on the road near Latayfiya. We had stopped at a U.S. roadblock, which is where Hekmat quit and said he couldn't go any farther. He was faking car trouble and said he couldn't get the car to start, but he had secretly thrown a switch under the dash to disable the ignition. If I'd found the switch I would have stolen the car. Traffic was backed up for miles because a patrol had found a roadside bomb and the Americans providing security for the sappers were nervous. They were standing in a row behind a coil of razor wire stretched across the asphalt with their weapons up, with rounds in the chambers. An Iraqi man walked forward with his four-year-old son in front of him until a soldier lowered his M-16. The man wanted to ask when the road would be clear. They didn't know. A young tanker yelled to me, "Hey, how's the sushi in California?" He wanted to know how reporters moved around the Mahdi Army areas. I told him about the safe-passage letters I carried and how they didn't work all the time, how the soldiers wouldn't let me through because their lieutenant hated reporters and the letters made them suspicious.

We listened to the sappers detonate the roadside bombs a mile down the highway. The sound was like a giant fist hitting a soft pillow. While I was trying to talk to the soldiers at the roadblock, Hekmat turned his car around and headed back to Baghdad. I caught a ride with some workers on a bus going to Iskandariya. The bus driver, who knew a way around the roadblock, turned off the highway into the patchwork of fields and irrigation canals around the town. A few minutes later, deep in this Euphrates River farmland, I saw a thin kid in a white dishdasha looking through windshields at the passengers in the cars. The kid had a walkie-talkie he was using to talk to fighters down the road about who was coming through their sector. He wasn't interested in the workers and the beat-up bus, and so he missed the foreigner. It was amazing how close you could get to the edge and still come back, like an amusement park ride or a submarine tour of the bottom of the ocean.

By late July 2004 the uprisings had spread across Iraq, pulling villages and major cities into open warfare, and the United States was calling in air strikes and heavy armor until we had the feeling that the whole thing was going to end in apocalypse, a great shout of blood and heat. The road south of Baghdad had rolled all the way out until it was the country itself.

While we drive toward Baghdad, twenty miles away, Moqtada al-Sadr wears a white martyr's shroud and prepares to speak to thousands of his followers in the courtyard of the vast Kufa mosque. It marks the place where Imam Ali, the first Shiite saint, was murdered. Moqtada's father, Mohammed Sadiq al-Sadr, gave sermons at this mosque until he was assassinated by security agents working for Saddam Hussein. Moqtada is the son of a martyr, and the shroud symbolizes his willingness to follow his father into death. On the grounds of the mosque there is no space to move: the courtyard is full of worshipers and perhaps ten thousand men cover the marble stones like a sea. They wait until a shattering sound comes from speakers in the minarets, the name of God in a hundred rising and falling notes. Its carrier wave is the breaking voice of a young man, one of the Mahdi revolutionaries. When the militiamen hear him, they stand absolutely still with their hands at their sides, the differences between the men washed away by the name of God. The muezzin's call holds them outside time until the voice they hear ceases to emanate from the singer; it now belongs to the myriad men in black shirts and sandals who no longer want to live in the corrupt world. The voice kills and resurrects. Hearing the call is like having electrical wires run through your veins. It sounds like heartbreak. They pray and touch their heads to the ground and rise again.

After the call, al-Sadr begins to speak. The cleric promises he will never leave his followers, that he is prepared to die for them. "I will never abandon you, no matter what, and I am close to you and living the same life as you." In his unrefined Arabic al-Sadr urges them forward into the guns of the Americans with the following chain of associations: I am like Imam Ali, the first martyr of the Shiites, and I am prepared to die. If you follow me, then you must also be prepared for death. In order to be a saint, you must die.

Death is the only way to free yourself from the corruption of the world. "There is no stench in paradise," a fighter told me when I asked what he thought death was like. "Things don't rot like they do here." In the mosque, the crowd of men in their black shirts stand under the crucible sun, hypnotized by their savior. It's a hundred and fifteen degrees, and the waves of sound from the public-address system are breaking on the high walls of the mosque. Al-Sadr tells them that the war against the Americans is going to begin, and he wants them to be ready.

The men believe al-Sadr is the disappeared twelfth imam, returning to deliver them from evil and injustice at the end of the world. "He is just like a lion. He is the Lion of God," one Mahdi Army fighter said to me during one of these faith rallies, his eyes ecstatic. They were all thinking the same thing, it didn't really matter whom you asked. Soon they would hallucinate. In the Kufa mosque, thousands of young men are kneeling in rows behind al-Sadr to pray while other, identical men standing on the walls of the Kufa mosque scan the dead horizon with rifle scopes. Many of the older fighters rose up against Saddam after the gulf war. When you met them in their homes, the first thing they showed you were the pictures they took in Abu Ghraib.

The ceasefire that has lasted for nearly a month is on the verge of collapse. The war will start in a matter of days, but we don't know it yet. There's a feeling of dread. U.S. forces have demanded that Mahdi Army forces withdraw from Najaf and Kufa, and the Mahdi Army demands that the Americans withdraw from Iraq. Ayatollah Sistani and the old sheikhs of the surrounding towns have said that they want the Mahdi Army to withdraw. Moqtada al-Sadr publicly refuses, saying he will follow the dictates of only the highest religious authorities. It's a strange statement to make. Sistani is the highest Shiite authority, and he is being ignored. The present uprising led by al-Sadr grew out of Shiite congregations all over the country but is fueled by young men who have nothing. Just before the uprisings started, Pro–Mahdi Army imams urged Iraqis to join the movement, to travel to Najaf and take a stand to defend their religion. Thousands obeyed.

The Well

In the evening, hordes of bats flew down from the tops of buildings to drink from the Hamra pool. The bats, falling and wheeling through the soft air, nicked the glassy surface of the water and then returned in a single arc to the rooftops of the buildings where they lived. Every night I watched their trajectories, amazed. The pool was the one place everyone went. It attracted and repelled. It was beautiful when the power went out. When the city's electricity failed, everything went black except the pool, radiating its silent blue reactor light.

South African mercenaries ended up there, and every time a mortar round went by overhead they would take defensive positions in the halls, crouching in corners. Some of these men were enormously fat and wore the gregarious faces of Down's syndrome. The older mercenaries had spent serious time in Angola, and the rifles in their giant meaty hands were like miniature theater props, useless. They smiled like children. It was surprising that a mortar never hit the pool. I wished for one in a perverse way — anything that would shut down the fucked-up conversation.

We heard things all the time. "You know, force is the only thing the Arabs understand." The man goes on, "Well, maybe Saddam was right to run the place with an iron fist. I mean, look at these people, look at how they live." The guy laughs, drinks his beer. The Abu Ghraib torture photographs are all over the news in every country of the world. "Now, Ahmed, for God's sake, bring some ketchup." The only thing to do was to find a table far from the mercenaries and pray they would get drunk.

When an attack finally came, it wasn't a mortar. It was a car bomb positioned near the hotel checkpoint that missed the Australian ambassador but killed a ten-year-old cigarette vendor named Ali. When the bomb went off, fifty yards from the Dulaimi Hotel, the hallways filled with dust and the windows were blown into the rooms. When I opened the door, the hallway stretched away in a long cloud. I thought something was wrong with my eyes. On another floor a woman was screaming. We ran outside, and since there was nothing else to do, we watched the car burn. Later that day, a funeral procession for Ali made its way through the Jadriya neighborhood in central Baghdad. The boy's house was only a few feet from where he was killed. His family wrapped the body in white, for martyrdom, and Ali's mother screamed at Bush for doing this to her son.

Everyone had their theories about the Iraqis. A skinny kid in the First Infantry Division told me that summer, "Hell, if it makes sense, Hajji don't do it. But he's getting pretty smart now. He's turning those PVC tubes you see all around here into launchers. I'm saying you gotta watch Hajji real close." Hajji, the honorific for older men or men who have made the pilgrimage to Mecca, is a term used for the enemy.

"You know what Hajji means, right?" I asked him.

"Yeah. We like to call 'em Hajjis."

We were on a First Cavalry base in Sadr City, and the soldier pointed toward some Iraqi workers milling around the store. "See those guys over there? They're probably spotting for the mortar teams on their cell phones. Shit, here comes another one." There was the cartoonish descending whistle, and the mortar hit near the command center. We huddled in the doorway of the aid station while shrapnel cut through the air. The guys laughed when more mortars came screaming down near the aid station from across the river, and they looked at me as if to say, See what we go through, buddy?

During evening prayers we listened to the imams broadcast bloody sermons, howling that the occupier was an enemy of God. A few weeks later, those same soldiers of the 1–5 Cav would be sent down to Najaf, into the vast necropolis with its million tombs, firing rounds at Mahdi Army positions next to the shrine walls. We would be only a few hundred feet apart during the siege, on opposite sides of the lines.

I was sitting by the pool in the warm evening air when Cho brought me a beer. He sat down next to me and said, "I have a good contact in Sadr City. Maybe he's the best one."

"Sure. I have contacts there too, Cho."

"Yes, but this one is different."

"They're all different."

"No. This guy is a really powerful guy, I call him Little Saddam, as a joke."

"Who is he?"

"He's a journalist, but he's more than a journalist. You can meet him if you want. I will arrange it."

"Tomorrow?"

"Tomorrow."

We drank our beers and I forgot about everything, and then I walked to the Dulaimi Hotel, the moldering wreck where second-rate Iraqi drivers waited for customers in the threadbare lobby. When kidnappers freed up most of the fourth floor, a wire-service report called it the "Eerie Dulaime," suggesting that the place was cursed. French TV crews came out to investigate.

We loved the place. It was a kingdom of stories and near misses. Because the rates were cheap, stringers and freelance photographers filled its rooms. Hamza Dulaime, the sheikh's son, would give freelancers a deal if he saw long-term prospects. When I was broke, Hamza waited for the money. "Don't worry about it," he said to me. This generosity, a willingness to discuss matters, is an Arab trait. It saved us. There were four filmmakers, a few writers, a gang of photographers. We left our doors open, friends stopped by with news, resistance contacts dropped by for coffee. In the hotel, we were all spied on and cajoled, given incredible information. At night, when the resistance was gone and the work was done, we got high and watched images of burning cars on the BBC. We turned the sound off, replaced it with Led Zeppelin.

I took the elevator to the third floor, to room 25. Its windows looked out over Jadriya Street. It had a pink linoleum dance floor, sharkskin-green furniture, a balcony from which one could possibly escape. From the windows I watched Apache helicopters hunt for mortar teams in the palm groves. These men would fire volleys of mortars at the Green Zone and disappear. At six in the morning, the dull thumps of bombs going off under American patrols woke us up.

Fatah al-Sheikh

At nine the next morning, I met Cho and we drove to the edge of Sadr City to meet his special contact, Fatah al-Sheikh. When we arrived at his office, in a small Internet café, Fatah, hoarse and barrel-chested, was on the phone arranging something. He talked about how he had just come back from Iran, showing us a photo album of snapshots taken with various officials. Fatah standing in front of an automated printing press. Fatah staring at the camera in front of a fountain. Fatah talking to a mullah. This man promotes himself, I thought. He gets around.

Our first meeting lasted half an hour, and I learned nothing, but

he learned a few things about us. While he was out of the room, his
lieutenants asked me what country I was from, the name of the paper I worked for, going over and over the same questions. "Do you
have another job besides journalist?" one of the men wanted to
know. I said no and explained that I was from Ireland. A lie. I
didn't know who they were.

Fatah was interested in talking. When I asked him to give an interview on tape, the sight of the black Panasonic video camera excited him so much that he went on for a full hour about his perse-
cution at the hands of Saddam. As he spoke, he spooled out
his history in a cheerful way, with no inflection, no pause for
thought. Fatah sounded upbeat when he described being tortured
by Saddam. Where were the signs of shame and trauma? Nowhere.
Fatah seemed to be an intelligent and optimistic man whose
phone rang every few minutes. He also made sure we knew that he
had access to fighters in the Mahdi Army, not just the political
leaders. I let him become my primary contact in Sadr City. I introduced him to colleagues, invited him back to the hotel for lunch.

A few days later, I stopped by the Internet café to give Fatah a
copy of his videotaped interview. Just before I left, possibly to return the favor, he went to his computer and said he had something
interesting to show me. Fatah printed out a document that had an
official Mahdi Army seal at the top. It was a mobilization order for
the followers of Moqtada al-Sadr. It said that the truce would end
in twenty-four hours. Fatah gave me a copy and smiled. This was
August 4, 2004. I took the document to a BBC reporter, and it was
broadcast that evening. By the following day, the truce that had
held for a month collapsed and major battles were raging in Najaf
and Sadr City. The siege had begun.

A week into the Shiite uprising, I was on my way to Fatah's office
when I got a telephone call from a friend who said that Cho had
been kidnapped in Sadr City. The only person we knew who had
enough leverage to get him out was Fatah. When I arrived at the
Internet café, Cho was sitting in the back room, badly beaten, his
face bleeding and his clothes torn. His attackers had destroyed his
Nikons and robbed him of everything else.

"What happened?"

Cho shook his head. "I can't tell you here."

Four attackers had fired at him while he was trapped in his car, then they pulled him out and pistol-whipped him. The men said they were going to kill him. After Cho left the café, I stayed behind because Fatah asked me to talk to him about what had happened. Around seven o'clock, just as it was getting dark, a white station wagon pulled up with the men who had attacked Cho. I was not allowed to go to the window when Fatah went out to greet them. Fatah had been the one who'd arranged the attack.

There are several reasons why he would benefit from that act of violence. He was a brutal and cunning man who used fear and secret-police methods to gather information. I learned later that he was not above outright murder. Fatah's method was simple: if he found a weakness, he exploited it by leaning on the compromised person to provide information about his friends. It was the signature style of a Baath Party agent, a member of the Mukhabarat, the Iraqi intelligence agency. Blackmail and carefully made threats were his instruments. A day after the attack on Cho, I met Fatah at a restaurant near his office and was interrogated. His precise and thorough questioning made it seem like a professional job.

"You are from which country? Tell me again."

"Ireland."

Pause.

"I heard that you are an American. Maybe you have dual nationality?"

Pause.

"Who said that?"

"The sheikh said it. He says that I do not know enough about you, that I am spending time with a man who is not truthful, and this was very embarrassing for me."

"Which sheikh?"

"You were acting suspiciously in Najaf, and there was an investigation."

"That's ridiculous."

Fatah was angry. "I need to see your passport immediately."

"I don't have it with me."

"No?"

"No. I don't carry it with me because of thieves."

"You can tell me if you are an American, because I am a sophisticated man."

"I am an American."

Fatah smiled. He was genuinely happy. He hated Americans. That was something I knew.

"You must tell me everything."

"That's all there is to tell, Fatah."

"You look sick. Are you afraid of something?"

"No."

"If you are afraid of something, and you run, then I know you are guilty."

Fatah held a cup of water and poured it out in a smear across the table. Dead light came off the surface. "You see? The problem is finished between us. That is how we finish things in Iraq."

It is possible that he had Cho beaten to coerce me into giving him information about our friends and colleagues. This Fatah incident is central to how we got to the shrine in Najaf during the siege. We went to Najaf because staying in Baghdad seemed like a bad idea. I was running from him.

How did Fatah know so much about us? A few of us at the Dulaime had had intelligence files under the previous government. Thorne Anderson, a photojournalist and close friend I'd met in Afghanistan, was deported by the Mukhabarat during the early days of the invasion. His partner, Kael Alford, also a photojournalist, was one of the few Westerners allowed to stay. Government minders and intelligence people had watched both of them closely because Thorne and Kael were also Americans. They had covered the Balkan wars, lived in impoverished eastern European countries, were fans of literature. We listened to the same weird music and lived in the Dulaime Hotel. Thorne played Daniel Johnston songs on a ruined guitar by the pool.

After the first session in the restaurant across from the Internet café, Fatah took me over to the Habaibna restaurant for the second phase of my interrogation.

"Now, tell me, who is the woman you were talking to at the Hamra pool a few days ago?"

"Which woman?"

"The pretty one, the blond one." Fatah was talking about Kael.

"I don't know who you mean."

"I know that you know her, she smiled at you. Remember? I saw you."

"I still don't know who you're talking about, Fatah. I'm sorry."

"Her husband — you know him?"

"No. I don't know them."

"Where are they from? Which country? Who do they work for?"

"I don't know who you are talking about. They are not my friends, Fatah."

"I think they are your friends. She smiled at you, the pretty one at the pool. I saw her."

"Maybe she smiled, Fatah. I say hello to everyone."

"You know her but you will not say." Fatah laughs. His lieutenants were watching me.

"That is not the case. I just don't know her."

"If you are afraid, you can leave now. But if you are very afraid, then there is certainly some problem, and then I cannot save you."

"I am not afraid."

Fatah smiles, because he knows fear when he sees it.

"Should we eat?" He calls the waiter over.

When I left Sadr City that night, we drove out through a maze of roadblocks formed by lines of burning fuel. Mahdi Army fighters were out pouring gasoline on the ground and setting it ablaze. When the asphalt melted, they dug shallow trenches and filled them with artillery shells. All the bombs were being laid at night. Fighters would wait for a U.S. patrol to drive by, then detonate a bomb from a nearby market stall or house. On the way out of Sadr City, I noticed that Mahdi Army checkpoints had appeared at every major street and intersection. We were stopped and questioned by nervous fighters, all of them looking for spies. The Mahdi Army was sowing Sadr City with explosives.

Back at the Dulaime, I spoke to Thorne and Kael about the Fatah interrogation and his involvement in the attack on Cho as news of the Shiite uprising poured out of the television. Cho, recovering from the pistol-whipping, had made plans to leave the country after talking to South Korean embassy officials. The innocent period in Baghdad was over, and I found that I couldn't easily write or work. I quickly suspected everyone of spying on us, especially drivers and translators. I stopped talking to Iraqis.

Meanwhile, Najaf was besieged by U.S. forces, and the few Western reporters who had found a way of getting into the old city

didn't stick around. I drifted around the hotel in Baghdad, falling
into a deep depression that lasted nearly two weeks. I felt locked
out of Najaf, where I'd had good contacts among the senior leadership of the Mahdi Army. All the time spent in the Shiite holy city
seemed wasted, and I'd missed the chance to get inside when the
door was still open. I became a prisoner of the Dulaime, paralyzed
and bitter.

To the Shrine

After August 5, 2004, U.S. forces closed in on the old city of Najaf,
but it was not a lightning attack. Elements of the First Cavalry Division sealed off major roads to the necropolis on the north side of
town and began pushing south, toward the shrine of Imam Ali in
central Najaf. Marine units moved in from the south and sealed off
Medina Street. Apache helicopters began launching attacks from
the floodplain in the west, called the Najaf Sea. At the start of the
siege, residents of Najaf heard loudspeaker announcements telling
them to leave the city, which sparked an exodus to the outlying
suburbs. Within hours, most of the city was empty except for
Mahdi Army soldiers and clerics loyal to Moqtada al-Sadr. U.S.
forces formed an unbroken ring outside the old city, with the
shrine at its center. Young men loyal to al-Sadr poured into Najaf
to reinforce the fighters. They had little equipment except their
faith in God.

  Most of the press was holed up in a hotel outside the U.S. cordon, too far away to see anything but flashes of light from the
pitched battle in the cemetery. We watched BBC broadcasts that
were little more than a rehash of what U.S. military commanders
were saying. What was happening at the center of the Mahdi Army
movement, inside the universe of the shrine, was hidden from
view. No information was leaving the old city.

When Shiite Muslims enter the shrine, they kiss the doorjambs of
the great wooden gates to greet Imam Ali, whose spirit they believe
resides there. Pilgrims speak to him as if he were alive. The shrine
is thought to have healing powers, and the old, the sick, and the
mad take shelter within its grounds. I had been there a number of
times. In the spring, a friend named Abu Hussein invited me to the

tomb. We walked through the gates and across a great expanse of polished marble, which reflected the sun, to a smaller building covered in gold plates. We took off our shoes and walked inside to an antechamber of green marble whose walls and vaulted ceilings were tiled with thousands of mirrors. Men prayed, edging closer to the tomb. Imam Ali is entombed behind a silver screen, behind glass, in darkness. Pilgrims circled the tomb, running their hands over the silver, pausing to kiss it and utter prayers. A twelve-year-old boy who was mentally ill chanted verses from the Koran, and the pilgrims assented, prayed with him, kissed the tomb every few steps. This is one of the most revered places on earth. Inside the tomb you feel surrounded by a collective consciousness that is dreaming of the past. Your image is reflected in ten thousand mirrored tiles that adorn the marble interior of the building. A few hundred feet away, more than a million people lie buried.

On August 16, Thorne Anderson knocked on the door of room 25. We were restless and sick of being holed up in the hotel. Thorne closed the door behind him and said, "What do you want to do?"

"I think we should go to Najaf," I said.

"How are we going to get in, if we get close enough?"

"There's a safe-passage letter from Sheikh Ahmed Sheibani I've been showing around."

Thorne thought about it and said he wanted to go. We decided to leave the next morning.

We didn't tell anyone about our plans to try to cross the siege lines. Other friends dropped by and asked what we were going to do, but we kept it an absolute secret. Kael Alford was already in Najaf, moving around the front lines near the old city, but she was unable to enter because her group was drawing fire. In the morning, we hired a translator named Basim and a driver to take us to Najaf, but they were not happy about making the trip. Basim said, "Phillip, I really think we should tell Fatah where we're going."

"No fucking way," I said. Fatah had threatened the translator, demanding reports on us.

"I think we are all going to die," Basim said in his strange high-pitched voice.

"Stop panicking, Basim."

We drove through the southern suburbs of Baghdad, past the black smoke-plume of the Doura power station. When Basim spoke again, he said, "Phillip, Iraq is like a universe without a god. There are no laws. The result is complete chaos."

In Kufa, a few kilometers from Najaf, a fighter motioned with his Kalashnikov for us to get out of the car. A cleric took us to the mosque, gave us water, and invited us to lunch. They treated us well, and we stuck around a commander's office for the rest of the afternoon, thinking we might be able to find out about an underground railroad to the shrine, starting at the mosque in Kufa.

The commander watched us. We waited in his office for four hours, begged for his help. He said he was sorry, but he couldn't help us. Thorne sat on the floor and made conversation with the commander. We dozed until a fighter came running in to show us a captured American antitank weapon. The missile had been fired, but he was proud — he wanted to show us the empty casing. We admired it. Then the fighter showed us his Strela antiaircraft missile launcher with the missile still in it. He'd come from the old city.

A stream of men arrived with donated food supplies that the commander received graciously, recording the items in a giant ledger before locking them away. I remember that an old man walked in and told us that he had come from the old city. This was the first break. A few minutes later, an assistant to the Mahdi Army commander of the Kufa mosque offered to take us across the lines. The assistant's name was Talib. He was a thin, serious man in his late thirties, a laborer who had fought against Saddam in the nineties. He seemed honest and straightforward.

Late in the afternoon, as the sun was going down, we took Talib with us and drove toward Najaf, winding our way through the dust-choked southern suburbs, stopping only when Bradleys were too close or tanks appeared around corners. At the edge of the city we got out of the car and listened to the deafening explosions coming from town. Pressure waves hit us in the chest. It was impossible to go forward because of the fighting on the routes leading into the city. Basim and the driver were panicking, and we slowly retraced our route out of town. Talib told us to stay in a hotel in Kufa run by his friends; we'd try again the next morning. Talib said he would come for us at seven when the bombing was less intense. It was like

waiting for a break in the weather. "Don't go outside, don't let anyone see you," he said as we unpacked the gear.

A few minutes later, Basim and our driver told us they were driving back to Baghdad without us. "You will die, one hundred percent. If you go in, you won't come out."

"Basim, aren't you a little panicky?" I asked.

"Absolutely not."

Thorne told Basim to take it easy, but there was no talking to
him. Basim was convinced of his own death.

By eight o'clock that night we were stranded in Kufa without a
driver or a translator. We ate a meal of shwarma sandwiches and
stayed away from the windows.

On the roof of the hotel in Kufa, Thorne put in a satellite call to
Mitch Prothero, another journalist at the Dulaime, and told him
we were stuck. Mitch said he would send a translator down for us
and to expect him in the morning. We expected nothing. At six-
thirty, Yassir opened the door of our room and found us after we'd
stayed up all night listening to gunfire outside the hotel. Yassir was
ready to go.

We took a cab to the edge of Najaf, retracing the route of the
previous day. In the dusty suburbs of the city we got out to walk the
three miles to the shrine. Yassir, calm and steady, walked next to us.
We thought there wouldn't be much fighting in the early morning,
but there was a great deal of it. Tympanum sounds. Tearing noises
that went beyond mere machinery. It was the sound of a battle between heaven and hell.

I tasted copper in my mouth as we walked. Clouds of dust rose
over the warren of houses in the old city. We heard fifty-caliber machine guns, rocket-propelled grenades, and Hellfire missiles fired
from attack helicopters. We made our way slowly toward the American lines at Medina Street, following a trickle of old men and
women. We walked north, talking to passing Najafis who warned us
away from snipers. One middle-aged man offered us water and
sanctuary. Men stood outside their houses with their sons, listening
to the war. A crowd followed us and then disappeared. We continued. Talib told us that if the Iraqi police caught us going into
Najaf, they would shoot us. They were worse than the Mahdi Army,
he said.

At one empty intersection, a man in Bedouin robes said we could cross Medina Street, explaining that he had just crossed the U.S. cordon without any problems. When we arrived at the open boulevard, between two Bradleys, we held our hands over our heads in surrender and stepped into the street. It was a weightless feeling.

A block farther in, the city was in ruins. Scorched shards of buildings faced streets filled with burned cars and fallen electrical cables. We had entered a no man's land between the two opposing forces. When we came across our second Bradley, Talib left us, turning back toward the suburbs. A few minutes later, some Mahdi boys replaced him, leading us deeper into the city. We followed them through a burned market, which smelled like death, bordered by the ruined Tho al Fikar Hotel. The boys laughed and ran ahead of us, shouting, "Which channel, which channel?"

When they yelled into the ruins, we heard shouts coming from empty windows in the buildings where the fighters were hiding. A head would appear wearing the green band of the Mahdi Army. Fighters waved to us. We waved back so they wouldn't shoot us. We came upon a small group of fighters who offered to help us reach the shrine. I told their commander that I wanted to speak to Sheikh Ahmed Sheibani, an adviser to Moqtada al-Sadr, and they agreed to send someone with us. Past the hotel, we arrived at the boundary of the old city, a wide-open boulevard we would have to cross.

When we were halfway to the other side, walking with our hands up, a sniper opened fire on us. Thorne was caught in the middle of the street and had to take cover. I ran behind a column and listened to the rounds slam into the concrete a few inches away. By the time we were out of the sniper's line of fire, we'd crossed into the old city, inside Mahdi lines. I gave the old letter of safe passage, written by Sheikh Ahmed, to a young man, and he told us to come with him.

The shrine's dome glowed in the sun about five hundred yards away. Rows of young men covered in ammunition belts, holding rifles and heavy weapons, hid in the shade of the long street. They shouted to us as we passed them. Ammunition and rockets were carefully stacked at their feet. We were at the shrine a few minutes later and, like devoted Shiites, when we crossed the threshold we touched the great carved wooden doors.

Inside the Walls

The shrine of Imam Ali is in the center of the old city, a few hundred feet south of the largest cemetery in the world. Its walls, laid out in a perfect square, are of deep red brick and at least fifty feet high. The outer walls are plain, but inside the gates, there is a sea of white marble that reflects the sun. The inner walls are covered in blue tiles that evoke the infinite forms of God. In the center of the courtyard is the tomb, covered in gold tiles. Caretakers continually wash the marble flagstones with water to keep them clean.

When we arrived after crossing the burned no man's land, the steps of the south-facing gate were smeared with the blood of fighters. The caretakers were busy because blood must not spill on the grounds of a mosque. They did not have much time to rest. Young Mahdi fighters running down Rasul Street were being blown to pieces by armored units firing from across Medina Street. Fighters loaded up the dead and wounded Mahdi volunteers in wooden carts and ran them up to the south gate, and a makeshift infirmary in the mosque. The doctors let us go inside. We watched one fighter carry a dead comrade to the infirmary, a severed forearm in a cigarette box, the stump of a leg jutting from his black dishdasha. The fighter, mad with grief, screamed at a doctor to save his friend, but the body was already the color of ashes. I watched the doctor pretend to take a pulse from the corpse to calm the fighter down. Blood ran on the marble floor as the fighters brought in another wounded militiaman, who made the victory sign with both hands as they treated him.

Sheikh Ahmed Sheibani, the Mahdi cleric and spokesman, wasn't in when we arrived, so the fighters gave us water and allowed us to wait in his office. We could hear the First Cavalry fighting in the cemetery, and there was a fierce battle between armored units, aircraft, and the militiamen hiding in underground tombs. With each passing hour, the Mahdi Army was losing ground, their men facing unbelievable American weapons with no hesitation. Most of the men who went into the cemetery to fight the Americans didn't come back. An Apache gunner named Joe Bruhl told me about the battle: "We'd fly over and I'd punch off a missile at one of their mortar teams, killing all of them. Then I'd see other guys run in and *pick up the weapons* the first guys dropped and start firing at me. I didn't know whether to call them crazy or tip my hat. I must have killed dozens of them a day."

Bruhl asked me why they did it, although as a devout Christian he could have easily answered his own question. It was the Mahdi Army's war at the end of the world.

No one knew the whereabouts of Moqtada al-Sadr, the Lion of God. I looked out for bodyguards and other signs that the man was nearby, but saw nothing. We would have known if he was in the shrine. He was hidden away somewhere, a kind of secret weapon who would never risk being martyred. After all his promises of sacrifice and bravery, he let the other young men walk into the blades of the killing machine for him.

Dead fighters were carried in a slow circuit around the tomb by their comrades. Wrapped in white martyr bags, the young men carried their friends and chanted, "There is no god but God." Because the cemetery was a battleground, the bodies were taken to the Islamic court, where they were left to rot in the basement. These processions happened every few minutes. The cycle was simple: fighters ran down Rasul Street, fought the Americans, were wounded or killed, then were hauled back to the shrine in the blood-stained wooden carts. The same scene was repeated over and over again.

We spoke to another cleric, Sayeed Hosam al-Husseini, and finally made contact with Sheikh Ahmed Sheibani when he returned from the main conference room. Men were now pouring through the gates of the mosque. When night came on, with no pause in the bombing, close to two thousand people had taken shelter inside the massive walls. Men sat on mats in small clusters according to which group they fought with, while the clerics sat with the commanders of the cells and planned the offensive. After evening prayers, when the stars came out, they stretched out to sleep. Thorne slept in the sheikh's office, and I found a place on a mat next to a group of fighters. All through the night, rounds passed over the walls, making weird zinging sounds.

As the Mahdi forces fell back toward the shrine walls, some of the men taking shelter in the mosque started to crack. There was nowhere to go. Marine snipers picked off men dashing across the street to the gates for shelter. Shards of metal slammed into the minarets, and the shock waves sent a rain of stunned birds down from the eaves. The mosque courtyard had become a hurricane's eye of machines and flying lead.

The fighting slowed when the militiamen came in for evening prayers. As night fell, the clerics would illuminate the gold dome, turning it into a beacon above the dark city. The lights stayed lit until the generator ran out of fuel. During one of these blackouts, on August 18, a thin young man began screaming, making a sound halfway between ecstasy and terror. The lights had just gone out, and the young man pointed to one of the archways in the second story of the mosque's western wall. At first we thought that Moqtada was going to appear on a balcony and address the thousands of men in the shrine. Yassir translated for the young man, who told us, "I just saw a vision of the Mahdi. He appeared there!"

"No, it was Imam Ali," another said.

A crowd collected around the visionary. Dozens of other fighters claimed to have seen the same image, a flickering saint in an alcove.

"What does it mean when the Mahdi returns?" I asked the fighter.

"It means he will come to deliver us from injustice and destroy our enemies with incredible weapons. America will be finished."

After some time, the crowd quieted down, but long after that I saw them looking at the balcony for another sign, anything that would have saved them.

MARILYNNE ROBINSON

Onward, Christian Liberals

FROM THE AMERICAN SCHOLAR

You shall be holy, for I the LORD your God am holy.
— *Leviticus 19:2*

I REALIZE THAT in attempting to write on the subject of personal
holiness, I encounter interference in my mind between my own
sense of the life of the soul and understandings that are now pervasive and very little questioned. The phrase "personal holiness," in
what at present is its received sense, suggests a preoccupation with
(usually) minor, namable, and numerable sins and the pious avoid-
ance of them where possible. It suggests a regime of pious behaviors whose object is the advantage of one's own soul. It suggests
also a sense of security concerning final things, which is understood as a virtue, though it is in fact a confidence not claimed even
by the Apostle Paul. If this is a view of the matter commonly held
by the unchurched and the irreligious, it is nevertheless a fair account of the thought and practice of many who do indeed aspire
to personal holiness, or who feel they have achieved it.

The approach to the issue I prefer is not original with me. It is
neither less Scriptural nor less theological nor less traditional than
the sense of the phrase I sketched above, though it has gone into
eclipse with the rise in this country of a culture of Christianity that
does not encourage thought. I intend this as a criticism not only of
the so-called fundamentalists but, more particularly, of the mainline churches, which have fairly assiduously culled out all traces of
the depth and learnedness that were for so long among their great-

est contributions to American life. Emily Dickinson wrote, "The abdication of belief / Makes the behavior small." There is a powerful tendency also to make belief itself small, whether narrow and bitter or feckless and bland, with what effects on behavior we may perhaps infer from the present state of the republic.

I believe in the holiness of the human person and of humanity as a phenomenon. I believe our failings, which are very great and very grave — after all, we have brought ourselves to the point of possible self-annihilation — are a cosmic mystery, a Luciferian disaster, the fall of the brightest angel. That is to say, at best and at worst we are within the field of sacred meaning, holy. I believe holiness is a given of our being that, essentially, we cannot add to or diminish, whose character and reality are fully known only to God and are fully valued only by him. What I might call personal holiness is, in fact, openness to the perception of the holy in existence itself and, above all, in one another. In other words, it is not my belief that personal holiness — sanctity, as the theologians call it — inheres in anyone in isolation or as a static quality. Acting with due reverence for the human situation, including the fact of one's own life, if that were possible, would be saintly. Instead we all struggle constantly with our insufficiency. To put the matter another way, we baffled creatures are immersed in an overwhelming truth. What is plainly before our eyes we know only in glimpses and through disciplined attention. Or again: to attempt obedience to God in any circumstance is to find experience opening on meaning, and meaning is holy.

I am speaking from the perspective of American liberal Protestantism. As I understand the history of this tradition, it departed in the mid-eighteenth century from the Calvinism its forebears had brought from England when it experienced the potent religious upheaval known as the First Great Awakening. The given of the movement was that people passed into a state of sanctity — and in effect were assured of their salvation — through an intense mystical/emotional experience, often a vision of Christ. The movement swept pre-Revolutionary America and left in its wake Princeton, Dartmouth, the temperance movement, a heightened sense of shared identity, and the model of revivalism as a norm of religious culture. There was criticism and reaction against extremes of enthusiasm, and an important Calvinist aversion to the idea that the fruits of salvation could be had by shaking the tree. And there was a period of quiet, which ended with the onset in the early nineteenth century of the Second Great Awakening, again based on the belief that salvation was realized in a mystical/emotional experience. It swept the Northeast, sending zealous New Yorkers and New Englanders out into the territories, and left in its wake the abolitionist movement, the women's suffrage movement, any number of fine colleges, a revived temperance movement, utopianism, Seventh-day Adventists, and Latter-day Saints. And also a literature on the treatment of an affliction they frankly called "religious mania."

Historically, mass religious excitements tend to be set off by plague and famine. The Great Awakenings were set off by preaching, in the first instance by the Congregationalist minister and metaphysician Jonathan Edwards, third president of Princeton, and in the second by the Presbyterian lawyer and abolitionist Charles Grandison Finney, who went on to serve as president of Oberlin College. While both movements were remarkable for benign and lasting consequences, as things go in this world, they left a heritage their own traditions rejected, the belief that salvation occurred in a discrete, unambiguous experience they called "conversion," which those who have retained the belief call "being born again." An important criticism of this model was that it created misery and despair among those called the "no hopers" — among whom Emily Dickinson found herself when a great revival swept through Mount Holyoke College. The liberal criticism, rejection of the idea that one could be securely persuaded of one's own salvation and could even apply a fairly objective standard to the state of others' souls, was in fact a return to Calvinism and its insistence on the utter freedom of God. That is to say, it was a rejection on theological grounds of a novel doctrine. So here has opened the great divide in American Protestant Christianity. I fall on the liberal side of this division.

History is a great ironist, though historians rarely seem to see the joke. The first two awakenings were the work of two eastern intellectuals. Anyone who has read Edwards's "Sinners in the Hands of an Angry God," the sermon often said to have kindled in his church in Northampton, Massachusetts, the movement that spread through the Colonies, knows that when he preached about damnation, he was preaching to the choir. That is, he did not encourage his flock to believe in their own special sanctity, nor did he encourage them to consider others to be in a more parlous state than they were themselves. Perhaps the whole great excitement passed as benignly as it did for that very reason. The excitement we are seeing now is called by some scholars a third great awakening, yet it is different from the other two in this crucial respect. It is full of pious aversion toward so-called secular culture — that is, whatever does not give back its own image — and toward those whose understanding and practice of religion fail to meet its standards. If Edwards's movement unified the Colonies, preparing the way for the Revolution, this may have been because his preachments encouraged people to believe that they themselves were the problem, not some hostile or decadent others who were corrupting the cultural atmosphere.

The Second Great Awakening, in which Charles Finney figured so prominently, was strongly focused on slavery and its abolition, and also on the education of women. Some part of its energies spun off into séances and experiments with marital arrangements, but in its main thrust it was profoundly progressive and reformist. It addressed inequality — of black and white, women and men, wealthy and poor — as a social sin to be overcome, especially through greatly increased access to education. The movement we are seeing now is notably devoid of interest in equality. Indeed, it passionately supports a government whose policies have created a sharp rise in the rate of poverty. For a self-declared Christian movement it shows startlingly little sense of responsibility for the vulnerable in society.

And here is the culminating irony. This movement, which calls itself fundamentalist, subscribes fervently to the principles of laissez-faire capitalism. It has helped to push American society toward what the English economist Herbert Spencer called "the survival of the fittest." Darwin borrowed that phrase from Spencer to name the dynamic of natural selection in the evolution of species, otherwise known as Darwinism. In other words, our anti-Darwinists are social Darwinists. The great defender of what were then called "the fundamentals" was William Jennings Bryan, a Democrat and a pacifist and a passionate campaigner against what he saw as the economic structures that created poverty. His "Cross of Gold" speech spoke of the poor of America as Christ crucified — not at all the kind of rhetoric we hear these days. Bryan, a liberal by any standard, opposed Darwinism because it was taken at the time, rightly or wrongly, to justify not only economic exploitation but also racism, colonialism, eugenics, and war. He feared the loss of belief in the sanctity of the human person, the only stay against these things.

The neo-fundamentalists treat the matter as if the central issue were the existence of God or the literal truth of the Bible. They seem to overlook the implications of the dignity conferred on every human being in the narratives of Creation. They speak of a right to life, an oddly disembodied phrase that, isolated as it is by them from human context, tends to devalue the incarnate person and is therefore as unbiblical a conception as Bergson's *élan vital*. It invokes Jefferson, but Jefferson posited a divine endowment to every person that includes liberty and the pursuit of happiness — terms that are difficult to define but that clearly imply dignity and hope and the exercise of meaningful agency. These are rights that, though "inalienable," have to be enabled and respected in society if they are to exist in fact. For example, they more or less require that one come through childhood in a reasonable state of health. Policies that spread and intensify poverty, besides being unbiblical, deprive individuals of what Jefferson called their God-given rights. The thought among anti-Darwinists was, and supposedly still is, that humankind is demeaned by the notion that God was not in every sense present and intentional in the creation of our first parents. The passionate loyalty of the neo-fundamentalists to the second chapter of Genesis (the first is startlingly compatible with the idea of evolution, though not with Darwinism) seems to have prevented them from reading on in the text. Were they to do so, they would find much to indicate that God continues to be present, and also intentional, in the lives of Eve's children.

Since these folk claim to be defenders of embattled Christianity (under siege by liberalism, as they would have it), they might be struck by the passage in Matthew 25 in which Jesus says, identifying himself with the poorest, "I was hungry, and ye fed me not." This is the parable in which Jesus portrays himself as eschatological judge and in which he separates "the nations." It should surely be noted that he does not apply any standard of creed, of purity, or of orthodoxy in deciding whom to save and whom to damn. This seems to me a valuable insight into what Jesus himself might consider fundamental. To those who have not recognized him in the hungry and the naked he says, "Depart from me, ye cursed, into the eternal fire which is prepared for the devil and his angels." Neo-fundamentalists seem to crave this sort of language — more than they might if they were to consider its context here. It is the teaching of the Bible *passim* that God has confided us very largely to one another's care, but that in doing so he has in no degree detached himself from us. Indeed, in this parable Jesus would seem to push beyond the image of God as final judge, to describe an immanence of God in humankind that makes judgment present and continuous and, in effect, makes our victim our judge. Neither here nor anywhere else in the Bible is there the slightest suggestion that our judge/victim would find a plea of economic rationalism extenuating. This supposed new awakening is to the first two awakenings, and this neo-fundamentalism is to the first fundamentalism, as the New Right is to the New Deal, or as matter is to antimatter.

Liberal that I am, I would not presume to doubt the authenticity of the religious experience of anyone at all. Calvinism encourages a robust sense of human fallibility, in particular forbidding the idea that human beings can set any limits to God's grace. I do wish to make very clear that it is a *religious* scruple that causes me to distance myself from the idea of an inhering personal holiness, a holiness realized otherwise than through God's good, and always mysterious, pleasure. I believe in a holiness visited upon any mortal as divinely imputed righteousness, to use the old language, or in the love of the father for his child, to use the old metaphor. The division between the liberals and the evangelicals is often treated as falling between the not really and the really religious, the dilettante Christians and those adhering to the true faith. This is the fault of the liberals in large part, because they have neglected their own tradition, or have abandoned it in fear that distinctiveness might scuttle ecumenism. Indeed, one of my hopes in writing this essay is to remind those generous spirits of *why* they believe as they do, since they themselves seem to have forgotten, more or less. And I hope also to draw a little attention to the fact that the old-time religion is not so old after all, and ought not be regarded as the Christian faith in a uniquely pure or classic form.

The liberal position on this matter could be seen as a softened predestinarianism. God alone judges, and the hearts of mortals can be known truly only by him, in the light of his grace. Like the old Calvinists, liberal Protestants reject the idea that anyone can achieve salvation by piety or moral rigor or by any other means. After all, Jesus did say, "Not everyone who says to me, 'Lord, Lord,' will enter the kingdom of heaven, but only the one who does the will of my Father in heaven. On that day many will say to me, 'Lord, Lord, did we not prophesy in your name, and cast out demons in your name, and do many deeds of power in your name?' Then I will declare to them, 'I never knew you; go away from me, you evildoers'" (Matthew 7:21–23). And Paul, perhaps alluding to this rather startling teaching of Christ and enlarging on it, said, "If I have prophetic powers, and understand all mysteries and all knowledge, and if I have all faith, so as to remove mountains, but do not have love, I am nothing" (1 Corinthians 13:2). Love is crucial here, and not highly compatible with the self-interest that can be expressed even in heroic self-sacrifice. Ironically, those who have claimed to be defenders of human freedom have tended to set requirements for salvation: being "born again," as they understand the phrase; being baptized at a certain age, under certain conditions, in a particular state of belief; being a member in good standing of a particular church; accepting the authority of a doctrinal system without reference to one's own knowledge or comprehension of it; availing oneself of the salvific benefits that are believed to be at the disposal of a church through its prayers and sacraments. Salvation "earned" by any of these means would itself depend on accidents of birth and culture, which, being accidents, would only imply predestination in another form, since after all, the great mass of human lives have come and gone without access to them. So the justice of God is vindicated, if at all, only locally by these intended empowerments of human beings. What can appear to be empowerments from one side are from another clearly conditions, even coercions. Better, liberally speaking, to trust the free grace of God than to attempt to make oneself proof against an arbitrariness it seems impious to ascribe to him.

Every old argument against predestination can be made against what I have called its softened form. (I intend no disparagement — the major traditions of Christianity are all softened at this point, less preoccupied with damnation than they have been historically and better for the change.) The argument has been made that the insistence on salvation by grace alone would free people to act however they pleased, the assumption being that they would turn to every sort of vice. Lutherans and Calvinists, whose traditions emphasize this teaching, have never been noted for libertinism, however. In general, their histories suggest that people are pleased to act well when they act freely, at least as often as they act well under any sort of coercion. In present terms, no statistics indicate that any of the vices or pathologies of modern life are more prevalent among liberal Protestants than among any other group.

It has been supposed that predestinarianism results in fatalism; that is, in a stoical passivity relative to the things of this world. But historically Calvinism is strongly associated with social reform as well as with revolution. This might seem a paradox at first glance, but the doctrine had its origins as a forthright teaching (Augustine, Aquinas, and Ignatius of Loyola were also predestinarians) in a context of profound skepticism as to the legitimacy of any number of human institutions and much questioning of their right to claim the Mandate of Heaven. The Reformation was not the work of fatalists. It is still true that liberal Protestants are disproportionately generous and active in support of social justice, a fact that makes them anathema to those who associate Christ with laissez-faire economics, as a surprising number of people do these days, absent any endorsement in Scripture. Despite their self-proclaimed Biblicism, they seem never to miss its endorsement.

There is an asymmetry in the relationship of liberal Protestants to their Christian detractors that is the result of the liberal understanding of the freedom of God. Liberals assume the existence of what is traditionally called "the invisible church." They believe that no institution is uniquely the people of God, that God knows his own whoever they are and wherever they are. And they believe, therefore, that this invisible church can, of course, include their Christian detractors. This view of things implies that no doctrinal tests exist to distinguish the true faith from the false, real Christians from poseurs, the orthodox from the erring. To object, to dispute, to counter text with text, all this is legitimate and necessary, though liberals have been far too hesitant to make their case, even among themselves. But to judge the state of any soul is to presume upon a prerogative God reserves to himself. As Paul says: "Who are you to pass judgment on the servants of another? It is before their own lord that they stand or fall. And they will be upheld, for the Lord is able to make them stand" (Romans 14:4). This is not relativism or lack of conviction. Certainly Paul was never guilty of either. It is deference toward God our Universal Father. And there is nothing easy about suspending judgment. On the contrary, the world is and has been ravaged by the very confident judgments people make of one another. More to the point, history is full of extraordinary acts of ferocity carried out by Christians against Christians. Self-styled defenders of the faith have left the faith sorely wounded, in its good name not least.

There is a Hebrew root, transliterated as *ndb*, which is rendered in English by such words as "free," "noble," "generous," "abundant," and "liberal," and their forms. It is used of God and of virtuous human beings and behaviors. It occurs in Isaiah 32:5, a messianic context. In the 1611 King James Version, it is rendered thus: "The instruments also of the churle are evill: he deviseth wicked devices, to destroy the poore with lying wordes even when the needie speaketh right. But the liberall deviseth liberall things, and by liberall things shall hee stand."

More modern translations render the word as "noble," which clarifies its meaning. In Deuteronomy 15:14 its use with reference to the poor is again very clear: "When you send a male slave out from you a free person, you shall not send him out empty-handed. Provide liberally out of your flock, your threshing floor, and your wine press, thus giving to him some of the bounty with which the Lord your God has blessed you."

Ndb — let us call it "liberality" — occurs in a context that continuously reinforces an ethic of liberality; that is, the Old Testament. The many economic laws God gives to Israel as a society are full of provisions for the widow and the orphan, the poor and the stranger. And the abuses the prophets decry most passionately are accumulations of wealth in contempt of these same laws.

And as for Jesus: a ruler asks him how he is to inherit eternal life, and Jesus replies, "Sell all that you own and distribute the money to the poor" (Luke 18:22). How on earth his teaching is to be reconciled with social conservatism I cannot imagine, though the question seems seldom to be asked. (I use the phrase "social conservatism," which might seem to imply moral conservatism, unless, like God, one considers generosity an essential part of morality.) There is a powerful contemporary Christianity that admires Dives and emulates him, and regards Lazarus as burdensome and reprehensible. Indeed, the supposed Christian revival of today has given something very like unlimited moral authority to money, though Jesus did say (and I think a literal interpretation is appropriate here if anywhere), "Woe to you who are rich!" (Luke 6:24). If this seems radical, dangerous, unfair, un-American, then those who make such criticisms should at least have the candor to acknowledge that their quarrel is with Jesus.

We all err, of course. We all come short of the glory of God, as Paul taught us. And as Christian liberalism teaches us as well. Calvin wrote about "total depravity," which has a terrible sound because of the modern meaning of a word that, when he used it (in the French and Latin it derives from), meant warped or distorted. He was rejecting the teaching of Catholic theology that baptism erased the consequences of the Fall from the higher functions, leaving only the lower functions, particularly sexuality, affected by it. No, there is always error in all our thinking and perceiving, according to Calvin. Or as Paul said, speaking to Christians as a Christian, "We see in a mirror dimly." This acknowledgment of the fact of inescapable fallibility has been called the origin of the scientific method, and in this form we know that doubt and self-doubt are allied with truth — teaching as they do that truth as we can know it remains forever partial and provisional.

This doctrine is very liberal in its consequences, an excellent basis for the harmony in diversity that is an essential liberal value now under attack as relativism or as an unprincipled concession to what is now called secularism. This secularism, which is supposed to alarm us, in fact may be nothing more alien to religion than the common space our many flourishing religious traditions have long been accustomed to share. In any case, it is worth remembering that such a common, nonjudgmental space is fully consistent with faithful doubt, as it were, which has not only the very humane consequence of allowing us to live together in peace and mutual respect, but also a strong theological and Scriptural grounding. It is first of all the responsibility of liberal or mainline Protestants to remember this, because insofar as it is an aspect of their tradition, they should understand it and be able to speak for it. A very great deal depends on its being understood and defended.

I may seem to have wandered from my original subject. What has personal holiness to do with politics and economics? Everything, from the liberal Protestant point of view. They are the means by which our poor and orphaned and our strangers can be sustained in real freedom, and graciously, as God requires. How can a Christian live without certainty? More fully, I suspect, than one can live with doctrines that constrict the sense of God with definitions and conditions.

It is vision that floods the soul with the sense of holiness, vision of this world. And it is reverent attention to this world that teaches us, and teaches us again, the imperatives of ethical refinement.

"We ought to embrace the whole human race without exception in a single feeling of love; here there is no distinction between barbarian and Greek, worthy and unworthy, friend and enemy, since all should be contemplated in God, not in themselves. When we turn aside from such contemplation, it is no wonder we become entangled in many errors." This is John Calvin, describing in two sentences a mystical/ethical engagement with the world that fuses truth and love and opens experience on a light so bright it expunges every mean distinction. There is no doctrine here, no setting of conditions, no drawing of lines. On the contrary, what he describes is a posture of grace, generosity, liberality.

RICHARD RODRIGUEZ

Disappointment

FROM CALIFORNIA

THOUGH JOHN STEINBECK was not, in my opinion, the best California writer of the last century, *The Grapes of Wrath* remains California's greatest novel. The native son imagined California from the outside, as a foreigner might; imagined wanting California desperately; imagined California as a remedy for the trial of the nation.

Otherwise, I might think of John Milton when I think of California and the writer's task. Milton devised that, after the Fall, the temperature in San Diego would remain at 75 degrees, but Adam and Eve's relationship to a perfect winter day would be changed to one of goose bumps.

The traditional task of the writer in California has been to write about what it means to be human in a place advertised as paradise. Not the Buckeye or the Empire, not the Can-do or the Show-me, California is the Postlapsarian State. Disappointment has always been the theme of California.

For example, my own.

I cannot afford to live here. I mean I do live here — I rent two large rooms, two stories above California. My light comes from the south. But if I had to move, I could not afford to live here anymore.

In San Francisco, small Victorians, small rooms, steep stairs, are selling for three or four million and are repainted to resemble Bavarian cuckoo clocks — browns and creams and the mute greens tending to blue. That is my mood. If I owned one of the Victorians, I would no doubt choose another comparison. It is like living on a street of cuckoo clocks — and all the cuckoos are on cell phones

— I won't say striking thirteen; nevertheless a version of post-modernity I had not anticipated. Only well-to-do futurists and stuffed T-shirts can afford to live in this nineteenth-century neighborhood.

My complaint with my city is that I am middle-aged.

The sidewalks in my neighborhood are uncannily empty save for Mexican laborers and Mexican nannies and Mexican caregivers, and women wearing baseball hats who walk with the exaggerated vigor of wounded pride (as do I). The streets are in disrepair; the city has no money; really, the streets have never been worse. And the city can no longer afford to maintain the park across the street. The park has never looked worse — the hedges are falling to ruin; are not trimmed; the grass is not watered. Can you imagine Adam and Eve grousing about rundown Eden?

California has been the occasion for disappointment since the 1850s, since men wrote home from the gold fields, from Auburn, from Tulare or Sonora, from tree stumps and tent hotels.

I have no doubt I will prevail here, but you may not think my thicker skin is the proper reformation of an Ohio son. The men here are rough, they grunt and growl and guard their plates with their arms. Now I reach past my neighbor, and grunt, too, and shove, too, and I would cuss just for the pleasure of saying something out loud. I don't believe I have said more than ten words since I came to this place. I realize any oath I might devise would pale next to the colorful flannel they run up here . . .

And yet the streets are clogged with pickups and delivery vans, cable vans, and the vans of construction workers — certain evidence of prosperity. Crews of men, recently from old countries, work to reconstruct the houses of futurists — houses that were reconstructed not two years ago. One cannot drive down any street without having to go around the pickups and the vans, without muttering under one's breath at the temporary No Parking signs that paper every street, because everyone knows the only reason for the No Parking permits is to enable construction workers to drive to work.

Men from every corner of the world converged on the gold fields in the 1850s, prompting Karl Marx to proclaim the creation of a global society in California, a society unprecedented in the world up to that time. The gold parliament was an achievement of necessity as much as of greed.

Kevin Starr, the preeminent historian of California from the 1850s to the end of the twentieth century, has described California as a chronology of proper names: Stanford. Atherton. Giannini. Disney.

Disappointment was arrival. Letters went out to the world, diaries, newspaper reports, warnings, laments, together with personal effects — eyeglasses, pen nibs, broken-backed Bibles — wrapped in soiled canvas. The stolen claim. Or the fortune squandered. (*Lottie, dear, I have wasted our dream* . . .) The trusting disposition. The false friend. The fog-shrouded wharf. The Spaniard Marquis, etc. The ring, the brooch, the opium den, etc.

Narratives of disappointment flowed eastward, like an auguring smoke, or bumped back over rutted trails, as coffins bump or buckboards slow, to meet the stories of the desolations of the prairie life, rolled over those, flowed back to the Atlantic shore, where the raw line separating the North and South was beginning to fester.

Nineteenth-century California rewarded only a few of its brotherhood, but it rewarded them as deliriously as an ancient king in an ancient myth would reward. The dream of a lucky chance encouraged a mass migration, toward "el norte" or "gold mountain," or from across the plains of America.

For, as much as California's story was a story of proper names or of luck or election, California was also a story of mass — mass migrations, unmarked graves, missing persons, accident. By the time he reaches the 1990s in his great work, Kevin Starr seems to sense an influential shift: the list of singular makers of California gives way to forces of unmaking — to gangs, earthquakes, riots, floods, propositions, stalled traffic.

Disappointment is a fine literary theme — "universal" — as the young high school English teacher, himself disappointed, was fond of saying, and it wears like leather.

Disappointment continued to be mined in California's literature throughout the twentieth century. Joan Didion gave us domestic broken dreamers, not so much driven as driving. In the great Didion essays of the sixties, the dystopian mother abandons her daughter on the median of the San Bernardino freeway; dirty dishes pile up in the sink; the hot wind blows from the desert.

Mike Davis gives us the California Club version of the broken dream — paper evidence that a deal was cut. The water, the electricity, the coastline — everything can be bought or sold in the promised land, and has been.

California's most influential prose has turned out to be that of mystery writers (more in line with John Milton), who regard Eden as only an occasion for temptation and fall. For example, the eighteen-year-old cheerleader from Sioux City returns her engagement ring, a poor-grade sapphire she got from a boy named Herbert (not after the president); cashes in her scholarship to the teachers' college; buys a ticket to L.A., enjoins herself to become the new, the next — *Whaddaya think?* — Jean Harlow. But she ends up a manicurist in Van Nuys; she ends up the blue, blond Jane Doe of the Month in the North Hollywood morgue. It requires a private investigator who is broke, dyspeptic, alcoholic, but also something of a puritan to want to incriminate California. The golden.

One of my favorite California essays is a disappointment essay, F. Scott Fitzgerald's "The Crack-Up," an incautious memoir, meticulous, snide.

What an unenviable prospect, though, to be forced to listen to the same lament — the Hollywood screenwriter's lament — at one o'clock in the morning in the Polo Lounge. I once suffered a very long evening thus, listening to a young man complain, in breath that smelled of boiled eggs for lunch, about the difficulty of being a "serious" writer in a town that idolized Spielberg. It was Spielberg that year; I imagine it still is Spielberg.

Francis Scott Fitzgerald at one o'clock in the morning: "I saw that the novel, which at my maturity was the strongest and supplest medium for conveying thought and emotion from one human being to another, was becoming subordinated to a mechanical and communal art that, whether in the hands of Hollywood merchants or Russian idealists, was capable of reflecting only the tritest thought, the most obvious emotion."

Many decades after Fitzgerald cracked up, I saw with my own eyes a still orbiting fragment of his legend. I saw Sheilah Graham, a tarnished blonde in a black cocktail dress. She floated from table to table at Mr. Chow's restaurant, myopic, bending at the waist to kiss the air behind the ears of revelers. As a public sinner, she was something of a disappointment.

What Fitzgerald was too aureate to imagine was that unfastidious merchants of Hollywood — the ham-fisted, the thick-fingered, the steak-minded — nevertheless could pay somebody (scale) to develop the screenwriter's complaint into a script — a picture about a pretty-boy screenwriter who ends up floating face-down in a swimming pool on Sunset Boulevard.

The question is, does California have anything left to say to America, or to the world, or even to itself, beyond disappointment? True, a vast literature is forming on the Dewey-decimal coast. Vietnamese-Californian, Japanese-Californian, Pakistani-Californian, Hispanics, all sorts, including my own. The question many people legitimately ask about this literature is whether our voices describe more than a hyphenated state.

My first literary recognition of California came from reading William Saroyan, because Saroyan described the world I recognized. It was as simple as that. Armenian Fresno was related to my Sacramento. It was as simple as that — the extreme valley heat (outlanders swore they never could stand it, or the flatness either, or the alfalfa green); also the taste of water from a garden hose — the realization that California, that any life, that my life, therefore, was potentially the stuff of literature.

Here is the quote from Saroyan that I typed and pasted on the inside of my bedroom door, a manifesto:

Try to learn to breathe deeply, really to taste food when you eat, and when you sleep, really to sleep. Try as much as possible to be wholly alive, with all your might, and when you laugh, laugh like hell, and when you get angry, get good and angry. Try to be alive. You will be dead soon enough.

That was Saroyan's "advice to a young writer." I took the advice at a time when I had no expectation of being a writer or any desire or sense of obligation. (It comes to me only now, as I type this, that Saroyan's advice has nothing to do with writing; it is advice for any mortal, sentient being.)

It would be another two decades before I came upon the words that made me think I had a story to tell — the opening words of Maxine Hong Kingston's *The Woman Warrior:*

"You must not tell anyone," my mother said, "what I am about to tell you."

The mother's prohibition to her daughter reminded me of my own mother's warning about spreading "family secrets." In the face of all California's fame for blatancy — in the face of pervasive light, ingenuousness, glass and aluminum housing, bikinis, billboards — Mrs. Hong recommended concealment. Her shrine is a published book.

At about this time, Aram Saroyan, William Saroyan's son, published a bitter memoir of his father's last years.

William Saroyan was not on any syllabus I ever saw at Stanford or Berkeley, nor, incidentally, was Steinbeck. Stanford, Berkeley — these were schools established in the nineteenth century by professors from the Ivy League who had come west, like Peace Corps volunteers, to evangelize California for the Atlantic Enlightenment. So perhaps it was not surprising that, even in the 1960s and 1970s, very little attention was paid to California in any university course, despite the fact that California in those years was at the center of the national imagination. The only California novel assigned in any course I took, either in college or graduate school, was Nathanael West's *The Day of the Locust,* probably because it fulfilled some East Coast expectation that California would come to doom.

And speaking of doom, the editor from *Time* magazine wanted an essay on California because it was a season (this was ten years ago) when the national newsweeklies were hitting the stands with titles like "Is the Golden State Tarnished?"

The *Time* editor wanted 750 words' worth of tarnish: "It would be nice if you could give us a Joan Didion essay."

"What's that?" I said.

"You know," she said. "Sardonic."

I unfold and refold that fraying *Time* story whenever I go to lunch with a California writer, handy to pull out if the conversation turns to New York. When the conversation inevitably turns to New York.

It is not sardonicism, sardony; it is the flat valley pitch. And it is precision.

Anyway, California is getting too old to play the unhappy child or even the sardonic — too rich, too glued, too Angelica Huston walking substantially down some steps into the garden, to play the exuberant, the naïf. And California has grown children of her own. Two of the most interesting cities in North America are California daughters. Las Vegas, the open-throttled city, mimics California's youth, when land was cheap and cities were built in opposition to nature. Tijuana wants so little, she terrifies us for needing so much.

And: New York, truly, I am sorry to say, is not New York anymore. I say this having once been the boy who strained — the antenna on our roof raked through the starlight — to catch any shred of conversation from New York. I watched James Baldwin interviewed by David Suskind. I watched Norman Mailer chafing at America on *The Dick Cavett Show.* New York was a conversation. I guess I am stuck there. Buckley and Galbraith, Yale and Harvard, W. H. Auden, and Hermione Gingold.

Unread copies of *The New Yorker* slip and slide on the opposite end of my couch — damn slippery things — opposite the end of the couch where I read. Still, every once in a while there's an essential article. I stopped my subscription to the *New York Review of Books* some years ago. When I was in college, in graduate school, and for many years after, the *NYRB* fed my ravenous appetite for Oxbridge-Manhattan conversation. But then — what? I got too old; the conversation got too old. And surely the world must be larger than New York and London. Even now, I could pick up right where I left off: *SWM seeks SWF, for argument's sake.*

On an April day in 1970, I saw Dwight Macdonald. We both were stranded on a concrete island in the middle of Broadway. He was an old man in a raincoat in the rain. I was a student. The rain was glorious, tall, immoderate. Everything was glorious. Broadway. No, I did not dare congratulate Macdonald for his bravery as a public intellectual, the best of his kind, and for whom the rain, that day, at least from the look of him, was just one more goddamned thing. Then the light changed.

Because Irving Kristol correctly predicted the light would change, that the intellectual center of America would shift from the shores of the Hudson to the Potomac.

For the writer, the problem of the absence of New York is the problem of the absence of a critical center, where opinion can be trusted to support talent or call down the falsely reasoned text. Washington think tanks are too far gone in the thrall to political power to provide that center. In the absence of critical structures, where does the young writer from California, or any writer, present himself for review; to what city does he apply for notice and contest? Nowadays, it is not Norman Mailer or James Baldwin who converses on television, it is Dr. Bill Frist or Harry Reid, and it is poor.

I was once interviewed on C-SPAN during the Los Angeles Times Book Festival. Five minutes max, the producer promised. Put this in your ear. Look over there. 5 . . . 4 . . . 3 . . . 2 . . . I was standing on a crowded plaza at UCLA between two stalls, one for African-American books, another for Latino books. I said to my interviewer, who was in Washington, D.C., which was inside an electronic button, which was inside my ear, that I regretted these two neighboring book booths represented so little understanding of what California is becoming.

The earphone remained as neutral as a can opener.

. . . I mean California's destiny is marriage. All the races of the world . . .

Two-second delay. Obviously I have wasted . . . the earphone asked if I was going to attend the Great Debate.

I'm sorry?

"Our viewers are going to watch a debate between California and New York," the earphone enthused (a brightening of tone).

(California would be "represented" by Ms. Ariana Huffington, New York by Mr. Pete Hamill.)

You'd do better to stage a conversation between Duluth and El Paso.

The earphone paused for an awful moment (cf. Bishop Proudie's wife, *Barchester Towers,* suspecting sarcasm) before leaping from my ear.

Americans have been promised — by God, by the Constitution of the United States, by Edna Ferber — that we shall enjoy liberty to pursue happiness. The pursuit constitutes what we have come to call the American Dream.

Americans feel disappointment so keenly because our optimism is so large and is so often insisted upon by historians. And so often justified by history. The stock market measures optimism. If you don't feel optimistic, there must be something wrong with you. There are pills for disappointment.

The California Dream was a codicil to the American Dream, an opening. Internal immigrants sought from California at least a softer winter, a wider sky, at least a thousand miles' distance between themselves and whatever dissatisfaction they felt with "home."

Midwestern California, the California of internal immigrants, was everywhere apparent when I was growing up, in the nervous impulse to build and to live in a house that had never been lived in or died in; where the old lady never spilled milk, the dog never bit, the bully never lurked behind the elm tree; where widows and discomfited children never stared at the moon through runny glass or listened to the wind at night. This California was created by newcomers from Illinois and Nebraska, and it shaped my life. This was California as America's America.

Simultaneous with midwestern California was the California of Maxine Hong Kingston and William Saroyan, and my Mexican mother and father and my Indian relatives, a California of private family secrets, yes, unorthodox ingredients, turmeric, cilantro, Santa Maria Purisima, but also some surpassing relief at having found in California a blind from tragedy. The relief California offered immigrants from other countries was comparable to the imagined restoration of the Joads. Ours was a California far removed from the drama of midwestern disappointment, from the all-new and the why-am-I-not-happy?, though we lived next door to it, to Nebraska and Illinois.

Thus, in my lifetime, I experienced two Californias concurrently. I discovered (because I was attuned to) a sort of hybrid of these two Californias in the writings of John Muir. Muir was born in Scotland; he moved with his family to Wisconsin when he was eleven. Muir saw California with a midwesterner's delight in the refulgence of it — he called California "the grand side of the mountain." Yet I recognized in John Muir as well the quiet, grateful voice of the immigrant from overseas. Muir sailed into California. He first saw the coastline as if through Pacific eyes; he saw immediately the implication of the coastline: California (and America) is finite.

When I grew up in the 1950s, freeways offered freedom from implication. California was neurotically rebuilding itself as an ever-rangier house in a farther-flung subdivision. As a loyal son of California, I believed in all this, in the "new" and the other "e-z" adjectives real estate agents employed to lure midwesterners. And though the advertisement the real estate developer placed in the midwestern newspaper was not a bluff, too many people believed, too many people came. The traffic on the freeway has slowed from Jetsons to "Now what?" to Sig Alert.

What is obsolete now in California is the future. For a century and a half Americans spoke of California as the future when they wanted to escape inevitability. Now the future attaches consequences and promises constriction. Technocrats in Sacramento warn of a future that is overwhelmed by students, pollution, immigrants, cars, fluorocarbons, old people. Or the future is diminished — water quality, soil quality, air quality, education quality, highway quality, life quality. There are not enough doctors for the state's emergency rooms, not enough blue parking spaces outside, not enough oil, not enough natural gas, not enough electricity. More blackouts, more brownouts, too many air conditioners, too few houses, frogs on the verge of extinction, a fugitive middle class. A state without a white center. To the rest of the nation California now represents what the nation fears to become.

The brilliance of midwestern California, the California that is founded upon discontent (and the reason why so much technological innovation springs from the West Coast), is that having confronted the finitude of the coastline, technologists in Silicon Valley have shrunk the needed commodity — the future (thousands of miles of Zen pathway) — to the size of a fleck of gold dust, to a microchip.

A few months ago, I went to have dinner in Menlo Park, where I met a young man who wore a linen jacket of the very blackest label and the scent of the winner's circle. He owns, very firmly owns, I imagine, on sheaves of legal-sized hard copy, electronic portals (virtual) through which the most ephemeral chatter and the finest thoughts of humankind pass as undifferentiated "content." (I imagine Ensor's painting of *Christ's Entry into Brussels* at the Getty.)

When I answered the young man's uninterested inquiry by identifying myself as a writer, his only response was to recommend that I consign every published sentence I now guard with copyright to the web and give it away. No one owns an idea in this age was his advice (and all of a sudden he sounded like someone one would have met on a riverboat). Except his idea, of course.

The young man's fortune comes, not from the "content" his technology conveys or conveys a quester toward, but rather from the means of conveyance — or, no, not even that. A sort of dock, is it? For swan boats. He will make more money by, at intervals, changing some aspect of conveyance or by padlocking the old portal (I imagine the Suez Canal) so that people have to pay to modify their means of access. He is set on weaning the minds of youth from the snares of merchandisers ("middlemen" he quaintly calls them). Young people are conveyed to the belief they should obtain intellectual property without paying for it, and without packaging. Packaging is sentimentality.

The young man is content to disassemble, by making "free," all intellectual property and factories of intellectual properties (recording studios, for example, or publishing houses), and all clearinghouses of intellectual properties (such as New York, such as Los Angeles), in order that he can charge more for his arch or his gondola or his Victorian bathing machine.

The technologist now publishes to the world that place is over. California used to be the summation of the expansionist dream; now we foretell constriction. The future has been condensed to the head of a pin. Not Go West, not even Go Home. Rather, stay at home. Run in place. You are still connected, whether you are in the air or on a train or never leave Wisconsin. The great invention — rather, the refinement — of Silicon Valley is portability.

For a long season, California was the most important purveyor of narrative to the world. Hollywood was filled with stories in the last century, stories bought and sold — more stories than anyone could listen to or use. When other lures to California were exhausted or quieted down, Hollywood became its own narrative, became the golden dream; people wanted, literally, "to get into the pictures."

Toward the end of dinner, the optimistic young man from Silicon Valley, having imbibed a liter or so of Napa Valley pish-posh '69, got around to his detestation of the congestion of California. In the end, it would appear, he has to live in a real body, in real space and in real time, and buckled into his hundred-thousand-dollar funk: "Traffic is a bitch every fucking morning."

. . . *When you get angry, get good and angry. Try to be alive. You will be dead soon enough.*

I, too, was an optimist. Well, I took Saroyan's pronouncement for optimism. Like many children of immigrant parents, Saroyan and I grew up among shadows, grotesque shadows thrown from a grandmother's stories, stories that might show us up as foreigners if they ever saw the light of day. How could the Saroyan boy not be beguiled in the direction of games and sunlight. And then limelight. And then Paris.

I saw him once, in a bookstore in San Francisco, a bookstore made of wood, now long gone. He dressed like a stage bohemian; he wore a walrus mustache and a fedora, and his cashmere coat rested upon his shoulders. He threw back his head to bellow, by which gesture he represented mirth. He was entirely admirable and theatrical. Saroyan's literary persona remained that of a carefree bon vivant, at ease with the world and delighted by it, tasting, breathing, laughing like hell. He'd never be a Princeton man — but so what?

The legend: William Saroyan of Fresno, California, and Paris, France, was haunted by the early promise of himself. Critics withheld from the middle-aged man the praise they had once lavished on the youth. He was the same man. What gives? He became darkminded and spiteful and stingy and mistrustful of friends and family and agents and stockbrokers and the IRS. The world smelled spoiled to him. He felt passed over by the world that mattered, the small, glittering, passing world.

The last time I was in Fresno, about a year ago, I gave a luncheon address at the African-American Cultural Center to a roomful of journalists from ethnic newspapers and radio and television stations, called, altogether, "New California Media." (The Pakistani radio station in San Diego. The Iranian television station in L.A. *The Oaxacan. The Mandarin.*) Everyone in the room spoke interestedly of a California that was crowded with voices, most of which they could not translate but they knew implicated them. No one knew what I was asking when I asked where Saroyan had lived.

The question for the night is the question of content, I think, not conveyance. A new generation of writers in California will not speak of separate neighborhoods, certainly not of brown hills and dairy cows, or the taste of water from a hose, or the sound of train whistles at night. Nor will they dote on New York, as I doted on

New York. Oh, maybe they will, why deny them that? Perhaps New York will be Shanghai.

In the time of your life, live was Saroyan's advice. I believe the difference between the literature of California's past and the literature to come will be the difference of expectation. There are children growing up in California today who take it as a given that the 101 North, the 405 South, and the 10 East are unavailable after two in the afternoon.

ELAINE SCARRY

Rules of Engagement

FROM BOSTON REVIEW

IN 1998, AN ARTICLE by Colonel Charles J. Dunlap Jr. appeared in the United States Air Force Academy's *Journal of Legal Studies* warning that a new form of warfare lay ahead. Because our military resources are so far beyond those of any other country, Dunlap argued, no society can today meet us through symmetrical warfare. Therefore, our twenty-first-century opponents will stop confronting us with weapons and rules that are the mirror counterparts of our own. They will instead use asymmetrical or "neo-absolutist" forms of warfare, resorting to unconventional weapons and to procedures forbidden by international laws.

What Dunlap meant by "unconventional weapons" is clear: the category would include not only outlawed biological, chemical, and nuclear weapons (the last of which, in the view of the United States, only itself and a small number of other countries are legally permitted to have) but also unexpected weapons such as civilian passenger planes loaded with fuel and flown into towering buildings in densely populated cities.

But the term "neo-absolutism," as used by Dunlap, applies not just to the use of unconventional weapons but to conduct that violates a sacrosanct set of rules — acts that are categorically prohibited by international law and by the regulations of the U.S. Air Force, Navy, and Army (along with the military forces of many other nations). For example, though warfare permits many forms of ruse and deception, it never permits the false use of a white flag of truce or a red cross. The white flag and red cross — along with a tiny number of other symbols and rules — are held to be inviolable, and their intentional misuse is regarded by the laws of nations as "perfidy," and, when employed to injure or kill, "treachery." A memorable example of such treachery occurred during the spring 2003 invasion of Iraq by the United States, when an Iraqi taxi driver allegedly displayed a white flag at a checkpoint and then, having gained the trust of the guards, exploded a car bomb, killing four American soldiers.[1] Though Iraqi forces were at that moment being attacked by American equipment whose power to injure was in vast excess of anything owned by the Iraqis, media in the United States and around the world rightly paused to express horror and indignation at the deceptive use of a white flag, as they would again pause to express horror a few months later, when an Iraqi truck carried explosives into the United Nations headquarters in Baghdad, a site that should have been treated as inviolable by both sides.

Dunlap's article, which so accurately predicted the coming era of neo-absolutist enemies, was *not* recommending that the United States reciprocate by itself succumbing to neo-absolutism. Precisely to the contrary, it urged that the U.S. military begin to prepare for asymmetrical warfare (of the kind we would experience three years later, on 9/11) so that it could maintain an unswerving conformity to international law while defeating its neo-absolutist opponent. Using the long-standing idiom of "chivalry" — a technical term by which international and military laws pay tribute to an overarching framework of civil laws that endure even in the midst of war — the article insisted that the United States must continue to be Sir Galahad even when confronted by Genghis Khan.

But has the United States continued to uphold the international prohibitions against treachery and other prohibitions against comparable acts of wrongdoing since 9/11? Or has it, without blinking, crossed over into the region of neo-absolutism? Often applied to monarchs and tyrants, the term "absolutism" has, over the last four centuries, been used in the political context to indicate an executive power that is unconstrained by rules or limits.

The gravest evidence against the United States resides in the now elaborately documented acts of torture at Abu Ghraib and the less fully documented acts of torture at interrogation centers in Bagram, Afghanistan (where one prisoner died of pulmonary embolism, another of a heart attack), in Qaim, Iraq (where an Iraqi general, who voluntarily entered a military camp to inquire about his four sons, died after interrogators beat him, put him head-first into a sleeping bag, and sat on his chest), on the British island of Diego Garcia, and at Guantánamo. We also know that the United States has repeatedly sent prisoners to interrogation centers with histories of torture in Syria, Saudi Arabia, Jordan, and Egypt.[2]

The willingness of the United States to torture might well absorb our full attention here. But because it is also the form of neo-absolutism about which most people are already acutely aware, I will only briefly review what we know about it.

In its 2005 annual report, Amnesty International called on national bodies to arrange for "a full and independent investigation" of the "use of torture . . . by U.S. officials" and called for the support of the International Criminal Court. Determining the degree of responsibility of government leaders for the events at Abu Ghraib must await such an inquiry, but it is important to recognize what the documentary evidence already makes clear: a stark line of influence from Washington to Guantánamo to Bagram to Abu Ghraib.

We know, first, that President George W. Bush and Secretary of Defense Donald Rumsfeld declared that detainees in Guantánamo were not lawful combatants and therefore not protected by international rules governing prisoners of war.[3]

Second, we know that President Bush officially announced that he *personally* had the power to suspend the Geneva Conventions in Afghanistan. A February 7, 2002, memo from the president to the vice president, secretary of state, secretary of defense, attorney general, CIA director, and chairman of the Joint Chiefs of Staff (among others) stated, "I have the authority under the constitution to suspend Geneva as between the United States and Afghanistan, but I decline to exercise that authority at this time . . . I reserve the right to exercise this authority in this or future conflicts."[4]

Third, we know that in Iraq, at Abu Ghraib, individual soldiers — men and women from the 800th Military Police Brigade and the 205th Military Intelligence Brigade — took it upon themselves to suspend Geneva rules and torture detainees. The investigative reports of their acts — the Taguba, Fay-Jones, and Schlesinger reports — take note of the fact that military-intelligence soldiers who had served in Guantánamo and Bagram later served in Abu Ghraib, carrying with them information about the suspendability of the Geneva Conventions. Key practices at Abu Ghraib — stripping prisoners naked and threatening them with attack dogs — coincide with practices explicitly authorized by Rumsfeld for Guantánamo detainees in a December 2002 memorandum.

The act of torture is such an extreme trespass against the laws of war that it may seem beside the point to wonder whether any other forms of wrongdoing have been carried out; additional acts cannot make a country that tortures worse than it already is, nor would the absence of additional acts diminish its culpability. Yet it is important to consider these others, and in particular perfidy and treachery, because every act that carries us into neo-absolutist territory blurs our vision, makes the boundary easier to cross, and puts us at ever-accelerating risk of carrying out moral harms (such as the use of nuclear weapons) from which we may not soon recover.

International law and military law identify only a tiny set of actions as treachery; it appears that we have committed — or have come perilously close to committing — each of them. Along with torture, the conduct described below reveals a pattern of indifference to even the most elementary moral and legal norms and a willingness to substitute the unbound dictates of men for the rule of law. A good case can be made that the United States has already violated these norms. But even if there have not been criminal violations, there is a pattern in the conduct I consider here, and that pattern suggests a pervasive unwillingness to take the most fundamental norms seriously as strictures that must not be violated. That indifference and that unwillingness are bound, sooner or later, to carry the country into fatal moral terrain.

Rule 1: White Flag, Red Cross

The misuse of a white flag or red cross is considered an act of perfidy. Perfidy is at its heart a misuse of signs or pieces of language, according to *International Law — The Conduct of Armed Conflict and Air Operations,* a 1976 pamphlet that is the air force's handbook on the laws of warfare. Yet most of the acceptable stratagems of deceit in warfare also involve an intentional misuse or falsification of language. Article 24 of the Hague Conventions, quoted in the air force handbook, Section 8–4, lists many legitimate falsifications of language: it is lawful to "use enemy signals and passwords" and to issue "bogus orders by an enemy commander"; one may "simulate quiet and inactivity" when a large force is gathering or, conversely, "simulate a large force" when only a small force is present. The list of permissible deceptions is vast. Fraud, as Machiavelli long ago realized, is the natural companion of force.

But the fraudulent use of a white flag or a red cross (or the equivalent of the red cross in other cultures — the red crescent or the red lion, for example) is prohibited for three reasons. First, some small pieces of language in war must remain wholly intact, uncompromised, unwavering, undiluted in their meaning. These few insignia are considered *hors de combat,* or "out of combat"; they constitute a civil structure that remains in place in the international sphere (in the same way that inside a country the military is kept within a civil frame). These small but sacrosanct pieces of language act as a location from which other true sentences can be spoken: without them, as Morris Greenspan observes in *Modern Law of Land Warfare,* neither party would "be able to place the slightest credence in the word of the other."

The second reason points to the future rather than the present, the period of peace rather than war. Unless certain pieces of language remain uncontaminated by war, no international framework of trust remains available for a truce or peace accord. These small pieces of language must be kept intact, then, because they will provide a bridge back to civilization.

The first and second reasons tell us that some pieces of language must carry the guarantee of truthfulness without telling us why *these particular* pieces of language must do so. This explanation is provided by a third principle, which is hard to formulate. One formulation states that no language can be used that "causes the enemy to refrain from violence he would otherwise surely exercise"; another formulation states that it is a "grave breach . . . when the use invites the confidence of the enemy with the intent to betray confidence." These descriptions are both still incomplete, because acceptable fraud, such as pretending that one's army is not present by moving quietly forward, is in fact intended to "cause the enemy to refrain from violence he would otherwise surely exercise" and also "invites the confidence of the enemy with the intent to betray confidence." What is key in cases of treachery is that one party invites its opponents to refrain from injuring others and to refrain from protecting themselves against injury by appealing to the higher frame of language, the *hors de combat* language, and then, thanks to the opponents' willingness to honor this higher call, injures them. The Iraqi taxi driver who lured the American soldiers toward him asked them to step away from the ground of combat, to stand with him above the battle, but did so only to maneuver the soldiers into harm's way.

So severe is the rule protecting the signs of truce and medical care that it cannot be suspended, even for the sake of escape, a circumstance that often permits a relaxation of the rules. For example, it is permissible, for the purpose of escape, to take off one's uniform and wear civilian clothes, an act impermissible in any other context.[5] In contrast, it is never permissible for uninjured soldiers to travel in an ambulance, whether they are moving forward into battle or trying to escape from it.

The stark prohibition on the false use of the red cross is derived from a logically prior and overarching prohibition: a Red Cross vehicle or building cannot itself be the target of assault. It is because all participants are obligated to regard the white flag and red cross as inviolable that a secondary obligation arises not to use either sign falsely. As the air force manual observes, "The rule prohibiting feigning *hors de combat* status, such as sickness, distress or death, in order to commit or resume hostilities is only a corollary rule to the principle prohibiting attacks on persons who are *hors de combat*."

What, then, are we to make of the joint army–navy–air force mission to storm Nasiriyah General Hospital to take back the injured prisoner of war Private Jessica Lynch? The people of the United States were asked by their government to bear collective witness to this mission — to take it, and honor it, as our national war story. If the narrative captivated national attention, it did so in part because the deeds were so fresh, so unheard-of — but they were fresh and unheard-of because such deeds are not ordinarily performed, and they are not ordinarily performed because to storm a hospital is to be guilty of perfidy: it is a violation of the primary and overarching prohibition from which the perfidy prohibition is derived.

Did anyone present at the planning session for this mission have a handbook of military rules available? Did anyone object to the plan?[6] For the U.S. Special Forces to drive up to the hospital in Nasiriyah in a fleet of ambulances would of course have been a clear act of perfidy. So too was it an act of perfidy to arrive at the threshold of the hospital in a fleet of military tanks and helicopters loaded with navy SEALs, army Rangers, and air force pilots, who spilled through the corridors at midnight, breaking down doors and blasting guns. Upon hearing the roar of approaching machinery, the hospital staff, according to their reports, fled to the basement. Inciting members of a medical staff to abandon their posts beside their patients for several hours is a concrete harm, though if they had not abandoned their posts, the United States might now have the slaying of medical personnel and hospital administrators on its hands.

The navy handbook on the law of naval warfare includes this specific prohibition: "Medical establishments and units, fixed or mobile, and vehicles of wounded and sick or of medical equipment may not be bombarded or attacked." Of the estimated three thousand Nasiriyan civilians who by that point in the war had been injured by U.S. armaments, sixty suffering from severed limbs and other serious wounds were housed in the hospital. Private Lynch was transferred to this civilian hospital from a military hospital by her Iraqi captors. Among many untrue elements included in the original dissemination of the story was the image of Iraqi soldiers hovering over Jessica Lynch, slapping her to extract information.[7] Both Private Lynch and the physicians and nurses who cared for her deny that any such incident ever took place. The inclusion of these details suggests that the people presenting the story to the American public understood that there was a stringent prohibition against attacking a hospital and therefore tried to convert the building into something other than a hospital, and to portray those hovering near her as brutal interrogators rather than nurses and physicians.

A basic principle governing hospitals in a time of war is *Hostes dum vulnerati, fratres,* or "Enemies while wounded are brothers," which is generally interpreted to mean that care of injured military forces must be carried out without regard to nationality.[8] This principle was honored at the Nasiriyah hospital, where, according to Private Lynch, one of her nurses soothed her body with talc while singing her lullabies. Of her main nurse Lynch said, "I loved her." Private Lynch credits her caretakers with giving her life: "I'm so thankful to those people, 'cause that's why I'm alive today," she told Diane Sawyer in a television interview. I am not suggesting that the medical treatment was in any way remarkable. Though some nurses or doctors may have done more than is necessary, decent medical treatment is required both by the Geneva Conventions and by the Red Cross's proposals for regulations on the "safeguard of an enemy *hors de combat*": "It is forbidden to kill, injure, ill treat or torture an adversary *hors de combat*. An adversary *hors de combat* is one who, having laid down his arms, no longer has any means of defense or has surrendered."

The fact that Private Lynch was receiving humane treatment in a hospital does not mean that her broken legs, arm, and spine could be as successfully mended in Iraq as they might be in an American or European hospital. The rules of war allow an injured enemy soldier to be transferred to medical care among her own countrymen, so long as the transfer can be safely made. The day before the Special Forces raided the hospital, the Iraqi medical staff — as physicians told the BBC and as Private Lynch told ABC — attempted to transport her to an American hospital, but the ambulance was fired on by American soldiers at a checkpoint and forced to turn around. An assault on an ambulance, like an assault on a hospital, is prohibited by national and international regulations. The U.S. soldiers might have thought that the ambulance was a ruse, though the public record does not document the misuse of ambulances by Iraqi forces in Nasiriyah.[9] At best, these actions can be interpreted as answering illegal acts with illegal acts; at worst, they represent the first step in the descent into neo-absolutism.

Some American newspapers called the episode a story of "smoke and mirrors," and, to their credit, the media soon collectively sorted through the story, correcting false information (that Private Lynch had gunshot and stab wounds rather than broken bones from the truck accident during the ambush; that she stood her ground, killing Iraqis and firing until the moment she was taken, rather than, as she describes, putting down her malfunctioning gun, lowering her head, and praying). The creation of an accurate record is the work of many people; it has depended most critically on Private Lynch herself, who demonstrates, among many other forms of valor, an unswerving commitment to the truth.

But what have often seemed to be at issue in these continual corrections are distracting questions about forms and degrees of heroism, whether on the part of Private Lynch or the Special Forces (who, though their mission was filmed as it took place, are prohibited from speaking about it) or the Nasiriyah medical staff. This constant readjustment of details has obscured basic questions: Is it now American practice to conduct raids on hospitals? If fedayeen soldiers stormed an American hospital in the middle of the night wearing blazing searchlights on their helmets, would we consider that action legal? admirable? If Al Jazeera dedicated several weeks to calibrating the exact level of heroism in the raid, would we believe that the Arab media and their audience were asking the right questions? Are U.S. hospitals, Iraqi hospitals, and International Red Cross facilities on the battlefield now legitimate targets?

Defenders of the American assault on the hospital might say that it was a legitimate rescue operation. They might say that the hospital was not itself the intended target; it only happened to be where Private Lynch was. The American forces had no choice about the location of the rescue, and the attack was therefore neither against the law nor demonstrative of an indifference to fundamental standards of law and morality.

This interpretation, however flattering to our self-understanding, is hard to reconcile with the facts. The Iraqis were willing to transfer Private Lynch; they were prevented from doing so by the American attack on the ambulance. Moreover, the U.S. government never expressed any regret about the "need" to attack a hospital in service of a rescue operation; instead the attack was mythologized and celebrated. A lawyer defending the American mission in a war crimes trial might win his case. But for American citizens who believe that their country should respect fundamental standards, the assault — and the surrounding attitudes — must be deeply troubling. Even if the American assault did not technically violate these standards, it showed no respect for them.

During the first year of the war, we had the numbers and names of U.S. soldiers killed in Iraq but almost no other information about what was happening on the ground. We did not know at that point even the numbers of Iraqi soldiers and civilians killed and injured, let alone the circumstances of their wounding. In the midst of this heartsickening vacuum, we were given one story — a story that, properly understood, reveals our own trespass into — or, at a minimum, perilous proximity to — neo-absolutism.

Rule 2: Flying a False Flag

If a country flies a flag that is not its own, the country whose flag it is will surely take offense. The United States has declared it unlawful for a foreign vessel to fly the American flag, and it exacts sanctions against any ship that violates this rule, denying it entry into U.S. ports for three months. During a period of warfare, a neutral country has a special interest in ensuring that its flag not be flown by one of the belligerents, since its use would falsely signal the country's participation on one side or the other, thus making its neutral population vulnerable to reprisal.[10]

But the rules against flying a false flag are not just left up to the special interests and vulnerabilities of particular countries. Chapter 8 of the air force handbook is dedicated to "Perfidy and Ruses." This chapter includes not only the category of falsified medical and truce signs ("The Misuse of Specified Signs, Signals, and Emblems which are Internationally Recognized") but also a second category: "Misuse of Enemy Flags, Insignia, and Uniform." Hague regulation 23(f) — the basis of the military prohibition — places the false flag in the same category as the misuse of the red cross and white flag: "It is especially prohibited to make improper use of a flag of truce, or the national flag, or of military insignias and uniform of the enemy, as well as of the distinctive signs of the Geneva Convention." Once more, these prohibited falsifications are very exceptional cases: almost all words and signs *can* legally undergo mystification during warfare; enemy flags and uniforms reside in that narrow region of language that cannot be misused without making the user guilty of perfidy.

Before the Abu Ghraib revelations, extensive *Washington Post* and *New York Times* reports on the alleged American practice of torture in the previous two years indicated that prisoners had been interrogated in rooms where false flags and national insignia were displayed. Gerald Posner's book *Why America Slept* includes a long description of the U.S. torture of the alleged Al Qaeda terrorist Abu Zubayda: it details the elaborate procedure American interrogators used to disguise themselves and their interrogation room as Saudi Arabian, with the result that the prisoner, believing he was being questioned by Saudis, revealed his close working relationship with an array of Saudi officials.[11] The CIA (according to Posner) refers to this method of torture as a false-flag interrogation.

Defenders of the event might say that although the Americans were surely flying a false flag, they were not necessarily flying the enemy's flag, or, more precisely, that it was only during the torture session that they learned that the flag they were flying may have belonged to an enemy. Defenders might also say that although many legal analysts before World War II endorsed a blanket prohibition on the use of an enemy flag, since World War II the misuse of the flag is prohibited only during combat.[12] Since torture takes place in a legal vacuum, it cannot be said to exist in the space of combat or the space of noncombat. Therefore, none of the Geneva, Hague, or military rules about uniforms, flags, and insignia apply.

These two arguments are obviously false. The stark illegality of torture does indeed place it in a space of moral reprehensibility outside the legal categories of combat and noncombat. But only the most abject cynic would claim that the zone of the morally reprehensible becomes, by virtue of its illegality, a free zone that is exempt from all other rules and laws. Furthermore, the Bush administration has repeatedly insisted that in a war on terrorism, the battlefield is everywhere: it would be odd for a country that unabashedly designated O'Hare International Airport in Chicago "a battlefield" when José Padilla was arrested to hold that a torture room is not a combat zone and therefore not subject to battlefield rules about false flags.

As the battlefield in the war on terrorism is simultaneously everywhere and nowhere, so our enemies are everyone and no one. If the flag we flew in the Zubayda torture room — the flag of Saudi Arabia — was not an enemy flag, it is because we have no enemy. Fifteen of the eighteen hijackers on 9/11 were from Saudi Arabia, so it is hard to see what country would stand ahead of Saudi Arabia in the line of candidates for the designation of "enemy." Are we to suppose that when the Saudi flag is introduced into an interrogation, it has been placed there as the insignia of an

American ally or neutral nation and not that of an opponent or suspected opponent? Is it not placed there because our enemy captive may well perceive it (as Zubayda did) as "friendly"?

The Bush administration has treated 9/11 as a shell game of shifting laws and norms. It could have treated the 9/11 attacks as criminal acts and gone after the perpetrators with criminal laws.[13] Instead it has treated them as acts of war and used a framework of war whose battlefields and enemies are everywhere but whose agents are nonstate actors and therefore not eligible for Geneva and Hague protections. If our opponents are nonstate actors, criminal law, and not a deformed version of the laws of war, should be used. But shuffling back and forth between two frameworks allows the administration to eliminate all national and international constraints on its increasingly debased power.

Before leaving the case of Abu Zubayda, we should take note that his treatment violated another elementary rule, beyond the false-flag principle: the requirement that the wounded be treated humanely.

Section 215 of the army's manual on the law of land warfare describes the "Protection and Care" due to the "Wounded and Sick":

> They shall be treated humanely and cared for by the Party to the conflict in whose power they may be, without any adverse distinction founded on sex, race, nationality, religion, political opinions . . . Any attempts upon their lives, or violence to their persons, shall be strictly prohibited; in particular, they shall not be . . . subjected to torture . . . they shall not be willfully left without medical assistance and care.

Whether the man being tortured actually was Zubayda was at the time uncertain (the man refused to say who he was), and whether Zubayda in turn was, as U.S. officials believed, a high-ranking Al Qaeda member was also uncertain (he had not stood trial). What was certain was that the captured man had a gunshot wound and was by virtue of his capture *hors de combat*. He therefore should have been subject to *Hostes dum vulnerati, fratres* and should have been cared for without regard for his nationality.

In September 2006, the U.S. Army issued a new handbook on interrogation, *Human Intelligence Collector Operations*. On page after page it forbids torture (invoking international, national, and military law), but it permits questioning that is free of force, even the questioning of a captive who is wounded, as long as the "questioning will not delay the administration of medication to reduce pain" or in any other way jeopardize the captive's medical well-being. In two separate sections it states the prohibition that was violated in the case of Zubayda: "Nor can [the questioner] state, imply, or otherwise give the impression that any type of medical treatment is conditional on the detainee's cooperation in answering questions."

Torture rooms and hospital rooms have come to be blurred in America's wars in Afghanistan and Iraq. Private Lynch was, by her own account and by the account of Nasiriyan physicians, nurses, and hospital administrators, treated in accordance with Section 215 of the army manual (and not, as Americans were at first led to believe, placed in a medical torture room). But the man called Zubayda, suffering from a gunshot wound in the groin, was placed not in a hospital but in a torture room, and his wound was enlisted into the method of extracting information.

A country at war must identify itself by flags, uniforms, and insignia on its planes. A country at war may not during combat fly a false flag. The United States may not fly the flag of Iraq or Saudi Arabia or Afghanistan or Pakistan. But may it continue to fly the flag of the United States? Can a country that breaks international and national rules — the Hague Conventions, the Geneva Conventions, and the regulations of its own army, navy, and air force — any longer fly the flag of the United States without being in danger of flying a false flag? The United States that most of us are committed to does not torture, does not conduct raids on the enemy's hospitals, does not shoot at ambulances, does not withhold a painkiller from a wounded enemy. Why should the small team of people carrying out such acts be permitted to continue flying our flag?

Rule 3: Wanted, Dead or Alive

On December 14, 2003, Paul Bremer, the American head of the Coalition Provisional Authority (wearing a large tie that looked like an American flag, with navy blue at the throat and flaring out into wide red and white stripes), stepped up to the microphone and, referring to the capture of Saddam Hussein, announced, "Ladies and gentlemen, we got him!"

The brief sections on perfidy and treachery in the rules-of-war handbooks of the air force, army, and navy contain one more regulation, derived from the Hague Conventions, Article 23(b). Here is the way the air force handbook formulates it:

> This article has been construed as prohibiting assassination, proscription or outlawry of an enemy, or putting a price upon an enemy's head, as well as offering a reward for any enemy "dead or alive."

The army handbook, composed earlier, uses almost identical language to describe the regulation in the section dedicated to "Forbidden Conduct with Respect to Persons." It is useful to look at the different phrasing used in Greenspan's *Modern Law of Land Warfare:*

> Under this rule are prohibited acts of assassination, the hiring of assassins, putting a price on an enemy's head, offering a reward for an enemy "dead or alive," proscription and outlawry of an enemy . . . Perpetrators of such acts should be tried as war criminals.

The first formal state prohibition of assassination and the promotion of assassination through the announcement of rewards was issued by President Abraham Lincoln in 1863, as General Order 100:

> The law of war does not allow proclaiming either an individual belonging to the hostile army, or a citizen, or a subject of the hostile government, an outlaw, who may be slain without trial by any captor, any more than the modern law of peace allows such international outlawry; on the contrary, it abhors such outrage. The sternest retaliation should follow the murder committed in consequence of such proclamation, made by whatever authority. Civilized nations look with horror upon offers of rewards for the assassination of enemies as relapses into barbarism.

This order influenced the creation of later international prohibitions (which have been incorporated into military law), as well as later American prohibitions in civil law (such as the current Executive Order 12,333).[14]

Against the backdrop of the tripartite prohibition (no assassination, no promise of a reward, no posting of "wanted, dead or alive"), it is useful to review the recent actions of President Bush.

On September 17, 2001, he announced to the country and the world that Osama bin Laden was "wanted, dead or alive." In his statement, made at a press conference, he referred to this as a phrase from a Wild West wanted poster, an allusion that has led at least one worried observer to excuse his statement as "a figure of speech." Nathan Canestaro, a member of the CIA's 2001 Afghanistan Task Force, writes in a law journal that "Bush's own suggestion that bin Laden was 'wanted, dead or alive,' strays dangerously close to those prohibited means of killing. Were the statement more than a figure of speech, it would constitute outlawry, rendering any resulting deaths as assassination under international law." But a call to treachery is not diminished by folksy phrasing.[15] Nor does Canestaro appear to have any reason (other than the wish to make Bush immune to the allegation of grave wrongdoing) to believe that the announcement was anything but literal.[16]

Soon, as if to reinforce the president's words, an official reward of $25 million was offered for Osama bin Laden. A later State Department clarification stressed that the reward was for information leading to bin Laden's capture rather than for his body, dead or alive; but the widely distributed wanted and reward posters did not always include that distinction. An article by Dayna Kaufman in the *Fordham Law Review* catalogues the ongoing forms of posting:

> The reward for bin Laden's capture is broadcast for 135 minutes a day in Afghanistan over the Voice of America radio system in Afghanistan's two main languages, Pashto and Dari. The length of the broadcast was expanded by thirty minutes to include daily crime alerts that promote the reward offer exclusively. In addition, the faces and other identifying characteristics of the wanted men [bin Laden and his inner circle] were placed on posters, matchbooks, fliers, and newspaper ads distributed around the world and dropped from United States military planes in Afghanistan.

Once more, the legal issues are arguably complicated, this time by questions about Osama bin Laden's status. Because bin Laden is not a combatant, the laws of war may not apply to him. Here again we see the shell game between criminal law and the laws of war. If bin Laden is a nonstate actor, if he is not a lawful combatant, he should be sought using criminal law.[17] Instead he is pursued as a war enemy, but the United States is exempt from following the laws of war because the enemy is not a combatant.

Of course, wanted and reward signs have continued to be posted even when the opponent has unquestionably been a state actor. When President Bush's attention pivoted from Afghanistan to Iraq, so did his posters. Perhaps in an attempt to sustain the Wild West saloon model, the U.S. military created a deck of cards naming and picturing the fifty-five most wanted men in Iraq. Unmindful of the air force and army regulations that forbid "putting a price on an enemy's head, offering a reward," the Bush administration offered, and paid, $15 million each for Uday and Qusay Hussein, the sons of Saddam Hussein, and $25 million for their father. A reward of $10 million was offered for Saddam Hussein's Baath Party deputy Izzat Ibrahim al-Douri. The reward for Abu Musab al-Zarqawi was initially set at $5 million, then raised to $10 million, and later to $25 million. Lesser amounts have been placed on the heads of other Iraqis. Speaking at a Coalition Provisional Authority briefing, Brigadier General Mark Kimmitt said that they put "specific amounts on specific people," though the amounts also depended on whether they were national ($1 million), regional ($200,000), or local ($50,000) terrorists.[18]

I have focused here on only the second and third elements of the tripartite ban (on assassination, on rewards, and on posting wanted signs) because the phrasing of those two bans is relatively uncontroversial, and the Bush administration's violation of — or straying near to violation of — the two bans is also relatively straightforward. Strong disagreements, in contrast, surround the question of precisely what national and international laws prohibit in the sphere of assassination, and such disagreements therefore also make it difficult to determine how close the Bush administration has come to assassination (in the killing of Uday and Qusay Hussein) or to attempted assassination (on the night before the beginning of the war in Iraq, when the United States, believing Saddam Hussein to be in a certain house, repeatedly bombed it). All sources agree that if a commander in chief or national leader or public figure participates in a battle and is killed in that battle (either intentionally or unintentionally), no act of assassination has occurred. If, however, one side goes behind the line of combat and intentionally kills a political leader on the other side, that act is widely understood to be an act of assassination.

But on this not everyone agrees. Several military analysts argue that the assassination of enemy leaders is legal under international law, that it is not in and of itself treacherous but only becomes so if it is treacherously carried out. This view is expressed by W. Hays Parks (writing in 1989 in *Army Lawyer*), by Air Force Major Michael N. Schmitt (writing in 1992 in the *Yale Journal of International Law*), and by Major Tyler J. Harder (writing in 2002 in *Military Law Review*). Although these men are military analysts, their interpretation appears to deviate from the air force and army handbooks' summaries of Hague regulation 23(b) by inverting the categories. These handbooks list assassination as a prohibited act of treachery (along with reward postings and "wanted, dead or alive" announcements). In other words, assassination is a subcategory of treachery. The two handbooks do not (as we might imagine from reading the cited articles) have a section on assassination that is divided into legal forms and illegal, treacherous forms. Parks, Schmitt, and Harder do not believe that there are acceptable and unacceptable "wanted, dead or alive" signs or acceptable and unacceptable reward postings, so it is odd that the third prohibited act, which occupies the same grammatical position in the sentence as the other two, is imagined in this way.

A second indication that this dissenting view is mistaken comes from the logical incoherence that it introduces into the relations between the three parts of the tripartite division. A treacherous assassination, in this view, involves "surprise"; it involves harm to someone who has reason to believe you wish him no injury (such as someone who agreed to meet you to discuss an armistice). Major Harder, arguing that only violations of confidence make assassination illegal, argues, "Treachery is a breach of confidence or perfidious act, that is, an attack on an individual who justifiably believes he has nothing to fear from the attacker."[19] But this view is starkly incompatible with the other two parts of the ban — the prohibition on wanted signs and rewards. What could be more open and unsurprising than a straightforward announcement that a country intends to have an enemy leader killed? A wanted sign or a reward poster constitutes just such an open announcement. Prohibiting assassination only if it entailed a violation of confidence or surprise would utterly contradict the ban on rewards and wanted postings.[20]

Even if one were to take the view offered by Harder, Parks, and Schmitt — that no act of intentionally killing political leaders will be deemed assassination unless it involves a betrayal of confidence

— the recent actions of the United States in Afghanistan and Iraq do not appear to stand entirely in the clear.[21] Once wanted signs, or their equivalents, have been posted, a political leader will almost certainly go into deep hiding. Who, then, is offered the reward for information leading to that leader's capture? It cannot be offered to random citizens of the country or passersby or taxi drivers or witnesses in the marketplace (since, once a reward is posted, the person will no longer travel on the public highways or walk in the marketplace); it cannot be offered to acquaintances or even to ordinary friends and family members. It is offered only to the one or two closest intimates in whom the leader places so much confidence that he has entrusted them with his hiding.[22]

The person who informed the U.S. military where they would find Uday and Qusay Hussein (and who has since collected the $30 million reward) was Nawaf al-Zaidan, in whose house the brothers had been staying for the twenty-two days before he revealed their location. Lists containing Nawaf al-Zaidan's name and the names of forty-eight of his relatives were later posted by Iraqis on the walls of Mosul as targeted for death because, as the *Guardian* explained, they were seen as having violated the host-guest relation: "Mr. Zaidan betrayed one of the most closely-held principles of tribal law: that a host has an obligation to protect his guests." While the prohibition on betraying the host-guest bond is indeed a principle of tribal law and may sound ancient to American ears, it must be noted how close it is to the prohibition on treachery in international law, since it involves injuring or killing someone who had reason to place confidence in you. Insofar as rewards and wanted signs are addressed to the hosts in whose care the wanted men have placed themselves, they are addressed to those who — in the eyes of the person in hiding — appear to be holding a white flag. Even if, therefore, we accept the Harder, Parks, and Schmitt doctrine that assassination is illegal only if it entails a violation of confidence, the United States may even be guilty by this narrow definition.

Where Do We Stand?

Our country tortures. It conducts raids on hospitals. It flies false flags. It makes "wanted, dead or alive" pronouncements. It posts rewards. It attempts (and sometimes carries out) assassinations. International law and military law do not put endless restraints on national actors. The sections on perfidy and treachery in the air force, army, and navy handbooks are in each case extremely brief — they put only three rules in front of us. Yet we have been unable to remain true to the three, or even two of the three, or even one of the three. We have violated, or have come perilously close to violating, each of them.

What judgments would we make if we altered the location and agent of these acts? Were we to look at Al Qaeda's literature and find there "wanted, dead or alive" postings for Western leaders or Western citizens, would we not regard those papers as documentary proof of neo-absolutism — proof of a complete disregard for international and military law? If a Saudi billionaire offered $30 million to any American who could identify a place in which an American leader or ordinary citizen could be captured or killed, what would we think? Would we say that the offer stays safely in the realm of legal practice because no one's confidence has been betrayed? Or because the offer only asked for information leading to capture? Would we say that it was just a figure of speech, an imitation of American rhetoric? If our opponents shot at our ambulances or if they raided our hospitals to retrieve their injured soldiers, what would we think?

The army manual, in Article 503, directly following a passage describing acts deemed "grave breaches" by the Geneva Conventions, quotes the conventions as saying, "No High Contracting Party [that is, a signatory nation] shall be allowed to absolve itself or any other High Contracting Party of any liability incurred by itself or by another High Contracting Party in respect of breaches referred to in the preceding Article." How, then, have we come to absolve ourselves of these breaches, or perhaps more to the point, how have we come to believe that no absolution is needed?

From the outset, the U.S. government's recognition that it might be guilty of wrongdoing has been visible in attempts not to right its conduct but to rewrite the rules. The correspondence between the White House and the Office of Legal Counsel during the winter of 2002 — specifically, Alberto Gonzales's January 25 memorandum and John Ashcroft's February 1 letter, both addressed to President Bush — shows an administration making legal decisions with the goal of making American officials immune to conviction of war crimes: Gonzales advises Bush to "[adhere] to your determination that [Geneva Convention III on the treatment of prisoners of war] does not apply," since that will "guard effectively against . . . misconstruction or misapplication of Section 2441 [the War Crimes Act]." Ashcroft writes, "A determination that the Geneva Convention does not apply will provide the United States with the highest level of legal certainty" so that our actions will be "foreclosed from judicial review."

The most effective way to make oneself immune to the charge of war crimes is to abstain from committing war crimes. Our alternative procedure might be called "cubing the violation": violate the rule in practice by carrying out actual harms to human beings, violate the rule in theory by deforming or revising the rule itself, violate the rule in metapractice by taking away from the courts the right to review the violations at levels one and two. The threefold injury to persons, rules, and courts has continued into the fall of 2006. President Bush attempted to write into a new detainee-treatment bill a provision granting immunity to war crime charges for its CIA counterterrorism officers, a provision Congress rejected. The CIA counterterrorism officers themselves are, according to the *Washington Post* and the *New York Times,* buying insurance policies in record numbers that will help cover their court costs should they eventually be tried for their acts during this period. The new detainee-treatment bill, called the Military Commissions Act, was signed into law on October 17, 2006, and permits the executive branch to rewrite the habeas corpus rule, thereby delivering a huge blow to persons and courts: it eliminates from our courts the right to review executive branch decisions about detainees by prohibiting prisoners from challenging their detention in court.

Often during the past five years it has been the military that has made the best — if ultimately unsuccessful — effort to protect our framework of national and international law: it was Colin Powell who held out the longest against the administration's pressure to give false evidence of Iraqi nuclear weapons; it was Specialist Joseph Darby who made the Abu Ghraib photographs available to the world; it was the judge advocates general who continually protested detainee treatment in Guantánamo until the Supreme

Court could act; it was Senator John McCain, explicitly on the basis of military experience, who repeatedly repelled President Bush's attempts to legalize torture.

But this resistance is imperfect and cannot always hold out, as became clear in Colin Powell's eventual UN testimony on Iraq's nuclear weapons and in John McCain's eventual endorsement of the devastating Military Commissions Act. The new army handbook on interrogation is a third case in point: it frequently reiterates the prohibition on torture and brainwashing, even explicitly listing and forbidding the elements (dogs, nakedness, hoods) that were designated permissible in Secretary Rumsfeld's December 2002 memorandum on detainee treatment in Guantánamo. But one practice that Rumsfeld permitted in his April 2003 memorandum to the Southern Command — the false-flag interrogation — has made its way into the handbook as an acceptable practice, as have other practices that should not be there.[23]

And what if the military does manage to hold the line? What if over time we come to see again and again that our civilian leaders do not obey the law and our military leaders do? And that our civilian leaders do not know how to safeguard the American population and our military leaders do? (Hurricane Katrina is an example: only when the military arrived did rescue begin.) Would this lead to our eventually preferring military over civilian leadership? It is exactly this situation that Charles Dunlap — the writer with whom we began — warns against in an earlier, 1992 article, "The Origins of the American Military Coup of 2012," which ought to be as widely read and debated in the civilian world as it has been in the military world.

But let us return to the immediate problem of neo-absolutism. To our earlier question — how have we come to believe that no acknowledgment of wrongdoing is needed? — three others can be added.

First, we know that our terrorist opponents resort to treachery because they cannot match our military force; they must choose between accepting defeat at the outset or else opposing us through asymmetrical warfare. But given our own military prowess, why do we resort to treachery?

Second, if the counterpart to treachery in the realm of weapons is unconventional weapons, why should we believe that our current leaders, willing to countenance torture and treachery, will refrain from using unconventional weapons? Though Iraq has no nuclear weapons, the United States has thousands. If our leaders have been willing to perform actions prohibited by our own military manuals, what will restrain us from performing actions that our military manuals assure us are legal? A version of the following sentence appears in the air force, army, and navy handbooks on the laws of war:

> There is at present no rule of international law expressly prohibiting States from the use of nuclear weapons in warfare. In the absence of express prohibition, the use of such weapons against enemy combatants and other military objectives is permitted.[24]

I believe there is every reason to worry that President Bush may use nuclear weapons.

Third, even if we ourselves successfully refrain from neo-absolutist practices, and even if those who oppose us eventually agree to give them up, is the situation that brought neo-absolutism into being at all tolerable? Is it tolerable that some one country in the world should have such uncontested military might that it can force every other country on earth to accept the boundaries that are now in place, the moral definitions that are now in place, the distribution of goods that is now in place? Most of the peace plans that have ever been written have included a provision that allows countries, after trying to settle disagreements peacefully, to go to war. Without this possibility, the world remains frozen in place in a way that arbitrarily advantages the country that at a single point in time became most powerful.

The sphere in which this question continues to be most important is that of nuclear weapons — their steady proliferation abroad and their vast and terrifying numbers on our own submarines and our own ground.

Notes

1. Though there was a strong reaction to the initial reports of this incident, eventually it became clear that the suicide-bomber taxi driver had not in fact used a white flag.

2. Rendition, like torture, is prohibited by the Geneva Conventions. Article 12

states that a signatory country can send prisoners only to other signatory countries; in transferring a prisoner, the first country has not transferred all responsibility.

3. For example, in his January 19, 2002, memorandum to the chairman of the Joint Chiefs of Staff, Rumsfeld states that detainees are "not entitled to prisoner of war status for the purposes of the Geneva Conventions." Later, in his April 16, 2003, memorandum to the commander of the U.S. Southern Command, he reiterates that "the provisions of Geneva are not applicable to unlawful combatants."

4. This memorandum and many others are reproduced in two books of documents: Mark Danner, *Torture and Truth: America, Abu Ghraib, and the War on Terror* (2004), and Karen J. Greenberg and Joshua L. Dratel, *The Torture Papers: The Road to Abu Ghraib* (2005).

5. This rule applies to nations with formal militaries and has complicated exceptions for popular uprisings, resistance fighters, and guerrilla fighters. During its consideration of "rules applicable in guerilla warfare" in a 1971 conference on international humanitarian law in armed conflict, members of the International Committee of the Red Cross worried about the way the absence of uniforms among these groups may, if they are taken prisoner, unfairly deprive them of prisoner-of-war status; it notes that these groups are still required to "conduct their operations in accordance with laws and customs of war."

6. It is reasonable to suppose that members of the military may well have seen, and voiced aloud their concern about, the trespass of rules. Often the civilian world learns belatedly, or not at all, of military objections to a country's undertakings: only in early March 2004, for example, did the public learn that British military leaders had, a year earlier, objected to the invasion of Iraq without a second UN resolution, for fear they would later be convicted of war crimes. It is also crucial to remember that we would still know nothing of torture at Abu Ghraib were it not for one soldier, Specialist Joseph Darby, who understood (and stood by) the rules.

7. During the weeks immediately following the event, the hospital was referred to, inaccurately, as "Saddam Hussein Hospital."

8. So strong is this nondiscrimination rule in the care of the sick that the Red Cross, which at one point had suggested that nurses in Red Cross hospitals be paired by nationality with patients when possible, later rescinded the recommendation.

9. The public record for this time does include a widely reported Iraqi misuse of a white flag: on March 23, 2003, an Iraqi artillery unit near Nasiriyah was said to have displayed a white flag, then fired on and killed nine U.S. Marines. But by the end of spring, the U.S. military acknowledged that these deaths were instead the result of American fratricide: an A-10 aircraft flying over the area misidentified, fired on, and killed the soldiers.

10. For more about these and other examples, see Myres S. McDougal and Florentino P. Feliciano's *Laws and Minimum World Public Order* (1961) and Robert W. Tucker's *The Law of War and Neutrality at Sea* (1957).

11. Because torture so often produces false information, U.S. officials could not act on the information Zubayda gave them about the Saudi officials without validating it independently. Their attempts to validate it failed, and Zubayda's information therefore proved useless.

12. Though the prohibition against using the enemy's flag or uniform is today widely recognized in the United States as applying only to battle, there is at least one

post–World War II regulation that asserts a blanket prohibition: Article 39 (2) of the 1977 Geneva Protocol. This blanket prohibition has been rejected by the United States. See Michael Matheson's 1987 essay "The United States Position of the Relation of Customary International Laws to the 1977 Protocols Additional to the Geneva Conventions," *American University Journal of International Law and Policy.*

Some of the pre–World War II arguments on behalf of the blanket prohibition continue to have considerable force: one scholar of international law, for example, points out the oddity of limiting the prohibition against using deceptive identifying marks to the very moment when one's actions make one's allegiance entirely evident — when one is firing on the enemy.

Of course, the display of national affiliation during battle not only announces one's intention to do harm but acknowledges responsibility for the injuries that follow. How important this act of acknowledgment is has in recent years become increasingly clear with the appearance of weapons that are decoupled from any human agent (unmanned planes) or that carry no national signature (electromagnetic transmissions that affect the equipment and people without leaving any trace of where the assault originated).

13. In the immediate aftermath of 9/11, this approach was urged by international law experts such as Richard Falk.

14. Major Tyler J. Harder, writing in the June 2002 issue of *Military Law Review,* argues that Executive Order 12,333 should be eliminated because it is redundant given Hague 23(b) prohibitions, but he simultaneously argues that it should be eliminated to give the U.S. executive and military more flexibility, thus proving that on some level Executive Order 12,333 is an effective, and needed, second brake on assassination, even if it does repeat international protocols.

15. A parallel instance of folksy Western phrasing appeared in President Bush's 2003 State of the Union address, as Hendrik Hertzberg noted in the February 10, 2003, issue of *The New Yorker.* After alluding to the arrest of three thousand suspected Al Qaeda terrorists, Bush said, "And many others have met a different fate. Let's put it this way: they are no longer a problem to the United States and our friends and allies." Hertzberg writes, "You could almost see the president blowing across the upturned barrel of his Colt .45." Hertzberg complains that the sentences are "tasteless," but a problem more grave than taste appears to be involved.

16. Threats against U.S. leaders are treated aggressively no matter how implausible or nonliteral. In October 2006, a fourteen-year-old girl who had temporarily posted on the MySpace website the words "Kill Bush" and a picture of a knife pointing toward the president's outstretched hand was visited by two Secret Service men who came first to her home, then to her school. They removed her from her eighth-grade biology class and questioned her harshly, telling her that she could be sent to juvenile hall.

17. Criminal law allows the posting of rewards and wanted signs, but not "wanted, dead or alive" announcements, since the alleged criminal must undergo a trial.

18. For an account of the January 13, 2006, "attempt to assassinate al Qaeda second-in-command Ayman Zawahiri in Pakistan" using a top-secret program of unmanned Predator drones, see Josh Meyer, "CIA Expands Uses of Drones in Terror War," *Los Angeles Times,* January 29, 2006. The attempt missed Zawahiri but killed eighteen civilians. Among those targeted and killed by Predator drones were, according to the *Times,* the military commander Mohammed Atef in Afghanistan,

Qaed Harithi in Yemen, Haitham Yemeni and Abu Hamza Rabia in Pakistan, and "a tall man in flowing robes" on the Pakistan-Afghanistan border who was wrongly thought to be Osama bin Laden. The Rabia killing included his seventeen-year-old son and the eight-year-old nephew of his landlord; the number of civilian deaths in the other targeted killings is not known.

19. Here Harder appears to have conflated the listing of assassination, rewards, and wanted announcements with the listing of red cross and white flag. It is indeed true to say that in war it is legal to shoot a gun at one's opponent but is treacherous to hold a white flag and shoot a gun at an opponent. But Harder concludes, using the foregoing as a template, that it must be legal to assassinate but treacherous to assassinate while holding a white flag (or otherwise enlisting the enemy's confidence). Were this an appropriate template, there would not be a need even to introduce the category of assassination, since the prohibition on assassinating while holding a white flag is already covered by the prohibition on the misuse of the white flag.

20. Though I have suggested two grounds that show the incoherence of requiring a violation of confidence to make assassination illegal, this idea has some plausible precedents that Schmitt offers in his richly detailed historical overview.

21. As Schmitt notes, a 1975 congressional investigation of attempted assassinations by the CIA records numerous attempts that certainly involved betrayal of confidence. For example, the air force handbook's Section 6.6(d) says that one must not injure enemy soldiers (or, needless to say, civilians) by using objects that enlist confidence — its example is putting an explosive in a fountain pen. The CIA attempted to kill Fidel Castro in the early 1960s by putting a lethal toxin in a cigar, placing an explosive device in a rare seashell deep under water (Castro was known to be an expert diver and lover of beautiful shells), and arming a fountain pen with a hypodermic needle so fine that he would not notice the injection.

22. The defense expert William Arkin, interviewed for a February 2004 Discovery Channel documentary on Osama bin Laden, said that offers of rewards are addressed to "close friends and associates."

23. Though interrogators are permitted to wear false military uniforms, they are explicitly prohibited from wearing false Red Cross uniforms: the two forms of false signs that were coupled in Article 23(f) of the Hague Conventions and the perfidy and treachery sections of the air force, army, and navy handbooks have therefore, in this new field manual, been decoupled from each other.

24. Section 6.5 of the air force handbook continues with a set of cautionary sentences: "The weapons have been the subject of intense international political interest and international regulation because of their potential for mass destruction, the historical fact of their recent development by only a very few powers with the ability to control their development and deployment, and international concern about possible proliferation." The section then lists the international treaties we have signed that may bear on the question of their use.

ROGER SCRUTON

A Carnivore's Credo

FROM HARPER'S MAGAZINE

THE TREATMENT OF ANIMALS, like much else that was once the prerogative of religion, has become a matter of ordinary morality, with no shortage of sermons directed at hunters, fur wearers, and carnivores by puritans who cannot abide the sight of sinful pleasure. Eating animals has become a test case for moral theory in Western societies. In confronting opponents of meat eating, we find ourselves exploring the grounds of moral judgments and the nature of the beings who make them.

The moral life, I believe, rests on three pillars: value, virtue, and duty. Some hold that all the weight can be made to rest on only one of them: value, according to utilitarians; duty, according to their deontological opponents. Whether or not any such reductions can be successfully carried out, we cannot give a coherent account of the moral life without doing justice to all the conceptions that support it — to value, virtue, and duty — and showing their place, for human beings, in the good life.

I have a strong urge to place at the very center of the subject, especially since the subject is our relation to the natural world, another aspect of human nature, often left out by the standard treatments of ethics: namely, piety. By this I mean a disposition to acknowledge our weak and dependent state and to face the surrounding world with due reverence and humility. It is the residue of religion in us all, whether or not we wish to admit it. It is the attitude that many people — environmentalists, conservationists, and animal welfare activists included — are attempting to recapture in a world where the results of human presumption are so depressingly apparent.

Unlike other animals, we are self-conscious. We do not live, as they do, only in the "world of perception," to use Schopenhauer's phrase. Our thoughts and feelings range over the actual and the possible, the probable and the necessary, what will be and what ought to be. Upon these basic facts — traditionally summarized by saying we are rational animals — other and more remarkable facts depend. We have moral, aesthetic, and religious experiences; we pray to things visible and invisible; we laugh, sing, and grieve; are indignant, approving, and dismayed. And we relate to one another in a special way. Human beings are actual or potential members of a moral community, regulated by concepts of right and duty, in which each member enjoys sovereignty over his own affairs, so long as he accords an equal sovereignty to others. With all this comes an immense burden of guilt. Morality and self-consciousness set us in judgment over ourselves, so that we see our actions constantly from outside, judged by ourselves as we are by others. We become cut off from our instincts, and even the spontaneous joy of fellowship is diminished by the screen of judgment through which it first must pass.

Animals rescue us from this predicament. Their mute lack of self-consciousness neutralizes our own possession of it and makes it possible to pour out on them the pent-up store of fellow feeling, without fear of reproach. At the same time, we are acutely aware of their moral incompetence. Their affection, if it can be won at all, is easily won, and based on nothing. However much a man may be loved by his dog, this love brings warmth and security but no release from guilt. It implies no moral approval and leaves the character of its object unassessed and unendorsed. For that very reason, a dog is a far easier companion than a person, and the temptation arises to believe that all animals are really like our pets, with the same moral claims and the same need for consideration that characterizes the animals on whom we depend for companionship. That which distinguishes us from animals — our predicament as self-conscious and judging creatures — leads us constantly to discount the difference, to act as though it were a marginal consideration on which nothing hangs when it comes to the real ethical questions.

But the difference comes immediately to life when we consider the question of eating. Whether or not we think eating people is wrong, we do not think it is on a par with eating other animals. We recoil from the idea that human beings might be on the daily menu along with cabbage, chicken, squirrel, and lentils. This brings to the fore the distinction between our attitude toward the human body, even when dead, and our attitude toward the bodies of other animals. Although elephants and dolphins engage in behavior that shows a partial resemblance to our feelings in the presence of the dead, the emotions with which we approach a corpse are emotions that only a self-conscious being can experience and must be characterized in terms such as "awe," "reverence," and "anxiety." They belong to the philosophically neglected realm of the psyche I have called piety. The corpse is not to be carelessly touched, not to be defiled, not to be abused. Its former occupant surrounds it like an aura, demanding to be mourned.

All this you will find beautifully evoked in the scene between Achilles and Priam in the *Iliad,* when the old king comes to beg for Hector's desecrated body. Not all cultures treat this predicament as the Homeric Greeks did, but in all cultures some form of piety is called forth by the human corpse. This is not some arbitrary or dispensable feature of our condition; it is a nonrational consequence of being rational. We can imagine a perfectly good functional justification for these feelings, but it would disappear if we thought of them in purely functional terms. Piety exists only so long as we don't ask the reason why: that, indeed, is its essence — a sense of duty that does not question what it receives as commands.

So far as I know, people do not eat their pets, even when the pets belong to species that are commonly eaten. Pets are honorary members of the human community and enjoy some imagined version of the nimbus that surrounds the human body — the nimbus Michelangelo presented in his versions of the Pietà. People bury their dogs and cats, often erecting tombstones over their bodies. And even when this seems absurd, some kind of piety is bestowed on an animal whose companionship has been enjoyed when it is a companion no longer.

Pious feelings survive also in the religious prohibitions that attach to the eating of meat. If God takes an interest in what we eat, it can only be because eating and ingesting are acts not only of the body but also of the soul. Yet dietary codes do not prohibit us from

defiling the corpses of other animals. They instruct us not to defile
ourselves by eating what is forbidden. This is further confirmation
of the dramatic way in which animals and people are distinguished
in our feelings.

The fact that eating, for us, is not what it is for other animals is related to the fact that we are moral beings. Eating has in every traditional society been regarded as a social, often religious, act,
embellished by ritual and enjoyed as a primary celebration of
membership. Rational beings are nourished on conversation, taste,
manners, and hospitality, and to divorce food from these practices
is to deprive it of its true significance. Rational beings rejoice less
in filling themselves than in the sight of food, table, and guests
dressed for a ceremonial offering. Their meals are also sacrifices;
some anthropologists have argued that the origin of our carnivo-
rous ways lies in the burnt offerings of ancient ritual. At any rate,
the giving of food is the core of hospitality.

In the fast-food culture, on the other hand, food is not given but
taken. The solitary stuffing of burgers, pizzas, and "TV dinners";
the disappearance of family meals and domestic cooking; the loss
of table manners — all these tend to obscure the distinction between eating and feeding. For many people, vegetarianism is a
roundabout way of restoring that distinction. Vegetables are gifts of
the earth: by eating them we reestablish contact with our roots.
They offer a way of reincorporating food into the moral life, hedg-
ing it in with moral scruples and revitalizing the precious sense of
shame. Meat eating cannot be vindicated without confronting the
deep feelings that prompt our dietary habits. The onus lies on the
carnivore to show that there is a way of incorporating meat into a
life that does not shame the human race, as it is shamed by the solitary "caveman" gluttony of the burger stuffer.

I have hinted that there might be a distinction between virtuous and vicious eating. Virtuous eating involves behavior that is
considerate of others and that permits and facilitates the easy con-
tinuation of dialogue. Good manners prevent that sudden and disturbing eclipse of the person by the animal, as the fangs sink themselves into the mess on the plate.

It is also a part of virtue to consider what benefits and harms are
promoted by your actions — not, I hasten to add, in the manner of

the utilitarian, seeking a comprehensive balance sheet of pleasure and pain, but in the manner of the humane person, who wishes to promote kindness and to oppose cruelty — in other words, to promote virtue over vice. The virtue of kindness cannot be understood without also invoking ideas of responsibility, duty, and right. Kindness means treating with gentleness and consideration all those with whom you have dealings, while also fulfilling your obligations toward them. To speak of it brings us to the fundamental question of deontology: What are our obligations, and do they permit us to eat animals?

Animals bred or kept for our uses are not honorary members of the moral community, as pets are. Nevertheless the use we make of them imposes a reciprocal duty to look after them, which spreads forward from the farmer to the slaughterer and from the slaughterer to the consumer, all of whom benefit from these animals and must therefore assume some part of the duty of care. To criticize battery pig farming as violating a duty of care is surely right and proper. But consider the traditional beef farmer, who fattens his calves for thirty months, keeping them on open pasture in the summer and in warm roomy barns in the winter, feeding them on grass, silage, beans, and maize, attending to their ailments, and sending them for slaughter, when the time comes, to the nearby slaughterhouse, where they are instantly dispatched by a humane killer. Such a farmer treats his cattle as well as cattle can be treated, and such animals are as happy as their nature allows. Anybody who cares for animals ought to see this kind of husbandry as a complex moral good, to be defended, on the one hand, against those who would forbid the eating of meat altogether and, on the other hand, against those carnivores who prefer the unseen suffering of the battery farm and the factory abattoir.

The relation between man and animal may not always be as harmonious as it appears in children's books devoted to life on the farm, but it is only one feature of the total ecology of the countryside. Traditional livestock farming involves the maintenance of pastureland, properly enclosed with walls or hedges. Wildlife habitats spring up as the near automatic byproducts of the boundaries and shady places required by cattle. This kind of farming has shaped the English landscape, ensuring it retains its dual character as producer of human food and a complex wildlife habitat with a beauty inextricably connected to its multifarious life. In this way, what is, from the point of view of agribusiness, a wasteful use of land becomes, from the point of view of the rest of us, one of the kindest uses of land yet devised. The animal brought to the table will have enjoyed the protection of the one who nurtured him, and his death will be like the ritual sacrifices described in the Bible and Homeric literature — a *singling out* of a victim for an important office to which a kind of honor is attached.

The real force of the vegetarian argument stems, I believe, from a revulsion at the vicious carnivore: the meat eater as he has evolved in the solipsistic fast-food culture, with the removal of food from its central place in domestic life and the winning of friends. From Homer to Zola, meat has been seen as the primordial gift to the stranger, the eruption into the world of human conflict of the divine spirit of peace. Reduce meat to an object of solitary greed like chocolate and the question naturally arises: Why should *life* be sacrificed just for this?

The question presents a challenge. It is asking the burger stuffer to *come clean:* to show why it is that his greed should be indulged in this way, why he can presume to kill again and again for the sake of a solitary pleasure that neither creates nor sustains any moral ties. To such a question it is always possible to respond with a shrug of the shoulders. But it is a real question, one of many that people now ask, as the old forms of piety dwindle. Piety is the remedy for religious guilt, and to this emotion we are all witting or unwitting heirs. And I suspect people become vegetarians for precisely that reason: by doing so they overcome the residue of guilt that attaches to every form of hubris, and in particular to the hubris of human freedom.

There is, however, a remedy more in keeping with the Judeo-Christian tradition. We should not abandon our meat-eating habits but *remoralize* them, by reincorporating them into affectionate human relations and using them as instruments of hospitality, conviviality, and peace. That was the remedy practiced by our parents, with their traditional "Sunday roast" coming always at midday, after they had given thanks. Those brought up on fast food are not used to making sacrifices: mealtimes, manners, dinner-table conversation, and the art of cookery itself have all but disappeared from their worldview. But all those things form part of a complex human good, and I cannot help thinking that, when added to the ecological benefits of small-scale livestock farming, they secure for us an honorable place in the scheme of things, and neutralize more effectively than the vegetarian alternative our inherited burden of guilt.

I would suggest that it is not only permissible for those who care about animals to eat meat; they have a duty to do so. If meat eating should ever become confined to those who do not care about animal suffering, then compassionate farming would cease. Where there are conscientious carnivores, there is a motive to raise animals kindly. Moreover, conscientious carnivores show their depraved contemporaries that there is a right and a wrong way to eat. Duty requires us, therefore, to eat our friends.

PETER SINGER

What Should a Billionaire Give — and What Should You?

FROM THE NEW YORK TIMES MAGAZINE

WHAT IS A HUMAN LIFE WORTH? You may not want to put a price tag on it. But if we really had to, most of us would agree that the value of a human life would be in the millions. Consistent with the foundations of our democracy and our frequently professed belief in the inherent dignity of human beings, we would also agree that all humans are created equal, at least to the extent of denying that differences of sex, ethnicity, nationality, and place of residence change the value of a human life.

With Christmas approaching, and Americans writing checks to their favorite charities, it's a good time to ask how these two beliefs — that a human life, if it can be priced at all, is worth millions, and that the factors I have mentioned do not alter the value of a human life — square with our actions. Perhaps this year such questions lurk beneath the surface of more family discussions than usual, for it has been an extraordinary year for philanthropy, especially philanthropy to fight global poverty.

For Bill Gates, the founder of Microsoft, the ideal of valuing all human life equally began to jar against reality some years ago, when he read an article about diseases in the developing world and came across the statistic that half a million children die every year from rotavirus, the most common cause of severe diarrhea in children. He had never heard of rotavirus. "How could I never have heard of something that kills half a million children every year?" he asked himself. He then learned that in developing countries, millions of children die from diseases that have been eliminated, or virtually eliminated, in the United States. That shocked him because he assumed that, if there are vaccines and treatments that could save lives, governments would be doing everything possible to get them to the people who need them. As Gates told a meeting of the World Health Assembly in Geneva last year, he and his wife, Melinda, "couldn't escape the brutal conclusion that — in our world today — some lives are seen as worth saving and others are not." They said to themselves, "This can't be true." But they knew it was.

Gates's speech to the World Health Assembly concluded on an optimistic note, looking forward to the next decade when "people will finally accept that the death of a child in the developing world is just as tragic as the death of a child in the developed world." That belief in the equal value of all human life is also prominent on the website of the Bill and Melinda Gates Foundation, where under "Our Values" we read: "All lives — no matter where they are being led — have equal value."

We are very far from acting in accordance with that belief. In the same world in which more than a billion people live at a level of affluence never previously known, roughly a billion other people struggle to survive on the purchasing power equivalent of less than one U.S. dollar per day. Most of the world's poorest people are undernourished, lack access to safe drinking water or even the most basic health services, and cannot send their children to school. According to UNICEF, more than 10 million children die every year — about 30,000 per day — from avoidable, poverty-related causes.

Last June the investor Warren Buffett took a significant step toward reducing those deaths when he pledged $31 billion to the Gates Foundation and another $6 billion to other charitable foundations. Buffett's pledge, set alongside the nearly $30 billion given by Bill and Melinda Gates to their foundation, has made it clear that the first decade of the twenty-first century is a new "golden age of philanthropy." On an inflation-adjusted basis, Buffett has pledged to give more than double the lifetime total given away by two of the philanthropic giants of the past, Andrew Carnegie and John D. Rockefeller, put together. Bill and Melinda Gates's gifts are not far behind.

Gates's and Buffett's donations will now be put to work primarily to reduce poverty, disease, and premature death in the developing world. According to the Global Forum for Health Research, less than 10 percent of the world's health research budget is spent on combating conditions that account for 90 percent of the global burden of disease. In the past, diseases that affect only the poor have been of no commercial interest to pharmaceutical manufacturers, because the poor cannot afford to buy their products. The Global Alliance for Vaccines and Immunization (GAVI), heavily supported by the Gates Foundation, seeks to change this by guaranteeing to purchase millions of doses of vaccines, when they are developed, that can prevent diseases like malaria. GAVI has also assisted developing countries to immunize more people with existing vaccines: 99 million additional children have been reached to date. By doing this, GAVI claims to have already averted nearly 1.7 million future deaths.

Philanthropy on this scale raises many ethical questions: Why are the people who are giving doing so? Does it do any good? Should we praise them for giving so much or criticize them for not giving still more? Is it troubling that such momentous decisions are made by a few extremely wealthy individuals? And how do our judgments about them reflect on our own way of living?

Let's start with the question of motives. The rich must — or so some of us with less money like to assume — suffer sleepless nights because of their ruthlessness in squeezing out competitors, firing workers, shutting down plants, or whatever else they have to do to acquire their wealth. When wealthy people give away money, we can always say that they are doing it to ease their consciences or generate favorable publicity. It has been suggested — by, for example, David Kirkpatrick, a senior editor at *Fortune* magazine — that Bill Gates's turn to philanthropy was linked to the antitrust problems Microsoft had in the United States and the European Union. Was Gates, consciously or subconsciously, trying to improve his own image and that of his company?

This kind of sniping tells us more about the attackers than the attacked. Giving away large sums, rather than spending the money on corporate advertising or developing new products, is not a sensible strategy for increasing personal wealth. When we read that someone has given away a lot of their money, or time, to help others, it challenges us to think about our own behavior. Should we be following their example, in our own modest way? But if the rich just give their money away to improve their image, or to make up for past misdeeds — misdeeds quite unlike any we have committed, of course — then, conveniently, what they are doing has no relevance to what we ought to do.

A famous story is told about Thomas Hobbes, the seventeenth-century English philosopher, who argued that we all act in our own interests. On seeing him give alms to a beggar, a cleric asked Hobbes if he would have done this if Christ had not commanded us to do so. Yes, Hobbes replied, he was in pain to see the miserable condition of the old man, and his gift, by providing the man with some relief from that misery, also eased Hobbes's pain. That reply reconciles Hobbes's charity with his egoistic theory of human motivation, but at the cost of emptying egoism of much of its bite. If egoists suffer when they see a stranger in distress, they are capable of being as charitable as any altruist.

Followers of the eighteenth-century German philosopher Immanuel Kant would disagree. They think an act has moral worth only if it is done out of a sense of duty. Doing something merely because you enjoy doing it, or enjoy seeing its consequences, they say, has no moral worth, because if you happened not to enjoy doing it, then you wouldn't do it, and you are not responsible for your likes and dislikes, whereas you are responsible for your obedience to the demands of duty.

Perhaps some philanthropists are motivated by their sense of duty. Apart from the equal value of all human life, the other "simple value" that lies at the core of the work of the Gates Foundation, according to its website, is "To whom much has been given, much is expected." That suggests the view that those who have great wealth have a duty to use it for a larger purpose than their own interests. But while such questions of motive may be relevant to our assessment of Gates's or Buffett's character, they pale into insignificance when we consider the effect of what Gates and Buffett are doing. The parents whose children could die from rotavirus care more about getting the help that will save their children's lives than about the motivations of those who make that possible.

Interestingly, neither Gates nor Buffett seems motivated by the possibility of being rewarded in heaven for his good deeds on earth. Gates told a *Time* interviewer, "There's a lot more I could be doing on a Sunday morning" than going to church. Put them together with Andrew Carnegie, famous for his freethinking, and three of the four greatest American philanthropists have been atheists or agnostics. (The exception is John D. Rockefeller.) In a country in which 96 percent of the population say they believe in a supreme being, that's a striking fact. It means that in one sense, Gates and Buffett are probably less self-interested in their charity than someone like Mother Teresa, who as a pious Roman Catholic believed in reward and punishment in the afterlife.

More important than questions about motives are questions about whether there is an obligation for the rich to give, and if so, how much they should give. A few years ago, an African-American cabdriver taking me to the Inter-American Development Bank in Washington asked me if I worked at the bank. I told him I did not but was speaking at a conference on development and aid. He then assumed that I was an economist, but when I said no, my training was in philosophy, he asked me if I thought the United States should give foreign aid. When I answered affirmatively, he replied that the government shouldn't tax people in order to give their money to others. That, he thought, was robbery. When I asked if he believed that the rich should voluntarily donate some of what they earn to the poor, he said that if someone had worked for his money, he wasn't going to tell him what to do with it.

At that point we reached our destination. Had the journey continued, I might have tried to persuade him that people can earn large amounts only when they live under favorable social circumstances, and that they don't create those circumstances by themselves. I could have quoted Warren Buffett's acknowledgment that society is responsible for much of his wealth. "If you stick me down in the middle of Bangladesh or Peru," he said, "you'll find out how much this talent is going to produce in the wrong kind of soil." The Nobel Prize–winning economist and social scientist Herbert Simon estimated that "social capital" is responsible for at least 90 percent of what people earn in wealthy societies like those of the United States or northwestern Europe. By social capital Simon meant not only natural resources but, more important, the technology and organizational skills in the community, and the presence of good government. These are the foundation on which the rich can begin their work. "On moral grounds," Simon added, "we could argue for a flat income tax of 90 percent." Simon was not, of course, advocating so steep a rate of tax, for he was well aware of disincentive effects. But his estimate does undermine the argument that the rich are entitled to keep their wealth because it is all a result of their hard work. If Simon is right, that is true of at most 10 percent of it.

In any case, even if we were to grant that people deserve every dollar they earn, that doesn't answer the question of what they should do with it. We might say that they have a right to spend it on lavish parties, private jets, and luxury yachts, or, for that matter, to flush it down the toilet. But we could still think that for them to do these things while others die from easily preventable diseases is wrong. In an article I wrote more than three decades ago, at the time of a humanitarian emergency in what is now Bangladesh, I used the example of walking by a shallow pond and seeing a small child who has fallen in and appears to be in danger of drowning. Even though we did nothing to cause the child to fall into the pond, almost everyone agrees that if we can save the child at minimal inconvenience or trouble to ourselves, we ought to do so. Anything else would be callous, indecent, and, in a word, wrong. The fact that in rescuing the child we may, for example, ruin a new pair of shoes is not a good reason for allowing the child to drown. Similarly if for the cost of a pair of shoes we can contribute to a health program in a developing country that stands a good chance of saving the life of a child, we ought to do so.

Perhaps, though, our obligation to help the poor is even stronger than this example implies, for we are less innocent than the passerby who did nothing to cause the child to fall into the pond. Thomas Pogge, a philosopher at Columbia University, has argued that at least some of our affluence comes at the expense of the poor. He bases this claim not simply on the usual critique of the barriers that Europe and the United States maintain against agricultural imports from developing countries but also on less familiar aspects of our trade with developing countries. For example, he points out that international corporations are willing to make deals to buy natural resources from any government, no matter how it has come to power. This provides a huge financial incentive for groups to try to overthrow the existing government. Successful rebels are rewarded by being able to sell off the nation's oil, minerals, or timber.

In their dealings with corrupt dictators in developing countries, Pogge asserts, international corporations are morally no better than someone who knowingly buys stolen goods — with the difference that the international legal and political order recognizes the corporations, not as criminals in possession of stolen goods but as the legal owners of the goods they have bought. This situation is, of course, beneficial for the industrial nations, because it enables us to obtain the raw materials we need to maintain our prosperity, but it is a disaster for resource-rich developing countries, turning the wealth that should benefit them into a curse that leads to a cycle of coups, civil wars, and corruption, and is of little benefit to the people as a whole.

In this light, our obligation to the poor is not just one of providing assistance to strangers but one of compensation for harms that we have caused and are still causing them. It might be argued that we do not owe the poor compensation, because our affluence actually benefits them. Living luxuriously, it is said, provides employment, and so wealth trickles down, helping the poor more effectively than aid does. But the rich in industrialized nations buy virtually nothing that is made by the very poor. During the past twenty years of economic globalization, although expanding trade has helped lift many of the world's poor out of poverty, it has failed to benefit the poorest 10 percent of the world's population. Some of the extremely poor, most of whom live in sub-Saharan Africa, have nothing to sell that rich people want, while others lack the infrastructure to get their goods to market. If they can get their crops to a port, European and U.S. subsidies often mean that they cannot sell them, despite — as for example in the case of West African cotton growers who compete with vastly larger and richer U.S. cotton producers — having a lower production cost than the subsidized producers in the rich nations.

The remedy to these problems, it might reasonably be suggested, should come from the state, not from private philanthropy. When aid comes through the government, everyone who earns above the tax-free threshold contributes something, with more collected from those with greater ability to pay. Much as we may applaud what Gates and Buffett are doing, we can also be troubled by a system that leaves the fate of hundreds of millions of people hanging on the decisions of two or three private citizens. But the amount of foreign development aid given by the U.S. government is, at 22 cents for every $100 the nation earns, about the same, as a percentage of gross national income, as Portugal gives and about half that of the United Kingdom. Worse still, much of it is directed where it best suits U.S. strategic interests — Iraq is now by far the largest recipient of U.S. development aid, and Egypt, Jordan, Pakistan, and Afghanistan all rank in the top ten. Less than a quarter of official U.S. development aid — barely a nickel in every $100 of our GNI — goes to the world's poorest nations.

Adding private philanthropy to U.S. government aid improves this picture, because Americans privately give more per capita to international philanthropic causes than the citizens of almost any other nation. Even when private donations are included, however, countries like Norway, Denmark, Sweden, and the Netherlands give three or four times as much foreign aid, in proportion to the size of their economies, as the United States gives — with a much larger percentage going to the poorest nations. At least as things now stand, the case for philanthropic efforts to relieve global poverty is not susceptible to the argument that the government has taken care of the problem. And even if official U.S. aid were better directed and comparable, relative to our gross domestic product, with that of the most generous nations, there would still be a role for private philanthropy. Unconstrained by diplomatic considerations or the desire to swing votes at the United Nations, private donors can more easily avoid dealing with corrupt or wasteful governments. They can go directly into the field, working with local villages and grass-roots organizations.

Nor are philanthropists beholden to lobbyists. As the *New York Times* reported recently, billions of dollars of U.S. aid is tied to domestic goods. Wheat for Africa must be grown in America, although aid experts say this often depresses local African markets, reducing the incentive for farmers there to produce more. In a decision that surely costs lives, hundreds of millions of condoms intended to stop the spread of AIDS in Africa and around the world must be manufactured in the United States, although they cost twice as much as similar products made in Asia.

In other ways, too, private philanthropists are free to venture where governments fear to tread. Through a foundation named for his wife, Susan Thompson Buffett, Warren Buffett has supported reproductive rights, including family planning and pro-choice organizations. In another unusual initiative, he has pledged $50 million for the International Atomic Energy Agency's plan to establish a "fuel bank" to supply nuclear-reactor fuel to countries that meet their nuclear-nonproliferation commitments. The idea, which has been talked about for many years, is widely agreed to be a useful step toward discouraging countries from building their own facilities for producing nuclear fuel, which could then be diverted to weapons production. It is, Buffett said, "an investment in a safer world." Though it is something that governments could and should be doing, no government had taken the first step.

Aid has always had its critics. Carefully planned and intelligently directed private philanthropy may be the best answer to the claim that aid doesn't work. Of course, as in any large-scale human enterprise, some aid can be ineffective. But provided that aid isn't actually counterproductive, even relatively inefficient assistance is likely to do more to advance human well-being than luxury spending by the wealthy.

The rich, then, should give. But how much should they give? Gates may have given away nearly $30 billion, but that still leaves him sitting at the top of the Forbes list of the richest Americans, with $53 billion. His 66,000-square-foot high-tech lakeside estate near Seattle is reportedly worth more than $100 million. Property taxes are about $1 million. Among his possessions is the Leicester Codex, the only handwritten book by Leonardo da Vinci still in private hands, for which he paid $30.8 million in 1994. Has Bill Gates done enough? More pointedly, you might ask: If he really believes that all lives have equal value, what is he doing living in such an expensive house and owning a Leonardo codex? Are there no more lives that could be saved by living more modestly and adding the money thus saved to the amount he has already given?

Yet we should recognize that, if judged by the proportion of his wealth that he has given away, Gates compares very well with most of the other people on the *Forbes* 400 list, including his former colleague and Microsoft cofounder, Paul Allen. Allen, who left the company in 1983, has given, over his lifetime, more than $800 million to philanthropic causes. That is far more than nearly any of us will ever be able to give. But *Forbes* lists Allen as the fifth-richest American, with a net worth of $16 billion. He owns the Seattle Seahawks, the Portland Trailblazers, a 413-foot oceangoing yacht that carries two helicopters and a 60-foot submarine. He has given only about 5 percent of his total wealth.

Is there a line of moral adequacy that falls between the 5 percent that Allen has given away and the roughly 35 percent that Gates has donated? Few people have set a personal example that would allow them to tell Gates that he has not given enough, but one who could is Zell Kravinsky. A few years ago, when he was in his mid-forties, Kravinsky gave almost all of his $45 million real estate fortune to health-related charities, retaining only his modest family home in Jenkintown, near Philadelphia, and enough to meet his family's ordinary expenses. After learning that thousands of people with failing kidneys die each year while waiting for a transplant, he contacted a Philadelphia hospital and donated one of his kidneys to a complete stranger.

After reading about Kravinsky in *The New Yorker,* I invited him to speak to my classes at Princeton. He comes across as anguished by the failure of others to see the simple logic that lies behind his altruism. Kravinsky has a mathematical mind — a talent that obviously helped him in deciding what investments would prove profitable — and he says that the chances of dying as a result of donating a kidney are about one in four thousand. For him this implies that to withhold a kidney from someone who would otherwise die means valuing one's own life at four thousand times that of a stranger, a ratio Kravinsky considers "obscene."

What marks Kravinsky from the rest of us is that he takes the equal value of all human life as a guide to life, not just as a nice piece of rhetoric. He acknowledges that some people think he is crazy, and even his wife says she believes that he goes too far. One of her arguments against the kidney donation was that one of their children may one day need a kidney, and Zell could be the only compatible donor. Kravinsky's love for his children is, as far as I can tell, as strong as that of any normal parent. Such attachments are part of our nature, no doubt the product of our evolution as mammals who give birth to children, who for an unusually long time require our assistance in order to survive. But that does not, in Kravinsky's view, justify our placing a value on the lives of our children that is thousands of times greater than the value we place on the lives of the children of strangers. Asked if he would allow his child to die if it would enable a thousand children to live, Kravinsky said yes. Indeed, he has said he would permit his child to die even if this enabled only two other children to live. Nevertheless, to appease his wife, he recently went back into real estate, made some money, and bought the family a larger home. But he still remains committed to giving away as much as possible, subject only to keeping his domestic life reasonably tranquil.

Buffett says he believes in giving his children "enough so they feel they could do anything, but not so much that they could do nothing." That means, in his judgment, "a few hundred thousand" each. In absolute terms, that is far more than most Americans are able to leave their children and, by Kravinsky's standard, certainly too much. (Kravinsky says that the hard part is not giving away the first $45 million but the last $10,000, when you have to live so cheaply that you can't function in the business world.) But even if Buffett left each of his three children a million dollars each, he would still have given away more than 99.99 percent of his wealth. When someone does that much — especially in a society in which the norm is to leave most of your wealth to your children — it is better to praise them than to cavil about the extra few hundred thousand dollars they might have given.

Philosophers like Liam Murphy of New York University and my colleague Kwame Anthony Appiah at Princeton contend that our obligations are limited to carrying our fair share of the burden of relieving global poverty. They would have us calculate how much would be required to ensure that the world's poorest people have a chance at a decent life, and then divide this sum among the affluent. That would give us each an amount to donate, and having given that, we would have fulfilled our obligations to the poor.

What might that fair amount be? One way of calculating it would be to take as our target, at least for the next nine years, the Millennium Development Goals, set by the United Nations Millennium Summit in 2000. On that occasion, the largest gathering of world leaders in history jointly pledged to meet, by 2015, a list of goals that include:

- Reducing by half the proportion of the world's people in extreme poverty (defined as living on less than the purchasing-power equivalent of one U.S. dollar per day).
- Reducing by half the proportion of people who suffer from hunger.
- Ensuring that children everywhere are able to take a full course of primary schooling.
- Ending sex disparity in education.
- Reducing by two thirds the mortality rate among children under five.
- Reducing by three quarters the rate of maternal mortality.
- Halting and beginning to reverse the spread of HIV/AIDS and halting and beginning to reduce the incidence of malaria and other major diseases.
- Reducing by half the proportion of people without sustainable access to safe drinking water.

Last year a United Nations task force, led by the Columbia University economist Jeffrey Sachs, estimated the annual cost of meeting these goals to be $121 billion in 2006, rising to $189 billion by 2015. When we take account of existing official development aid promises, the additional amount needed each year to meet the goals is only $48 billion for 2006 and $74 billion for 2015.

Now let's look at the incomes of America's rich and superrich and ask how much they could reasonably give. The task is made easier by statistics recently provided by Thomas Piketty and Emmanuel Saez, economists at the École Normale Supérieure, Paris-Jourdan, and the University of California, Berkeley, respectively, based on U.S. tax data for 2004. Their figures are for pretax income, excluding income from capital gains, which for the very rich are nearly always substantial. For simplicity I have rounded the figures, generally downward. Note too that the numbers refer to "tax units" — that is, in many cases, families rather than individuals.

Piketty and Saez's top bracket comprises 0.01 percent of U.S. taxpayers. There are 14,400 of them, earning an average of $12,775,000, with total earnings of $184 billion. The minimum annual income in this group is more than $5 million, so it seems reasonable to suppose that they could, without much hardship, give away a third of their annual income, an average of $4.3 million each, for a total of around $61 billion. That would still leave each of them with an annual income of at least $3.3 million.

Next comes the rest of the top 0.1 percent (excluding the category just described, as I shall do henceforth). There are 129,600 in this group, with an average income of just over $2 million and a minimum income of $1.1 million. If they were each to give a quarter of their income, that would yield about $65 billion and leave each of them with at least $846,000 annually.

The top 0.5 percent consists of 575,900 taxpayers, with an average income of $623,000 and a minimum of $407,000. If they were to give one fifth of their income, they would still have at least $325,000 each, and they would be giving a total of $72 billion.

Coming down to the level of those in the top 1 percent, we find 719,900 taxpayers with an average income of $327,000 and a minimum of $276,000. They could comfortably afford to give 15 percent of their income. That would yield $35 billion and leave them with at least $234,000.

Finally, the remainder of the nation's top 10 percent earn at least $92,000 annually, with an average of $132,000. There are nearly 13 million in this group. If they gave the traditional tithe — 10 percent of their income, or an average of $13,200 each — this would yield about $171 billion and leave them a minimum of $83,000.

You could spend a long time debating whether the fractions of income I have suggested for donation constitute the fairest possible scheme. Perhaps the sliding scale should be steeper, so that the superrich give more and the merely comfortable give less. And it could be extended beyond the top 10 percent of American families, so that everyone able to afford more than the basic necessities of life gives something, even if it is as little as 1 percent. Be that as it may, the remarkable thing about these calculations is that a scale of donations that is unlikely to impose significant hardship on anyone yields a total of $404 billion — from just 10 percent of American families.

Obviously, the rich in other nations should share the burden of relieving global poverty. The United States is responsible for 36 percent of the gross domestic product of all Organization for Economic Cooperation and Development nations. Arguably, because the United States is richer than all other major nations, and its wealth is more unevenly distributed than wealth in almost any other industrialized country, the rich in the United States should contribute more than 36 percent of total global donations. So somewhat more than 36 percent of all aid to relieve global poverty should come from this country. For simplicity, let's take half as a fair share for the United States. On that basis, extending the scheme I have suggested worldwide would provide $808 billion annually for development aid. That's more than six times what the task force chaired by Sachs estimated would be required for 2006 in order to be on track to meet the Millennium Development Goals, and more than sixteen times the shortfall between that sum and existing official development aid commitments.

If we are obliged to do no more than our fair share of eliminating global poverty, the burden will not be great. But is that really all we ought to do? Since we all agree that fairness is a good thing, and none of us like doing more because others don't pull their weight, the fair-share view is attractive. In the end, however, I think we should reject it. Let's return to the drowning child in the shallow pond. Imagine it is not one small child who has fallen in, but fifty children. We are among fifty adults, unrelated to the children, picnicking on the lawn around the pond. We can easily wade into the pond and rescue the children, and the fact that we would find it cold and unpleasant sloshing around in the knee-deep muddy water is no justification for failing to do so. The "fair share" theorists would say that if we each rescue one child, all the children will be saved, and so none of us have an obligation to save more than one. But what if half the picnickers prefer staying clean and dry to rescuing any children at all? Is it acceptable if the rest of us stop after we have rescued just one child, knowing that we have done our fair share, but that half the children will drown? We might justifiably be furious with those who are not doing their fair share, but our anger with them is not a reason for letting the children die. In terms of praise and blame, we are clearly right to condemn, in the strongest terms, those who do nothing. In contrast, we may withhold such condemnation from those who stop when they have done their fair share. Even so, they have let children drown when they could easily have saved them, and that is wrong.

Similarly, in the real world, it should be seen as a serious moral failure when those with ample income do not do their fair share toward relieving global poverty. It isn't so easy, however, to decide on the proper approach to take to those who limit their contribution to their fair share when they could easily do more and when, because others are not playing their part, a further donation would assist many in desperate need. In the privacy of our own judgment, we should believe that it is wrong not to do more. But whether we should actually criticize people who are doing their fair share, but no more than that, depends on the psychological impact that such criticism will have on them, and on others. This in turn may depend on social practices. If the majority are doing little or nothing, setting a standard higher than the fair-share level may seem so demanding that it discourages people who are willing to make an equitable contribution from doing even that. So it may be best to refrain from criticizing those who achieve the fair-share level. In moving our society's standards forward, we may have to progress one step at a time.

For more than thirty years, I've been reading, writing, and teaching about the ethical issue posed by the juxtaposition, on our planet, of great abundance and life-threatening poverty. Yet it was not until, in preparing this article, I calculated how much America's top 10 percent of income earners actually make that I fully understood how easy it would be for the world's rich to eliminate, or virtually eliminate, global poverty. (It has actually become much easier over the past thirty years, as the rich have grown significantly richer.) I found the result astonishing. I double-checked the figures and asked a research assistant to check them as well. But they were right. Measured against our capacity, the Millennium Development Goals are indecently, shockingly modest. If we fail to achieve them — as on present indications we well might — we have no excuses. The target we should be setting for ourselves is not halving the proportion of people living in extreme poverty, and without enough to eat, but ensuring that no one, or virtually no one, needs to live in such degrading conditions. That is a worthy goal, and it is well within our reach.

JERALD WALKER

Dragon Slayers

FROM THE IOWA REVIEW

I WAS AT A CHRISTMAS PARTY with a man who wanted me to hate him. I should hate *all* whites, he felt, for what they have done to me. I thought hard about what whites have done to me. I was forty, old enough to have accumulated a few unpleasant racial encounters, but nothing of any significance came to mind. The man was astonished at this response. "How about *slavery?*" he asked. I explained, as politely as I could, that I had not been a slave. "But you *feel* its effects," he snapped. "Racism, discrimination, and prejudice will *always* be a problem for you in this country. White people," he insisted, "are your *oppressors.*" I glanced around the room, just as one of my oppressors happened by. She was holding a tray of canapés. She offered me one. I asked the man if, as a form of reparations, I should take two.

It was midway through my third year in academia. I had survived mountains of papers, apathetic students, cantankerous colleagues, boring meetings, sleep deprivation, and two stalkers, and now I was up against a man who had been mysteriously transported from 1962. He even looked the part, with lavish sideburns and solid, black-rimmed glasses. He wasn't an academic, but rather the spouse of one. In fact, he had no job at all, a dual act of defiance, he felt, against a patriarchal and capitalistic society. He was a fun person to talk with, especially if, like me, you enjoyed driving white liberals up the wall. And the surest way to do that, if you were black, was to deny them the chance to pity you.

He'd spotted me thirty minutes earlier while I stood alone at the dining room table, grazing on various appetizers. My wife, Brenda, had drifted off somewhere, and the room buzzed with pockets of conversation and laughter. The man joined me. I accepted his offer of a gin and tonic. We talked local politics for a moment, or rather he talked and I listened, because it wasn't something I knew much about, before moving on to football, our kids, and finally my classes. He was particularly interested in my African-American literature course. "Did you have any black students?" he inquired.

"We started with two," I said, "but ended with twenty-eight." I let his puzzled expression linger until I'd eaten a stuffed mushroom. "Everyone who takes the course has to agree to be black for the duration of the semester."

"Really?" he asked, laughing. "What do they do, smear their faces with burnt cork?"

"Not a bad idea," I said. "But for now they simply have to think like blacks, but in a way different from what they probably expect." I told him that black literature is often approached as records of oppression, but that my students don't focus on white cruelty but rather its flip side: black courage. "After all," I continued, "slaves and their immediate descendants were by and large heroic, not pathetic, or I wouldn't be standing here."

The man was outraged. "You're letting whites off the hook," he said. "You're absolving them of responsibility, of the obligation to atone for past and present wrongs . . ." He went on in this vein for a good while, and I am pleased to say that I goaded him until he stormed across the room and stood with his wife, who, after he'd spoken with her, glanced in my direction to see, no doubt, a traitor to the black race. That was unfortunate. I'd like to think I betray whites, too.

More precisely, it's the belief that blacks are primarily victims that I betray, a common view held by both races. I, too, held it for many years. When I was in my early twenties and making my first crude attempts at writing fiction, I'd sit at my word processor and pound out stories brimming with blacks who understood only anger and pain. My settings were always ghettos, because that was what I knew, and the plots centered on hardship and suffering, because I knew that, too. And I also knew this: white society was responsible for the existence of this miserable world, and it was my duty as a black artist to make this clear. Three of these stories gained me acceptance into the Iowa Writers' Workshop. It was there that my awakening occurred.

My first course was with Frank Conroy, the program's director. He was brutally honest and harbored a militant obsession with clarity. Most of the two-hour-long classes were spent with him shredding the stories and our egos. We squirmed in our seats and wiped our brows as he did his infamous line-by-line, zeroing in on words and phrases that confused the work's meaning or failed to make unequivocal sense. It was the most intense and best writing class that I'd ever had. I went into the second semester confident that my prose had improved and that the most difficult course was behind me.

Randomly, I decided to take a workshop with James Alan Mc-Pherson. During the break before classes resumed, I read for the first time his books *Hue and Cry* and *Elbow Room*. The impact his writing had on me was profound. He, too, chronicled the lives of African Americans, and he had done it in short story form, my genre of choice; this was the model I'd been searching for. I read the stories over and over again, convinced that I had found my literary father.

The contrast between Conroy and McPherson could not have been more stark. Conroy was tall, white, and boisterous; McPherson was short, black, and shy. Conroy cursed, yelled, laughed, and joked; McPherson rarely spoke at all, and when he did his voice was so quiet you often couldn't hear him. The students dominated his workshops. I was disappointed. McPherson was a Pulitzer Prize winner, after all, the first African American to receive that honor for fiction. He was the recipient of a MacArthur "genius" grant and countless other awards. I wanted his wisdom. I wanted his insight. He gave it midsemester, when it was time to workshop my first story.

"Before we begin today," he said, "I'd like to make a few comments." This was new; he'd never prefaced a story before. A smile crept on my face as I allowed myself to imagine him praising me for my depiction of a den of heroin addicts, for this was not easy to do, requiring, among other things, an intimate knowledge of heroin addicts and a certain flair for profanity.

"Are you all familiar with gangster rap?" McPherson asked. We were, despite the fact that, besides me, all of the students were white and mostly middle to upper class. While we each nodded our familiarity with the genre, McPherson reached into a shopping bag he'd brought and removed a magazine. He opened it to a premarked page on which was a picture of a rapper, cloaked in jewelry and guns and leaning against the hood of a squad car. Behind him was a sprawling slum. "This person raps about the ghetto," McPherson said, "but he doesn't live in the ghetto. He lives in a wealthy white suburb with his wife and daughter. His daughter attends a predominantly white private school. That's what this article is about." He closed the magazine and returned it to the bag. "What some gangster rappers are doing is using black stereotypes because white people eat that stuff up. But these images are false, they're dishonest. Some rappers are selling out their race for personal gain." He paused again, this time to hold up my story. "That's what this writer is doing with his work." He set my story back on the table. "Okay, that's all I have to say. You can discuss it now."

For a few seconds, the only sound in the room was of my labored breathing. And then someone said, "McPherson's right. The story is garbage."

"Complete rubbish," said another.

And so it went from there.

I did not sleep that night. At eight A.M., when I could hold out no longer, I called McPherson at home and demanded a conference. He agreed to meet me in his office in ten minutes.

He was there when I arrived, sitting behind his desk. The desk was bare except for a copy of my story, and the office was bare except for the desk and two chairs. The built-in bookshelves held nothing, and nothing hung on the walls. There was no dressing on the window, no telephone, and no computer. It might have been the janitor's office, a place to catch a few winks while the mopped floors dried. And McPherson might have been the janitor. His blue shirt was a mass of wrinkles and his eyes were bloodshot. His trademark hat, a beige straw Kangol, seemed to rest at an odd angle on his head; from beneath it a single long braid had worked its way free and dangled rebelliously behind his right ear. He noticed me staring at it and poked it back into concealment.

"Are you okay?" he asked. His voice was gentle, full of concern. "You sounded like a crazy man on the phone."

"Well, I'm *not* a crazy man." I reached forward to tap my finger on my story and proceeded to rant and rave as only a crazy man could. "I did not make this stuff up," I insisted. "I'm *from* the ghetto." I went through the characters one by one, citing various relatives on whom they were based, and I mentioned that, just the week before, my younger brother had been shot in the back while in McDonald's. I told him I had another brother who was in and out of prison, a heroin addict sister-in-law, that I had once been arrested for car theft (falsely, but that was beside the point), and that many, many of my friends were still living in the miserable community in which I'd been raised. "You misread my story," I said in conclusion, "and you misread *me*." I leaned back and folded my arms across my chest, waiting for his apology. Instead, I watched as he sprang from his chair and hurried from the room. He turned left into the hall, and a moment later he passed going right, with Frank Conroy calling after him, and then they passed left again, now with Connie Brothers, the program's administrator, in tow, and after two more passes this awful parade came to an end somewhere out of view. Now Connie stood before me, looking as nauseated as I felt. "Jim is the kindest soul on this earth," she said quietly. "Why, why would you insult him?"

For an instant, I saw myself at twelve, looking at a closed front door, behind which was my first love, who had just dumped me and left me standing on her porch, trying unsuccessfully not to cry.

Connie magically produced a tissue and handed it to me. She rubbed my shoulders while I rambled incoherently, something about sleep deprivation and McPherson being my father. "It's okay, sweetie," Connie said. "I'll talk to him."

McPherson returned momentarily. I apologized. He told me it was okay, that workshops can make people uptight and sensitive. It had been difficult for him too, he explained, when he was a student there in the seventies. There was a lull in the conversation before he said, "So, where're your people from?"

He still doesn't believe me, I thought. I mumbled, "Chicago."

"No, no. That's where they *are*. Where are they *from?*"

"Oh, sorry. Arkansas."

"Mine are from Georgia," he said. He smiled and added, "That place is a *motherfucker.*"

The essence of black America was conveyed in that response, a toughness of spirit, humor laced with tragedy, but at that moment all I saw was the man who had rejected my vision. Defeated, I thanked him for agreeing to meet with me as I rose to leave. He

stood and shook my hand. As I was walking out the door, he called
my name. I turned to face him.

"Stereotypes are valuable," he said. "But *only* if you use them to
your advantage. They present your readers with something they'll
recognize, and it pulls them into what appears to be familiar territory, a comfort zone. But once they're in, you have to move them
beyond the stereotype. You have to show them what's real."

"What's real?" I asked.

Without hesitation, he said, "You."

It was one of those things that you instantly recognize as profound, and then, because you don't quite understand it, try to forget as quickly as you can. It was also one of those things that you
cannot forget. And so it roamed freely in my subconscious, occasionally coming into sharp focus to remind me of its presence, but
I allowed myself to be consumed by it no more than I would a
housefly. For about a year. And then I went to see him again.

"I was wondering," I said, "if you wouldn't mind supervising an
independent project."

"That depends," he responded, "on what you'd like to study."

"Me," I said. "I want to study me."

We started with black folklore and history. Next we moved on to
blues and jazz, and then we covered a broad range of black literature and culture. We studied black intellectuals and philosophers,
sociologists, anthropologists, activists, filmmakers, and ex-cons.
For four years, we dissected nearly every aspect of black life and
thought, and in the process a theme emerged that had been there
all along: *life* is a motherfucker; living it anyway, and sometimes
laughing in the process, is where humanity is won.

And this is what I learned about me: I had become my own stereotype, a character in one of my short stories who insisted on seeing himself primarily as a repository of pain and defeat, despite
overwhelming evidence to the contrary. The very people with
whom I had been raised and whom I had dedicated myself to rendering in prose had become victims of my myopia. My stories
showed people being affected by drug addiction, racism, poverty,
murder, crime, violence, but they said nothing about the spirit
that, despite being confronted with what often amounted to certain defeat, would continue to struggle and aspire for something
better. That old slave song "We Shall Overcome" pretty much says
it all.

The course work I conducted with McPherson ultimately contributed to a doctorate in interdisciplinary studies. McPherson served as my dissertation chair. I knew when I started my academic career that I owed him a debt to teach black literature in a certain way. "Less time needs to be spent on the dragons," he told me once, "and more on our ability to forge swords for battle, and the skill with which we've used them."

The man at the Christmas party, of course, would rather that I talk about the dragons. And at first, when students take my class, they are surprised, even a bit disappointed, to see the course will not head in that direction. But by the end of the semester, they are invariably uplifted by the heroic nature of African Americans, in part, perhaps, because it is the nature found in us all. Sometimes students thank me for this approach. On occasion they ask me where I got the idea. I tell them I got it from my father.

EDWARD O. WILSON

Apocalypse Now

FROM THE NEW REPUBLIC

The following is a letter from the eminent Harvard biologist Edward O. Wilson, winner of the National Medal of Science and two Pulitzer Prizes, to an imagined Southern Baptist pastor — and the larger evangelical community.

DEAR PASTOR:

We have not met, yet I feel I know you well enough to call you a friend. First of all, we grew up in the same faith. As a boy, I too answered the altar call; I went under the water. Although I no longer belong to that faith, I am confident that if we met and spoke privately of our deepest beliefs, it would be in a spirit of mutual respect and goodwill. I know we share many precepts of moral behavior. Perhaps it also matters that we are both Americans and, insofar as it might still affect civility and good manners, we are both Southerners.

I write to you now for your counsel and help. Of course, in doing so, I see no way to avoid the fundamental differences in our worldviews. You are a strict interpreter of Christian Holy Scripture; I am a secular humanist. You believe that each person's soul is immortal, making this planet a waystation to a second, eternal life; I think heaven and hell are what we create for ourselves, on this planet. For you, the belief in God made flesh to save mankind; for me, the belief in Promethean fire seized to set men free. You have found your final truth; I am still searching. You may be wrong; I may be wrong. We both may be partly right.

Do these differences in worldview separate us in all things? They do not. You and I and every other human being strive for the same imperatives of security, freedom of choice, personal dignity, and a cause to believe in that is larger than ourselves. Let us see, then, if we can meet on the near side of metaphysics in order to deal with the real world we share. You have the power to help solve a great problem about which I care deeply. I hope you have the same concern. I suggest that we set aside our differences in order to save the Creation. The defense of living nature is a universal value. It doesn't rise from, nor does it promote, any religious or ideological dogma. Rather, it serves without discrimination the interests of all humanity. Pastor, we need your help. The Creation — living nature — is in deep trouble.

Scientists estimate that, if habitat conversion and other destructive human activities continue at their present rates, half the species of plants and animals on earth could be either gone or at least fated for early extinction by the end of the century. The ongoing extinction rate is calculated in the most conservative estimates to be about one hundred times above that prevailing before humans appeared on earth, and it is expected to rise to at least one thousand times greater (or more) in the next few decades. If this rise continues unabated, the cost to humanity — in wealth, environmental security, and quality of life — will be catastrophic.

Surely we can agree that each species, however inconspicuous and humble it may seem to us at this moment, is a masterpiece of biology and well worth saving. Each species possesses a unique combination of genetic traits that fits it more or less precisely to a particular part of the environment. Prudence alone dictates that we act quickly to prevent the extinction of species and, with it, the pauperization of the earth's ecosystems.

With all the troubles that humanity faces, why should we care about the condition of living nature? *Homo sapiens* is a species confined to an extremely small niche. True, our minds soar out to the edges of the universe and contract inward to subatomic particles — the two extremes encompassing thirty powers of ten in space. In this respect, our intellects are godlike. But, let's face it, our bodies stay trapped inside a proportionately microscopic envelope of physical constraints. Earth provides a self-regulating bubble that sustains us indefinitely without any thought or contrivance of our own. This protective shield is the biosphere, the totality of life, creator of all air, cleanser of all water, manager of all soil — but is itself a fragile membrane that barely clings to the face of the planet. We depend upon its razor-thin health for every moment of our lives. We belong in the biosphere, we were born here as species, we are closely suited to its exacting conditions — and not all conditions either, but just those in a few of the climatic regimes that exist on some of the land. Environmental damage can be defined as any change that alters our surroundings in a direction contrary to humanity's inborn physical and emotional needs. We must be careful with the environment upon which our lives ultimately depend.

In destroying the biosphere, we are destroying unimaginably vast sources of scientific information and biological wealth. Opportunity costs, which will be better understood by our descendants than by ourselves, will be staggering. Gone forever will be undiscovered medicines, crops, timber, fibers, soil-restoring vegetation, petroleum substitutes, and other products and amenities. Critics of environmentalism forget, if they ever knew, how the rosy periwinkle of Madagascar provided the alkaloids that cure most cases of Hodgkin's disease and acute childhood leukemia; how a substance from an obscure Norwegian fungus made possible the organ transplant industry; how a chemical from the saliva of leeches yielded a solvent that prevents blood clots during and after surgery; and so on through the pharmacopoeia that has stretched from the herbal medicines of Stone Age shamans to the magic-bullet cures of present-day biomedical science.

These are just a few examples of what could be lost if *Homo sapiens* pursue our current course of environmental destruction. Earth is a laboratory wherein nature — God, if you prefer, Pastor — has laid before us the results of countless experiments. We damage her at our own peril.

You may well ask at this point, Why me? Simply because religion and science are the two most powerful forces in the world today, and especially in the United States. If religion and science could be united on the common ground of biological conservation, the problem might soon be solved.

It may seem far-fetched for a secular scientist to propose an alliance between science and religion. But the fact is that environmental activists cannot succeed without you and your followers as allies. The political process in American democracy, with rare exceptions, does not start at the top and work its way down to the voting masses. It proceeds in the opposite direction. Political leaders are compelled to calculate as precisely as they can what it will take to win the next election. The United States is an intensely religious nation. It is overwhelmingly Judeo-Christian, with a powerful undercurrent of evangelism. We secularists must face reality. The National Association of Evangelicals has thirty million members; the three leading American humanist organizations combined have, at best, a few thousand. Those who, for religious reasons, believe in saving the Creation have the strength to do so through the political process; acting alone, secular environmentalists do not. An alliance between science and religion, forged in an atmosphere of mutual respect, may be the only way to protect life on earth, including, in the end, our own.

Yes, the gulf separating our worldviews is wide. The Abrahamic religions — Judaism, Christianity, and Islam — believe that the universe was constructed to be relevant to humanity. The discoveries of science, in unintended opposition, have reduced the earth to an infinitesimal speck within an immensity of space unrelated to human destiny. The Abrahamic religions envisage a supreme ruler who, while existing outside the material universe, nevertheless oversees an agenda for each and every one of our immortal souls. Science can find no evidence of an agenda other than that fashioned by the complex interaction of genes and environment within parallel evolving cultures. Religious creation stories have a divinely engineered beginning and a divinely ordained ending. According to science, in contrast, humans descended from apish ancestors; our origin was basically no different from that of other animals, played out over geological time through a tortuous route of mutation and environmentally driven natural selection. In addition, all mainstream religious belief, whether fundamentalist or liberal, is predicated upon the assumption that humanity is not alone, and we are here for a life and purpose beyond our earthly existence. Science says that, as far as verifiable evidence tells, we are alone, and what significance we have is therefore of our own making. This is the heart of the agonizing conflict between science and religion that has persisted for the past five hundred years.

I do not see how the difference in worldview between these two great productions of human striving can be closed. But for the purposes of saving the Creation, I am not sure that it needs to be. To make the point in good gospel manner, let me tell the story of a young man, newly trained for the ministry and so fixed in his Christian faith that he referred all questions of morality to readings from the Bible. When he visited the Atlantic rainforest of Brazil, he saw the manifest hand of God, and in his notebook he wrote, "It is not possible to give an adequate idea of the higher feelings of wonder, admiration, and devotion which fill and elevate the mind." That was Charles Darwin in 1832, early into the voyage of the HMS *Beagle*, before he had given any thought to evolution. And here is Darwin, concluding *On the Origin of Species* in 1859, having first abandoned Christian dogma and then, with his newfound intellectual freedom, formulated the theory of evolution by natural selection: "There is grandeur in this view of life, with its several powers, having been originally breathed into a few forms or into one; and that, whilst this planet has gone cycling on according to the fixed law of gravity, from so simple a beginning endless forms most beautiful and most wonderful have been, and are being, evolved." Darwin's reverence for life remained the same as he crossed the seismic divide that separated his religious phase and his scientific one. And so it can be for the divide that today separates mainstream religion and scientific humanism. And that separates you and me.

Indeed, despite all that divides science from religion, there is good reason to hope that an alliance on environmental issues is possible. The spiritual reach of evangelical Christianity is nowadays increasingly extended to the environment. While the Old Testament God commands humanity to take dominion over the earth, the decree is not (as one evangelical leader recently affirmed) an excuse to trash the planet. The dominant theme in Scripture as interpreted by many evangelicals is instead stewardship. Organizations like the Green Cross and the Evangelical Environmental Network (the latter a coalition of evangelical Christian agencies and institutions) are expanding their magisterium to include conservation — in religious terms, protection of the living Creation.

This evangelical interest in the environment is part of a worldwide trend among religions. In the United States, the umbrella National Religious Partnership for the Environment works with evangelical groups and other prominent organizations, including the U.S. Conference of Catholic Bishops, the National Council of Churches of Christ, and the Coalition on the Environment and Jewish Life. In 2001, the Archbishop of Canterbury urged that "it may not be time to build an Ark like Noah, but it is high time to take better care of God's creation." Three years earlier, Bartholomew I, Patriarch of the Greek Orthodox Church, had gone further: "For humans to cause species to become extinct and to destroy the biological diversity of God's creation . . . these are sins." He and Pope John Paul II later issued a "Common Declaration" that "God has not abandoned the world. It is His will that His Design and our hope for it will be realized through our co-operation in restoring its original harmony. In our own time we are witnessing a growth of an ecological awareness which needs to be encouraged, so that it will lead to practical programs and initiatives." Unfortunately, a corresponding magnitude of engagement has not yet occurred in Islam or the Eastern religions.

Every great religion offers mercy and charity to the poor. The poor of the world, of whom nearly a billion exist in the "poverty trap" of absolute destitution, are concentrated in the developing countries — the home of 80 percent of the world's population and most of the earth's biodiversity. The solution to the problems of both depends on the recognition that each depends on the other. The desperately poor have little chance to improve their lives in a devastated environment. Conversely, natural environments, where most of the Creation hangs on, cannot survive the press of land-hungry people who have nowhere else to go.

To be sure, some leaders of the religious right are reluctant to support biological conservation, an opposition sufficient to create a wedge within the evangelical movement. They may be partly afraid of paganism, by which worship of nature supplants worship of God. More realistically and importantly, opposition rises from the perceived association of environmental activism with the political left. For decades, conservatives have defined environmentalism as a movement bent on strangling the United States with regulations and bureaucratic power. This canard has dogged the U.S. environmental movement and helped keep it off the agenda of the past two presidential campaigns.

Finally, however, opinion may be changing. The mostly evangelical religious right, which, along with big business, has been the decisive source of power in the Republican Party, has begun to move care of the Creation back into the mainstream of conservative discourse. The opportunity exists to make the environment a universal concern and to render it politically nonpartisan.

Still, for all the positive signs, I remain puzzled that so many religious leaders have hesitated to make protection of the Creation an important part of their magisterium. Pastor, help me understand: Do they believe that human-centered ethics and preparation for the afterlife are the only things that matter? Do they believe that the Second Coming is imminent and that therefore the condition of the planet is of little consequence? These and other similar doctrines are not gospels of hope and compassion. They are gospels of cruelty and despair.

You and I are both humanists in the broadest sense: human welfare is at the center of our thought. So forget our disagreements, I say, and let us meet on common ground. That might not be as difficult as it first seems. When you think about it, our metaphysical differences have remarkably little effect on the conduct of our separate lives. My guess is that you and I are about equally ethical, patriotic, and altruistic. We are products of a civilization that rose from both religion and the science-based Enlightenment. We would gladly serve on the same jury, fight the same wars, and sanctify human life with the same intensity. Surely we also share a love of the Creation — and an understanding that, however the tensions play out between our opposing worldviews, however science and religion wax and wane in the minds of men, there remains the earthborn yet transcendental obligation we are both morally bound to share.

Contributors' Notes

Jo Ann Beard received fellowships in nonfiction writing from the John Simon Guggenheim Foundation and the New York Foundation for the Arts in 2005 and a Whiting Foundation Award in 1996.

Ian Buruma is the author of a novel, *Playing the Game,* and several books of nonfiction that cover Asian and European culture and politics, such as *God's Dust; The Wages of Guilt; Behind the Mask; A Japanese Mirror; Voltaire's Coconuts, or Anglomania in Europe; The Missionary and the Libertine;* and *Inventing Japan: From Empire to Economic Miracle, 1853–1964.* His latest book is *Murder in Amsterdam: The Death of Theo van Gogh and the Limits of Tolerance.* In 2003 he became the Henry R. Luce Professor of Democracy, Human Rights, and Journalism at Bard College.

Mark Danner has been reporting on and writing about war and politics for two decades, mostly for the *New York Review of Books* and for *The New Yorker,* where he was a staff writer. He has covered conflicts in Central America, Haiti, the Balkans, and the Middle East, among other stories. Among his books are *The Massacre at El Mozote: A Parable of the Cold War; Torture and Truth: America, Abu Ghraib, and the War on Terror;* and *The Secret Way to War.* Danner's work has received many honors, including a National Magazine Award, three Overseas Press Awards, an Emmy, and a MacArthur fellowship. He teaches at the University of California, Berkeley, and at Bard College. His work can be found at www.markdanner.com.

W. S. Di Piero is the author of numerous volumes of poetry, essays, and translations. His latest book is *Chinese Apples: New and Selected Poems.*

GEORGE GESSERT is an artist and writer. He has exhibited widely in the United States, Australia, and Europe. His writings have appeared in several anthologies, including *Biomediale, Art et Biotechnologies,* and *The Aesthetics of Care.* He was awarded a Pushcart Prize in 2005. Currently he is editor for art and biology for *Leonardo.*

MALCOLM GLADWELL is a staff writer for *The New Yorker.* He is also the author of two books, *The Tipping Point: How Little Things Make a Big Difference* and *Blink: The Power of Thinking Without Thinking.*

MARK GREIF is a cofounder and editor of the journal $n + 1$ and a senior correspondent for *The American Prospect.* He holds degrees from Harvard and Oxford and a Ph.D. from Yale. His essay "Against Exercise" appeared in *The Best American Essays 2005.* His writing has appeared in *Harper's Magazine,* the *London Review of Books, Dissent,* the *New York Times,* and elsewhere. "Afternoon of the Sex Children" is part of a continuing project about the history of morality. He lives on Cape Cod.

MARIONE INGRAM was born in Hamburg, Germany, in 1935 and today lives in Washington, D.C. "Operation Gomorrah" is taken from her memoir about the Second World War and her later work as a civil rights activist in Mississippi. Her fiber art and constructions have been exhibited at galleries in Europe and the United States.

GARRET KEIZER is the author of *Help, The Enigma of Anger, God of Beer, A Dresser of Sycamore Trees,* and *No Place but Here.* His work has appeared in *The Best American Science and Nature Writing* and *The Best American Poetry.* A contributing editor of *Harper's Magazine,* he is currently writing a book about noise with the support of a Guggenheim fellowship. He lives with his family in northeastern Vermont.

JOHN LAHR, the senior drama critic of *The New Yorker* since 1992, is the author of eighteen books, including *Notes on a Cowardly Lion* (on his father, Bert Lahr), *Prick Up Your Ears* (on the British playwright Joe Orton, which was also made into a movie by Stephen Frears), and *Sinatra: The Artist and the Man.* His critical books include *Light Fantastic: Adventures in the Theater, Show and Tell:* New Yorker *Profiles of Star Turns,* and *Honky Tonk Parade:* New Yorker *Profiles of Show People.* He has also edited the diaries of Joe Orton and Kenneth Tynan. In 2002, for his coauthorship of *Elaine Stritch at Liberty,* he became the first drama critic to receive a Tony Award. Lahr, who divides his time between London and New York, has twice won the George Jean Nathan Award for Drama Criticism.

LOUIS MENAND is the author of *The Metaphysical Club,* which won the 2002 Pulitzer Prize for history, and *American Studies,* a collection of essays. He is the Anne T. and Robert M. Bass Professor of English at Harvard. He was a contributing editor at the *New York Review of Books* from 1994 to 2001. Since 2001 he has been a staff writer for *The New Yorker.*

DANIEL OROZCO's stories have appeared in the *Best American Short Stories, Best American Mystery Stories,* and *Pushcart Prize* anthologies, and in *Harper's Magazine, Zoetrope All-Story, McSweeney's,* and other publications. He is the recipient of a National Endowment for the Arts fellowship. He teaches in the creative writing program at the University of Idaho. About "Shakers," he says: "I was born in California, and I don't live there anymore, and so writing this particular piece — recollecting and reimagining the landscapes and vistas, the terra not-so-firma of a place I miss a lot — was lonely and gratifying work for me. My thanks to the MacDowell Colony and to Marie Hayes at *StoryQuarterly.*"

CYNTHIA OZICK is the author of nine works of fiction, most recently the novels *The Puttermesser Papers* and *Heir to the Glimmering World,* which was a New York Times Notable Book, a Book Sense pick, and was chosen by NBC's *Today* Book Club. Her essay collections are *Art & Ardor, Metaphor & Memory, Fame & Folly,* a finalist for the 1996 Pulitzer Prize, *Quarrel & Quandary,* the winner of the 2001 National Book Critics Circle Award, and *The Din in the Head,* which was published in 2006. She served as guest editor of *The Best American Essays 1998.* "Out from Xanadu" originally appeared under the title "A Youthful Intoxication."

MOLLY PEACOCK is the author of a memoir, *Paradise, Piece by Piece,* as well as five volumes of poetry, including *Cornucopia: New and Selected Poems.* She is also the editor of *The Private I: Privacy in a Public World* (Graywolf Forum, 2001). Her articles on poetry, gardens, and her choice not to have children have appeared in *Elle, House & Garden, Ms., New York Magazine,* and *O, The Oprah Magazine.* She is a member of the graduate faculty of the Spalding University Brief Residency M.F.A. Program in Creative Writing. When she is not touring with her one-woman show in poems, *The Shimmering Verge,* she lives in Toronto with her husband, Professor Michael Groden. "Passion Flowers in Winter" is the prelude to a book about Mrs. Delany. Peacock's website is www.mollypeacock.org.

PHILLIP ROBERTSON has covered the wars in Afghanistan and Iraq for Salon.com. He has also reported for BBC Radio, National Public Radio, and the *Christian Science Monitor.*

MARILYNNE ROBINSON's 2005 novel, *Gilead,* won the Pulitzer Prize and the National Book Critics Circle Award.

RICHARD RODRIGUEZ is the author of an intellectual autobiography, *Hunger of Memory: The Education of Richard Rodriguez; Days of Obligation: An Argument with My Mexican Father,* which was nominated for the Pulitzer Prize; and *Brown: The Last Discovery of America,* a finalist for the National Book Critics Circle Award. A native Californian, he received his B.A. from Stanford, an M.A. from Columbia, and was a Ph.D. candidate in English renaissance literature at Berkeley. He has appeared for more than a decade as an essayist on *The NewsHour with Jim Lehrer,* for which he received the 1997 George Foster Peabody Award. He is writing a book about monotheism and the desert.

ELAINE SCARRY, the Walter M. Cabot Professor of Aesthetics and the General Theory of Value at Harvard University, is the author of *The Body in Pain, On Beauty and Being Just, Dreaming by the Book,* and a series of articles on war and the social contract.

ROGER SCRUTON is a writer and philosopher who divides his time between rural Wiltshire, in southwestern England, and rural Virginia. He is currently a research professor at the Institute for the Psychological Sciences in Arlington, Virginia, and has taught previously in London, Cambridge, Boston University, and Princeton. He is the author of thirty-five books, including *On Hunting, Animal Rights and Wrongs,* and *Gentle Regrets.* He is married, with two children, six horses, five chickens, and two pigs.

PETER SINGER was born in Melbourne, Australia, and studied philosophy there and at Oxford University. His books include *Animal Liberation, Practical Ethics, How Are We to Live?, Rethinking Life and Death, Ethics into Action, One World: The Ethics of Globalization, Pushing Time Away: My Grandfather and the Tragedy of Jewish Vienna,* and most recently *The Way We Eat: Why Our Food Choices Matter.* He is the Ira W. DeCamp Professor of Bioethics at the Center for Human Values at Princeton University.

JERALD WALKER's works have appeared in *The Iowa Review, The North American Review,* and other publications. "Dragon Slayers" is from *Notes from the Promised Land,* an in-progress collection of essays on being a black academic. He is a graduate of the Iowa Writers' Workshop, a recipient of a James A. Michener fellowship, a member of the Columbia Scholastic Press Association's Board of Judges, the director of literature of Imago's Fine Arts and Crafts Gallery in Warren, Rhode Island, and founder of the award-winning literary arts journal *The Bridge.* He is an assistant professor of English at Bridgewater State University, where he founded and co-coordinates the annual Festival of Arts. He lives in Bridgewater, Massachusetts, with his wife and their two sons.

EDWARD O. WILSON is the Pellegrino University Professor Emeritus at Harvard University. A native of Alabama, he was named by *Time* magazine in 1995 as one of America's twenty-five most influential people. His many books include *Insect Societies, Sociobiology: The New Synthesis, The Diversity of Life, In Search of Nature, Consilience,* and most recently *The Creation: An Appeal to Save Life on Earth* and *Nature Revealed: Selected Writings, 1949–2006.* A member of the National Academy of Science, he received the Pulitzer Prize in 1979 for *On Human Nature* and again in 1991 for *The Ants* (with Bert Hölldobler). Other awards include the National Medal of Science, the Crafoord Prize, the Nierenberg Prize, and in 2007 the TED Prize, which honors three individuals who show they can make a positive impact on the world.

Notable Essays of 2006

SELECTED BY ROBERT ATWAN

MARCIA ALDRICH
Garbo and the Norns. *Northwest Review*, 44/1.
SHERMAN ALEXIE
My Encounters with the Homeless People of the Pacific Northwest. *Willow Springs*, Fall.
BROOKE ALLAN
Jefferson the Skeptic. *Hudson Review*, Summer.
WILLIAM ALBERT ALLARD
Solace at Surprise Creek. *National Geographic*, June.
CHRIS AMANI
Resisting the Anomie: Exile and the Romantic Self. *Witness*, 20.
ANONYMA
Lust, Impotence, Porn. *Frontiers: A Journal of Women Studies*, 27/1.
CHRIS ARTHUR
Room, Empty. *Southwest Review*, 92/3.
SARAH ASWELL
The Art of War. *Gettysburg Review*, Winter.
PAUL AUSTIN
The Devil Is a Beautiful Man. *Gettysburg Review*, Spring.

POE BALLANTINE
World of Trouble. *The Sun*, February.
DENNIS BARRINGER
The Names in the Case. *Hobart*, Summer.
ANN BEATTIE
Always on Sunday. *Five Points*, 9/3.
GEOFFREY BENT
Claude Monet: Le Roi de la France. *Boulevard*, Spring.
SVEN BIRKERTS
Serving the Sentence. *Raritan*, Winter.
CARA BIRNBAUM
The Fight Club. *Elle*, July.
EULA BLISS
Letter to Mexico. *Gulf Coast*, Fall.
WILL BLYTHE
The Art of Hatred. *Oxford American*, Winter.
MICHAEL P. BRANCH
Endlessly Rocking. *Ecotone*, Fall/Winter.
JOHN BURNSIDE
How to Fly. *Granta*, Summer.

KEN CHEN
Four Essays on Luck. *Pleiades*, 26/2.

CHRISTOPHER CLAUSEN
The New Ivory Tower. *Wilson Quarterly,* Autumn.

MICHAEL COHEN
Location, Location, Location. *Briar Cliff Review,* 18.

NEIL COHEN
Love, Jerry. *Playboy,* December.

ANN COPELAND
Six Bagatelles for Dancers. *Iowa Review,* Fall.

PAUL CRENSHAW
Concrete. *North American Review,* May–August.

MICHAEL CUNNINGHAM
Scheherazade Nights. *Washington Post Magazine,* July 9.

RENÉE E. D'AOUST
Blue Mao Hat. *Under the Sun,* Summer.

STEVE DAVENPORT
Murder on Gasoline Lake. *Black Warrior Review,* Fall/Winter.

MELISSA DELBRIDGE
West Greene and River Bend: Gun and Bait. *Antioch Review,* Fall.

DENNIS DILLINGHAM
A Fool's Faith. *Hobart,* Summer.

ELIZABETH DODD
The Scribe in the Woods. *Fourth Genre,* Spring.

WENDY DONIGER
Many Masks, Many Selves. *Daedalus,* Fall.

SEAN THOMAS DOUGHERTY
Killing the Messenger. *Massachusetts Review,* Winter.

BRIAN DOYLE
Fishering. *Ecotone,* Fall/Winter.

MARTHA DUNCAN
So Have I Been a Good Stepmother? *Gettysburg Review,* Autumn.

OMAR EBY
A Distraught Woman. *River Teeth,* Fall.

MARK EDMUNSON
Fadeaway Jumper. *American Scholar,* Winter.

STEPHEN ELLIOTT
Just Always Be Good. *Tin House,* Winter.

JAMES ELLROY
My Mother and the Dahlia. *Virginia Quarterly Review,* Summer.

JOSEPH EPSTEIN
New Leader Days. *Weekly Standard,* September 18.

RANDY FERTEL
Katrina Five Ways. *Kenyon Review,* Summer.

GARY FINCKE
The Handmade Court. *Ecotone,* Fall/Winter.

MOE FOLK
32nd Running of the Tempus Stakes. *New Letters,* 72/2.

STEVE FRIEDMAN
Lonely at the Top. *Backpacker,* April.

GUY GALLO
Gifts from Nola. *Bomb,* Summer.

JOHN GAMEL
A Quiet Departure. *Boulevard,* Spring.

MARJORIE GARBER
Loaded Words. *Critical Inquiry,* Summer.

J. MALCOLM GARCIA
Draft Notice. *Alaska Quarterly Review,* Fall/Winter.

WILLIAM H. GASS
Half a Man, Half a Metaphor. *Harper's Magazine,* August.

CHRISTINE GELINEAU
Gifts That Cannot Be Refused. *Iron Horse Literary Review,* 8/1.

JOHN O'CONNOR
Oedipus Wreck. *Quarterly West,*
Spring/Summer.

REBECCA K. O'CONNOR
Mercy. *South Dakota Review,* Summer.

ARIKA OKRENT
A Visit to Esperantoland. *American
Scholar,* Winter.

MARY OLIVER
Foods for Thought. *Country Living,*
June.

JAMES OLNEY
Remembering Richard,
Remembering Mlle. Marty.
Cincinnati Review, Summer.

CAROLYN OSBORN
My Father's Guns. *Hotel Amerika,*
Spring.

ANNE PANNING
Secondhand. *Alaska Quarterly Review,*
Fall/Winter.

VINCE PASSARO
Voluntary Tyranny, or Brezhnev at
the Mall. *Open City,* Fall.

ANN PATCHETT
Love Sustained. *Harper's Magazine,*
November.

GAYLE PEMBERTON
My Tourette's. *Massachusetts Review,*
Summer.

ADAM PHILLIPS
The Dream Horizon. *Raritan,*
Summer.

SAM PICKERING
Shadows. *Harvard Review,* 31.

STEVEN PINKER
Groups and Genes. *New Republic,*
June 26.

ROBERT PINSKY
On Translation. *Literary Review,* Fall.

MARSHALL POE
The Hive. *Atlantic Monthly,*
September.

AIMEE POGSON
The Dance I Danced for You. *Lake
Effect,* Spring.

MAXIMILLIAN POTTER
The Prodigal Father. *Best Life,* June.

RICHARD PRESTON
Tall for Its Age. *The New Yorker,*
October 9.

LIA PURPURA
On Looking Away: A Panoramic.
Sonora Review, 50.

JOHN PURUGGANAN
You're in Prison. *The Sun,* October.

DANIEL RAEBURN
Vessels. *The New Yorker,* May 1.

IRAJ ISAAC RAHMIM
My American Fantasy. *Gulf Coast,*
Winter/Spring.

CHERRI RANDALL
As I Fold My Ego Origami-Style.
Sojourn, 19.

WENDY RAWLINGS
Spectacular Mistakes. *Agni,* 64.

KATHRYN RHETT
Our So-Called Illustrious Past.
Harvard Review, 30.

REBECCA EMLINGER ROBERTS
In Praise of Complaint. *Massachusetts
Review,* Spring.

ROBERT ROOT
The Pattern of Life Indelible.
Ecotone, Winter/Spring.

EDWARD ROTHSTEIN
Mozart: In Search of the Roots of
Genius. *Smithsonian,* February.

JUDY ROWLEY
The Color of Sound. *Bellevue Literary
Review,* Spring.

JULIAN RUBINSTEIN
Final Cut. *5280,* June.

SHERMAN APT RUSSELL
My Life as a Pantheist. *Camas,*
Winter.

ARTHUR SALTZMAN
Duck-Rabbit Variations. *Baltimore Review,* Summer/Fall.

SCOTT RUSSELL SANDERS
Conscience. *Orion,* January/February.

JANE SANDOR
Ingenting. *Calyx,* Summer.

ROBERT M. SAPOLSKY
A Natural History of Peace. *Foreign Affairs,* January/February.

JILLIAN SCHEDNECK
Schmates: A Memoir of Words. *Alligator Juniper,* 2006.

ROGER SCHMIDT
Thirteen Ways of Looking at a Blackboard. *Raritan,* Winter.

BRANDON R. SCHRAND
The Enders Hotel. *Green Mountains Review,* 19/2.

MIMI SCHWARTZ
Off the Record. *Missouri Review,* Fall.

A. O. SCOTT
Falling-Down Funny. *New York Times Magazine,* November 12.

JEREMY SEABROOK
Twins. *Granta,* Fall.

DAVID SEDARIS
Road Trips. *The New Yorker,* November 27.

PETER SELGIN
Restaurant. *Bellevue Literary Review,* Fall.

HEATHER SELLERS
Tell Me Again Who You Are? *Alaska Quarterly Review,* Fall/Winter.

FRED SETTERBERG
She's Gone: The Eternal Ache of the Love Song. *Southern Review,* Winter.

ALAN SHAPIRO
My Tears See More Than My Eyes: My Son's Depression and the Power of Art. *Virginia Quarterly Review,* Fall.

JEFF SHARLET
Through a Glass, Darkly. *Harper's Magazine,* December.

DAVID SHIELDS
The Thing About Life Is That One Day You'll Be Dead. *Conjunctions,* Spring.

SUE WILLIAM SILVERMAN
Tramping the Land of Look Behind. *Hotel Amerika,* Spring.

SHARA SINOR
Ghost of Ten. *Post Road,* 13.

FLOYD SKLOOT
Cover Stories. *Prairie Schooner,* Winter.

REBECCA SKLOOT
Taking the Least of You. *New York Times Magazine,* April 16.

LAUREN SLATER
Tongue and Groove. *Iowa Review,* Spring.

JANNA MALAMUD SMITH
Smarrita. *Threepenny Review,* Fall.

RANJIT SOURI
Fireworks and Beethoven. *India Currents,* July.

MICHELLE STACEY
Clash of the Time Lords. *Harper's Magazine,* December.

MICHAEL STEINBERG
Working Out: A Cautionary Tale. *Paterson Literary Review,* 35.

DONNA STEINER
Cold. *Isotope,* Spring/Summer.

M. G. STEPHENS
Seven Wonders. *Fourth Genre,* Fall.

SUSAN STERLING
Radiation Blooms. *Crab Orchard Review,* Winter/Spring.

SHERYL ST. GERMAIN
Inside Passages: A Cajun in Alaska. *Southern Humanities Review,* Spring.

CHERYL STRAYED
The Boy with Blue Hair. *The Sun,* January.

NED STUCKEY-FRENCH
South Side. *The Pinch,* Fall.
IRA SUKRUNGRUANG
A World of Adjusters. *River Styx,* 73.
LEONARD SUSSKIND
Fighting the Cultural War.
Chattahoochee Review, Winter/
Spring.
LISA SZEFEL
Beauty and William Braithwaite.
Callaloo, Spring.

BARRY TARGAN
Journal Making. *New Letters,* 72/3 &
4.
MICHAEL TAUSSIG
What Color Is Sacred? *Critical
Inquiry,* Autumn.
ELLA TAYLOR
Family Viewing. *LA Weekly,* February
24–March 2.
JUSTIN TAYLOR
Fort Smith, Arkansas: A Monologue.
Barrelhouse, 2.
KERRY TEMPLE
Hot August Night. *Notre Dame
Magazine,* Winter.
RICHARD TERRILL
Yet Again to the Lake. *Colorado
Review,* Fall/Winter.
PAUL THEROUX
Living with Geese. *Smithsonian,*
December.
ABIGAIL THOMAS
Guilt. *Subtropics,* Winter/Spring.
CHRISTINA THOMPSON
Smoked Heads. *Salmagundi,* Fall.
JOHN THORN
Cardboard Gods. *Woodstock Times,*
October 12.
CALVIN TRILLIN
Alice, Off the Page. *The New Yorker,*
March 27.

ROBERT VIVIAN
Hotel Auschwitz. *First Intensity,* 21.

VIVIAN WAGNER
Under the Gun. *The Pinch,* Spring.
GARRY WALLACE
The Big Table Club. *Owen Wister
Review,* Spring.
RICHARD WARD
My Mother. *Gettysburg Review,*
Spring.
BILL WASIK
My Crowd. *Harper's Magazine,*
March.
ED WEATHERS
Hitting the Façade. *Elysian Fields,*
23/3.
PAUL WEST
Fatherhood. *Five Points,* 10/1 & 2.
W. D. WETHERELL
Yellowstone Autumn. *Ascent,* Fall.
CLAIRE NICOLAS WHITE
And Then There Was Light.
Commonweal, December 15.
JOAN WICKERSHAM
An Attempt at a Biographical Essay.
Agni, 63.
ALEC WILKINSON
Secret Tunnels. *The Believer,*
February.
JOY WILLIAMS
Literature Unnatured. *American
Short Fiction,* Winter.
SANDY WOODSON
A Pure and Lovely Flame. *Bellevue
Literary Review,* Spring.

JONATHAN YARDLEY
Sharp Pencils. *Smithsonian,*
November.
AMY YELIN
Torn. *Baltimore Review,* Summer/
Fall.

JOSHUA ZEITS
1964: The Year the Sixties Began.
American Heritage, October.
PAUL ZIMMER
Hyacinthe and the Bear. *Georgia
Review,* Summer.

Notable Special Issues of 2006

Antioch Review, Memoirs True and False, ed. Robert S. Fogarty, Fall.

The Believer, Games Issue, ed. Heidi Julavits, Ed Park, Vendela Vida, September.

Callaloo, Hip-Hop Music and Culture, ed. R. Scott Heath and Charles Henry Rowell, Summer.

Cream City Review, Memoir, ed. Phong Nguyen, Fall.

Creative Nonfiction, Our Roots Are Deep with Passion: New Essays by Italian American Writers, ed. Lee Gutkind and Joanna Clapps Herman, 30.

Daedalus, On Identity, ed. James Miller and Akeel Bilgrami, Fall.

Five Points, Tenth Anniversary Issue, ed. Megan Sexton, 10/1 & 2.

Granta, Loved Ones, ed. Ian Jack, Fall.

Indiana Review, Latina and Latino Writers, ed. Grady Jaynes, Summer.

Iowa Review, Nonfiction Conference Issue, ed. David Hamilton, Spring.

Massachusetts Review, The Messy Self, guest ed. Jennifer Rosner, Summer.

Mississippi Review, The Prose Poem, guest ed. Julia Johnson, 34/3.

Oxford American, Best of the South, ed. Marc Smirnoff, Spring.

Natural Bridge, Dream Issue, guest ed. Howard Schwartz, Spring.

New Literary History, Reading and Healing, ed. Ralph Cohen, Summer.

North Dakota Quarterly, Hemingway: Places and People, ed. Robert W. Lewis, Winter/Spring.

Shenandoah, Traditional Music Issue, ed. R. T. Smith, Fall.

Southern Review, All Nonfiction Issue, ed. Bret Lott, Winter.

TriQuarterly, The Violence, guest ed. Leigh Buchanan Bienen, 124.

Witness, Exile in America, ed. Peter Stine, 20.

THE B·E·ST AMERICAN SERIES®

THE BEST AMERICAN SHORT STORIES® 2007. STEPHEN KING, editor, HEIDI PITLOR, series editor. This year's most beloved short fiction anthology is edited by Stephen King, author of sixty books, including *Misery, The Green Mile, Cell,* and *Lisey's Story,* as well as about four hundred short stories, including "The Man in the Black Suit," which won the O. Henry Prize in 1996. The collection features stories by Richard Russo, Alice Munro, William Gay, T. C. Boyle, Ann Beattie, and others.

ISBN-13: 978-0-618-71347-9 • ISBN-10: 0-618-71347-6 $28.00 CL
ISBN-13: 978-0-618-71348-6 • ISBN-10: 0-618-71348-4 $14.00 PA

THE BEST AMERICAN NONREQUIRED READING™ 2007. DAVE EGGERS, editor, introduct. ꞌn by SUFJAN STEVENS. This collection boasts the best in fiction, nonfiction, altᵣnative comics, screenplays, blogs, and "anything else that defies categorization" ⟨ꞌISA Today⟩. With an introduction by singer-songwriter Sufjan Stevens, this volume features writing from Alison Bechdel, Scott Carrier, Miranda July, Lee Klein, Matthew Klam, and others.

ISBN-13: 978-0-618-90276-7 • ISBN-10: 0-618-90276-7 $28.00 CL
ISBN-13: 978-0-618-90281-1 • ISBN-10: 0-618-90281-3 $14.00 PA

THE BEST AMERICAN COMICS™ 2007. CHRIS WARE, editor, ANNE ELIZA-BETH MOORE, series editor. The newest addition to the Best American series — "A genuine salute to comics" (*Houston Chronicle*)— returns with a set of both established and up-and-coming contributors. Edited by Chris Ware, author of *Jimmy Corrigan: The Smartest Kid on Earth,* this volume features pieces by Lynda Barry, R. and Aline Crumb, David Heatley, Gilbert Hernandez, Adrian Tomine, Lauren Weinstein, and others.

ISBN-13: 978-0-618-71876-4 • ISBN-10: 0-618-71876-1 $22.00 CL

THE BEST AMERICAN ESSAYS® 2007. DAVID FOSTER WALLACE, editor, ROBERT ATWAN, series editor. Since 1986, *The Best American Essays* has gathered outstanding nonfiction writing, establishing itself as the premier anthology of its kind. Edited by the acclaimed writer David Foster Wallace, this year's collection brings together "witty, diverse" (*San Antonio Express-News*) essays from such contributors as Jo Ann Beard, Malcolm Gladwell, Louis Menand, and Molly Peacock.

ISBN-13: 978-0-618-70926-7 • ISBN-10: 0-618-70926-6 $28.00 CL
ISBN-13: 978-0-618-70927-4 • ISBN-10: 0-618-70927-4 $14.00 PA

THE BEST AMERICAN MYSTERY STORIES™ 2007. CARL HIAASEN, editor, OTTO PENZLER, series editor. This perennially popular anthology is sure to appeal to mystery fans of every variety. The 2007 volume, edited by best-selling novelist Carl Hiaasen, features both mystery veterans and new talents. Contributors include Lawrence Block, James Lee Burke, Louise Erdrich, David Means, and John Sandford.

ISBN-13: 978-0-618-81263-9 • ISBN-10: 0-618-81263-6 $28.00 CL
ISBN-13: 978-0-618-81265-3 • ISBN-10: 0-618-81265-2 $14.00 PA

THE B·E·S·T AMERICAN SERIES®

THE BEST AMERICAN SPORTS WRITING™ 2007. DAVID MARANISS, editor, GLENN STOUT, series editor. "An ongoing centerpiece for all sports collections" (*Booklist*), this series stands in high regard for its extraordinary sports writing and topnotch editors. This year David Maraniss, author of the critically acclaimed biography *Clemente*, brings together pieces by, among others, Michael Lewis, Ian Frazier, Bill Buford, Daniel Coyle, and Mimi Swartz.

ISBN-13: 978-0-618-75115-0 • ISBN-10: 0-618-75115-7 $28.00 CL
ISBN-13: 978-0-618-75116-7 • ISBN-10: 0-618-75116-5 $14.00 PA

THE BEST AMERICAN TRAVEL WRITING™ 2007. SUSAN ORLEAN, editor, JASON WILSON, series editor. Edited by Susan Orlean, staff writer for *The New Yorker* and author of *The Orchid Thief*, this year's collection, like its predecessors, is "a perfect mix of exotic locale and elegant prose" (*Publishers Weekly*) and includes pieces by Elizabeth Gilbert, Ann Patchett, David Halberstam, Peter Hessler, and others.

ISBN-13: 978-0-618-58217-4 • ISBN-10: 0-618-58217-7 $28.00 CL
ISBN-13: 978-0-618-58218-1 • ISBN-10: 0-618-58218-5 $14.00 PA

THE BEST AMERICAN SCIENCE AND NATURE WRITING™ 2007. RICHARD PRESTON, editor, TIM FOLGER, series editor. This year's collection of the finest science and nature writing is edited by Richard Preston, a leading science writer and author of *The Hot Zone* and *The Wild Trees*. The 2007 edition features a mix of new voices and prize-winning writers, including James Gleick, Neil deGrasse Tyson, John Horgan, William Langewiesche, Heather Pringle, and others.

ISBN-13: 978-0-618-72224-2 • ISBN-10: 0-618-72224-6 $28.00 CL
ISBN-13: 978-0-618-72231-0 • ISBN-10: 0-618-72231-9 $14.00 PA

THE BEST AMERICAN SPIRITUAL WRITING™ 2007. PHILIP ZALESKI, editor, introduction by HARVEY COX. Featuring an introduction by Harvey Cox, author of the groundbreaking *Secular City*, this year's edition of this "excellent annual" (*America*) contains selections that gracefully probe the role of faith in modern life. Contributors include Robert Bly, Adam Gopnik, George Packer, Marilynne Robinson, John Updike, and others.

ISBN-13: 978-0-618-83333-7 • ISBN-10: 0-618-83333-1 $28.00 CL
ISBN-13: 978-0-618-83346-7 • ISBN-10: 0-618-83346-3 $14.00 PA

 HOUGHTON MIFFLIN COMPANY www.houghtonmifflinbooks.com